The Active Template Library:

A DEVELOPER'S GUIDE

The Active Template Library:

A DEVELOPER'S GUIDE

Tom Armstrong

An Imprint of IDG Books Worldwide, Inc.
An International Data Group Company
Foster City, CA ✦ Chicago, IL ✦ Indianapolis, IN ✦ Southlake, TX

The Active Template Library: A Developer's Guide

Published by

M&T Books, an imprint of IDG Books Worldwide, Inc.

An International Data Group Company
919 E. Hillsdale Blvd, Suite 400
Foster City, CA 94404

www.idgbooks.com (IDG Books Worldwide Web site)

Library of Congress Catalog Card No.: 98-70061

ISBN: 1-55851-580-1

Printed in the United States of America

10 9 8 7 6 5 4 3 2

XX/RW/QR/ZY/NY

Distributed in the United States by IDG Books Worldwide, Inc.

Distributed by Macmillan Canada for Canada; by Transworld Publishers Limited in the United Kingdom; by IDG Norge Books for Norway; by IDG Sweden Books for Sweden; by Woodslane Pty. Ltd. for Australia; by Woodslane Enterprises Ltd. for New Zealand; by Longman Singapore Publishers Ltd. for Singapore, Malaysia, Thailand, and Indonesia; by Simron Pty. Ltd. for South Africa; by Toppan Company Ltd. for Japan; by Distribuidora Cuspide for Argentina; by Livraria Cultura for Brazil; by Ediciencia S.A. for Ecuador; by Addison-Wesley Publishing Company for Korea; by Ediciones ZETA S.C.R. Ltda. for Peru; by WS Computer Publishing Corporation, Inc., for the Philippines; by Unalis Corporation for Taiwan; by Contemporanea de Ediciones for Venezuela; by Computer Book & Magazine Store for Puerto Rico; by Express Computer Distributors for the Caribbean and West Indies. Authorized Sales Agent: Anthony Rudkin Associates for the Middle East and North Africa.

For general information on IDG Books Worldwide's books in the U.S., please call our Consumer Customer Service department at 800-762-2974. For reseller information, including discounts and premium sales, please call our Reseller Customer Service department at 800-434-3422.

For information on where to purchase IDG Books Worldwide's books outside the U.S., please contact our International Sales department at 415-655-3200 or fax 415-655-3295.

For information on foreign language translations, please contact our Foreign & Subsidiary Rights department at 415-655-3021 or fax 415-655-3281.

For sales inquiries and special prices for bulk quantities, please contact our Sales department at 415-655-3200 or write to the address above.

For information on using IDG Books Worldwide's books in the classroom or for ordering examination copies, please contact our Educational Sales department at 800-434-2086 or fax 817-251-8174.

For press review copies, author interviews, or other publicity information, please contact our Public Relations department at 415-655-3000 or fax 415-655-3299.

For authorization to photocopy items for corporate, personal, or educational use, please contact Copyright Clearance Center, 222 Rosewood Drive, Danvers, MA 01923, or fax 508-750-4470.

An Imprint of IDG Books Worlwide, Inc.
An International Data Group Company

ABOUT IDG BOOKS WORLDWIDE

Welcome to the world of IDG Books Worldwide.

IDG Books Worldwide, Inc., is a subsidiary of International Data Group, the world's largest publisher of computer-related information and the leading global provider of information services on information technology. IDG was founded more than 25 years ago and now employs more than 8,500 people worldwide. IDG publishes more than 275 computer publications in over 75 countries (see listing below). More than 60 million people read one or more IDG publications each month.

Launched in 1990, IDG Books Worldwide is today the #1 publisher of best-selling computer books in the United States. We are proud to have received eight awards from the Computer Press Association in recognition of editorial excellence and three from *Computer Currents'* First Annual Readers' Choice Awards. Our best-selling *...For Dummies*® series has more than 30 million copies in print with translations in 30 languages. IDG Books Worldwide, through a joint venture with IDG's Hi-Tech Beijing, became the first U.S. publisher to publish a computer book in the People's Republic of China. In record time, IDG Books Worldwide has become the first choice for millions of readers around the world who want to learn how to better manage their businesses.

Our mission is simple: Every one of our books is designed to bring extra value and skill-building instructions to the reader. Our books are written by experts who understand and care about our readers. The knowledge base of our editorial staff comes from years of experience in publishing, education, and journalism — experience we use to produce books for the '90s. In short, we care about books, so we attract the best people. We devote special attention to details such as audience, interior design, use of icons, and illustrations. And because we use an efficient process of authoring, editing, and desktop publishing our books electronically, we can spend more time ensuring superior content and spend less time on the technicalities of making books.

You can count on our commitment to deliver high-quality books at competitive prices on topics you want to read about. At IDG Books Worldwide, we continue in the IDG tradition of delivering quality for more than 25 years. You'll find no better book on a subject than one from IDG Books Worldwide.

John Kilcullen
CEO
IDG Books Worldwide, Inc.

Steven Berkowitz
President and Publisher
IDG Books Worldwide, Inc.

Eighth Annual Computer Press Awards ≥1992

Ninth Annual Computer Press Awards ≥1993

Tenth Annual Computer Press Awards ≥1994

Eleventh Annual Computer Press Awards ≥1995

IDG Books Worldwide, Inc., is a subsidiary of International Data Group, the world's largest publisher of computer-related information and the leading global provider of information services on information technology. International Data Group publishes over 275 computer publications in over 75 countries. Sixty million people read one or more International Data Group publications each month. International Data Group's publications include: **ARGENTINA:** Buyer's Guide, Computerworld Argentina, PC World Argentina; **AUSTRALIA:** Australian Macworld, Australian PC World, Australian Reseller News, Computerworld, IT Casebook, Network World, Publish, Webmaster; **AUSTRIA:** Computerwelt Osterreich, Networks Austria, PC Tip Austria; **BANGLADESH:** PC World Bangladesh; **BELARUS:** PC World Belarus; **BELGIUM:** Data News; **BRAZIL:** Annuário de Informática, Computerworld, Connections, Macworld, PC Player, PC World, Publish, Reseller News, Supergamepower; **BULGARIA:** Computerworld Bulgaria, Network World Bulgaria, PC & MacWorld Bulgaria; **CANADA:** CIO Canada, Client/Server World, ComputerWorld Canada, InfoWorld Canada, NetworkWorld Canada, WebWorld; **CHILE:** Computerworld Chile, PC World Chile; **COLOMBIA:** Computerworld Colombia, PC World Colombia; **COSTA RICA:** PC World Centro America; **THE CZECH AND SLOVAK REPUBLICS:** Computerworld Czechoslovakia, Macworld Czech Republic, PC World Czechoslovakia; **DENMARK:** Communications World Danmark, Computerworld Danmark, Macworld Danmark, PC World Danmark, Techworld Denmark; **DOMINICAN REPUBLIC:** PC World Republica Dominicana; **ECUADOR:** PC World Ecuador; **EGYPT:** Computerworld Middle East, PC World Middle East; **EL SALVADOR:** PC World Centro America; **FINLAND:** MikroPC, Tietoverkko, Tietoviikko; **FRANCE:** Distributique, Hebdo, Info PC, Le Monde Informatique, Macworld, Reseaux & Telecoms, WebMaster France; **GERMANY:** Computer Partner, Computerwoche, Computerwoche Extra, Computerwoche FOCUS, Global Online, Macwelt, PC Welt; **GREECE:** Amiga Computing, GamePro Greece, Multimedia World; **GUATEMALA:** PC World Centro America; **HONDURAS:** PC World Centro America; **HONG KONG:** Computerworld Hong Kong, PC World Hong Kong, Publish in Asia; **HUNGARY:** ABCD CD-ROM, Computerworld Szamitastechnika, Internetto online Magazine, PC World Hungary, PC-X Magazin Hungary; **ICELAND:** Tolvuheimur PC World Island; **INDIA:** Information Communications World, Information Systems Computerworld, PC World India, Publish in Asia; **INDONESIA:** InfoKomputer PC World, Komputek Computerworld, Publish in Asia; **IRELAND:** ComputerScope, PC Live!; **ISRAEL:** Macworld Israel, People & Computers/Computerworld; **ITALY:** Computerworld Italia, Macworld Italia, Networking Italia, PC World Italia; **JAPAN:** DTP World, Macworld Japan, Nikkei Personal Computing, OS/2 World Japan, SunWorld Japan, Windows NT World, Windows World Japan; **KENYA:** PC World East African; **KOREA:** Hi-Tech Information, Macworld Korea, PC World Korea; **MACEDONIA:** PC World Macedonia; **MALAYSIA:** Computerworld Malaysia, PC World Malaysia, Publish in Asia; **MALTA:** PC World Malta; **MEXICO:** Computerworld Mexico, PC World Mexico; **MYANMAR:** PC World Myanmar; **NETHERLANDS:** Computer! Totaal, LAN Internetworking Magazine, LAN World Buyers Guide, Macworld Netherlands, Net, WebWereld; **NEW ZEALAND:** Absolute Beginners Guide and Plain & Simple Series, Computer Buyer, Computer Industry Directory, Computerworld New Zealand, MTB, Network World, PC World New Zealand; **NICARAGUA:** PC World Centro America; **NORWAY:** Computerworld Norge, CW Rapport, Datamagasinet, Financial Rapport, Kursguide Norge, Macworld Norge, Multimediaworld Norge, PC World Ekspress Norge, PC World Nettverk, PC World Norge, PC World ProduktGuide Norge; **PAKISTAN:** Computerworld Pakistan; **PANAMA:** PC World Panama; **PEOPLE'S REPUBLIC OF CHINA:** China Computer Users, China Computerworld, China InfoWorld, China Telecom World Weekly, Computer & Communication, Electronic Design China, Electronics Today, Electronics Weekly, Game Software, PC World China, Popular Computer Week, Software Weekly, Software World, Telecom World; **PERU:** Computerworld Peru, PC World Profesional Peru, PC World SoHo Peru; **PHILIPPINES:** Click!, Computerworld Philippines, PC World Philippines, Publish in Asia; **POLAND:** Computerworld Poland, Computerworld Special Report Poland, Cyber, Macworld Poland, Networld Poland, PC World Komputer; **PORTUGAL:** Cerebro/PC World, Computerworld/Correio Informático, Dealer World Portugal, Mac*In/PC*In Portugal, Multimedia World; **PUERTO RICO:** PC World Puerto Rico; **ROMANIA:** Computerworld Romania, PC World Romania, Telecom Romania; **RUSSIA:** Computerworld Russia, Mir PK, Publish, Seti; **SINGAPORE:** Computerworld Singapore, PC World Singapore, Publish in Asia; **SLOVENIA:** Monitor; **SOUTH AFRICA:** Computing SA, Network World SA, Software World SA; **SPAIN:** Communicaciones World España, Computerworld España, Dealer World España, Macworld España, PC World España; **SRI LANKA:** Infolink PC World; **SWEDEN:** CAP&Design, Computer Sweden, Corporate Computing Sweden, Internetworld Sweden, it.branschen, Macworld Sweden, MaxiData Sweden, MikroDatorn, Natverk & Kommunikation, PC World Sweden, PCaktiv, Windows World Sweden; **SWITZERLAND:** Computerworld Schweiz, Macworld Schweiz, PCtip; **TAIWAN:** Computerworld Taiwan, Macworld Taiwan, NEW ViSiON/Publish, PC World Taiwan, Windows World Taiwan; **THAILAND:** Publish in Asia, Thai Computerworld; **TURKEY:** Computerworld Turkiye, Macworld Turkiye, Network World Turkiye, PC World Turkiye; **UKRAINE:** Computerworld Kiev, Multimedia World Ukraine, PC World Ukraine; **UNITED KINGDOM:** Acorn User UK, Amiga Action UK, Amiga Computing UK, Apple Talk UK, Computing, Macworld, Parents and Computers UK, PC Advisor, PC Home, PSX Pro, The WEB; **UNITED STATES:** Cable in the Classroom, CIO Magazine, Computerworld, DOS World, Federal Computer Week, GamePro Magazine, InfoWorld, I-Way, Macworld, Network World, PC Games, PC World, Publish, Video Event, THE WEB Magazine, and WebMaster; online webzines: JavaWorld, NetscapeWorld, and SunWorld Online; **URUGUAY:** InfoWorld Uruguay; **VENEZUELA:** Computerworld Venezuela, PC World Venezuela; and **VIETNAM:** PC World Vietnam.   3/24/97

Credits

Associate Publisher: Paul Farrell

Managing Editor: Shari Chappell

Editor: Andy Neusner

Copy Edit Manager: Karen Tongish

Production Editor: Paul Aljian

Technical Editor: Stuart Bessler

Copy Editor: Betsy Hardinger

To Nicole, Jessica, and Eric, with love.

Acknowledgments

I first have to thank the gang at M&T Books for doing most of the work required to publish this book. My editor, Andy Neusner, kept me focused and provided needed encouragement—all without pushing too hard. Thanks Andy, and good luck with your new job. A special thanks to my copy editor, Betsy Hardinger. Betsy edited one of my previous books and did a fantastic job; I was happy to hear that she would be doing this one as well. Betsy is a wonderfully "technical" copy editor, and somehow knows what I'm trying to say even when I can't quite write it correctly. Several times I've gone back to rewrite a technical idea, only to find that Betsy has already fixed it with my *exact* words! Thanks also to my production editor, Paul Aljian, who worked hard laying out these pages.

Thanks to Stuart Bessler my technical editor. Stuart and I have corresponded routinely since he used my first book in a course he taught at the University of California. Stuart provided wonderful feedback and helped clarify many of the difficult topics presented herein.

Thanks to Mark Nelson who graciously let me use our DDJ article as the basis of Chapter 9 on transparent ActiveX controls. Mark is a well-known author and a partner in Addisoft Consulting (*www.addisoft.com*) where I teach an occasional COM/ActiveX class. Thanks also to Ron Patton of Midwest Independent Consultant's Group. Ron wrote most of Appendix B introducing COM+ and I'm grateful for his help in this area.

Thanks to Chuck Reeves. A great friend who continues to teach and challenge me in many aspects of my life. Chuck recently accepted a job with Microsoft and I wish him well in this new adventure.

And finally, I'm most thankful for my beautiful wife Nicole and my two children, Jessica and Eric. They add inspiration, hope, and especially joy, to everything I do.

Tom Armstrong
tom@widgetware.com
Independence, Missouri
December, 1997

Contents at a Glance

Contents

CHAPTER 4 Interfaces, IDL, and Marshaling 133

CHAPTER 5   Containment and Aggregation 177

CHAPTER 7   **Events and Connection Points** 253

CHAPTER 8   ActiveX Controls .287

CHAPTER 9   **Transparent Controls and Asynchronous Download** **349**

Introduction

This book is about one of Microsoft's most important new development tools: the Active Template Library (ATL). ATL is a C++–based framework that facilitates the development of small and efficient software components based on Microsoft's Component Object Model (COM). ATL is similar to Microsoft's Foundation Class libraries (MFC), the most popular C++–based framework on the Windows platform. MFC has been around for about six years and has grown to be the dominant framework for developing Windows applications. In many cases, ATL is now the preferred framework to use when developing Windows–based software.

MFC will not go away overnight; in fact, MFC can be used with the ATL, but existing MFC features will probably be merged with ATL over time. Microsoft developed the new ATL framework primarily for one reason: a new application development architecture called the Component Object Model (COM).

COM is Microsoft's system-level object-oriented technology that is used extensively within its products and tools. COM provides several features that software developers need. COM provides language independence, which allows developers to reuse their C++ modules in Visual Basic, Delphi, or virtually any other development environment. COM provides location transparency, which allows a software module to execute anywhere in a distributed network environment. COM also provides the standard object-oriented characteristics of encapsulation, polymorphism, and inheritance. COM is the future of all Microsoft–based development, and ATL is one of the most important tools that developers can use to take advantage of this shift in technology.

The primary focus of ATL is to enable the creation of small COM–based software modules. These modules are then assembled to create larger applications. As developers move to this new component–based development model, they will use ATL. Microsoft is also committed to delivering COM on non-Windows platforms such as UNIX, Sun's Solaris, and Digital's VMS—ATL is one approach to providing a cross-platform COM development tool.

The history of ATL began in the fall of 1996 when Microsoft released version 1.0 as a freely, downloadable add-on for Visual C++ (Version 4.2 at the time), and version 1.1 followed shortly thereafter. ATL version 2.1, which added a significant amount of new functionality, was released as part of Visual C++ 5.0.

The purpose of this book is to help you understand and adopt one of the most important developments in Windows–based development: the move to COM–based application development. ATL is a powerful tool in this new environment, and this book provides in-depth coverage of what you need to know.

CHAPTER ORGANIZATION

The chapters are probably best read in succession, although the first two chapters can be skimmed if you familiar with C++ templates and COM. Chapter 1 covers C++ template–based development. Chapter 2 provides an in-depth introduction to the Component Object Model (COM), and introduces the examples that we will use throughout the book.

With the exception of Chapters 1 and 11, each chapter is divided into two primary sections. The first section provides a conceptual, code–based discussion of the topic, while the second section walks you through developing one or more sample applications that demonstrate the techniques described. This allows you to read the book for the concepts, and when you actually need to use them in your projects, you can go back and read the explicit implementation section.

Following are brief introductions to each chapter.

Chapter 1: C++ Templates

ATL uses templates throughout its implementation and Chapter 1 provides an introduction to this new approach to building reusable C++ classes.

Chapter 2: The Component Object Model

A general overview and detailed discussion of COM. The example is a simple C++ COM client and server. In later chapters, this example is reimplemented and enhanced using ATL with various COM techniques.

Chapter 3: The Active Template Library

ATL is about building COM–based applications. This chapter introduces ATL with a discussion of its template–based implementation and its wizards. The chapter also includes coverage of ATL's classes and idioms.

Chapter 4: Interfaces, IDL, and Marshaling

Chapter 4 goes a bit deeper into the various interface mechanisms provided by COM. In particular, we cover the Interface Definition Language (IDL) and something called marshaling. After that, we cover some miscellaneous COM details, such as error handling, memory management, and basic data types. Of course, this is all discussed in the context of ATL.

Chapter 5: Containment and Aggregation

One important feature of COM is its support for software module reuse at a binary level. In Chapter 5 we look at COM's binary reuse techniques: containment and aggregation. After a quick introduction to the two techniques, we examine how ATL provides support for developing components that support and/or use containment and aggregation.

Chapter 6: Automation

Automation is the COM–based technology that almost all Windows developers are familiar with, at least from a user's perspective. Visual Basic uses Automation extensively and ActiveX controls expose their functionality through Automation. Chapter 6 covers Automation in detail including a discussion of early and late binding, dual interfaces, and how ATL handles support for Automation.

Chapter 7: Events and Connection Points

Chapter 7 covers a very important topic for those developers using COM in their development projects: events and connection points. Today, COM interface calls are by nature synchronous. However, by using various techniques, COM components can provide pseudo-asynchronous behavior through support for interface callbacks and connection points. We cover these techniques along with the ATL implementation in Chapter 7.

Chapter 8: ActiveX Controls

ActiveX controls play a major role in Microsoft's component–based future. ActiveX controls are COM–based components that implement a number of standard, Microsoft-defined interfaces. It's actually quite hard to articulate what an ActiveX control is, primarily because the definition has changed frequently over the years, but in this chapter we cover what is called a full control. A *full control* is one that works in the popular development environments (such as Visual Basic), and implements at least 20 different COM interfaces.

Chapter 9: Asynchronous Downloading and Transparency

ActiveX controls can be used to deliver software functionality in both intranet and Internet environments. Chapter 9 covers many of the issues encountered when developing components that target these environments. Items such as transparency, asynchronous download, embedding controls within HTML documents, and security are covered.

Chapter 10: ATL and Threads

COM threading is one of the most misunderstood (and feared) COM topics. There's no doubt that multithreading is a difficult topic in itself, and by introducing COM into the equation, it becomes even more difficult. Chapter 10 first covers the basics of COM threading and then moves into a discussion of ATL's support for the various COM threading models. Chapter 10 ends with an example of a multithreaded math component that supports asynchronous method calls.

Chapter 11: MFC and ATL

The primary focus of this book is ATL–based development. However, most Windows developers are already familiar with, and probably use, the MFC libraries. MFC has become the most popular Windows development framework. In fact, MFC is probably where many developers first experienced working with COM, OLE, or ActiveX. In Chapter 11, we discuss some pros and cons of developing your applications and components with ATL or MFC, cover how both frameworks can be used together, and finally discuss some issues we encountered when converting MFC–based ActiveX controls to use ATL instead.

THE EXAMPLES

Because of the ubiquity and low cost of the World Wide Web, technical books no longer come with (or need) a CD-ROM containing the example code. Instead, you can download all the examples along with other supporting material from my Website. The majority of the examples use C++ and ATL and are combined into one large Visual C++ workspace (*ATL_Examples.dsw*). There are also a number of Visual Basic examples, which are combined into one Visual Basic workspace (*VB_Projects.vbg*). Visit the following URL for complete details:

HTTP//www.widgetware.com

COMMENTS AND BUG REPORTS

I welcome and encourage comments, suggestions, and bug reports at the following e-mail address. You can contact me via email or through my Website. The site contains examples, FAQs, pointers to other COM/OLE/ActiveX sites, discussions, and other material concerning COM, ATL, and ActiveX technology.

tom@WidgetWare.com

Chapter

C++ Templates

As its name implies, the Active Template Library (ATL) uses C++ templates as a principal feature of its implementation. For that reason, in this chapter, we'll take a quick look at C++ templates and discuss how developing with templates is a bit different from what you may be used to.

TEMPLATES

Templates are a fairly new addition to the C++ language. They provide a generic way to develop reusable code by allowing parameterized types. There are two basic types of templates: function templates and class templates. Using function templates is similar to using the C++ preprocessor. Class templates allow you to write generic, type-safe classes.

Function Templates

Function templates allow you to write type-safe functions. To implement a type-safe MAX function without templates, you must provide overloaded functions:

```
long MAX( long a, long b )
{
   if ( a > b )
      return a;
   else
      return b;
}

double MAX( double a, double b )
{
   if ( a > b )
      return a;
   else
      return b;
}
```

For each type that you would like to use with the MAX function, you must provide an explicit implementation. Using a function template, however, you can instead do this:

```
template <class Type>
Type MAX( Type a, Type b )
{
    if ( a > b )
        return a;
    else
        return b;
}
```

If this is the first template you have seen, it may look a little strange. The template keyword identifies this as a template. The values between the less-than and greater-than characters specify the parameterized type, which is indicated by the class keyword. The type is then replaced at compile-time with a type specified by the function user. Here's what it looks like:

```
int main( int argc, char *argv[] )
{
    int     iMax = MAX<int>( 10, 12 );
    long    lMax = MAX<long>( 10, 12 );
    double dMax = MAX<double>( 10.0, 12.0 );

    return 0;
}
```

Again, the syntax is a bit arcane, but after inspection it should make sense. When calling the function, we provide the type as a parameter to the function. Templates are compile-time constructs and basically expand for each specified type. As an example, the preceding code would expand to something like this:

```
int main( int argc, char *argv[] )
{
    int MAXint( int a, int b )
    {
        if ( a > b )
            return a;
        else
            return b;
    }
    int iMax = MAXint( 10, 12 );
    ...
}
```

This is the expansion for only one function type, but you should get the idea. Function templates give you the flexibility of the C preprocessor and the type safety of writing a specific function for every possible type. Class templates provide the same flexibility at the class level.

Class Templates

Class templates are similar to function templates in that they allow the user of a class to specify a type at instantiation time. A generic class can be developed that operates on a user-defined type, and that provides type safety. The most difficult aspect of template-based development is figuring out the syntax.

EXAMPLE: A TEMPLATE-BASED STACK CLASS

To demonstrate the basic features of template-based programming, let's build an example class that implements a stack. I know this has been done before, but the example is short, and it will allow us to focus on how templates work.

To begin, a stack provides a FILO (first-in-last-out) structure in which to store elements of the same type. Stacks are used extensively at the hardware level, but they are also useful in software. What we would like to do is design a stack class that can store any data type. Without C++ templates this is impossible to do, at least in a straightforward way. Without templates, we would have to design a class for each data type. Here's what an integer stack might look like:

```
class StackInt
{
public:
    StackInt()
    {
        m_sPos = 0;
    }
    ~StackInt() {}

    void    Push( int iValue );
    int     Pop();

    bool IsEmpty()
    {
        return( m_sPos == 0 );
    }
    bool IsFull()
    {
        return( m_sPos == 100 );
    }
    bool HasElements()
    {
        return( m_sPos != 0 );
    }
```

(code continued on next page)

```
private:
   int    m_data[100];
   short m_sPos;
};

void StackInt::Push( int iValue )
{
   m_data[ sPos++ ] = iValue;
}

int StackInt::Pop()
{
   return m_data[ --sPos ];
}
```

There we have it—a nice, simple class that implements a stack. It has the typical Push and Pop methods as well as a few others that allow the user to determine the state of the stack (whether the stack is empty or full, and so on). Here's how you might use the class:

```
int MAIN( int argc, char *argv[] )
{
   StackInt stack;

   stack.Push( 100 );
   stack.Push( 200 );
   stack.Push( 300 );

   while( stack.HasElements() )
   {
      cout << stack.Pop() << endl;
   }

   return 0;
}
```

The class is easy to use, and it does just what we want. However, it has few problems. First, there isn't much error checking, but this is by design so as to keep the code small and easy to follow. Second, the stack supports only integers. Third, the size of the stack is explicitly set to 100. What if the user needs a larger stack? Well, we can use a parameterized constructor such as this one:

```
class StackInt
{
public:
   StackInt()
   {
      m_sSize = 100;
```

```
      m_data = new int[ m_sSize ];
      m_sPos = 0;
   }
   StackInt( short sSize )
   {
      m_sSize = sSize;
      m_data = new int[ m_sSize ];
      m_sPos = 0;
   }
   ~StackInt() {}

   void      Push( int iValue );
   int       Pop();

   bool IsEmpty()
   {
      return( m_sPos == 0 );
   };
   bool HasElements()
   {
      return( m_sPos != 0 );
   }
   bool IsFull()
   {
      return( m_sPos == m_sSize );
   }
private:
   short m_sSize;
   int* m_data;
   short m_sPos;
};

void StackInt::Push( int iValue )
{
   m_data[ m_sPos++ ] = iValue;
}

int StackInt::Pop()
{
   return m_data[ --m_sPos ];
}
```

That makes the class more general because the user can now specify the size of the stack, but we still have the problem that it only supports integers. What if the user of the class wants a stack that manages doubles or strings or some other class, such as MFC's CWnd or a user-defined class such as CBankAccount? We would have to rewrite the class completely. It wouldn't be hard, and with a bit of cut-and-paste, we would have the class built in no time.

For example, to build a class for doubles, we can do something like this:

```
class StackDouble
{
public:
   StackDouble()
   {
      m_sSize = 100;
      m_data = new double[ m_sSize ];
      m_sPos = 0;
   }
   StackDouble( short sSize )
   {
      m_sSize = sSize;
      m_data = new double[ m_sSize ];
      m_sPos = 0;
   }
   ~StackDouble() {}
   void      Push( double dValue );
   int       Pop();
   bool IsEmpty()
   {
      return( m_sPos == 0 );
   };
   bool HasElements()
   {
      return( m_sPos != 0 );
   }
   bool IsFull()
   {
      return( m_sPos == m_sSize );
   }
private:
   short m_sSize;
   double* m_data;
   short m_sPos;
};
```

Now we have a class that implements a stack for doubles. I've highlighted the code that we changed (in boldface type) and, as you can see, we changed only three items: the name of the class, the parameter type of the *Push* method, and the actual type stored in our array.

This seems simple. Isn't it something the compiler could do for us? Yes, and that's exactly what C++ templates do. Templates give you a compile-time substitution mechanism at the class level.

By providing substitution of types (and constants) at compile time, templates allow you to build generic classes that do not use a specific data type. Instead, the data type can be provided by the class user when an instance of the class is instantiated. At compile time, the template is "expanded" with the user-specified type, and that generates a completely new and type-safe class. Let's look at the stack example again. This time, though, we'll use C++ templates:

```
template <class T>
class Stack
{
public:
    Stack()
    {
        m_sPos = 0;
    }
    ~Stack() {}

    void Push( T value );
    T    Pop();

    bool IsEmpty()
    {
        return( m_sPos == 0 );
    };
    bool HasElements()
    {
        return( m_sPos != 0 );
    }
    bool IsFull()
    {
        return( m_sPos == 100 );
    }

private:
    T m_data[100];
    short m_sPos;
};
```

The syntax for class templates is very similar to that of function templates. We use the `template` keyword to indicate that the class is a template class. Next, we provide one or more template parameters. Each parameter can be a *type*, indicated by the class keyword, or a *constant*, indicated by an existing, valid type. We'll cover parameterized constants in the next example.

The syntax within the class declaration is to use the "type" (in our case T) wherever you would like it substituted at compile time. In the preceding example, we need to substitute the type of our array as well as the parameter and return types for the Push and Pop methods.

MEMBER SYNTAX

The syntax for implementing member functions (methods) outside the class declaration is a bit different. Following are the definitions for the Push and Pop methods. You must use the template keyword and the type name when defining the methods.

```
template <class T>
void Stack<T>::Push( T value )
{
    m_data[m_sPos++] = value;
}

template <class T>
T Stack<T>::Pop()
{
    return m_data[--m_sPos];
}
```

The syntax for constructors and destructors for templated classes is also different. Here's what our Stack constructor and destructor should look like if they are defined outside the class declaration:

```
Template <class T>
Stack<T>::Stack()
{
    sPos = 0;
}

Template <class T>
Stack<T>::~Stack()
{
}
```

NOT JUST TYPES

Templates also allow you to provide parameterized constants when building generic classes. In the stack example, we can specify the size of the stack as part of the template. Again, this gives both the implementer and the user of the class more freedom. Here's what the stack class looks with a short that specifies the stack size:

```cpp
template <class T, short sSize = 100>
class Stack
{
public:
   Stack()
   {
      m_sPos = 0;
   }
   ~Stack() {}

   void Push( T value );
   T    Pop();

   bool IsEmpty()
   {
      return( m_sPos == 0 );
   };
   bool HasElements()
   {
      return( m_sPos != 0 );
   }
   bool IsFull()
   {
      return( m_sPos == sSize );
   }
   long GetSize()
   {
      return sSize;
   }
private:
   T m_data[ sSize ];
   short m_sPos;
};

template <class T, short sSize = 100>
void Stack<T>::Push( T value )
{
   m_data[ m_sPos++ ] = value;
}

template <class T, short sSize = 100>
T Stack<T>::Pop()
{
   return m_data[ --m_sPos ];
}
```

One difference in this implementation is that we need not dynamically create our array when the class is instantiated as we did with the version that doesn't use templates. Non-type template parameters are constants that are evaluated at compile time. That makes things a bit more efficient, because we don't have to maintain a member to hold the actual size of our array.

Here's how we might use the new class:

```
int main( int argc, char *argv[] )
{
    // Create a stack of doubles with a max size of
    // 20 elements
    Stack< double, 20 > doubleStack;

    cout << "doubleStack size is " << doubleStack.GetSize() << endl;

    doubleStack.Push( 1.1 );
    doubleStack.Push( 2.2 );
    doubleStack.Push( 3.3 );
    while( doubleStack.HasElements() )
    {
        cout << doubleStack.Pop() << endl;
    }

    // A dynamically created stack
    Stack<long>* plongStack = new Stack<long, 10>;

    plongStack->Push( 1000 );
    plongStack->Push( 2000 );

    delete plongStack;

    return 0;
}
```

As you can see, we provide a parameter for both the stack type and its size. Both techniques are used extensively within ATL. The last part of the preceding example demonstrates the syntax for creating template-based objects using the new operator. Again, it's a bit different from what we're used to, but the syntax is consistent in most circumstances.

TEMPLATE-BASED REUSE

Template-based reuse is different from inheritance-based reuse. If you've been developing with C++, you no doubt understand the concept of reuse by inheritance. With inheritance-based reuse, you reuse a class's implementation by deriving a new class and modifying its behavior by overriding the base class's methods, and so on. The key is to inherit as much functionality as possible.

With templates, you reuse a class by generating a new class implementation based on parameterized types. You achieve reuse by letting the compiler generate code for you. In the early days of templates, they were criticized because they increased compile times and bloated the resulting code; every new class produced its own object code. Today's compilers handle these issues much more efficiently, and templates have become an effective way to develop generic, reusable code. As you'll see, the Active Template Library is a great demonstration of this new approach to C++ development.

ON TO THE COMPONENT OBJECT MODEL

Now that you have a good understanding of C++ templates, let's move on to understanding what Microsoft's Component Object Model (COM) is all about. COM is an important new technology for Windows developers. Chapter 2 provides a detailed introduction.

2

The Component Object Model

Before we start developing software with ATL, we need to first understand the details of Microsoft's Component Object Model. COM is at the center of almost everything Microsoft does. Microsoft uses COM extensively within its own applications, tools, and operating systems, and most new Windows functionality is now delivered as a set of COM components instead of a series of API calls.

If you develop Windows software, a solid understanding of COM is a must, and the focus of this chapter is to provide you with all the gory details. ATL is about developing COM components. After going through this chapter and its examples, you'll be ready to dig into the details of the ATL framework.

SOFTWARE COMPONENTS

COM is about designing, building, and using software components. COM is a system-level technology provided in all of Microsoft's current 32-bit operating systems. By building software using COM, a developer gets a significant amount of built-in functionality. In particular, COM endows a software module with the following attributes: language independence, robust versioning, location transparency, and object orientation. Let's go through each one.

Language Independence: A Binary Standard

Although this book focuses primarily on building COM components with C++, COM components need not be written in any specific language. In fact, other languages, such as Visual Basic and Java, make it easy to develop as well as use COM-based components. The kicker here, though, is that the client (or user) of a COM component is oblivious to how or in what language the component was implemented.

In other words, COM-based software modules are language independent. We can write a component using C++ and use it from Visual Basic. We can write a component in Visual Basic and use it from Java, C++, or Visual FoxPro. It doesn't matter.

One of COM's most important features is that it gives us a technique to write object-oriented code in any language we choose and deliver this functionality to users of any other language. COM supports a *binary standard*. We can deliver a component housed within a DLL or EXE (a binary) and the component's functionality can be used from Visual Basic, Java, C++, or even COBOL. Of course, the language implementation must support COM, and nearly every language used in the Windows environment supports COM.

Because this book is about ATL, we will use the C++ language to implement our COM objects. We will also write most of our *client* applications (a software entity that uses a component) using C++, but we will also demonstrate COM-based development using Visual Basic.

Robust Versioning

Another important feature of COM is its support for component versioning. One difficult aspect of delivering software modules, especially in environments that are shared among multivendor applications, is the problem of handling new versions of software. COM addresses this problem by providing a robust versioning technique that is based on COM's most fundamental entity: the component's interface.

COM enables robust versioning via its support for multiple interfaces on the same component. In other words, a component's functionality can be partitioned into small, distinct areas, each of them a specific COM interface. Version support is then provided by allowing a component to expose slight variations of the same interface, thereby allowing older applications to run unchanged and newer applications to take advantage of a component's new features.

Location Transparency

Another important COM feature is *location transparency*. It means that a component user—the client—need not know where a component's functionality is located. A client application uses the same COM services to instantiate and use a component no matter where the component resides.

The component may reside directly within the client's process space (a DLL), it may reside in another process on the same machine (an executable), or it may reside on a machine located hundreds of miles away (a distributed object). COM and Distributed COM provide this location transparency.

The client interacts with a COM-based component in exactly the same way no matter where the component resides. The client interface does not change. Location transparency allows developers to build scalable, distributed, multitier applications.

Object-Oriented Characteristics

COM enables a component to deliver its functionality in an object-oriented way. Most older interoperability techniques (such as DLL exports and DDE) do not provide the typical object-oriented characteristics that C++ developers use daily. COM provides the three fundamental object-oriented characteristics of encapsulation, inheritance, and polymorphism and does so in a language-independent way. We'll discuss each of these characteristics in more detail later.

WHERE IS COM IMPLEMENTED?

COM is a model for implementing object-oriented, language-independent, location-transparent components or software modules. The model is described in Microsoft's *Component Object Model Specification*. Anyone can provide an implementation of COM's model. However, because Microsoft specifies it and has ultimate control over it, Microsoft has provided the initial implementation through its 32-bit operating systems (such as Windows 95, Windows 98, and Windows NT). Support for COM is built into the operating system. There is no need to distribute additional software to use COM within your Windows applications.

Microsoft's implementation of COM is a small set of Win32 API functions and a large number of COM interface declarations (language-independent header files). The use of these APIs and interfaces is the focus of this chapter and is revisited throughout the book, because ATL is primarily concerned with developing COM-based software.

CLIENTS AND SERVERS

It is important to understand the relationship between a component and the software entity using its services. A COM component provides services to some other entity and so is viewed as a *server*. A software entity using a component's services is deemed the *client*. This seems straightforward, but, as you'll see, in many cases a server is also a client and a client is routinely a server. It has to do with interfaces. COM is about interfaces.

A software module that *implements* an interface is said to be the server. In other words, it provides a set of services through the implemented interface. A software module that uses, or *consumes*, an interface is said to be a client of that interface. It is using the services implemented by the server. Also, in many cases a component will be both an implementer and a consumer of a number of COM interfaces. It behaves as both a client and server.

OLE, ACTIVEX, AND ALL THE REST

There is a lot of confusion about COM, OLE, and ActiveX and how they differ. COM is a *system*-level standard that provides basic object model services on which to build higher-level services. It's basically a software interoperability standard. OLE and ActiveX are examples of higher-level services built on top of this standard. OLE and ActiveX provide application-level features but are built using COM's services. So the terms *COM*, *OLE*, and *ActiveX* are somewhat interchangeable in that their capabilities and features are closely related. However, each term describes a separate set of high-level technologies, although there is a lot of crossover. Here's a quick history of OLE and ActiveX.

When OLE was first introduced (circa 1991), the term was an acronym for *object linking and embedding*. Its primary purpose was to provide object linking and embedding support for Windows applications. This *compound document* functionality allowed users to embed Excel spreadsheets directly within Word documents and so on.

Then, with the release of OLE 2.0 (circa 1993), OLE was no longer used as an acronym; instead, it was an umbrella term for several technologies based on COM. Many of the new capabilities provided by OLE 2.0 had nothing to do with linking and embedding. A good example of this is OLE automation (now called simply *automation*), whose primary purpose is to promote component and application interoperability through language and tool independence. It has nothing to do with compound documents.

In April 1996, Microsoft embraced the Web wholeheartedly and coined the term *ActiveX* to indicate a new direction in its product line. However, the majority of the new ActiveX technologies existed long before April 1996; they were just categorized under a different name: OLE. In general, *ActiveX* replaced *OLE* to describe the majority of Microsoft's COM-based technologies. As a result, OLE could again be used to describe only those technologies related to compound documents and object linking and embedding and so has reverted its former status as an acronym.

THE ESSENCE OF COM: INTERFACES

COM's implementation contains a handful of Win32 APIs, but the purpose of these APIs is basically to bootstrap the COM environment. After that, COM is about implementing and using *interfaces*.

As a C++ developer, you implement and use interfaces all the time. As the implementer of a C++ class, a developer encapsulates the details of the class's implementation by using the `public`, `protected`, and `private` keywords. A user of the C++ class interacts with a class instance only through its public interface. This interface acts as a contract between the developer and the user of the class. The class implementer can change the internal implementation of the class, because it is encapsulated. However, if the public interface is changed, it forces the user of the class to recompile his or her application. For this reason, the public interface should not change. Following is a simple C++ class declaration that demonstrates a public interface with four methods.

```
class Math
{
public:
    long Add( long, long );
    long Subtract( long, long );
    long Multiply( long, long );
    long Divide( long, long );

private:
    // Implementation here...
};
```

A COM interface is very similar to a C++ class's public interface. It lets you describe methods and properties (data members) and fully encapsulate the details of the underlying implementation. However, unlike C++, COM does this in a language-independent fashion.

C++ Virtual Function Tables

COM interfaces are built using a C++ *Vtable*, which is short for *virtual function table*. A virtual function table is used in C++ to provide late binding of an instance's functionality. Before we move into describing the implementation of a COM interface, let's review virtual functions.

Virtual functions allow C++ programs to resolve function calls dynamically, at run time, instead of statically, at compile time. This powerful feature of C++ provides for many of its object-oriented capabilities.

In early-binding languages such as C, the specific function address to call in any particular instance is determined at compile time. C programs can support run-time binding, but the developer must do all the work (by using pointers to functions). C++ makes it much easier. Virtual functions allow the implementation of *polymorphism*, or the ability of an object to respond differently to the same method or member function at run time depending on the object's type.

These virtual functions don't do much if you declare them in only one class. The strength of virtual functions is manifest only as you augment existing base classes by creating subclasses. The following example demonstrates the power of using virtual functions.

```
class Fruit {
public:
   void    put_Color( string str )
   {
      m_strColor = str;
   }
   string  get_Color()
   {
      return m_strColor;
   }

   virtual void  Draw() {};
private:
   string   m_strColor;
};
```

Our Fruit class contains a virtual method, Draw, that returns void and does nothing. The base Fruit class does not have an implementation for Draw, because each particular type of fruit should implement its own Draw method. For example, let's derive some fruit from the Fruit class.

```
class Apple : public Fruit
{
   virtual void  Draw()
   {
     cout << "I'm an Apple" << endl;
   }
};

class GrannySmith : public Apple
{
   virtual void  Draw()
   {
     cout << "I'm a Granny Smith Apple" << endl;
   }
};

class Orange : public Fruit
{
   virtual void  Draw()
   {
      cout << "I'm an Orange" << endl;
   }
};

class Grape : public Fruit
{
   virtual void  Draw()
   {
      cout << "I'm a Grape" << endl;
   }
};
```

Each class that is derived directly or indirectly from Fruit implements its own Draw function that prints that particular fruit's type. In itself, this isn't anything spectacular, but look at the following code.

```
int main()
{
   Fruit* pFruitList[4];
   pFruitList[0] = new Apple;
   pFruitList[1] = new Orange;
   pFruitList[2] = new Grape;
   pFruitList[3] = new GrannySmith;

   for( int i = 0; i < 4; i++ )
      pFruitList[i]->Draw();
}
```

```
// Produces this output
>
> I'm an Apple
> I'm an Orange
> I'm a Grape
> I'm a Granny Smith Apple
>
```

The preceding code illustrates the power of virtual functions. We've declared an array of pointers of type Fruit, the base class, and have assigned to each element the address of an instance of a particular derived fruit type. As the line pFruitList[i]->Draw() is executed, the program dynamically, at run time, determines which member function to invoke. This dynamic binding is implemented with a virtual function table.

Pure Virtual Functions and Abstract Classes

An *abstract* class provides a model, or template, for all classes that derive from it. In our Fruit example, the base class Fruit is a good abstract class candidate. A "fruit" is itself an abstract thing. In real life we cannot instantiate a general fruit object, something that has the broad characteristics of a fruit but isn't a specific kind of fruit. Abstract classes are used by developers to categorize and classify things that have similar characteristics. Our base Fruit class contains the essence of all fruits but nothing specific.

```
class Fruit
{
public:
   void put_Color( string str )
   {
      m_strColor = str;
   }
   string  get_Color()
   {
      return m_strColor;
   }

   virtual void Draw() = 0;
private:
   string m_strColor;
};
```

Abstract classes provide those properties and actions shared by all deriving classes. Abstract classes can choose not to implement specific member functions, requiring instead that deriving classes implement those functions. In the example, the Draw function is declared as pure virtual by using the notation = 0. This indicates that all deriving classes must implement some form of the Draw function.

By declaring a pure virtual function within a class, the class designer also makes the class abstract, meaning that the class cannot be directly instantiated. Although the class itself cannot be instantiated, pointers to the class can be used, and this proves to be an important characteristic. Recall the example with the array of Fruit pointers.

```
int main()
{
   // Now we can't do this
   Fruit fruit;

   // But we can still do this, and it produces the same output
   // as the earlier example.
   Fruit* pFruitList[4];
   pFruitList[0] = new Apple;
   pFruitList[1] = new Orange;
   pFruitList[2] = new Grape;
   pFruitList[3] = new GrannySmith;

   for( int i = 0; i < 4; i++ )
     pFruitList[i]->Draw();
}
```

The ability to determine object behavior at run time instead of only at compile time is a major improvement over C and provides the polymorphic behavior required by object-oriented development.

Understanding Vtables

As we described earlier, virtual functions allow C++ programs to invoke functions dynamically instead of statically. Other terms for dynamic and static function invocation are *late* and *early* binding, which refer to binding the function address either at run time or at compile time. Whenever you declare a function as virtual, the compiler adds a pointer to your class structure called the *vptr*, or virtual pointer. The vptr points to a Vtable structure that contains the addresses of any virtual functions in your class as well as any base classes. Figure 2.1 depicts the vptr and Vtable entries for the following class definition:

```
class Fruit {
public:
   void     put_Color( string str )
   {
      m_strColor = str;
   }
   string   get_Color()
   {
```

```
        return m_strColor;
    }

    virtual void    Draw() {};
private:
    string    m_strColor;
}
class Apple : public Fruit
{
public:
    void Draw()
    {
        cout << "I'm an Apple" << endl;
    }
}
class GrannySmith : public Apple
{
public:
    void Draw()
    {
        cout << "I'm a Granny Smith Apple" << endl;
    }
}
```

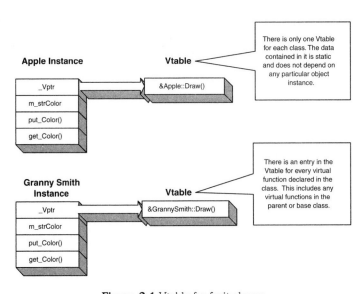

Figure 2.1 Vtable for fruit classes.

This late binding of function addresses at run time is important to object-oriented languages. Some object-oriented languages, in particular Smalltalk and Java, bind all functions late. Others, including C++, leave it to the developer to decide which functions should bind late. C++ does this for performance reasons. There is overhead in providing the late binding necessary for polymorphic behavior. For every class that has at least one virtual function, a Vtable is needed for the class and a vptr is needed for each instance. The vptr must be initialized for each instance, and run-time overhead of function lookup is incurred every time a virtual function is called.

How COM Uses Vtables

C++ uses Vtables for implementing polymorphic behavior. COM, however, uses the C++ Vtable structure to build a COM interface. Because a Vtable is a table that holds function addresses, it is a good candidate for such an application. A COM interface is actually a pointer to a class's Vtable structure. This arrangement provides a convenient way to encapsulate the functionality of a component class.

A user of a COM interface has access only to the public methods of a component. Because COM uses a Vtable pointer, this also means that a component's interface can contain only methods. This relationship is shown in Figure 2.2. A component implementer cannot expose data members directly, although COM provides a way to simulate data members through its concept of properties.

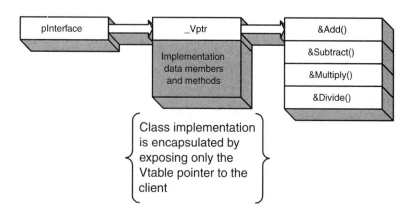

Figure 2.2 COM and the Vtable.

The COM designers probably chose to use this C++ construct because most of them were C++ developers and because it would allow C++ compilers to efficiently produce components based on COM. It doesn't really matter. They had to choose some technique, and by picking the C++ Vtable they made it easier for C++ developers to understand.

In the next few sections, we'll convert the C++ Math class shown next into a COM component that will expose a basic interface with its public methods. To demonstrate COM's support for multiple interfaces, we'll also add another math-based interface.

```
class Math
{
public:
   long Add( long, long );
   long Subtract( long, long );
   long Multiply( long, long );
   long Divide( long, long );

private:
   // Implementation here...
};
```

COM Interfaces

Now that we understand that COM uses Vtables to implement its interfaces, let's go through the details by implementing our simple Math class as a COM component. The first step is to build a Vtable that exposes our component's public interface. Here's the declaration:

```
class IMath
{
public:
   virtual long   Add( long Op1, long Op2 ) = 0;
   virtual long   Subtract( long Op1, long Op2 ) = 0;
   virtual long   Multiply( long Op1, long Op2 ) = 0;
   virtual long   Divide( long Op1, Op2 ) = 0;
};
```

Next, we derive from this abstract class and provide the implementation just as we did before.

```
class Math : public IMath
{
public:
   long   Add( long Op1, long Op2 );
   long   Subtract( long Op1, long Op2 );
   long   Multiply( long Op1, long Op2 );
   long   Divide( long Op1, Op2 );
};
```

This is the first step in making our class available to non-C++ users. COM-based technologies, such as OLE and ActiveX, are composed primarily of interfaces such as our IMath class. Our new class is abstract, so it contains at least one pure virtual function and contains only the public methods of our component class. In other words, its purpose is to completely describe the layout of a C++ Vtable.

In IMath, the I indicates that it is an interface declaration. COM uses this nomenclature throughout its implementation. The IMath class provides an external interface declaration for the Math component. The most important aspect of the new IMath class is that it forces the creation of a C++ Vtable in any derived classes.

The use of virtual functions in a base class is central to the design of COM. The abstract class definition provides a Vtable that contains only the public methods (the interface) of the class. The IMath class contains no data members and no implementation functions. Its only purpose is to force the derived class, Math, to implement, virtually, the methods of the component's interface.

COM provides access to its components only through a Vtable pointer, so access to the component's implementation is impossible. Study this example. It is simple, but it contains the core concept of COM: the use of Vtables to provide the interface to a component's functionality. In the end, a COM interface is just a pointer to a pointer to a C++-style interface (or Vtable). Figure 2.3 depicts this relationship for our math component.

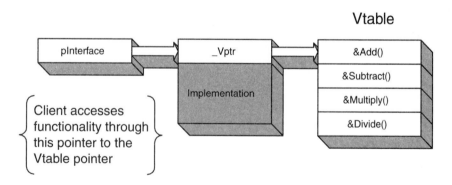

Figure 2.3 COM interfaces and the Vtable.

In our example, several concepts need to be understood. First, all COM-based technologies, such as ActiveX and OLE, contain a number of abstract interface definitions just as our IMath class does. Ultimately, your job as the developer is to provide an *implementation* for those interfaces. That's one reason ActiveX is a standard. ActiveX provides the interface declarations, and you provide the implementation. Several developers can provide different implementations for a standard ActiveX component by providing their own unique implementations. This is the concept behind ActiveX controls and all Active(X) technologies. The COM, OLE, and ActiveX specifications define the abstract classes that you must implement to create a COM-based component.

For example, if we were to put our abstract IMath class in a header file and then distribute it with various Windows development tools, we could call it a *math component standard*. Then any developer could build a component based on our IMath interface. Also, because it would be a standard, other developers could develop software to use the IMath interface. In this way, we would produce an environment in which anyone could implement a component that provided functionality via IMath and anyone could use a component that implemented IMath. Without writing one line of executable code, we would produce a standard. This is basically what COM does.

Accessing a COM Interface

Now that you've seen how a COM interface is described, let's take a look at how a client application might access and use the interface. We haven't yet covered all the details, but getting a look at both sides of the equation is important at the beginning. One of the most important COM API functions is CoCreateInstance. As its name implies, CoCreateInstance is used by a client application to create an instance of a component. The client provides some basic information about the component it wants to create, and COM handles all the details of finding the component, launching it, and returning the requested interface pointer. Here's a quick example of how a client application might create an instance of our math component and use its IMath interface:

```
// Create an instance and return the IMath interface
IMath* pMath;
HRESULT hr = CoCreateInstance( CLSID_Math,
                  NULL,
                  CLSCTX_INPROC,
                  IID_IMath,
                  (void**) &pMath );

// Use IMath
long lResult = pMath->Multiply( 44, 33 );
```

We declare a pointer to our abstract IMath class and then ask COM to create an instance of a component identified by its class identifier of CLSID_Math. We haven't covered the details yet, but the important point here is that COM creates the component instance and returns a pointer to a pointer to a Vtable structure described by our abstract IMath class. Once we have the pointer, we can access any functionality exposed through the IMath interface.

The other technique of accessing a component's interface is through a standard interface that we will discuss shortly. As the next section describes, most components have more than one interface, and a mechanism is needed to allow clients to access a specific one. Briefly, here's what it looks like:

```
IMath* pMath;
hr = pUnk->QueryInterface( IID_IMath, (void**) &pMath );
pUnk->Release();
if ( FAILED( hr ))
{
    cout << "QueryInterface() for IMath failed" << endl;
    CoUninitialize();
    return -1;
}
```

Multiple Interfaces per Component

One of COM's most important features is the ability for a component to implement multiple interfaces. This feature is key to COM's support for robust component versioning. For developers new to COM, multiple interfaces per component is also one of the most difficult aspects to understand.

To begin, take a look at the following C++ class declaration. It declares a Math component with a few new features:

```
class Math
{
public:
    long Add( long lOp1, long lOp2 );
    long Subtract(long lOp1, long lOp2 );
    long Multiply(long lOp1, long lOp2 );
    long Divide( long lOp1, long lOp2 );

    long Factorial( short sOp );
    long Fibonacci( short sOp );

    void Draw();

private:
    // Implementation here...
};
```

The class now sports the ability to do advanced math functions such as the factorial or Fibonacci of a given number, and it also has a new Draw method. A user of the class interacts with an instance via its public interface, which contains seven methods.

However, there is a certain implied grouping of the interface methods. The first four methods do simple math operations, the next two methods provide advanced math operations, and the Draw method provides a visual representation of the instance.

One of the drawbacks of C++ is that it can expose only one large interface to its users, and this is where COM adds significantly to the design of components. COM provides the ability to partition a component's functionality into multiple interfaces, each one exposing a small, well-defined set of functionality. The client of the component can then interact directly with the piece of functionality that it needs. For example, here's what the component might look like as a COM-based component:

```
class IMath
{
public:
    virtual long   Add( long Op1, long Op2 ) = 0;
    virtual long   Subtract( long Op1, long Op2 ) = 0;
    virtual long   Multiply( long Op1, long Op2 ) = 0;
    virtual long   Divide( long Op1, Op2 ) = 0;
};

class IAdvancedMath
{
public:
    virtual long   Factorial( short sOp ) = 0;
    virtual long   Fibonacci( short sOp ) = 0;
};

class IDraw
{
public:
    virtual void Draw() = 0;
};

class Math : public IMath, public IAdvancedMath, public IDraw
{
public:
    // Implementation of each interface here
    ...
}
```

The `Math` class multiply inherits from three interface classes. Remember, because the classes are pure abstract classes they don't provide any implementation to the `Math` class, which is still responsible for providing the complete implementation.

C++ implements multiple inheritance by building multiple Vtables for the class, and that is exactly what we want. Our C++ class now has three Vtables. In other words, it now contains three COM-based interfaces. We're getting a bit ahead of ourselves, but I felt this example might help with your understanding of multiple interfaces. The important point is that our class can now expose its functionality in a more useful way. If a client wants only to draw the math component, then it need access and understand only the component's `IDraw` interface.

N O T E There are several ways to provide a C++ class with multiple Vtables. The technique used by ATL is multiple inheritance. However, other Microsoft frameworks, such as MFC, use a concept called C++ class nesting. A third option is to use something called interface implementations, which is similar to C++ class nesting. In both cases, an additional C++ class is used to implement each COM interface. These implementation classes are then instantiated or embedded within an outer class through which their Vtables are exposed. See Designing and Using ActiveX Controls (M&T Books) for full coverage of MFC's class nesting idiom.

COM's support for multiple interfaces is also useful from a component implementer's view. As we'll see, a COM component will typically implement a number of interfaces already defined by Microsoft. By choosing from a large number of small, well-defined interfaces, a component can expose only the important functionality. There is no need to implement methods that do not pertain to the functionality it supports.

Multiple interfaces also provide COM's robust support for component versioning. Continuing with our `Math` component example, let's say we want to add a new method to the `IAdvancedMath` interface to calculate the circumference of a circle. At first glance, it's easy—we just add the method to our `IAdvancedMath` interface. But wait—we can't do this, because it will break any existing client application that uses `IAdvancedMath`. Why? Because the client has bound, at compile time, the structure of the `IAdvancedMath` Vtable.

COM requires us to implement a new interface—let's call it `IAdvancedMathEx`—whenever we change an existing interface. Any change to the interface, be it a new method or a new parameter added to an existing method, requires a new interface. Here's our new IAdvancedMathEx interface:

```
class IAdvancedMathEx : public IAdvancedMath
{
public:
   virtual long   Circumference( short sRadius ) = 0;
};
```

We derive the new interface from the old one and add the new method. The most important point is that our component will now expose *both* interfaces. In this way, we can distribute a newer version of the component without breaking any existing clients that use the older IAdvancedMath interface. New clients can take advantage of the new functionality by using the newer IAdvancedMathEx interface. The trick is to provide both implementations within one component and supply a mechanism whereby the client can "ask" for a specific interface. COM provides this functionality through the most important interface of all: IUnknown.

STANDARD COM INTERFACES

The Math component that we've been describing is not yet an actual COM component. All COM components are required to implement a standard COM interface (pulled in by **WINDOWS.H**) called IUnknown. IUnknown serves two purposes. The first is to provide a standard way for the component user (or client) to ask for a specific interface within a given component. QueryInterface, a method of IUnknown, provides this capability. The second purpose of IUnknown is to help in the management of the component's lifetime. The IUnknown interface provides two methods—AddRef and Release—that implement lifetime management of a component instance. We will discuss this in more detail shortly. Following is the definition of IUnknown.

```
class IUnknown
{
   virtual HRESULT   QueryInterface( REFIID riid, void** ppv ) = 0;
   virtual ULONG     AddRef() = 0;
   virtual ULONG     Release() = 0;
};
```

As you can see, IUnknown is an abstract class that provides the requirements for all classes that derive from it. It mandates that the three methods be implemented in the deriving class. It also ensures that the deriving class will have a Vtable, just as in the IMath interfaces we examined earlier.

QueryInterface returns a pointer to a specific interface (such as IUnknown, IMath, and IDraw) contained within a component. The first parameter, REFIID, is a reference to the specific interface ID, which is a unique identifier for the particular interface we are querying for. The second parameter, void**, is where the interface pointer is returned. The return value, HRESULT, is the handle to a COM-specific error structure that contains any error information.

HRESULTs

Most COM interface methods and API functions return an HRESULT (the exceptions are AddRef and Release). An HRESULT in Win32 is defined as a DWORD (32 bits) that contains information about the result of a function or method call. The high-order bit indicates the success or failure of the function. The next 15 bits indicate the facility and provide a way to group related return codes according to the Windows subsystem that generated the error, and the lowest 16 bits provide specific information on what occurred. The structure of HRESULT is identical to the status values used by the Win32 API (see Figure 2.4).

HRESULT structure

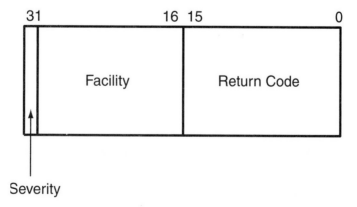

Figure 2.4 HRESULT structure.

COM provides several macros to help in determining the success or failure of a method call. The SUCCEEDED macro evaluates to TRUE if the function call was successful, and the FAILED macro evaluates to TRUE if the function failed. These macros aren't specific to COM and ActiveX but are used throughout the Win32 environment and are defined in **WINERROR.H**. Return values in Win32 are prefixed with S_ when they indicate success, and E_ to indicate failure. Here's a look at **WINERROR.H**.

```
// From WINERROR.H
...
// Generic test for success on any status value (non-negative numbers
// indicate success).
//

#define SUCCEEDED(Status) ((HRESULT)(Status) >= 0)

//
// and the inverse
//

#define FAILED(Status) ((HRESULT)(Status)<0)
...
//
// Create an HRESULT value from component pieces
//

#define MAKE_HRESULT(sev,fac,code) \
    ((HRESULT) (((unsigned long)(sev)<<31) |
                ((unsigned long)(fac)<<16) | ((unsigned long)(code))) )
```

Throughout this chapter, you'll see these macros used extensively. We'll discuss HRESULTs and COM error handling in more detail in Chapter 4.

Implementing IUnknown

In our Math example, users who require the services of our component request one of the component's interfaces. This request can be made either through an existing IUnknown interface (on an existing Math component) or during the component's instantiation (which we'll discuss shortly). COM requires that the IUnknown interface be present in any COM object and that all COM interfaces also contain the IUnknown interface. In this way, a component user can obtain an interface pointer to any interface within the component by querying any existing interface on that component. Here's our Math example with the IUnknown interface added to its implementation.

```
// public interface definition
// An abstract class that derives from IUnknown
class IMath : public IUnknown
{
public:
   virtual long    Add( long Op1, long Op2 ) = 0;
   virtual long    Subtract( long Op1, long Op2 ) = 0;
   virtual long    Multiply( long Op1, long Op2 ) = 0;
   virtual long    Divide( long Op1, Op2 ) = 0;
};

class IAdvancedMath : public IUnknown
{
public:
   virtual long    Factorial( short sOp ) = 0;
   virtual long    Fibonacci( short sOp ) = 0;
};

// The actual implementation
class Math : public IMath, public IAdvancedMath
{
// We also have to implement IUnknown's methods
public:
   HRESULT  QueryInterface( REFIID riid, void** ppv );
   ULONG    Release();
   ULONG    AddRef();

   // IMath
   long    Add( long Op1, long Op2 );
   long    Subtract( long Op1, long Op2 );
   long    Multiply( long Op1, long Op2 );
   long    Divide( long Op1, Op2 );

   // IAdvancedMath
   long    Factorial( short sOp );
   long    Fibonacci( short sOp );
};
```

The addition of deriving IMath from IUnknown requires that we implement seven methods: three from IUnknown and the four original IMath class methods. Every COM interface requires an implementation of IUnknown. Our IAdvancedMath interface also derives from it. Because of the way C++ implements multiple inheritance, we need implement our IUnknown methods only once.

Figure 2.5 shows the Vtable layout for the IMath interface. Our component actually has two Vtables; the IAdvancedMath Vtable is very similar to Figure 2.5.

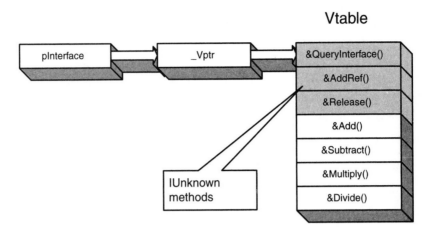

Figure 2.5 IMath interface with IUnknown Added.

Following is the implementation of IUnknown::QueryInterface for the Math component.

```
HRESULT Math::QueryInterface( REFIID riid, void** ppv )
{
    *ppv = 0;

    if ( riid == IID_IUnknown )
        *ppv = (IMath*) this;
    else  if ( riid == IID_IMath )
        *ppv = (IMath*) this;
    else  if ( riid == IID_IAdvancedMath )
        *ppv = (IAdvancedMath*) this;

    if ( *ppv )
    {
        AddRef();
        return( S_OK );
    }
    return (E_NOINTERFACE);
}
```

The basic purpose of QueryInterface is to return a Vtable pointer for the requested interface. One interesting aspect of the preceding code is the way we handle a request for the IUnknown interface. Both IMath and IAdvancedMath implement IUnknown, but we must choose only one implementation to return. This is because one of COM's rules states that an IUnknown interface pointer can be used to identify a specific component instance. So

QueryInterface must always return the same address in response to a request for an IUnknown interface. This arrangement allows client applications to determine whether they are working with the same instance of a component by comparing IUnknown* addresses.

Again, here is an example of a client instantiating and accessing a component's functionality through its COM interfaces. We create the component and ask for its IUnknown interface. After this call succeeds, we query through the IUnknown pointer for the IMath interface and subsequently use its functionality.

```
// Create an instance and return its IUnknown interface
IUnknown* pUnk;
HRESULT hr = CoCreateInstance( CLSID_Math,
                    NULL,
                    CLSCTX_INPROC,
                    IID_IUnknown,
                    (void**) &pUnk );

// Query for IMath
IMath* pMath;
pUnk->QueryInterface( IID_IMath, (void**) &pMath );

// Use IMath
long lResult = pMath->Multiply( 44, 33 );
```

There is a standard way of depicting COM objects and their interfaces. Figure 2.6 depicts our Math class with its interfaces. IUnknown is shown on the upper-right corner because it is always required and so will be present in any COM object. Other interfaces are usually shown on the left-hand side of the component. Remember, though, that every interface on the left also contains an IUnknown interface, because every COM interface also implements IUnknown.

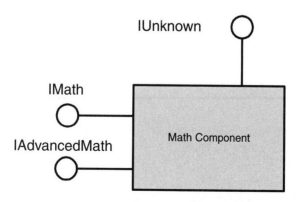

Figure 2.6 COM object representation.

COMPONENT LIFETIMES

We've learned that access to a component's interface is obtained through IUnknown::QueryInterface. Lifetime management of components is handled with the other two methods provided by IUnknown: AddRef and Release. A typical COM component has several interfaces, and each one could be connected to multiple external clients. In our example, the component is a C++ class, and what we're discussing is managing the lifetime of a specific C++ class instance.

The user will create the instance through a mechanism provided by COM and will use the capabilities of that instance through its COM-based interfaces. Because we're using C++ to implement our example component, the instance will be created with the C++ new operator. We'll first describe how and when the instance will be deleted; we'll discuss how it's created in a moment.

Because an instance of a COM component can have multiple interfaces connected to multiple clients, we need a reference-counting capability. Each time a client requests an interface, we increment a counter; when the client is finished with the interface, we decrement the counter. Eventually, when the outstanding interface reference count reaches zero, our COM object instance can go away. IUknown::AddRef and IUnknown::Release provide a way for a client to increment and decrement the instance's internal counter.

In our math class example, we will need to maintain an internal reference counter. When we return an interface, we'll increment the counter, and the client application must then decrement the counter by calling IUnknown::Release when finished with the interface.

The component user cannot directly delete our C++ instance, because the user has only a pointer to our C++ Vtable. In reality, the client shouldn't try to delete the object anyway, because other clients (such as a C++ instance) could be accessing the same component object. Only the component itself, based on its internal reference count, can determine when it can or should be deleted. Following is the implementation of AddRef and Release in our math component.

```
Math::Math()
{
   // Initialize our reference counter
   m_lRef = 0;
}

ULONG Math::AddRef()
{
   return InterlockedIncrement( &m_lRef );
}
```

(code continued on next page)

```
ULONG Math::Release()
{
    if ( InterlockedDecrement ( &m_lRef ) == 0 )
    {
        delete this;
        return 0;
    }

    return m_lRef;
}
```

Our example uses the Win32 API functions `InterlockedIncrement` and `InterlockedDecrement`. These functions provide atomic access to our internal counters and make our component's reference counting thread-safe. We'll discuss other details about thread safety later.

NOTE

To support the `AddRef` and `Release` methods of `IUnknown`, we added a member variable, `m_lRef`, that keeps a count of the current references, or outstanding interface pointers, to our object. The `AddRef` and `Release` methods directly affect a COM interface, but an interface is not an instance of the object itself. This object can have any number of users of its interfaces at a given time and must maintain an internal count of its active interfaces. When this count reaches zero, it is free to delete itself.

It is important that component users diligently call `AddRef` and `Release` to increment and decrement the component's reference count when appropriate. The `AddRef/Release` pair is similar to the `new/delete` pair used to manage memory in C++. Whenever a user obtains a new interface pointer or assigns its value to another variable, `AddRef` should be called through the `new` pointer. You have to be careful, though; some COM interface functions return pointers to interfaces, and, in these cases, the functions themselves call `AddRef` through the returned pointer. The most obvious example is `QueryInterface`. It always calls `AddRef` after returning an interface pointer, so it isn't necessary to call `AddRef` again. Another important example is the COM API function `CoCreateInstance`. It always returns an interface pointer and, before doing so, will call `AddRef` through the returned interface pointer.

GLOBALLY UNIQUE IDENTIFIERS OR GUIDs

In distributed-object and component-based environments, unique identification of components and their interfaces is paramount. COM uses a technique described in the distributed computing environment (DCE) standard for remote procedure calls (RPC). The standard describes something called a Universally Unique Identifier (UUID). The Win32 RPC implementation is based on the OSF (Open Software Foundation) RPC standard and so uses this concept extensively.

A UUID is a 128-bit value that is unique with a very high probability. Note: For complete details on how GUIDs are generated, including complete C source code for a sample generator, see: ftp://ftp.isi.edu/internet-drafts/draft-leach-uuids-guids-00.txt. It combines a unique network address (48 bits) with a very granular time stamp (down to 100 nanoseconds). COM's implementation of the UUID is called a globally unique identifier (GUID) and is basically identical to a UUID. GUIDs are used by COM to identify component classes (CLSID), interfaces (IID), type libraries, and component categories (CATID), to name a few. Following are the GUIDs used by our math component example:

```
// {A888F560-58E4-11d0-A68A-0000837E3100}
DEFINE_GUID( CLSID_Math,
             0xa888f560, 0x58e4, 0x11d0, 0xa6, 0x8a, 0x0,
             0x0, 0x83, 0x7e, 0x31, 0x0);
// {A888F561-58E4-11d0-A68A-0000837E3100}
DEFINE_GUID( IID_IMath,
             0xa888f561, 0x58e4, 0x11d0, 0xa6, 0x8a, 0x0,
             0x0, 0x83, 0x7e, 0x31, 0x0);

// {A888F562-58E4-11d0-A68A-0000837E3100}
DEFINE_GUID( IID_IAdvancedMath,
             0xa888f562, 0x58e4, 0x11d0, 0xa6, 0x8a, 0x0,
             0x0, 0x83, 0x7e, 0x31, 0x0);
```

The DEFINE_GUID macro creates a global constant that can be used throughout your programs, both on the client side and the server side. However, you can define the value only once. COM provides a set of macros to make management of this process easy. At the point in your programs where you want to define a GUID structure, you must include **INITGUID.H** before the header file that includes the declarations. Here's how it works in our math example.

```
//
// imath.h
//

// {A888F560-58E4-11d0-A68A-0000837E3100}
DEFINE_GUID( CLSID_Math,
             0xa888f560, 0x58e4, 0x11d0, 0xa6, 0x8a, 0x0,
             0x0, 0x83, 0x7e, 0x31, 0x0);
// {A888F561-58E4-11d0-A68A-0000837E3100}
DEFINE_GUID( IID_IMath,
             0xa888f561, 0x58e4, 0x11d0, 0xa6, 0x8a, 0x0,
             0x0, 0x83, 0x7e, 0x31, 0x0);
```

(code continued on next page)

```
// {A888F562-58E4-11d0-A68A-0000837E3100}
DEFINE_GUID( IID_IAdvancedMath,
             0xa888f562, 0x58e4, 0x11d0, 0xa6, 0x8a, 0x0,
             0x0, 0x83, 0x7e, 0x31, 0x0);

class IMath : public IUnknown
{
public:
    ...
};

class IAdvancedMath : public IUnknown
{
    ...
};

//
// Client.cpp
//

#include <windows.h>

// Define the included GUIDs
#include <initguid.h>
#include "imath.h"
```

By including **INITGUID.H**, you change the meaning of the DEFINE_GUID macro. It not only declares the GUID's variable but also defines and initializes it.

In our math example, we need three GUIDs. The CLSID identifies our component's class or type, and the two IIDs uniquely identify our COM Vtable interfaces: IMath and IAdvancedMath. There are a number of ways to generate GUIDs for your components. When you're using Visual C++'s AppWizard and ATL Object wizard, the GUIDs will be generated automatically for you. You can programmatically generate them using COM's CoCreateGuid function. You can also generate them using two programs provided with Visual C++. UUIDGEN is a command-line utility that you can use if you need to generate a sequence of GUIDs for your projects. The following command line will generate a list of 50 GUIDs and write them to the specified file.

```
c:\devstudio\vc\bin\uuidgen -n50 > Project_Guids.txt
```

The other program, GUIDGEN, is graphical and provides several formatting methods for the created GUIDs. In our case we need the DEFINE_GUID format. By using the **Copy to clipboard** option, you can paste the GUID definition directly into your source. Figure 2.7 shows the GUIDGEN program.

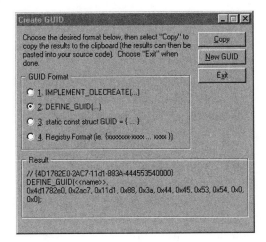

Figure 2.7 GUIDGEN utility.

The COM API provides several functions for comparing GUIDs, creating GUIDs, and converting GUID types. Some of the more useful ones are shown in Table 2.1.

Table 2.1 Useful GUID Helper Functions

FUNCTION	PURPOSE
CoCreateGuid(GUID* pGuid)	Programmatic way of generating one unique GUID
IsEqualGUID(REFGUID, REFGUID)	Compares two GUIDs
IsEqualIID(REFIID, REFIID)	Compares two IIDs
IsEqualCLSID(REFCLSID, REFCLSID)	Compares two CLSIDs
CLSIDFromProgID(LPCOLESTR, LPCLSID)	Returns the CLSID for the given ProgID
ProgIDFromCLSID(REFCLSID, LPOLESTR*)	Returns the ProgID from the CLSID

Programmatic Identifiers (ProgIDs)

A component is uniquely identified by its CLSID, but remembering a component's CLSID can be difficult. COM provides another mechanism for naming a component: the programmatic identifier, or ProgID. A ProgID is a simple character string that is associated through the registry with the component's CLSID.

For example, we've chosen a ProgID of "Chapter2.Math" for our math component. Using the ProgID it's much easier to specify an understandable component name, as in this Visual Basic code.

```
Dim objMath as Object
Set objMath = CreateObject( "Chapter2.Math" )
objMath.Add( 100, 100 )
Set objMath = Nothing
```

The Visual Basic `CreateObject` statement takes as a parameter the component's ProgID. Internally, the statement uses the COM `CLSIDFromProgID` function to convert the ProgID into the component's actual CLSID. `CreateObject` then uses `CoCreateInstance` to create an instance of the component.

THE REGISTRY

Information needed by COM and client applications to locate and instantiate components is stored in the Windows registry. The registry provides nonvolatile storage for component information. Browser applications can determine the number and type of components installed on a system and so on.

The registry orders information in hierarchical manner and has several predefined, top-level keys. The one that is most important to us in this chapter is HKEY_CLASSES_ROOT. This section of the registry stores component information.

An important HKEY_CLASSES_ROOT subkey is CLSID (class identifier). It describes every component installed on the system. For example, our math component requires several registry entries before it will work:

```
REGEDIT
HKEY_CLASSES_ROOT\Chapter2.Math.1 = Chapter2 Math Component
HKEY_CLASSES_ROOT\Chapter2.Math.1\CLSID = {A888F560-58E4-11d0-A68A-
0000837E3100}
HKEY_CLASSES_ROOT\Chapter2.Math = Chapter2 Math Component
HKEY_CLASSES_ROOT\Chapter2.Math\CurVer = Chapter2.Math.1
HKEY_CLASSES_ROOT\Chapter2.Math\CLSID = {A888F560-58E4-11d0-A68A-0000837E3100}

HKEY_CLASSES_ROOT\CLSID\{A888F560-58E4-11d0-A68A-0000837E3100} = Chapter2 Math
Component
HKEY_CLASSES_ROOT\CLSID\{A888F560-58E4-11d0-A68A-0000837E3100}\ProgID =
Chapter2.Math.1
HKEY_CLASSES_ROOT\CLSID\{A888F560-58E4-11d0-A68A-
0000837E3100}\VersionIndependentProgID = Chapter2.Math
HKEY_CLASSES_ROOT\CLSID\{A888F560-58E4-11d0-A68A-0000837E3100}\InprocServer32 =
server.dll
```

The first five lines create a programmatic identifier for our math component. A component's CLSID is its unique identifier, but it is hard to read and hard to remember. COM provides the concept of a ProgID to make it easier for us humans to interact with components. The third line provides a mapping from the ProgID, directly to the corresponding CLSID.

The final lines add all the information necessary for COM to locate our component housing. There's a cross-reference to our ProgID along with component version information. The most important entry is the `InProcServer32` key. It describes the exact location of a component's housing. (We'll discuss this in a moment.) Table 2.2 describes each of the keys in more detail, and Figure 2.8 shows the registry entry relationships.

Table 2.2 Important Registry Key Entries.

ENTRY	PURPOSE
ProgID	Identifies the ProgID string for the COM class. It must contain no more than 39 characters and can contain periods.
InprocServer32	Contains the path and filename of the 32-bit DLL. It does not have to contain the path, but if it does not, it can be loaded only if it resides within the Windows **PATH**. 16-bit versions do not include the '32' extension.
VersionIndependentProgID	Indicates the latest version of a component
LocalServer32	Contains the path and filename of the 32-bit EXE.
CurVer	The ProgID of the latest version of the component class.

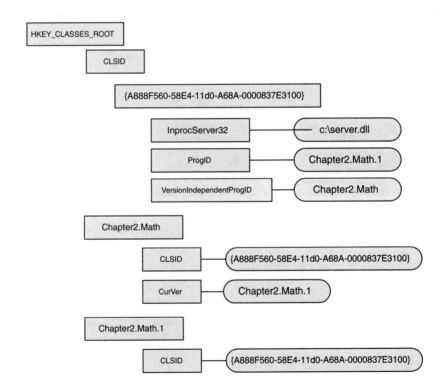

Figure 2.8 COM registry entries.

Component Categories

Basic registry entries provide only limited information about a component. In the early days of COM-based technologies, a few registry entries were all that were needed to specify gross functionality of a component. The absence or existence of a subkey provided a lot of information. With the large number of COM-based components now installed on a typical machine, however, a more granular and useful approach to categorizing the capabilities of components is needed.

Microsoft has responded to this need by providing a new mechanism for describing a component's functionality. The new specification, called *component categories*, provides system-defined and user-defined categories for various components. The information is still stored in the registry, but a new component is provided that makes it easy to add and remove entries without any knowledge of the registry itself. We'll discuss this in more detail in Chapter 8.

OLEVIEW

A good tool for inspecting the registry from a COM perspective is the OLEVIEW utility provided with Visual C++ (and the Platform SDK). OLEVIEW provides several different views of the components on your system as well as a number of other useful capabilities. Figure 2.9 shows OLEVIEW in action.

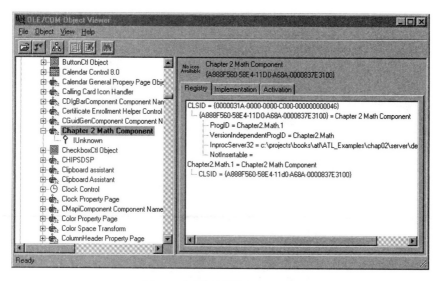

Figure 2.9 OLEVIEW in action.

COMPONENT HOUSINGS

So far we've discussed the requirements for a COM-based component. Once a component is designed and implemented with a specific language (C++ in our case), it must then execute within the context of an operating system process. COM-based components are housed within either an executable (EXE) or a Windows dynamic link library (DLL). Each housing type has its own characteristics. Component developers must implement certain functions differently depending on the particular housing if they're not using a framework that encapsulates these details.

The term *local server* is used to describe a component housing that is an executable. The executable may contain functionality in addition to supporting COM-based components. For example, Microsoft Word is a local server. It provides word processing capabilities for users but also exposes a number of COM components that other applications can access.

An *in-process server* is a Windows DLL that houses COM-based components. A DLL executes in the context of the calling process, so the client process has direct memory access to any DLL-based components. This concept will become important when we discuss COM-based custom interfaces and marshaling.

A *remote server* is a housing that loads and executes on a remote machine. Typically, a remote server is implemented within an executable, although this is not a requirement. Components housed only within DLLs can be accessed remotely. COM provides a *surrogate* process in which the remote DLL can execute.

One of COM's benefits is that it provides location transparency for client processes (the user of the component). As we described earlier, COM-based services can be implemented in three different configurations: in-process via a DLL on the local machine, across-process on the same machine (local server), or on a remote machine via a DLL or executable. The client process, however, requires no knowledge of how the component is implemented or where the service is located. The client creates an instance of a component, and it's up to COM to locate and launch the housing. This makes COM-based components inherently multitier.

You should consider two primary factors when determining how to implement your components. The first is performance. Because in-process servers execute in the address space of the client process, they provide the best performance. No marshaling of method parameters is required. We'll discuss marshaling in a later chapter. The second, is client robustness. By implementing your component in an in-process housing, you can potentially crash the client. Major errors in an out-of-process component will not bring down the client application.

CLASS FACTORIES

Because COM objects can be located outside the client's process space and must be accessed from various languages, a language-independent way of instantiating a component is required. In C++ the new operator is used to create an instance of an object, but this is just an implementation detail of the component. COM supplies a standard interface, IClassFactory, that components must provide if they are to be externally instantiated. Following is the definition of IClassFactory. Like all COM interfaces, it must implement IUnknown.

```
class IClassFactory : public IUnknown
{
    virtual HRESULT CreateInstance( LPUNKNOWN pUnk,
                                    REFIID riid, void** ppv ) = 0;
    virtual HRESULT LockServer( BOOL fLock ) = 0;
};
```

A class factory is a COM object whose sole purpose is to facilitate the creation of other, more useful COM objects. The CreateInstance method does what it says: it creates an instance of the specified component class and returns the requested interface on that instance. The LockServer method provides a way for a client to lock a server in memory. By locking a server in memory, the client ensures that it will be available when needed even when there are no instantiated components within the server. It is typically done for performance reasons. Following is the class factory implementation for our Math component.

```
MathClassFactory::MathClassFactory()
{
    m_lRef = 0;
}

MathClassFactory::~MathClassFactory()
{
}

STDMETHODIMP MathClassFactory::QueryInterface( REFIID riid, void** ppv )
{
    *ppv = 0;

    if ( riid == IID_IUnknown || riid == IID_IClassFactory )
        *ppv = this;

    if ( *ppv )
    {
        AddRef();
        return S_OK;
    }
}
```

```
      return( E_NOINTERFACE );
}

STDMETHODIMP_(ULONG) MathClassFactory::AddRef()
{
    return InterlockedIncrement( &m_lRef );
}

STDMETHODIMP_(ULONG) MathClassFactory::Release()
{
    if ( InterlockedDecrement( &m_lRef ) == 0 )
    {
       delete this;
       return 0;
    }

    return m_lRef;
}

STDMETHODIMP MathClassFactory::CreateInstance
      ( LPUNKNOWN pUnkOuter, REFIID riid, void** ppvObj )
{
    Math*      pMath;
    HRESULT    hr;

    *ppvObj = 0;

    // Create our component instance
    pMath = new Math;

    if ( pMath == 0 )
       return( E_OUTOFMEMORY );

    hr = pMath->QueryInterface( riid, ppvObj );

    if ( FAILED( hr ) )
       delete pMath;

    return hr;
}

STDMETHODIMP MathClassFactory::LockServer( BOOL fLock )
{
    if ( fLock )
       InterlockedIncrement( &g_lLocks );
    else
       InterlockedDecrement( &g_lLocks );

     return S_OK;
}
```

In most cases, COM will handle the details of creating a component instance when the client uses the CoCreateInstance API call. However, a client can gain direct access to a component's class factory by using COM's CoGetClassObject function. In most cases, the CoGetClassObject function will return a pointer to the component's IClassFactory interface. Here's an example:

```
int main()
{
    IClassFactory* pCF;
    IMath* pMath;
    HRESULT hr;

    // Get the class factory for the Math class
    hr = CoGetClassObject( CLSID_Math,
                           CLSCTX_INPROC,
                           NULL,
                           IID_IClassFactory,
                           &pCF );

    // using the class factory interface create an instance of the
    // component and return the IMath interface.
    pCF->CreateInstance( NULL, IID_IMath, &pMath );

    // Release the class factory
    pCF->Release();

    // Use the component to do some work
    long lResult = pMath->Add( 100, 433 );

    // Release it when we're finished
    pMath->Release();
}
```

CoGetClassObject is a COM API function that returns the class factory of the requested component (identified by the CLSID). CoGetClassObject then returns the class factory interface so that we can create an instance of the Math component class. Once we've used the class factory, we call Release, which then deletes the class factory instance. This three-step process is performed often, so COM provides a helper function, CoCreateInstance that encapsulates the steps. By using CoCreateInstance, you don't have to deal with the class factory interface; you just call CoCreateInstance with the specific component interface that you require.

Figure 2.10 depicts what we've built so far. We have two components, each with a number of interfaces. What we need now is a way of delivering or housing this functionality. COM provides mechanisms for this as well.

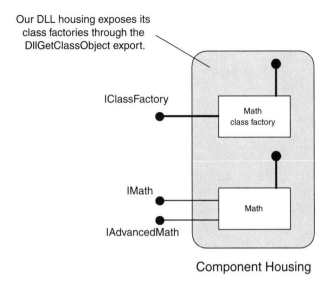

Our DLL housing exposes its
class factories through the
DllGetClassObject export.

IClassFactory

Math
class factory

IMath

Math

IAdvancedMath

Component Housing

Figure 2.10 Our Math component and its class factory.

COM-BASED REUSE

COM provides two methods for reusing component class objects: containment and aggregation. They are similar to C++ reuse techniques, but COM provides *binary* reuse as opposed to the compile-time or source-code-dependent reuse provided by C++. We aren't going to cover these methods in detail here, because we have a chapter on this topic later. Here we provide a brief description, because we will encounter the terms in almost every chapter.

Containment

COM *containment* is similar to the C++ technique of class composition. Class composition is the technique in which you embed a class instance inside your own class. For example, you might implement a stack component by using an array object inside your stack class. In this way, you are "containing" the array class. A user of the class does not have direct access the array's methods unless you explicitly expose them through your stack class's public interface.

Containment and composition achieve reuse by using the services of a COM object or C++ class internally. The interface of the contained component is exposed only indirectly (if at all) via methods provided by the containing (or *outer*) component. The internal (or *inner)* COM component's interfaces are used by the outer COM object in the implementation of its interfaces. The outer object can, if it chooses, expose the inner object's interfaces as well. The lifetime of the inner object is controlled completely by the outer component, just as in C++. A COM object does not have to do anything to support being used as an inner or contained object.

Aggregation

COM object *aggregation* is similar to COM containment except that the interface of the inner or contained COM object is directly exposed. The aggregate object doesn't need or use the functionality of the contained object internally but instead exposes the inner object's interfaces as if they were its own. The IUnknown interface of the outer aggregate object provides access to all the interfaces of the inner object. This detail makes it complicated to implement aggregation at times.

The management of the lifetimes of the outer and inner objects must be coordinated through the IUnknown implementation. Successful lifetime management of the aggregate object requires that the inner object provide support for a *controlling unknown*: the outer object in aggregation. When an inner COM object is created as part of an aggregate, it is passed a pointer to the outer object's IUnknown implementation. The inner object then defers its IUnknown implementation to that of the outer object's. This arrangement provides a consistent approach to the management of the aggregate object's lifetime. A COM object supports aggregation if it includes support for deferring its IUnknown implementation to that of a controlling unknown.

COM APIs

Microsoft provides a number of Win32 API functions specific to COM, ActiveX, and OLE. There are more than 100 COM-specific calls and we can't cover them all here. By studying the major COM API functions, however, we can garner a good understanding of how COM works. The COM API functions provide the basis of higher-level services such as OLE and ActiveX. Remember that COM is a bunch of interface definitions that must be implemented by you, and these API calls get things started. Table 2.3 shows the API functions that we'll be using in this chapter.

Table 2.3 Basic COM Functions

FUNCTION	PURPOSE
CoInitialize, CoInitializeEx	Initializes the COM libraries for use by a process.
CoUninitialize (client and server)	Releases the COM libraries when their services are no longer needed. Not used by in-process servers.
CoGetClassObject (client)	Get an instance of a class factory for a specific COM object.
CoCreateGUID (client and server)	Creates a new unique GUID.
CoCreateInstance (client), CoCreateInstanceEx (client)	Creates an instance of a specific COM object, which may be on a remote machine.
CoRegisterClass (server)	Registers the existence of a class factory for a particular COM object.
DllCanUnloadNow (in-process server)	Called periodically by COM to determine whether the DLL can be unloaded (when there are no objects instantiated within the DLL housing). Implemented by in-process servers.
DllGetClassObject (server)	Entry point implemented by in-process servers so that its class factory interfaces can be obtained by client processes.

CoInitialize and CoInitializeEx

CoInitialize initializes the COM libraries and DLLs so that the other APIs can be used. CoInitialize takes one parameter, which currently is reserved and should be NULL.

CoInitializeEx was added to support the various COM threading models. Before NT 4.0, COM supported only the *apartment* threading model, which is the default threading model for CoInitialize. CoInitializeEx takes two parameters. The first parameter is reserved and should be NULL, and the second parameter specifies one of the threading models from the COINIT enumeration. We'll discuss COM threading in detail in a later chapter.

```
typedef enum tagCOINIT{
   COINIT_APARTMENTTHREADED = 0x2,   // Apartment model
   COINIT_MULTITHREADED     = 0x0,   // OLE calls objects on any thread.
   COINIT_DISABLE_OLE1DDE   = 0x4,   // Don't use DDE for Ole1 support.
   COINIT_SPEED_OVER_MEMORY = 0x8,   // Trade memory for speed.
} COINIT;
```

CoUninitialize

CoUninitialize is called to free the use of the COM libraries and DLLs. CoUninitialize should be called only if CoInitialize has previously been called successfully. Also, every call to CoInitialize should be balanced with a corresponding call to CoUninitialize.

CoRegisterClassObject

CoRegisterClassObject is called by an out-of process server to register its class factories as available. CoRegisterClassObject must be called for every class factory provided by an executable. This should be done as soon as possible before processing the Windows message loop. CoRegisterClassObject is only used by executables. In-process servers export the DllGetClassObject function to expose its component's class factories.

Table 2.4 CoRegisterClassObject Parameters

PARAMETER	DESCRIPTION
REFCLSID rclsid	The CLSID for the component class being registered.
LPUNKNOWN pUnk	The IUnknown pointer for the component class being registered.
DWORD dwClsContext	The requested context for the executable. This can be one of the following:
	CLSCTX_INPROC_SERVER
	CLSCTX_INPROC_HANDLER
	CLSCTX_LOCAL_SERVER
	CLSCTX_REMOTE_SERVER
DWORD flags	REGCLS flags specify how multiple instances of the component should be created. One of the following:
	REGCLS_SINGLEUSE
	REGCLS_MULTIPLEUSE
	REGCLS_MULTI_SEPARATE
LPDWORD lpdwRegister	A value returned that must be used when deregistering the class object using the CoRevokeClassObject function.

CoGetClassObject

CoGetClassObject is used by a COM client to obtain a pointer to the IClassFactory interface of the specified component class. The IClassFactory pointer can then be used to create multiple instances of the component class.

COM will ensure that the server is either loaded (DLL) or running (EXE). If the component is housed within a DLL, COM loads the DLL and retrieves the requested interface by calling its exported `DllGetClassObject` function. If the component is contained within an executable that is not running, COM launches the executable, either locally or remotely, waits for the server to register its class factories with `CoRegisterClassObject`, and then returns the requested interface to the client.

For NT 4.0 and later, the COSERVERINFO parameter is used to allow instantiation on remote systems. The COSERVERINFO structure allows specification of the server name as a UNC name (for example, `\\twa_nt`), DNS name (such as `www.WidgetWare.com`), or IP address (such as `191.51.33.1`).

```
typedef struct _COSERVERINFO
{
    DWORD dwReserved1;
    LPWSTR pwszName;
    COAUTHINFO *pAuthInfo;
    DWORD dwReserved2;
} COSERVERINFO;
```

In most cases, the client should use the shorthand `CoCreateInstance` function described next. There are two cases when a client application might use `CoGetClassObject`. First, suppose that the client application intends to create several instances of the component object. In this case, it would be efficient to retrieve only one copy of the class factory for the creation of these components. The second case occurs when the client application requires access to the `IClassFactory::LockServer` method to lock the component housing in memory, typically for performance reasons. Table 2.5 lists the `CoGetClassObject` parameters.

Table 2.5 `CoGetClassObject` Parameters

PARAMETER	DESCRIPTION
REFCLSID rclsid	A reference to the CLSID for the specific component.
DWORD dwClsContext	The requested context for the server housing. This can be one, two, or all of the following:
	CLSCTX_INPROC_SERVER
	CLSCTX_INPROC_HANDLER
	CLSCTX_LOCAL_SERVER
	CLSCTX_REMOTE_SERVER
COSERVERINFO pServerInfo	Pointer to COSERVERINFO structure.
REFIID riid	A reference to an IID for the specific interface to be returned from the created class object. This will normally be IClassFactory so that the client can create an instance of the required component.
VOID** ppvObj	A void pointer to return the specified interface.

CoCreateInstance

CoCreateInstance is used by the client application to create an instance of the specified component class. It is a helper function that calls CoGetClassObject to get a class factory for the component and then uses the IClassFactory::CreateInstance method to create the component instance. You should use CoCreateInstance instead of performing the three-step process shown next, unless your requirements match those discussed previously.

```
// What CoCreateInstance does internally
CoGetClassObject(..., &pCF );
pCF->CreateInstance(..., &pInt );
pCF->Release();
```

CoCreateInstance's parameters are similar to those required by CoGetClassObject. The only difference is that the client using CoCreateInstance will ask for the specific interface on the component (such as IDispatch) instead of an IClassFactory pointer.

To support distributed COM, the CoGetClassObject method uses a previously reserved parameter to pass the COSERVERINFO parameter. However, CoCreateInstance did not have one reserved, so a new method, CoCreateInstanceEx, is required. CoCreateInstanceEx is used to create an instance of the COM object on a remote machine. The fourth parameter supports the new COSERVERINFO parameter. The format is the same as described earlier with the CoGetClassObject function.

To improve performance when creating a component instance, the MULTI_QI structure was added to allow the client to query the interface for multiple interfaces in one call. The MULTI_QI structure allows you to provide an array of IIDs. This array will be returned with the array of interfaces. The parameters for CoCreateInstance and CoCreateInstanceEx are shown in Tables 2.6 and 2.7.

```
typedef struct _MULTI_QI
{
    const IID*    pIID;
    IUnknown *    pItf;
    HRESULT       hr;
} MULTI_QI;
```

Table 2.6 CoCreateInstance Parameters

PARAMETER	DESCRIPTION
REFCLSID rclsid	A reference to the CLSID for the specific component.
IUnknown* pUnkOuter	The controlling outer unknown when aggregation is used.
DWORD dwClsContext	The requested context for the server housing. This can be one, two, or all of the following:
	CLSCTX_INPROC_SERVER
	CLSCTX_INPROC_HANDLER
	CLSCTX_LOCAL_SERVER
	CLSCTX_REMOTE_SERVER
REFIID riid	A reference to an IID for the specific interface to be returned from the created component object.
VOID** ppvObj	A void pointer to return the specified interface.

Table 2.7 CoCreateInstanceEx Parameters

PARAMETER	DESCRIPTION
REFCLSID rclsid	A reference to the CLSID for the specific component.
IUnknown* pUnkOuter	The controlling outer unknown when aggregation is used.
DWORD dwClsContext	The requested context for the server housing. This can be one, two, or all of the following:
	CLSCTX_INPROC_SERVER
	CLSCTX_INPROC_HANDLER
	CLSCTX_LOCAL_SERVER
	CLSCTX_REMOTE_SERVER
COSERVERINFO* pServerInfo	Information about the remove server machine.
ULONG	Number of QueryInterfaces to perform for the MULTI_QI structure.
MULTI_QI	An array of MULTI_QI structures. This makes it more efficient to retrieve a series of interfaces from the create call.

DllCanUnloadNow

DllCanUnloadNow is implemented by in-process servers. Its purpose is to allow COM to periodically check to determine whether the DLL can be unloaded. DllCanUnloadNow takes no parameters and returns either S_FALSE, indicating that the DLL cannot be unloaded, or S_OK, which indicates that the DLL can be unloaded.

DllGetClassObject

DllGetClassObject is implemented by in-process servers to expose the class factories for its component objects. When a client application requests a component housed within an in-process server, COM calls the DllGetClassObject entry point within the DLL with the parameters shown in Table 2.8.

Table 2.8 DllGetClassObject Parameters

PARAMETER	DESCRIPTION
REFCLSID rclsid	A reference to the CLSID for the specific component.
DWORD dwClsContext	The requested context for the DLL. This can be one of the following:
	CLSCTX_INPROC_SERVER
	CLSCTX_INPROC_HANDLER
	CLSCTX_LOCAL_SERVER
LPVOID pvReserved	Reserved. Must be NULL
REFIID riid	A reference to an IID for the specific interface to be returned from the created COM object. This will normally be IClassFactory so that the client can create an instance of the requested component.
VOID** ppvObj	A void pointer to return the specified interface.

MISCELLANEOUS COM DETAILS

The purpose of this chapter is to give you an effective introduction to COM. It's hard to cover such a large topic in one chapter, and we will continue to build on the concepts presented here in the later chapters. However, there are a few more details that need to be cleared up before we move on.

COM C++ Macros: STDMETHOD and STDMETHODIMP

To this point, we haven't been using the standard COM and OLE macros when declaring interfaces, because for instructional purposes they get in the way of understanding what's going on. COM and ATL use C/C++ macros extensively to hide the implementation details of the various platforms. We're getting ready to write some real code, so it's time I explained the macros that we'll be using. There are four macros for COM interface declarations and definitions: STDMETHOD, STDMETHODIMP, STDMETHOD_, and STDMETHODIMP_. You'll use the first two macros nearly all of the time, because they indicate an HRESULT return from a method. Those that end with an underscore are used only with IUnknown's AddRef and Release, and indicate a user-specified return value. In an earlier example of IMath we declared it this way:

```
// public interface definition of our Math component
// An abstract class
class IMath
{
public:
    virtual long   Add( long Op1, long Op2 ) = 0;
    virtual long   Subtract( long Op1, long Op2 ) = 0;
    virtual long   Multiply( long Op1, long Op2 ) = 0;
    virtual long   Divide( long Op1, Op2 ) = 0;
};
```

Before we convert the preceding code to use the macros, we need to understand one more thing about COM. As we described earlier with only two exceptions every COM interface method should return an HRESULT. But so far we've been returning longs from our IMath methods. At this point, we must move the result of our computation from a return value to a pass-by-pointer parameter. This step is important and is required because we must return an HRESULT.

N O T E

Requiring all interface methods to return HRESULTs seems strange and restrictive at first, especially if you like the idea of using the return value as part of your implementation. However, it isn't a big problem because there are ways to enable a client application to treat a method parameter as a return value. We'll discuss this in detail later.

Using COM's macros and moving our return value to the end as a pointer, our interface is declared as follows.

```
class IMath : public IUnknown
{
public:
    STDMETHOD(Add)( long, long, long* )      PURE;
    STDMETHOD(Subtract)( long, long, long* ) PURE;
    STDMETHOD(Multiply)( long, long, long* ) PURE;
    STDMETHOD(Divide)( long, long, long* )   PURE;
};
```

The actual expansion of STDMETHOD_ depends on the target platform and whether you're using C or C++. The expansion for Win32 using C++ is as follows:

```
// OBJBASE.H

#define STDMETHODCALLTYPE          __stdcall
...
#define STDMETHOD(method)          virtual HRESULT STDMETHODCALLTYPE method
#define STDMETHOD_(type,method)    virtual type STDMETHODCALLTYPE method
#define PURE                       = 0

#define STDMETHODIMP               HRESULT STDMETHODCALLTYPE
#define STDMETHODIMP_(type)        type STDMETHODCALLTYPE
```

As you can see, our earlier example is very similar to the expanded macro version except for the additional return type __stdcall. This Microsoft-specific calling convention is used by the Win32 API functions. It specifies that the callee will clean up the stack after the call. It isn't crucial to our understanding, but it's interesting reading. As you can see, PURE equates to = 0 and is another way of making a function pure virtual.

The STDMETHOD macro is also used in the declaration of interface methods within the implementing class. The only difference is that you don't need the PURE qualifier. The STD-METHODIMP macros are used when you actually implement the interface function, usually in your .CPP file. Following are the declarations of our IMath methods within the Math class.

```
Math : public IMath, public IAdvancedMath
{
    // IMath
    STDMETHOD(Add) ( long, long, long* );
    STDMETHOD(Subtract) ( long, long, long* );
    STDMETHOD(Multiply) ( long, long, long* );
    STDMETHOD(Divide) ( long, long, long* );
};
```

When we implement the functions in our **.CPP** file, we use the STDMETHODIMP macros:

```
STDMETHODIMP Math::Add( long lOp1, long lOp2, long* pResult )
{
    *pResult = lOp1 + lOp2;
    return S_OK;
}

STDMETHODIMP Math::Subtract( long lOp1, long lOp2, long* pResult )
{
    *pResult = lOp1 - lOp2;
    return S_OK;
}
...
```

The primary purpose of the STDMETHODIMP macro is to prepend the HRESULT return type to the method implementation.

COM and Unicode

All COM functions and standard interface methods require Unicode strings. Unicode strings, which are also referred to as *wide character strings*, store characters as two bytes, primarily to enable support for international character sets such as Kanji. The Windows NT operating system also implements its APIs using native Unicode strings. When you build a Visual C++ application, you have the option of building an ANSI- or Unicode-based application.

Windows 95 provides native ANSI support, so if you want your application or component to run on both Windows 95 and Windows NT, you must use the ANSI build. If you will always run your applications on Windows NT, however, you can build your applications in straight Unicode and gain a slight performance improvement.

Most of us must target both operating systems and so do our work with ANSI, or multibyte, strings. As a result, we must convert our strings from ANSI to Unicode whenever we pass them to a COM function or through a COM interface method. There are several techniques that you can use to perform this conversion.

First, if you are passing a literal, you can simply add an *L* to the front of the string. The C++ compiler supports wide strings indicated in this manner. Here's an example.

```
// Get the unique CLSID from the ProgID
HRESULT hr = ::CLSIDFromProgID( L"Chapter2.Math.1", &clsid );
```

Second, you can use the native Win32 APIs to convert from Unicode to ANSI and back. Here's an example of converting an ANSI string (multibyte) to Unicode (wide).

```
// Convert the ProgID to Unicode
char* szProgID = "Chapter2.Math.1";
WCHAR  szWideProgID[128];
CLSID  clsid;
long lLen = MultiByteToWideChar( CP_ACP,
                    0,
                    szProgID,
                    strlen( szProgID ),
                    szWideProgID,
                    sizeof( szWideProgID ) );
// Terminate the returned string
szWideProgID[ lLen ] = '\0';
```

Third, you can use one of the many macros supplied by MFC or ATL. We haven't gotten into either of these frameworks yet, but we're discussing it, so we might as well take a quick look at an example.

```
USES_CONVERSION;

// Get the unique CLSID from the ProgID
char* szProgID = "Chapter2.Math.1";
HRESULT hr = ::CLSIDFromProgID( A2W( szProgID ), &clsid );
```

The USES_CONVERSION macro supplies temporary variables for the conversion, and, as you can see, the A2W macro converts from ANSI to Unicode, in place. There is a corresponding W2A and a number of macros for converting other string types. See **\DevStudio\VC\ALT\INCLUDE\ATLCON.H** for more details.

COM and Polymorphism

COM supports the object-oriented concept of polymorphism, but it isn't easy to get this across to most new students. Typically, what they need is a concrete example. Earlier in this chapter, we demonstrated the use of Vtables using a simple C++ Fruit class. To refresh your memory, here it is:

```
int main()
{
   Fruit* pFruitList[4];
   pFruitList[0] = new Apple;
   pFruitList[1] = new Orange;
   pFruitList[2] = new Grape;
   pFruitList[3] = new GrannySmith;

   for( int i = 0; i < 4; i++ )
      pFruitList[i]->Draw();
}

// Produces this output
>
> I'm an Apple
> I'm an Orange
> I'm a Grape
> I'm a Granny Smith Apple
>
```

Polymorphism is the ability of an object to respond differently to the same message (in C++, a message is basically a method). Another way to look at it is to say that the user of an object uses the same methods independent of the object's underlying implementation.

In the example, each of the four different objects (such as Apple and Orange) have each implemented the Draw method described in the base Fruit class. A client application can then interact with each object using exactly the same methods. However, each object is free to implement its Draw in any way it deems necessary and can also respond differently to the Draw method. Here's an example:

```
class IFruit {
   virtual void Draw() = 0;
   ...
};

IFruit* pFruit[4];
CoCreateInstance( CLSID_Apple, IID_IFruit, ..., (void**) &(pFruit[0]));
CoCreateInstance( CLSID_Orange, IID_IFruit, ..., (void**) &(pFruit[1]));
CoCreateInstance( CLSID_Grape, IID_IFruit, ..., (void**) &(pFruit[2]));
CoCreateInstance( CLSID_GrannySmith, IID_IFruit, ..., (void**) &(pFruit[3]));

for( I = 0; I < 3; I++ )
   pFruit->Draw();
```

There we have it: four different COM objects, each possibly implemented by a different vendor, and all of them supporting the IFruit interface. From the client's perspective, it can interact with each component in exactly the same way.

AN EXAMPLE: THE SIMPLE COM CLIENT AND SERVER

We have discussed a number of COM's features and attributes. Most of the demonstration code from this chapter comes from the example that is described next. What follows are the step-by-step details of creating a C++ COM client and server application. Although the Math component is simple, building the infrastructure to support the component takes quite a bit of code, and much of the support code is the same for every COM component you build. That is why frameworks such as ATL are popular. They encapsulate the tedious, routine code and allow you to focus on providing your components unique functionality.

To get a solid understanding of how COM is implemented, I recommend that you download the code for this example (see the Preface for details) and step through it in debug mode. You can also follow along and type all the code by hand; that is what my students do. They complain but are quite appreciative when everything finally works. The understanding gained by typing the code and getting it to work will help as you read the forthcoming chapters.

Create the Visual C++ Project

Start Visual C++ and create a new project, selecting **Win32 Dynamic-Link Library**. Give it the name "**Server**"

The initial project does not contain any files. We must build each of them ourselves. I told you it would be tedious at first.

Create IMATH.H

The next step is to declare the component's interfaces as abstract classes. Before we do that, however, we need three new GUIDs: one to uniquely identify the component and the other two to uniquely identify our component's custom interfaces. Use the GUIDGEN utility (shown in Figure 2.11) to create three GUIDs. Copy each one to the clipboard and then paste it into your **IMATH.H** file (described next). Be sure to use the DEFINE_GUID format.

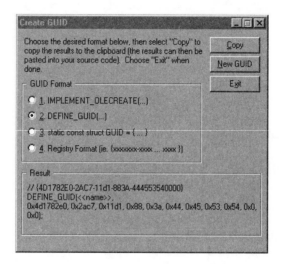

Figure 2.11 The GUIDGEN utility.

The GUIDGEN utility is located in the **\DevStudio\VC\BIN** directory.

NOTE

Type the following and save it in a file called **IMATH.H**. You should replace the GUIDs shown with those that you've created using GUIDGEN.

```
//
// imath.h
//
```

```
// {A888F560-58E4-11d0-A68A-0000837E3100}
DEFINE_GUID( CLSID_Math,
             0xa888f560, 0x58e4, 0x11d0, 0xa6, 0x8a, 0x0, 0x0, 0x83, 0x7e,
0x31, 0x0);
// {A888F561-58E4-11d0-A68A-0000837E3100}
DEFINE_GUID( IID_IMath,
             0xa888f561, 0x58e4, 0x11d0, 0xa6, 0x8a, 0x0, 0x0, 0x83, 0x7e,
0x31, 0x0);

// {A888F562-58E4-11d0-A68A-0000837E3100}
DEFINE_GUID( IID_IAdvancedMath,
             0xa888f562, 0x58e4, 0x11d0, 0xa6, 0x8a, 0x0, 0x0, 0x83, 0x7e,
0x31, 0x0);
class IMath : public IUnknown
{
public:
    STDMETHOD(Add)( long, long, long* )      PURE;
    STDMETHOD(Subtract)( long, long, long* ) PURE;
    STDMETHOD(Multiply)( long, long, long* ) PURE;
    STDMETHOD(Divide)( long, long, long* )   PURE;
};

class IAdvancedMath : public IUnknown
{
public:
    STDMETHOD(Factorial)( short, long* ) PURE;
    STDMETHOD(Fibonacci)( short, long* )  PURE;
};
```

We separate our interface definition, CLSID, and IIDs from the actual implementation so that we can provide just this information to the client program. With only this information, the client can access our component's functionality. Remember, the primary purpose of the preceding declarations is to provide potential clients with the correct Vtable layout and parameter types so that they can access our component's interfaces.

The client doesn't need the CLSID—we will access the component through its ProgID—but it doesn't hurt to put it here. The PURE macro equates to = 0 to make the methods abstract.

Declare the Component and Class Factory

Next, we declare our component class and a class factory for the component. Create a new file called **MATH.H** and enter the following code:

```
//
// math.h
//

#include "imath.h"

extern long g_lObjs;
extern long g_lLocks;

class Math : public IMath, public IAdvancedMath
{
protected:
    // Reference count
    long          m_lRef;

public:
    Math();
    ~Math();

public:
    // IUnknown
    STDMETHOD(QueryInterface( REFIID, void** ));
    STDMETHOD_(ULONG, AddRef());
    STDMETHOD_(ULONG, Release());

    // IMath
    STDMETHOD(Add)( long, long, long* );
    STDMETHOD(Subtract)( long, long, long* );
    STDMETHOD(Multiply)( long, long, long* );
    STDMETHOD(Divide)( long, long, long* );

    // IAdvancedMath
    STDMETHOD(Factorial)( short, long* );
    STDMETHOD(Fibonacci)( short, long* );
};

class MathClassFactory : public IClassFactory
{
protected:
    long      m_lRef;

public:
    MathClassFactory();
    ~MathClassFactory();

    // IUnknown
    STDMETHOD( QueryInterface(REFIID, void** ));
    STDMETHOD_(ULONG, AddRef());
    STDMETHOD_(ULONG, Release());
```

```
   // IClassFactory
   STDMETHOD(CreateInstance)(LPUNKNOWN, REFIID, void**);
   STDMETHOD(LockServer)(BOOL);
};
```

We derive our math class from both of our abstract interface classes—IMath and IAdvancedMath, which also derive from IUnknown. We then provide non-abstract declarations for the interface methods. The two global variables keep track of the total number of component instances within the DLL and the number of calls that have been made to IClassFactory::LockServer.

Implement the Component and Class Factory Classes

Create a **MATH.CPP** file for the component's implementation and add the following:

```
//
// Math.cpp
//

#include <windows.h>
#include "math.h"

//
// Math class implementation
//
Math::Math()
{
   m_lRef = 0;

   // Increment the global object count
   InterlockedIncrement( &g_lObjs );
}

// The destructor
Math::~Math()
{
   // Decrement the global object count
   InterlockedDecrement( &g_lObjs );
}
```

In our constructor, we initialize the internal reference counter to zero and increment the global instance count for the DLL. Our destructor then decrements the global count. Next, add the following:

```
STDMETHODIMP Math::QueryInterface( REFIID riid, void** ppv )
{
    *ppv = 0;
```

(code continued on next page)

```
    if ( riid == IID_IUnknown )
        *ppv = (IMath*) this;
    else  if ( riid == IID_IMath )
        *ppv = (IMath*) this;
    else  if ( riid == IID_IAdvancedMath )
        *ppv = (IAdvancedMath*) this;

    if ( *ppv )
    {
        AddRef();
        return( S_OK );
    }
    return (E_NOINTERFACE);
}

STDMETHODIMP_(ULONG) Math::AddRef()
{
    return InterlockedIncrement( &m_lRef );
}

STDMETHODIMP_(ULONG) Math::Release()
{
    if ( InterlockedDecrement( &m_lRef ) == 0 )
    {
        delete this;
        return 0;
    }

    return m_lRef;
}
```

This code provides the implementation of our three IUnknown methods. Our component supports three interfaces: the required IUnknown and our two custom interfaces. QueryInterface checks to see that the client has requested one that is supported and returns a pointer to a pointer to the appropriate Vtable. Remember, when using multiple inheritance you must explicitly cast the instance to get the correct Vtable. Before returning, we increment the internal reference count by calling AddRef.

Next, add the implementations for each exposed interface method.

```
STDMETHODIMP Math::Add( long lOp1, long lOp2, long* pResult )
{
    *pResult = lOp1 + lOp2;
    return S_OK;
}
```

```
STDMETHODIMP Math::Subtract( long lOp1, long lOp2, long* pResult )
{
   *pResult = lOp1 - lOp2;
   return S_OK;
}

STDMETHODIMP Math::Multiply( long lOp1, long lOp2, long* pResult )
{
   *pResult = lOp1 * lOp2;
   return S_OK;
}

STDMETHODIMP Math::Divide( long lOp1, long lOp2, long* pResult )
{
   *pResult = lOp1 / lOp2;
   return S_OK;
}

// IAdvancedMath interface
long calcFactorial( short n )
{
   // The factorial of 0 is 1
   if ( n <= 1 )
      return 1;

   return n * calcFactorial( n - 1 );
}

STDMETHODIMP Math::Factorial( short sOp, long* pResult )
{
   *pResult = calcFactorial( sOp );
   return S_OK;
}

long calcFibonacci( short n )
{
   if ( n <= 1 )
      return 1;

   return calcFibonacci( n - 1 ) + calcFibonacci( n - 2 );
}

STDMETHODIMP Math::Fibonacci( short sOp, long* pResult )
{
   *pResult = calcFibonacci( sOp );
   return S_OK;
}
```

The preceding code is our no-brainer implementation, but at least it doesn't get in the way of our understanding of COM at this point. Next, we have the implementation of the class factory class.

```
MathClassFactory::MathClassFactory()
{
    m_lRef = 0;
}

MathClassFactory::~MathClassFactory()
{
}

STDMETHODIMP MathClassFactory::QueryInterface( REFIID riid, void** ppv )
{
    *ppv = 0;

    if ( riid == IID_IUnknown || riid == IID_IClassFactory )
        *ppv = this;

    if ( *ppv )
    {
        AddRef();
        return S_OK;
    }

    return( E_NOINTERFACE );
}

STDMETHODIMP_(ULONG) MathClassFactory::AddRef()
{
    return InterlockedIncrement( &m_lRef );
}

STDMETHODIMP_(ULONG) MathClassFactory::Release()
{
    if ( InterlockedDecrement( &m_lRef ) == 0 )
    {
        delete this;
        return 0;
    }

    return m_lRef;
}

STDMETHODIMP MathClassFactory::CreateInstance
      ( LPUNKNOWN pUnkOuter, REFIID riid, void** ppvObj )
{
    Math*       pMath;
    HRESULT     hr;

    *ppvObj = 0;

    pMath = new Math;
```

```
   if ( pMath == 0 )
      return( E_OUTOFMEMORY );

   hr = pMath->QueryInterface( riid, ppvObj );

   if ( FAILED( hr ) )
      delete pMath;

   return hr;
}

STDMETHODIMP MathClassFactory::LockServer( BOOL fLock )
{
   if ( fLock )
      InterlockedIncrement( &g_lLocks );
   else
      InterlockedDecrement( &g_lLocks );

    return S_OK;
}
```

We've covered most of this already. The only exception is the implementation of the LockServer method. Our server housing (the DLL implementation) maintains a count of calls to lock the server. We'll use this counter in our housing implementation next.

Create the Component's Housing (SERVER.CPP)

After saving **MATH.CPP,** create a new file and call it **SERVER.CPP**. It will provide the housing code for our component. **IMATH.H, MATH.H,** and **MATH.CPP** constitute our component implementation. We now need housing code to wrap the component. Here it is:

```
//
// server.cpp : Defines the initialization routines for the DLL.
//

#include <windows.h>

#include <initguid.h>
#include "math.h"

long    g_lObjs = 0;
long    g_lLocks = 0;

// This entry point provides COM a standard way of accessing the housing's
// class factories.
STDAPI DllGetClassObject( REFCLSID rclsid, REFIID riid, void** ppv )
{
   HRESULT              hr;
   MathClassFactory     *pCF;
```

(code continued on next page)

```
    // Make sure the CLSID is for our Math component
    if ( rclsid != CLSID_Math )
        return( E_FAIL );

    pCF = new MathClassFactory;

    if ( pCF == 0 )
        return( E_OUTOFMEMORY );

    hr = pCF->QueryInterface( riid, ppv );

    // Check for failure of QueryInterface
    if ( FAILED( hr ) )
        delete pCF;

    return hr;
}
STDAPI DllCanUnloadNow(void)
{
    if ( g_lObjs || g_lLocks )
        return( S_FALSE );
    else
        return( S_OK );
}
```

First, we include **INITGUID.H** to define the GUIDs used by the DLL. Next, we define the two global variables that maintain our housing reference counts. Remember, COM requires that a DLL export two functions to be a true component housing. (Actually, there are four functions, but we'll discuss them in the later examples.) First, we implement DllGetClassObject. COM calls this entry point on behalf of a client to access a component's class factory.

We first check to make sure that the client is requesting a component that our housing supports. If we recognize it, we create an instance of our math class factory and call QueryInterface on the interface requested by the client. Our Math class factory supports only IUnknown and IClassFactory. If the client, or COM, requests anything else, we return an error.

Thanks to our two global variables, our implementation of DllCanUnloadNow is easy. We check to see whether there are any outstanding instances of the math component and determine the number of calls that have been made to LockServer. If either value is nonzero, the DLL cannot be unloaded.

Export `DllGetClassObject` and `DllCanUnloadNow`

There is one remaining step. To export our two functions in **SERVER.CPP**, we need a **SERVER.DEF** file. Create a file so named and add the following:

```
;
; Server.def : Declares the module parameters for the DLL.
;

LIBRARY      "SERVER"
DESCRIPTION  'SERVER Windows Dynamic Link Library'

EXPORTS
    ; Explicit exports can go here
    DllGetClassObject   PRIVATE
    DllCanUnloadNow     PRIVATE
```

Insert the Files into the Project and Build It

Before building the project, use the **Insert/Files into project** menu item to insert the **MATH.CPP**, **SERVER.CPP**, and **SERVER.DEF** files into the project. If it compiles cleanly on the first try, great. Once you have a DLL, you must register the component.

Build or Modify SERVER.REG

The final step is to register the math component. The downloadable example contains a **SERVER.REG** file that looks similar to this:

```
REGEDIT
HKEY_CLASSES_ROOT\Chapter2.Math.1 = Chapter2 Math Component
HKEY_CLASSES_ROOT\Chapter2.Math.1\CLSID = {A888F560-58E4-11d0-A68A-
0000837E3100}
HKEY_CLASSES_ROOT\Chapter2.Math = Chapter2 Math Component
HKEY_CLASSES_ROOT\Chapter2.Math\CurVer = Chapter2.Math.1
HKEY_CLASSES_ROOT\Chapter2.Math\CLSID = {A888F560-58E4-11d0-A68A-0000837E3100}

HKEY_CLASSES_ROOT\CLSID\{A888F560-58E4-11d0-A68A-0000837E3100} = Chapter2 Math
Component
HKEY_CLASSES_ROOT\CLSID\{A888F560-58E4-11d0-A68A-0000837E3100}\ProgID =
Chapter2.Math.1
HKEY_CLASSES_ROOT\CLSID\{A888F560-58E4-11d0-A68A-
0000837E3100}\VersionIndependentProgID = Chapter2.Math
HKEY_CLASSES_ROOT\CLSID\{A888F560-58E4-11d0-A68A-0000837E3100}\InprocServer32 =
d:\server\debug\server.dll
```

If you used the existing GUIDs in our example, all you have to modify in the **SERVER.REG** file is the location of **SERVER.DLL** via the InProcServer32 entry. However, if you generated your own GUIDs, you'll have to update all the CLSID entries with the new GUID. After you've typed in or updated **SERVER.REG**, merge it into the registry using REGEDIT or by double-clicking on the file in Explorer.

NOTE

The registry editor program is **REGEDIT.EXE**. You can register **.REG** files by double-clicking the file icon Windows Explorer. Because this is managed through a file association, you can also type **start server.reg** from the command line.

Now that we've built the simple COM-based math component, let's build a client application to test its functionality.

Test the Math Component with OLEVIEW

Before we build a real client program, let's give our server a quick test. Start OLEVIEW, make sure **Expert Mode** is on, and click on the **All Objects** node. You should find your component under **Chapter2 Math Component**. Once you find it, try to expand it. If all succeeds, you will see something like Figure 2.12. Otherwise, some debugging is in order.

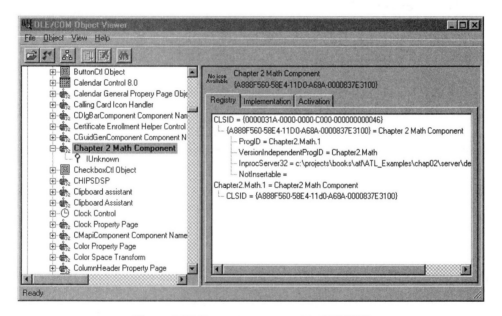

Figure 2.12 Our `Math` component in OLEVIEW.

A SIMPLE COM CLIENT

Our client application is a simple Win32 console application. Using AppWizard, create a **Win32 Console Application** and name it **Client**. Because AppWizard will supply only the project's make file, we must create the actual code files.

Next, create a file called **CLIENT.CPP** and add the following code:

```
//
// Client.cpp
//

#include <windows.h>
#include <tchar.h>
#include <iostream.h>

#include <initguid.h>
#include "..\server\imath.h"

int main( int argc, char *argv[] )
{
   cout << "Initializing COM" << endl;

   if ( FAILED( CoInitialize( NULL )))
   {
      cout << "Unable to initialize COM" << endl;
      return -1;
   }

   // Get the unique CLSID from the ProgID
   HRESULT hr = ::CLSIDFromProgID( L"Chapter2.Math.1", &clsid );
   if ( FAILED( hr ))
   {
      cout.setf( ios::hex, ios::basefield );
      cout << "Unable to get CLSID from ProgID. HR = " << hr << endl;
      return -1;
   }

   // Get the class factory for the Math class
   IClassFactory* pCF;
   hr = CoGetClassObject( clsid,
                          CLSCTX_INPROC,
                          NULL,
                          IID_IClassFactory,
                          (void**) &pCF );
   if ( FAILED( hr ))
   {
      cout.setf( ios::hex, ios::basefield );
      cout << "Failed to GetClassObject server instance. HR = " << hr << endl;
      return -1;
   }
```

(code continued on next page)

```
// using the class factory interface create an instance of the
// component and return the IUnknown interface.
IUnknown* pUnk;
hr = pCF->CreateInstance( NULL, IID_IUnknown, (void**) &pUnk );

// Release the class factory
pCF->Release();

if ( FAILED( hr ))
{
   cout.setf( ios::hex, ios::basefield );
   cout << "Failed to create server instance. HR = " << hr << endl;
   return -1;
}

cout << "Instance created" << endl;

IMath* pMath = NULL;
hr = pUnk->QueryInterface( IID_IMath, (void**) &pMath );
pUnk->Release();
if ( FAILED( hr ))
{
   cout << "QueryInterface() for IMath failed" << endl;
   CoUninitialize();
   return -1;
}

long result;
pMath->Multiply( 100, 8, &result );
cout << "100 * 8 is " << result << endl;

pMath->Subtract( 1000, 333, &result );
cout << "1000 - 333 is " << result << endl;

// Try IAdvancedMath, QI through IMath
IAdvancedMath* pAdvMath = NULL;
hr = pMath->QueryInterface( IID_IAdvancedMath, (void**) &pAdvMath );
if ( FAILED( hr ))
{
   cout << "QueryInterface() for IAdvancedMath failed" << endl;
   pMath->Release();
   CoUninitialize();
   return -1;
}

pAdvMath->Factorial( 10, &result );
cout << "10! is " << result << endl;

pAdvMath->Fibonacci( 10, &result );
cout << "The Fibonacci of 10 is " << result << endl;
```

```
    cout << "Releasing IMath interface" << endl;
    pMath->Release();

    cout << "Releasing IAdvancedMath interface" << endl;
    pAdvMath->Release();

    cout << "Shuting down COM" << endl;
    CoUninitialize();

    return 0;
}
```

We start by including the **IMATH.H** header file from the server project. Before doing so, we include **INITGUID.H** so that the component's GUIDs will be defined. In main, we first initialize the COM libraries. Our example uses the component's ProgID to determine the correct CLSID. Before we can call CLSIDFromProgID, however, we must first convert the ANSI ProgID into a Unicode string. All COM, OLE, and ActiveX calls have native Unicode implementations, so all strings must be converted to Unicode before they are passed to any COM API functions.

After retrieving the CLSID for the component, we call CoGetClassObject and request a pointer to the class factory interface for the math component. We then create an instance of the math component by calling CreateInstance. After we create the instance, we release the class factory interface. CreateInstance returns an IUnknown pointer, through which we finally query for IMath. Once we have an IMath pointer, we use the component's services to do some simple calculations.

When we're finished, we release our IMath and IAdvancedMath interface pointers. We then call CoUninitialize before the application terminates.

Build the Client Project

After entering the preceding code, insert **CLIENT.CPP** into the client project and build it. By running the client in debug mode, you can step into our server code. Take your time and really understand this simple COM-based client/server example. It contains the essence of COM-based development.

Debugging the Server

Debugging the client and server applications is easy. First, load the server project. Select the menu item **Build/Start Debug/Go**. The first time you attempt to debug the DLL, you will be asked to specify the **Executable for Debug Session**. Enter the path to **CLIENT.EXE**, and you're ready to debug. You can also specify the executable through the **Project/Settings** menu item.

If you get errors, they'll probably be in the form of HRESULTs. To look them up, start Visual C++'s Error Lookup component (**Tools/Error Lookup**) and type the HRESULT in hex as shown in Figure 2.13.

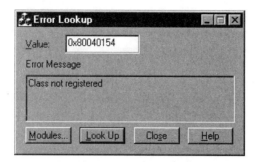

Figure 2.13 Visual C++ Error Lookup.

WHAT THE EXAMPLE IS MISSING

The example in this chapter implements a true COM component and shows how a client program might access its functionality. However, it is missing a few items that most COM-based components should provide: good error handling, support for self-registration, support for interface marshaling, and self-description through a type library. In the next few chapters we will add these elements to the math example. Here's a list of what we have yet to do:

- Cover COM error handling so that we can handle divide by zero and similar errors.

- Add self-registration to our component so that we don't have to distribute or manually register the component via a **.REG** file.

- Add marshaling support so that the component can be used in cross-thread, cross-process, and cross-machine environments. Right now the math component can be used only in-process.

- Add a type library so that potential clients can programmatically investigate and display the component's capabilities.

We'll add most of these capabilities in Chapter 3, although we'll use ATL. ATL provides most of these elements by default, and so we'll do a lot less typing.

ON TO THE ACTIVE TEMPLATE LIBRARY

With this introduction to the Component Object Model, we are now ready to delve into developing COM-based modules using the Active Template Library in Chapter 3.

Chapter 3

The Active Template Library

This book is about Microsoft's latest C++ framework: the Active Template Library. Microsoft developed ATL so that developers could build small, COM-based components. ATL uses the new template-based features of C++ and is provided with source code as part of the Visual C++ development environment. Visual C++'s Developer Studio IDE also includes a number of Visual C++ wizards that make it easier to start using ATL in your projects. In this chapter, we'll cover the basics of ATL by implementing our `Math` component using ATL's features.

BASIC ATL FEATURES

ATL provides support for implementing the core aspects of a COM-based component. Many of the tedious implementation details that we had to deal with in Chapter 2 are taken care of by the ATL template classes. Here's a quick list of what ATL provides.

- AppWizard, which creates the initial ATL project.
- Object Wizard, which produces code for basic COM components.
- Built-in support for elementary COM functionality such as `IUnknown`, class factories, and self-registration.
- Support for Microsoft's Interface Definition Language (IDL). This provides marshaling support for custom Vtable interfaces as well as component self-description through a type library.
- Support for `IDispatch` (automation) and dual interfaces.
- Support for developing efficient ActiveX controls.

Many of these terms may sound foreign to you, but they will make more sense as we move through the chapters.

Comparison to the Microsoft Foundation Class Libraries

The purpose of ATL is to facilitate the creation of small, COM-based components. The purpose of MFC is to speed development of larger, Windows-based applications, which generally have large GUIs. There is some overlap in functionality, primarily in the area of OLE and ActiveX support.

For example, you can create ActiveX controls with both ATL and MFC. By using MFC and its Control wizard, you can create a fully functional ActiveX control by adding just a few lines of code to the thousands already provided by MFC. However, the controls that you develop depend on the existence of the MFC run-time DLL, which is more than 1MB in size.

ATL also provides complete support for ActiveX controls. The difference is that you must write a lot of the code yourself, and to do so you need a solid understanding of COM and the ActiveX control specification. We'll develop such a control in a later chapter. One of the useful things about ATL is that you can develop a full-function control that depends only on the standard C run-time DLL. This DLL is installed as part of the operating system, so your control is easier to distribute in low-bandwidth environments such as the Internet.

When you're developing a COM-based component that has little or no visual aspect, ATL is usually the way to go. If you're developing a Windows-based application with lots of visual functionality, you'll probably want to use MFC. This is just a guideline, though, and I recommend that you get some experience with both frameworks before making a final decision. This book is about ATL, so we won't discuss MFC very much, except in Chapter 11.

The ATL Philosophy

The developers of ATL had one primary purpose in mind: to develop a framework that makes it easy to create small, lightweight COM objects. In other words, the aim was to give software developers the flexibility to implement their components without any dependencies on secondary DLLs, including the standard C run-time DLL. Another important goal was to make components developed with ATL as small and fast as possible.

The developers of ATL succeeded, but I can tell you this: Their success at making ATL small, fast, and efficient has made it hard to understanding the ATL implementation. At times, it can make you want to pull your hair out. That's what happens when you put a bunch of smart people on a project and ask them to save every byte possible. As we encounter those aspects of ATL that are difficult to comprehend, I'll add an extra note that tries to explain the ATL group's reasons for doing what they did as well as explain what it is actually going on.

A Quick Overview of the ATL Framework

ATL is C++ class library, or framework, that handles many of the routine details of COM-based development. For example, we know that a COM component needs either a DLL or EXE housing and that the component requires a class factory. We also know that the implementation of these requirements is basically the same for every component. A framework such as ATL provides this basic component support. All we have to do is use it. If you've used MFC at all, you no doubt understand this concept well.

ATL's Implementation

Because ATL is a template-based framework, you will include ATL's implementation as part of your implementation. In other words, to get at ATL's built-in functionality, you don't necessarily link to a series of DLLs. Instead, you include header files that compile directly into object code within your DLL or executable. In fact, ATL is basically a series of header files that contain a number of template classes. The implementation is included directly in your project. There are only a few exceptions.

Again, one of the design goals of ATL was to allow the building of small and independent components. This approach makes your executables bigger, but ATL provides several options to give you flexibility.

If you dissect a basic ATL project you'll see that you use its include files this way:

```
//
// STDAFX.H
//
#define _ATL_APARTMENT_THREADED

#include <atlbase.h>
#include <atlcom.h>
...

//
// STDAFX.CPP
//

#include "stdafx.h

// Include ATL's implementation code
#include <atlimpl.cpp>
...

//
// YourImplementation.cpp
//

#include "stdafx.h"
...
```

ATL's use of **STDAFX.H** and **STDAFX.CPP** is similar to the way they are used in most Visual C++ projects. The **STDAFX** files include the basic requirements of the project type, and you then include **STDAFX.H** in all your implementation files. The important point in the preceding example is that ultimately all ATL projects include **ATLBASE.H, ATLCOM.H,** and **ATLIMPL.CPP.** By including **ATLIMPL.CPP,** the majority of ATL's implementation becomes an explicit part of your project and its object code becomes part of your executable.

Table 3.1 describes each of the header and implementation files that are part of ATL.

Table 3.1 ATL's Implementation Files

FILE	DESCRIPTION
ATLBASE.H	Basic include file for ATL projects.
ATLCOM.H	All ATL projects must include **ATLCOM.H,** because it provides most of ATL's basic behavior.
ATLIMPL.CPP	The actual implementation of the classes and methods declared in **ATLBASE.H** and **ATLCOM.H.**
ATLCTL.H, ATLCTL.CPP	ATL's support for ActiveX controls. Again, both files will be included in your project when you're using ATL's control support.
ATLWIN.H, ATLWIN.CPP	ATL's support for windows and dialog boxes.
STATREG.H, STATREG.CPP	The implementation files for ATL's Registrar component. Depending on preprocessor symbols, the code is either compiled to produce part of **ATL.DLL** or is included directly within your component's implementation.
ATLIFACE.IDL, ATLIFACE.H	Support files for ATL's Registrar component. The header file contains the output that results from running the IDL through the MIDL compiler.

ATLBASE.H, ATL_DLL_, and ATL.DLL

When you're developing with ATL, most of its functionality is included as part of your implementation, so there is no need to link to any external DLLs (other than system DLLs and possibly the C run time, which is delivered with the OS anyway). However, ATL implements some of its basic APIs in a module appropriately named **ATL.DLL.** The functions implemented in **ATL.DLL** are primarily helper functions for ATL's classes. To give you an idea of what's in **ATL.DLL,** following is the output of the **DUMPBIN /EXPORTS** command.

```
c:\winnt\system32>dumpbin /exports atl.dll

Microsoft (R) COFF Binary File Dumper Version 5.02.7132
Copyright (C) Microsoft Corp 1992-1997. All rights reserved.

Dump of file atl.dll
```

File Type: DLL

    Section contains the following Exports for ATL.DLL

           0 characteristics
    32E97F0B time date stamp Fri Jan 24 21:33:31 1997
       0.00 version
        1 ordinal base
      32 number of functions
      27 number of names

    ordinal hint   name

ordinal	hint	name
10	0	AtlAdvise (00002B6F)
30	1	AtlComPtrAssign (00002A1E)
31	2	AtlComQIPtrAssign (00002A47)
26	3	AtlCreateTargetDC (000033C5)
29	4	AtlDevModeW2A (00002635)
12	5	AtlFreeMarshalStream (00002A6E)
27	6	AtlHiMetricToPixel (000034E3)
32	7	AtlInternalQueryInterface (00002946)
13	8	AtlMarshalPtrInProc (00002A8A)
15	9	AtlModuleGetClassObject (00002EB0)
16	A	AtlModuleInit (00002DAC)
17	B	AtlModuleRegisterClassObjects (00002DFD)
18	C	AtlModuleRegisterServer (00002FD2)
19	D	AtlModuleRegisterTypeLib (000031FB)
20	E	AtlModuleRevokeClassObjects (00002E80)
21	F	AtlModuleTerm (00002F72)
22	10	AtlModuleUnregisterServer (0000303B)
23	11	AtlModuleUpdateRegistryFromResourceD (00003082)
28	12	AtlPixelToHiMetric (00003546)
25	13	AtlSetErrorInfo (00002C46)
11	14	AtlUnadvise (00002BDC)
14	15	AtlUnmarshalPtr (00002ACF)
24	16	AtlWaitWithMessageLoop (00002B03)
1	17	DllCanUnloadNow (00001378)
2	18	DllGetClassObject (00001387)
3	19	DllRegisterServer (000013A0)
4	1A	DllUnregisterServer (000013AF)

As you can see, there are a number of exported functions that appear to handle COM-like tasks for ATL. When building an ATL project you have several options. One is to use these helper functions from **ATL.DLL** and distribute it as part of your software. Or you can choose to include the implementation of these helper functions directly within your module.

If you define the ATL_DLL_ symbol, your project will depend on **ATL.DLL**. If you do not define ATL_DLL_, the **ATLIMPL.CPP** file will include the implementations as part of your module. We'll have more to say about this is a later section.

Component Housing Support

ATL encapsulates a component's housing support in its CComModule class. ATL hides most of the differences between the two housing types (DLL or EXE) from the developer. Also, the ATL AppWizard generates the housing code for you. Typically, you don't modify the housing support code because the default implementation provides everything your component needs.

Support for IUnknown

As you'll see in a moment, ATL's support for the IUnknown methods is a bit difficult to understand. However, it is encapsulated pretty well, and typically you won't have to delve into the details of what's going on. In this chapter, we'll take a look at how QueryInterface, AddRef, and Release are implemented by ATL. The most important aspect of ATL's IUnknown implementation is to understand which macros to use within your implementation.

Support for Class Factories

When using ATL, you need not implement class factories for your components. ATL provides support for basic class factories in CComClassFactory, licensed class factories through CComClassFactory2, and singleton class factories through CComClassFactorySingleton. You add support for these various construction methods through the use of ATL macros.

Support for Other Aspects of COM Development

At this point we've briefly examined ATL's support for component housings, the IUnknown interface, and class factories, but ATL provides basic support for much more. We'll examine ATL's support for the other aspects of COM development in later chapters. Table 3.2 gives you a glimpse of the rest of ATL.

Table 3.2 ATL's Support for COM

COM FUNCTIONALITY	ATL SUPPORT CLASSES
ActiveX controls	CComControl, IOleControlImpl, IOleObjectImpl, and so on to support the development of controls. IPropertyPageImpl and ISpecifyPropertyPageImpl for support of property pages.
Automation	IDispatchImpl handles both automation and dual interfaces.
COM data types	CComBSTR and CComVariant.
Interface pointer management	CComPtr and CComQIPtr.
Error handling	ISupportErrorInfoImpl and CComObject.
Connection points	IConnectionPointContainerImpl and IConnectionPointImpl.
Asynchronous property download	CBindStatusCallback.
Self-registration	The ATL Registrar object (IRegistrar) provides self-registration support for your components.
Windows and dialog boxes	CWindow, CWindowImpl, CDialogImpl, and CMessageMap.

USING ATL'S WIZARDS

In this book our goal is to understand how ATL makes it easier to develop COM-based applications. When you're first learning a large framework such as ATL, it's nice to have some base code from which to begin, and this is what ATL's wizards provide.

The wizards hide many of the implementation details, and this is good when you're just learning ATL. But later, when something breaks, you really need to understand what the wizards are doing for you. In the next few sections we'll cover the details of creating ATL projects using the Visual C++ wizards, but after that we'll focus mostly on the ATL code.

The ATL COM AppWizard

The ATL COM AppWizard (Figure 3.1) is a Visual C++ wizard that steps you through the initial creation of an ATL-based project. You will use AppWizard only once per project. The purpose of AppWizard is to create the initial housing code for your components. After the project is created you use the ATL Object wizard to add components to your project. We'll discuss the files created by AppWizard shortly.

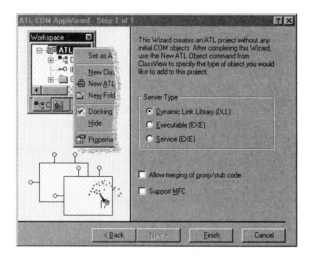

Figure 3.1 Creating an ATL project.

When creating a project using AppWizard, you have only a few simple options. The first is **Server Type**. You can select one of three options: a DLL or EXE housing for your components, or an EXE housing that executes as an NT service.

If you choose the DLL option, you can then select **Allow merging of proxy/stub code** and **Support MFC** if you wish. We haven't discussed proxy/stubs (we will in Chapter 4). This option allows your component's housing to act also as the proxy/stub DLL if you're going to provide marshaling. In other words, by checking this option and doing a bit more work, you can distribute one less DLL. If you select **Support MFC**, the wizard will add #includes for MFC's header files as well as additional code for MFC's CWinApp class. We'll discuss this in Chapter 11.

The ATL Object Wizard

The initial project created using the ATL AppWizard provides only basic housing support for your components and does not supply the files needed for building a specific component. To do that, you must use the new ATL Object wizard. It is accessed through the Visual C++ **Insert/Add ATL Component** menu item.

The main Object wizard dialog box is shown in Figure 3.2. There are three categories of objects that you can add to your project: **ATL Controls**, **ATL Miscellaneous**, and **ATL Objects**. The **ATL Controls** category provides two basic control types and a **Property Page** object. We'll discuss them in detail in a later chapter. The **ATL Miscellaneous** section allows you to create a COM-based object that is a Windows dialog box.

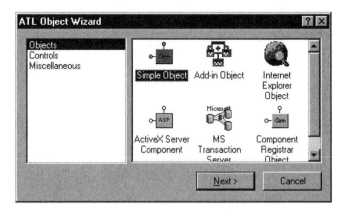

Figure 3.2 The ATL Object wizard.

Object Wizard Names

A series of dialog boxes is presented depending on the object type selected. For a simple COM object, information for two dialog boxes—Name and Attributes—must be populated. For more-complex object types, such as ActiveX controls, additional information is required. Again, we'll cover these objects in more detail when we build an ActiveX control with ATL in a later chapter.

Figure 3.3 shows the Object wizard's Names dialog box. Table 3.3 lists the purpose of each option.

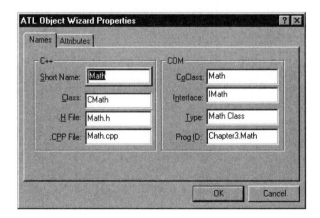

Figure 3.3 ATL Object wizard names.

Table 3.3 Object Wizard Name Options

FIELD	DESCRIPTION
Short Name	This entry provides the basis, or prefix, for the rest of the entries on the page. It does not map directly to any particular attribute. As you change this value the entries for the rest of the page also changes.
Class	The name used for the C++ class that implements the object.
.H File and .CPP File	The header and implementation files.
CoClass	The name of the COM class. This name will be used by external clients as the "type" of the component.
Interface	The name of the interface to create for your object. Our object will initially expose the IMath interface that we described in Chapter 2.
Type	The human-readable name of the component that will be placed in the registry. This has no programmatic value.
Prog ID	This is the programmatic identifier for the component. Clients may use this identifier to locate and instantiate a component.

Object Wizard Attributes

The Attributes dialog box allows specification of basic COM support options for a component. Many of the details of each option are beyond the scope of this chapter, because we haven't covered things such as COM threading models and the concept of COM aggregation. Figure 3.4 shows the Attributes dialog box, and the following sections describe each option.

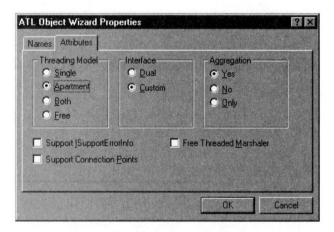

Figure 3.4 ATL Object wizard attributes.

Threading Model

Several threading models are available for COM-based components. We'll discuss each of them in Chapter 10, giving a quick introduction here. For our initial examples, we'll use the **Apartment** option.

- **Single**. COM clients must interact with the component only through their primary thread.
- **Apartment**. Instances of the component can reside within their own apartment thread.
- **Free**. The component supports the free threading model. In other words, it can reside with other threads in the multithreaded apartment (or MTA).
- **Both.** Specifies that the component can support both the apartment model and the free threading model.

Interface

There are two interface options: custom and dual. A *custom* interface is the standard Vtable interface that we've been discussing so far. We haven't yet discussed the concept of a *dual* interface; Microsoft recommends that components support a dual interface if possible. A dual interface implements both a Vtable interface and the standard automation interface. In this way, the client can choose how it will access the component's functionality. We'll discus this in more detail in Chapter 6.

Aggregation

Aggregation is a COM technique that allows one component to incorporate, or reuse, the functionality of another component. The internal component must explicitly support this technique by delegating its `IUnknown` implementation. These options allow a component to decide whether to support aggregation. The Object wizard has several support options, each of which we'll discuss in Chapter 5.

Support for `ISupportErrorInfo`

If you select this option, the Object wizard will provide a default implementation for the `ISupportErrorInfo` interface. This arrangement provides a robust server-to-client error-reporting mechanism. If you haven't guessed by now, we'll also be covering this in a later chapter. I don't want to overload you with details yet. Hang in there.

SUPPORT CONNECTION POINTS

By selecting this option, you direct the wizard to provide a default implementation of COM's connection point interfaces. Connection points allow a client and server to communicate on a peer-to-peer basis. In other words, connection points support server callbacks or events. Again, we'll have a whole chapter (Chapter 7) on this later.

FREE THREADED MARSHALER

Free threaded marshaling provides default marshaling of interface pointers between threads in a single process. More on this in Chapter 10.

Other Object Wizard Options

Depending on the object type that you're inserting, the Object wizard can display as many as four different tabbed dialogs. We've discussed the two pages that will always display. The other two pages are used primarily for developing ActiveX controls, and we'll discuss them in a later chapter.

AN EXAMPLE SERVER

To demonstrate some of the basic features of ATL, we will convert our math example from Chapter 2 to use the ATL framework. The steps for creating the Math component are at the end of this chapter. In the next few sections, we'll go over each line that ATL's AppWizard and Object wizard create for a basic COM server.

By placing the cookbook-style steps at the end of the chapter, we can focus on ATL's basic implementation. One approach might be to create the example by quickly following the steps and then to come back here as we go through ATL's implementation. Another approach might be to follow along and get a sense of what ATL is doing and then step through the example when you get to it. It's up to you.

THE STRUCTURE OF AN ATL PROJECT

After you run the ATL AppWizard, the initial ATL project contains files that support the component's housing. Then additional files are added for each component through the Object wizard. Table 3.4 briefly describes each file produced by AppWizard.

Table 3.4 ATL AppWizard Project Files

FILE	DESCRIPTION
ProjectName.cpp	The main project file. This file contains the support functions required by COM to provide a housing for our components.
ProjectName.h	The interface declarations for the components in the housing. This file is created by the MIDL compiler. The project's IDL file is compiled to produce it.

Table 3.4 *(continued)*

FILE	DESCRIPTION
ProjectName.idl	The IDL file for our project. You will add interface and method definitions here. The MIDL compiler will process this file to create a type library for the project. There is one IDL file per project, so all the components in the project share the IDL file.
ProjectName.tlb	The binary type library for the housing. This file is produced by compiling the IDL file with the MIDL compiler.
ProjectName.def	Windows definition file. For DLL projects, it contains the exposed entry points. This file is not created for EXE projects.
*ProjectName*_i.c	A file, produced by compiling the IDL file, that contains definitions for all the CLSIDs and IIDs defined in the project.
*ProjectName*_p.c	The proxy/stub code for the project. This file is produced by the MIDL compiler.
*ProjectName*PS.mk	The command-line make file for the project's proxy/stub DLL.
*ProjectName*PS.dll	The proxy/stub DLL created by the above make file.
DLLDATA.C	DLL defines for the proxy/stub DLL project.
RESOURCE.H	The resource definition file for the project.
ProjectName.rc	The resource file the project.
STDAFX.H and STDAFX.CPP	Definitions and includes for the ATL framework.

For each component that you add through the Object wizard, you get the files listed in Table 3.5. Each component within the housing shares many of the files described in Table 3.4. We'll go over the files created by the Object wizard when we describe ATL's support for IUnknown, housings, class factories, and self-registration. The files provide us with basic component support, and we then add our specific implementation.

Table 3.5 Files Created by the Object Wizard

FILE	DESCRIPTION
ObjectName.h, *ObjectName*.cpp	The object's header and implementation files.
ObjectName.rgs	The object's Registrar script. This file contains the registry entries to self-register the component.

STDAFX.H and STDAFX.CPP

As we discussed earlier, every file in an ATL project will include the **STDAFX.H** header file, which pulls in ATL's header files. When using template-based frameworks such as ATL, you generally include all the code that your implementation needs. For example, here's a look at **STDAFX.H** and **STDAFX.CPP**. Notice the inclusion of **ATLIMPL.CPP**. This is where the majority of ATL's implementation is pulled into your code.

```
// stdafx.h : include file for standard system include files,
//      or project-specific include files that are used frequently
//      but are changed infrequently

#if !defined(AFX_STDAFX_H__88126992_1CC8_11D1_883A_444553540000__INCLUDED_)
#define AFX_STDAFX_H__88126992_1CC8_11D1_883A_444553540000__INCLUDED_

#if _MSC_VER >= 1000
#pragma once
#endif // _MSC_VER >= 1000

#define STRICT

#define _WIN32_WINNT 0x0400
#define _ATL_APARTMENT_THREADED

#include <atlbase.h>
//You may derive a class from CComModule and use it if you want to override
//something, but do not change the name of _Module
extern CComModule _Module;
#include <atlcom.h>

//{{AFX_INSERT_LOCATION}}
// Microsoft Developer Studio will insert additional declarations immediately
// before the previous line.

#endif // !defined(AFX_STDAFX_H__88126992_1CC8_11D1_883A_444553540000__INCLUDED)

//
// stdafx.cpp : source file that includes just the standard includes
//
#include "stdafx.h"

#ifdef _ATL_STATIC_REGISTRY
#include <statreg.h>
#include <statreg.cpp>
#endif

#include <atlimpl.cpp>
```

I've highlighted one of the comment lines to point something out. The comment warns you not to change the name of the global CComModule instance. This warning is there because many ATL's classes have the _Module name hard-coded as part of their implementation. In other words, ATL depends heavily on the fact that there is a global class named _Module.

RESOURCE.H and ProjectName.rc

As a Windows developer, you should be familiar with the **RESOURCE.H** file. It primarily defines symbols for the project's resources. A basic ATL project such as the one we're studying in this chapter has only a few resources defined, because nonvisual components such as our math component don't need a lot of GUI-type resources. Following is a quick glance at the **RESOURCE.H** file for our ATL-based math component.

```
//{{NO_DEPENDENCIES}}
// Microsoft Developer Studio generated include file.
// Used by Chapter3_Server.rc
//
#define IDS_PROJNAME                    100
#define IDR_MATH                        101

// Next default values for new objects
//
#ifdef APSTUDIO_INVOKED
#ifndef APSTUDIO_READONLY_SYMBOLS
#define _APS_NEXT_RESOURCE_VALUE        201
#define _APS_NEXT_COMMAND_VALUE         32768
#define _APS_NEXT_CONTROL_VALUE         201
#define _APS_NEXT_SYMED_VALUE           102
#endif
#endif
```

I've highlighted two lines that are specific to our project. The `IDS_PROJNAME` symbol was added by AppWizard. It identifies a string-table string that contains the name of our project. The `IDR_MATH` symbol identifies a binary resource that contains self-registration information for our project. This involves the ATL Registrar, which we'll discuss in a moment.

A basic ATL project stores four items in its ***projectname*.rc** file: version information for the housing, a binary resource containing a Registrar script, a string table with the name of the project, and a binary resource that contains the type library for the component.

ProjectName.CPP, ProjectName.H, and ProjectName.DEF

These files implement the basic housing support for ATL. For DLLs, this support would include the `DllMain` entry point and the other exports required by COM. For executables (EXEs), it would include the `WinMain` function and the primary message loop for the application. We cover the details of this implementation in our housing discussion later.

ProjectName.IDL

The IDL file in an ATL project is very important. In fact, many of the files that the project depends on are created by running the IDL file through another compiler (**MIDL.EXE**). We haven't discussed what an IDL file is, but here is a brief introduction. In Chapter 4, we'll cover IDL and the files that MIDL creates.

Interface Definition Language

Microsoft's Interface Definition Language (IDL) is based on the DCE RPC specification. In general, IDL is used to described remote procedure call interfaces, but Microsoft has extended the specification to include support for COM-based interfaces. The primary purpose of IDL, at least in the context of COM-based components, is to define, in a language-independent way, a component's interfaces (its methods and parameters). This definition can then be used by clients of the component. Because IDL is also used to support RPC-like capabilities, it can produce marshaling code so that a component's interfaces can be used across process and network boundaries.

NOTE

Before the widespread support of IDL, Microsoft used the Object Description Language (ODL). ODL was designed specifically for automation. Today, IDL is used instead. It is more functional than ODL and still provides support for the older ODL language.

IDL uses a C-style syntax, so defining a component's interface is similar to declaring the C++ class. You can define structure types, enumerated types, and so on using IDL. Following is the IDL file for our math component in this chapter.

```
//
// Chapter3_Server.idl : IDL source for Chapter3_Server.dll
//

// This file will be processed by the MIDL tool to
// produce the type library (Chapter3_Server.tlb) and marshaling code.

import "oaidl.idl";
import "ocidl.idl";

[
   object,
   uuid(8812699C-1CC8-11D1-883A-444553540000),
   helpstring("IMath Interface"),
   pointer_default(unique)
]
interface IMath : IUnknown
{
   [helpstring("method Add")]
     HRESULT Add(long lOp1, long lOp2, long* plResult);
   [helpstring("method Subtract")]
     HRESULT Subtract(long lOp1, long lOp2, long* plResult);
   [helpstring("method Multiply")]
     HRESULT Multiply(long lOp1, long lOp2, long* plResult);
   [helpstring("method Divide")]
     HRESULT Divide(long lOp1, long lOp2, long* plResult);
};
```

```
[
   object,
   uuid(6AF3DF1E-C48F-11D0-A769-D477A4000000),
   helpstring("IAdvancedMath Interface"),
   pointer_default(unique)
]

interface IAdvancedMath : IUnknown
{
   HRESULT Factorial( [in] short sFact, [out, retval] long* pResult );
   HRESULT Fibonacci( [in] short sFib, [out, retval] long* pResult );
};

[
   uuid(8812698E-1CC8-11D1-883A-444553540000),
   version(1.0),
   helpstring("Chapter3_Server 1.0 Type Library")
]
library CHAPTER3_SERVERLib
{
   importlib("stdole32.tlb");
   importlib("stdole2.tlb");

   [
      uuid(8812699D-1CC8-11D1-883A-444553540000),
      helpstring("Math Class")
   ]
   coclass Math
   {
      [default] interface IMath;
      interface IAdvancedMath;
   };
};
```

The first section defines our IMath interface. IDL definitions are preceded with an attribute block. These attributes, enclosed within brackets ([]), provide additional information about the ensuing definition. Our IMath interface definition begins with three attributes:

```
[
   object,
   uuid(8812699C-1CC8-11D1-883A-444553540000),
   helpstring("IMath Interface"),
   pointer_default(unique)
]
```

The object attribute specifies that we are describing a COM custom interface and not a DCE/RPC-based interface. The IDL is also used to describe RPC interfaces. The uuid keyword, specifies the GUID of our interface, and the helpstring keyword specifies some text that a object browser might display.

The pointer_default attribute sets the default pointer attribute for any pointers defined within the interface. We specify a default pointer attribute of **unique**. The unique attribute specifies that whenever a pointer is passed through an interface method, the memory associated with the pointer can not be modified elsewhere in our application. In other words, the memory pointed to can only be changed by the method that operates on it. This is the typical case and makes marshaling more efficient. Next, we have the interface definition.

```
interface IMath : IUnknown
{
    [helpstring("method Add")]
        HRESULT Add( [in] long lOp1, [in] long lOp2,
                     [out, retval] long* plResult);
    [helpstring("method Subtract")]
        HRESULT Subtract( [in] long lOp1, [in] long lOp2,
                          [out, retval] long* plResult);
    [helpstring("method Multiply")]
        HRESULT Multiply( [in] long lOp1, [in] long lOp2,
                          [out, retval] long* plResult);
    [helpstring("method Divide")]
        HRESULT Divide( [in] long lOp1, [in] long lOp2,
                        [out, retval] long* plResult);
};
```

The interface describes the COM-based interface in our component. This code matches almost exactly with our C++ class declaration. The major differences are in the listing of the parameters. IDL has several keywords that can be applied to method parameters. The in and out keywords specify the direction of the parameter. By providing this information, you provide COM with information that will help make the parameter marshaling process more efficient. The retval keyword specifies that the parameter should be treated as the return value for the method. The remaining IDL lines pertain to the housing and its contained components.

```
[
    uuid(8812698E-1CC8-11D1-883A-444553540000),
    version(1.0),
    helpstring("Chapter3_Server 1.0 Type Library")
]
library CHAPTER3_SERVERLib
{
    importlib("stdole32.tlb");
    importlib("stdole2.tlb");
```

```
[
   uuid(8812699D-1CC8-11D1-883A-444553540000),
   helpstring("Math Class")
]
coclass Math
{
   [default] interface IMath;
   interface IAdvancedMath;
};
};
```

The attribute block describes the type library as a whole. It has a GUID, a version, and a help string. The help string provides textual information for component browser applications. The `library` keyword specifies the name of the library and typically encloses all the definitions for the specific housing. It may have interface, module, type, and component definitions. Our example server contains only one math component, and it is specified using the `coclass` keyword. The `coclass` keyword specifies individual components and the interfaces that they support. Our math component exposes both the `IMath` and the `IAdvancedMath` interfaces. Table 3.6 summarizes the basic IDL keywords.

Table 3.6 Basic IDL Keywords

KEYWORD	DESCRIPTION
object	Begins the definition for a COM-based custom interface. The `object` keyword is followed by several attributes that describe additional interface capabilities.
uuid	The GUID that uniquely defines the given interface, type library, or component class.
helpstring	Specifies a string that can be displayed by tools such as component and interface viewers.
interface	Specifies the name of an interface. The name is then used in the `coclass` section to specify the interfaces supported by a component.
coclass	Describes the interfaces supported by a given COM object. The GUID specifies the component itself.
default	Specifies the default component interface. A component object can have at most two default interfaces: one for the source and a second one for the sink programmable interfaces.
in/out/retval	For method calls, this keyword indicates the direction of each parameter. The `retval` keyword describes which parameter should be treated as the return value of the method.

Now we have an idea of how IDL describes our component and its interfaces, but the IDL file is used for much more. In fact, in our ATL projects the IDL file provides three important things. Each one is described briefly next, and these relationships are depicted in Figure 3.5. The important fact is that the IDL file is parsed by the MIDL compiler to produce several files for our components.

- The IDL file is compiled to produce C++ header files that declare and define the interfaces, class identifiers, and interface identifiers for the project.
- The IDL (or those items in the *library* section) file is compiled into a binary representation called a *type library*. This type library (**.TLB**) can be inspected by component users to determine how they should access and interact with it.
- The IDL file produces a series of C files and a make file to generate a proxy/stub DLL. This DLL provides marshaling support for component interfaces. We'll discuss this in detail in Chapter 4.

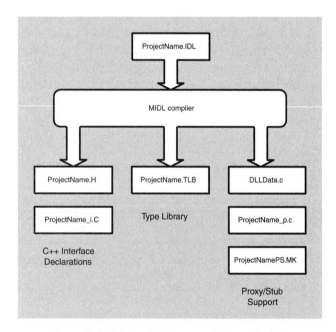

Figure 3.5 Relationship between IDL and its files.

BUILDING AN ATL PROJECT

The ATL AppWizard creates a basic ATL project that has several build options. Most of the options are the same ones you usually get when you use Visual C++, but there are a few extras related to code size and external DLL dependencies. Table 3.7 lists the various build options.

Table 3.7 ATL Project Build Options

PROJECT OPTION	DESCRIPTION
Win32 Debug	The typical debug build.
Win32 Release MinSize	Builds the module with the minimal size option. This option defines `ATL_DLL_` and `ATL_MIN_CRT`.
Win32 Release MinDependencies	Similar to the MinSize option but defines the ATL_STATIC_REGISTRY symbol. By selecting this option, your module will not require distribution of the ATL Registrar component. This option also does not define ATL_DLL_, which removes any module dependencies on ATL.DLL.
Win32 Unicode Release MinSize **Win32 Unicode Release MinDependencies** **Win32 Unicode Debug**	Same as preceding options but builds the project using the _UNICODE symbol. Using a pure Unicode code build provides faster execution on native Unicode machines such as Windows NT, but it will not execute on an ANSI operating system such as Windows 95.

ATL's Basic Housing Support: `CComModule`

ATL's `CComModule` class provides basic housing support for COM objects. Remember that every COM object must execute within the context of a Windows process. In the Windows environment, there are two ways to deliver object code: in a DLL or an executable. ATL's `CComModule` class encapsulates the differences between the two housing types. We used a DLL housing in Chapter 2 and will do so again here. In Chapter 4 we'll cover EXE housings.

NOTE ATL's `CComModule` class provides similar functionality to that provided by MFC's `CWinApp` class. Both classes attempt to insulate the developer from differences between the two Windows housing types. For example, `CWinApp::InitInstance` implements `WinMain` for executables and `DllMain` for DLLs.

When the ATL AppWizard generated our main project file, **CHAPTER3_SERVER.CPP**, it added a global instance of the `CComModule` class with the name _Module. The _Module instance is a global C++ object and is created as soon as the module is executed.

```
//
// Chapter3_Server.cpp : Implementation of DLL Exports.
//

// Note: Proxy/Stub Information
//        To build a separate proxy/stub DLL,
//        run nmake -f Chapter3_Serverps.mk in the project directory.
```

(code continued on next page)

```
#include "stdafx.h"
#include "resource.h"
#include "initguid.h"
#include "Chapter3_Server.h"

#include "Chapter3_Server_i.c"
#include "Math.h"

CComModule _Module;
```

You can ignore the proxy/stub comments, which we'll discuss in detail in Chapter 4. We covered most of the header files earlier in the chapter. The **INITGUID.H** file is included to initialize our CLSIDs and IIDs just as we described in Chapter 2. After the include files there is a global instance of ATL's CComModule class, _Module. We'll see references to that instance throughout.

Next, we encounter our first series of ATL macros.

```
BEGIN_OBJECT_MAP(ObjectMap)
    OBJECT_ENTRY(CLSID_Math, CMath)
END_OBJECT_MAP()
```

The BEGIN_OBJECT_MAP and OBJECT_ENTRY Macros

These macros set up a table of CLSIDs and their associated ATL implementation classes (i.e., components). This table of "objects" is used to implement several aspects of an ATL component. First, ATL uses the table to update the registry with information for each component within the housing. The class's UpdateRegistry method is called. UpdateRegistry is automatically implemented by ATL through its series of DECLARE_REGISTRY macros, which we'll discuss in a moment.

Second, the object map is also used to create instances of a component. In other words, it provides the component's class factory. Two addresses are placed in the map. The _ClassFactoryCreatorClass::CreateInstance call returns a class factory instance, and _CreatorClass::CreateInstance creates an instance of the component class itself. We'll have a lot more to say about this later, too.

Third, the class::GetObjectDescription method provides an implementation of the IComponentRegistrar::GetComponents method but does nothing by default. Here's a quick look at the expanded macros.

```
#define BEGIN_OBJECT_MAP(x) static _ATL_OBJMAP_ENTRY x[] = {
#define OBJECT_ENTRY(clsid, class) {
        &clsid,
        &class::UpdateRegistry,
```

```
            &class::_ClassFactoryCreatorClass::CreateInstance,
            &class::_CreatorClass::CreateInstance,
            NULL, 0, &class::GetObjectDescription },
#define END_OBJECT_MAP()    {NULL, NULL, NULL, NULL}};
```

The remaining entries in our housing implementation file deal with ATL's housing support module: CComModule. By taking a look at it, you'll find the housing implementation easier to understand.

CComModule

The implementation of CComModule is provided in **ATLBASE.H** and **ATLIMPL.CPP**. The class has a number of methods and data members that are used throughout ATL. Table 3.8 lists the most important methods and their purposes.

Table 3.8 Commonly Used CComModule Methods

Method	Description
Init	Initializes the CComModule instance, generally initializing internal data members and getting everything ready to go. It ultimately calls AtlModuleInit().
GetClassObject	This method is used only within DLL housings. It creates an instance of a component's class factory. In other words, it provides the implementation of our DLL housing's DllGetClassObject function.
RegisterClassObjects	The preceding method is for DLLs only, and this method is for EXEs only. As we'll see in Chapter 4, EXEs must register their class factories explicitly, and that is what this method does.
RevokeClassObjects	The Revoke method deregisters the class factories when the EXE is shutting down.
Lock, Unlock	Increments or decrements the module's global lock count. In Chapter 2, we maintained a global variable in our DLL to keep track of calls to IClassFactory::LockServer. These methods provide the implementation for our ATL-based housing.
RegisterServer, UnregisterServer	Adds and removes registry entries for each component in the housing.

The following code implements the standard entry points for a DLL-based COM server. The DllMain entry point initializes our module on startup and shuts down properly when the DLL is unloaded. The other four entry points implement those required by a well-behaved COM DLL housing. DllCanUnloadNow checks the global lock count, DllGetClassObject returns the requested class factory, and the DllRegisterServer and DllUnregisterServer functions handle self-registration.

```
//////////////////////////////////////////////////////////////////////////
// DLL Entry Point

extern "C"
BOOL WINAPI DllMain(HINSTANCE hInstance, DWORD dwReason, LPVOID /*lpReserved*/)
{
   if (dwReason == DLL_PROCESS_ATTACH)
   {
      _Module.Init(ObjectMap, hInstance);
      DisableThreadLibraryCalls(hInstance);
   }
   else if (dwReason == DLL_PROCESS_DETACH)
      _Module.Term();
   return TRUE;      // ok
}
//////////////////////////////////////////////////////////////////////////
// Used to determine whether the DLL can be unloaded by OLE

STDAPI DllCanUnloadNow(void)
{
   return (_Module.GetLockCount()==0) ? S_OK : S_FALSE;
}

//////////////////////////////////////////////////////////////////////////
// Returns a class factory to create an object of the requested type

STDAPI DllGetClassObject(REFCLSID rclsid, REFIID riid, LPVOID* ppv)
{
   return _Module.GetClassObject(rclsid, riid, ppv);
}
//////////////////////////////////////////////////////////////////////////
// DllRegisterServer - Adds entries to the system registry

STDAPI DllRegisterServer(void)
{
   // registers object, typelib, and all interfaces in typelib
   return _Module.RegisterServer(TRUE);
}
//////////////////////////////////////////////////////////////////////////
// DllUnregisterServer - Removes entries from the system registry

STDAPI DllUnregisterServer(void)
{
   _Module.UnregisterServer();
   return S_OK;
}
```

As you can see, ATL's `CComModule` class provides basic housing functionality. With that in place we can focus on ATL's support for components themselves.

ATL's Support for Components

The ATL AppWizard provides the basic housing support that COM components need. After we have the housing set up, you use the ATL Object wizard to add basic components to your housing. All COM objects have several things in common. Each COM object must support the `IUnknown` interface along with others that will expose its specific functionality. It must provide a class factory so that it can be created by client applications, and it should support self-registration. ATL provides built-in support for each of these requirements. In the next few sections we will investigate this aspect of an ATL-based component.

ATL's `IUnknown` Support

ATL's support for COM's `IUnknown` methods is rather difficult to understand, so we'll spend quite a bit of time on it. To understand ATL's implementation of `IUnknown`, we'll examine a number of ATL's implementation classes. The most important point to remember is that the implementation (executable code) of the three `IUnknown` methods isn't determined until an instance of our component class is actually created. ATL provides a lot of flexibility as to how an object's lifetime is managed. In most cases, the creator of the object, and not the implementer, knows how an object's lifetime should be handled. We won't get into the details of this until later when we discuss creators and class factories, but it's important to begin with this thought.

`CComObjectRootEx` and `CComObjectRootBase`

Each ATL class that will become a COM object must derive from the `CComObjectRootEx` class. There is also a `CComObjectRoot` class, but it's just a typedef that we will discuss in a moment. `CComObjectRootEx` indirectly provides reference counting and `QueryInterface` support for the component. As we described earlier, the real implementation of the `IUnknown` methods is deferred until an instance of a component is created.

Before we can look at `CComObjectRootEx`, we must take a look at `CComObjectRootBase`, from which it derives. Following is most of the declaration for `CComObjectRootBase`.

```
class CComObjectRootBase
{
public:
    CComObjectRootBase()
    {
        m_dwRef = 0L;
    }
```

(code continued on next page)

```
static HRESULT WINAPI InternalQueryInterface(void* pThis,
    const _ATL_INTMAP_ENTRY* pEntries, REFIID iid, void** ppvObject)
{
    HRESULT hRes = AtlInternalQueryInterface(pThis, pEntries, iid, ppvObject);
}

ULONG OuterAddRef()
{
    return m_pOuterUnknown->AddRef();
}
ULONG OuterRelease()
{
    return m_pOuterUnknown->Release();
}
HRESULT OuterQueryInterface(REFIID iid, void ** ppvObject)
{
    return m_pOuterUnknown->QueryInterface(iid, ppvObject);
}
union
{
    long m_dwRef;
    IUnknown* m_pOuterUnknown;
};
};
```

CComObjectRootBase contains the reference count variable used to maintain our object's outstanding interface references, but as you can see it's part of a union. When a component is aggregated with another component, the lifetime of the first component is tied to that of the second, so there is no need for the first (or inner) component to maintain its own reference count. Instead, it must maintain a pointer to the aggregating component's IUnknown implementation, so only one member of the union will be used per instance.

An instance that has been aggregated must also delegate any IUnknown method calls to its outer or aggregating component, and that's exactly what the three Outer methods do here in CComObjectRootBase. CComObjectRootBase provides basic support for aggregation in components, and CComObjectRootEx provides support for the non-aggregate IUnknown methods. Here's a look at its declaration:

```
template <class ThreadModel>
class CComObjectRootEx : public CComObjectRootBase
{
public:
    typedef ThreadModel _ThreadModel;
    typedef _ThreadModel::AutoCriticalSection _CritSec;
```

```
    ULONG InternalAddRef()
    {
        return _ThreadModel::Increment(&m_dwRef);
    }
    ULONG InternalRelease()
    {
        return _ThreadModel::Decrement(&m_dwRef);
    }

    void Lock() {m_critsec.Lock();}
    void Unlock() {m_critsec.Unlock();}
private:
    _CritSec m_critsec;
};
```

CComObjectRootEx provides the InternalAddRef and InternalRelease methods. These methods are used when the component has not been aggregated or does not support aggregation. We have not yet seen the actual implementation of IUnknown::AddRef and IUnknown::Release, but we're getting there. Before we do, though, let's look at how our math component uses CComObjectRootEx.

```
class ATL_NO_VTABLE CMath :
    public CComObjectRootEx<CComSingleThreadModel>,
    public CComCoClass<CMath, &CLSID_Math>,
    public IMath,
    public IAdvancedMath
{
    ...
};
```

As you can see, the first class that we derive from in our CMath implementation is CComObjectRootEx. It provides basic IUnknown support. But what about that CComSingleThreadModel stuff?

The CComObjectRootEx class is template-based, and the template parameter is the threading model to use for the component. We'll discuss the various threading models in more detail in a later chapter. For now, just understand that you specify the threading models supported by your component through a parameter when building your implementation class. ATL does this so that you can easily change the threading models supported by your components.

CComObjectRoot and Threading

That brings us to the CComObjectRoot class, which is a simple typedef of CComObjectRootEx with a parameter of CComObjectThreadModel.

```
typedef CComObjectRootEx<CComObjectThreadModel> CComObjectRoot;
```

The `CComObjectThreadModel` parameter is defined via a preprocessor symbol. Here's how it gets set:

```
// From ATLBASE.H
#if defined(_ATL_SINGLE_THREADED)
     typedef CComSingleThreadModel CComObjectThreadModel;
     typedef CComSingleThreadModel CComGlobalsThreadModel;
#elif defined(_ATL_APARTMENT_THREADED)
     typedef CComSingleThreadModel CComObjectThreadModel;
     typedef CComMultiThreadModel CComGlobalsThreadModel;
#else
     typedef CComMultiThreadModel CComObjectThreadModel;
     typedef CComMultiThreadModel CComGlobalsThreadModel;
#endif
```

By changing a compiler directive, you can change the threading model for all the components in your project. By using `CComObjectRoot` instead of `CComObjectRootEx`, we could have declared our class this way instead:

```
// From MATH.H
class ATL_NO_VTABLE CMath :
   //public CComObjectRootEx<CComSingleThreadModel>,
   public CComObjectRoot,
   public CComCoClass<CMath, &CLSID_Math>,
   public IMath,
   public IAdvancedMath
```

This approach would allow us to change the threading model of our component without modifying the source in any way. However, as we'll see later, to build a truly multithreaded component you must make sure that your component is thread-safe. ATL can help, but you must do some work, too.

Where are AddRef and Release?

We've discussed how ATL implements `IUnknown` support, but we still haven't found the important `AddRef` and Release methods. Where are they? Here's the scoop. The implementation of the reference counting methods is provided by another set of ATL classes. In other words, ATL implements reference counting in two phases. `CComObjectRootEx` manages reference counting through its Internal and Outer methods, and the `CComObject` series of classes handles the implementation of the exposed `IUnknown` methods. The problem, as you can see in the following code, is that there is no `CComObject` class in our implementation.

```
// From MATH.H
class ATL_NO_VTABLE CMath :
    public CComObjectRootEx<CComSingleThreadModel>,
    public CComCoClass<CMath, &CLSID_Math>,
    public IMath,
    public IAdvancedMath
{
...
};
```

The trick is that our CMath class is still not complete. You cannot instantiate CMath directly because it is still an abstract class. To instantiate our math implementation, we must derive one more template-based class. Here's a simple example of how you might instantiate an instance of the CMath class:

```
IMath* pIMath = new CComObject<CMath>
```

Maybe a picture will help. Figure 3.6 shows the classes necessary to implement our math component.

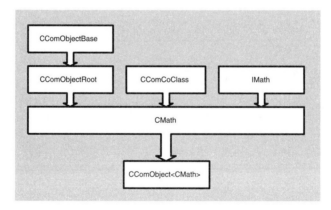

Figure 3.6 Basic ATL implementation.

For a basic, non-aggregation example, CComObjectRoot gives us InternalAddRef, InternalRelease, and InternalQueryInterface, CComCoClass provides class factory support, and IMath and IAdvancedMath provide our abstract interface classes. All these are combined to produce our CMath class. Then ATL goes one step further. To create instances, it uses CMath as a template parameter to CComObject, causing CComObject to derive from CMeth.

CComObject

CComObject is one of a number of classes that are the final destination in ATL's inheritance chain. Following is the majority of the implementation of CComObject.

```
// From ATLCOM.H
template <class Base>
class CComObject : public Base
{
public:
...
    STDMETHOD_(ULONG, AddRef)() {return InternalAddRef();}
    STDMETHOD_(ULONG, Release)()
    {
        ULONG l = InternalRelease();
        if (l == 0)
            delete this;
        return l;
    }
    STDMETHOD(QueryInterface)(REFIID iid, void ** ppvObject)
    {
        return _InternalQueryInterface(iid, ppvObject);
    }
};
```

Finally, we have found the declaration and implementation for the three IUnknown methods. Notice that for CComObject they call directly to the internal methods (such as InternalAddRef) implemented by CComObjectRootEx and so do not support aggregation.

There are ten CComObject-like classes that can be used to create an actual, instantiable class using ATL, and each one is described briefly in Table 3.9. Each one has a specific use.

Table 3.9 CComObject Classes

CLASS NAME	DESCRIPTION
CComObject	Used for most typical COM components. The object does not support aggregation and handles reference counting as a typical object does. It deletes itself when the reference count reaches zero.
CComObjectNoLock	Like CComObject except that the lifetime of the object does not affect the component housing's lock count. ATL uses this class in its implementation of a housing's class factories, because their lifetimes should not affect the lifetime of the housing.
CComAggObject	Supports aggregation only. The IUnknown implementation delegates to the outer component.

Table 3.9 *(continued)*

Class Name	Description
CComContainedObject	Similar to an aggregate object because it delegates all calls to its outer or parent object. However, this class can be used when the class is contained within your implementation. In other words, you aren't performing explicit aggregation.
CComPolyObject	Supports either aggregation or standard implementation. It is basically a space-saving implementation.
CComObjectStack	This implementation does not support reference counting at all. It is intended for use with COM objects that are created on the stack. The scope of their lifetimes is limited and well understood.
CComObjectGlobal	The lifetime of a CComGlobalObject is equivalent to the lifetime of the component's housing. In other words, it's just like a global C++ object. The lifetime is based on the housings global lock count.
CComObjectCached	Once created, this object will remain in a cache of objects. ATL uses this to implement a component's class factory.
CComTearOffObject, CComCachedTearOffObject	Tear-off objects provide a mechanism to create classes only when necessary.

Why are there so many ways to create classes? Good question. As we've discussed, ATL is about creating the most efficient COM objects possible. By providing ten different way of implementing a component's IUnknown support, the designers of ATL have given us maximum efficiency and flexibility in our implementations. It's a headache trying to figure out which one to use, but, hey, that's why we make the big money.

Following are some ways that you might access our math component using C++. Remember that this code is not *client* code. COM clients almost always create a component through their class factories. What we're studying here is how you might implement a component that uses other COM components using ATL. COM client code will use CoCreateInstance and QueryInterface, as we discussed in Chapter 2 and will return to at the end of this chapter.

```
SomeFunction()
{
   // Create an component on the stack
   // It's lifetime is limited to this function
   CComObjectStack<CMath> tempMath;

   // Create an instance in the heap
   CComObject<CMath> *pMath;
   pMath = new CComObject<CMath>

   // Use the static CreateInstance method
   // We'll discuss this in a moment
   CComObject<CMath> *pMath;
   HRESULT hr = CComObject<CMath>::CreateInstance( &pMath );

}
```

NOTE

Use of CreateInstance is the preferred technique especially if your implementation makes use of ATL's FinalConstruct idiom. We'll discuss this in Chapter 5.

Interfaces and Multiple Inheritance

If you look again at the class declaration for our math component, you'll see that CMath derives from four other classes. ATL uses multiple inheritance extensively in its implementation. We get IUnknown support from CComObjectRootEx, class factory support from CComCoClass, and the method signatures from each of our component's unique interfaces (such as IMath and IAdvancedMath). Here's our declaration again:

```
// From MATH.H
class ATL_NO_VTABLE CMath :
    public CComObjectRootEx<CComSingleThreadModel>,
    public CComCoClass<CMath, &CLSID_Math>,
    public IMath,
    public IAdvancedMath
{
...
// IMath
public:
    STDMETHOD(Divide)(long lOp1, long lOp2, long* plResult);
    STDMETHOD(Multiply)(long lOp1, long lOp2, long* plResult);
    STDMETHOD(Subtract)(long lOp1, long lOp2, long* plResult);
    STDMETHOD(Add)(long lOp1, long lOp2, long* plResult);

// IAdvancedMath
public:
    STDMETHOD(Factorial)( short, long* );
    STDMETHOD(Fibonacci)( short, long* );
};
```

We get some functionality from the first two derivations, but by deriving from IMath and IAdvancedMath all we get is *interface inheritance*. Absolutely no functionality is provided by IMath and IAdvancedMath. Their only purpose is to provide our component with Vtables so that we can expose IMath and IAdvancedMath as COM interfaces. We covered this in detail in Chapter 2. The concept is still here, although in the ATL implementation of IUnknown it's a bit obscured.

ATL_NO_VTABLE

Our CMath class is created by inheriting from multiple ATL template classes. Before we go on, let's look at ATL_NO_VTABLE. ATL_NO_VTABLE equates to __declspec(novtable).

This directive tells the compiler not to produce or initialize a Vtable structure for the class, something that makes the class's construction and destruction code smaller.

But don't we need a Vtable for our class? Yes, we do—at least in our final, constructed class. But remember, our implementation class is still abstract at this point. The ATL_NO_VTABLE option allows the compiler to defer building the Vtable structure until a true instance is created, and that requires CComObject to ultimately provide its IUnknown implementation. In other words, we don't need a Vtable until we reach the end of our derivation chain, so ATL_NO_VTABLE saves us some bytes as well as code.

There are number of restrictions to remember when you're using the ATL_NO_VTABLE option. In general, you should not call virtual functions or functions that will result in a virtual call in the class constructor or destructor. You can remove the ATL_NO_VTABLE macro from the declaration if you're not sure whether your class follows the rules. It's just an attempt to reduce the size of the generated code.

NOTE As we discussed in Chapter 2, COM interfaces are built using C++ Vtables. ATL is about building COM components, so what is this stuff about ATL_NO_VTABLE? The designers of ATL took great pains to develop a framework that would not compromise performance, and this is one example.

ATL's CLASS FACTORY SUPPORT: CComCoClass

Our CMath class also derives from CComCoClass. CComCoClass provides class factory support, and basic methods to retrieve its CLSID and component-specific error information. If you're developing a component that does not need a class factory because it does not support external creation, you won't need to include CComCoClass in your implementation.

As you can see from the code below, we provide the name of our implementation class as well as the actual CLSID of our component via template parameters to CComCoClass.

```
// From MATH.H
class ATL_NO_VTABLE CMath :
   public CComObjectRootEx<CComSingleThreadModel>,
   public CComCoClass<CMath, &CLSID_Math>,
   public IMath,
   public IAdvancedMath
{
...
};
```

When the template expands, you get something like the following: (I've highlighted those items that are affected by our template parameters.)

```
class CComCoClass
{
public:
    DECLARE_CLASSFACTORY()
    DECLARE_AGGREGATABLE( CMath )
    typedef CMath _CoClass;
    static const CLSID& WINAPI GetObjectCLSID() {return &CLSID_Math;}
    static LPCTSTR WINAPI GetObjectDescription() {return NULL;}
    static HRESULT WINAPI Error(LPCOLESTR lpszDesc,
                                const IID& iid = GUID_NULL,
                                HRESULT hRes = 0)
    {
        return AtlReportError(GetObjectCLSID(), lpszDesc, iid, hRes);
    }
...
};
```

The important thing to notice here is that CComCoClass provides our component's class factory support through the DECLARE_CLASSFACTORY macro. This macro eventually expands to provide the class with a typedef that is used by ATL's OBJECT_ENTRY macro that we described earlier. The OBJECT_ENTRY macro is used to build a map of creator functions for each component within a housing.

ATL's class factory support is very difficult to understand, so I'm going to quickly summarize it here, and then we'll work through each of the macros. By presenting it twice, I hope to make it a bit easier to understand.

To begin, CComCoClass contains two macros: DECLARE_CLASSFACTORY and DECLARE_AGGREGATABLE that provide typedefs for the OBJECT_ENTRY macro

```
#define DECLARE_CLASSFACTORY
    typedef CComCreator<CComObjectCached<CComClassFactory> > \
        _ClassFactoryCreatorClass;
#define DECLARE_AGGREGATABLE( x )
    typedef CComCreator2<CComCreator<CComObject<x> >, \
        CComCreator<CComAggObject<x> > > _CreatorClass;
```

The _ClassFactoryCreatorClass and _CreatorClass, which are *creator* classes, contain static CreateInstance methods, through with the instances are created. The object map will look like this:

```
{
    &CLSID_CMATH,
    &CMath::UpdateRegistry,
    &CMath::_ClassFactoryCreatorClass::CreateInstance,
    &CMath::_CreatorClass::CreateInstance,
    ...
}
```

When a client calls CoCreateInstance, COM calls DllGetClassObject. This eventually calls AtlModuleGetClassObject, which searches the object map for the CLSID_Math entry. Upon finding it, AtlModuleGetClassObject calls &CMath::_ClassFactoryCreatorClass::CreateInstance passing &CMath::_CreatorClass::CreateInstance as a parameter. This parameter is cached in the m_pfmCreateInstance member of CComClassFactory.

The &CMath::_ClassFactoryCreatorClass::CreateInstance call instantiates CComClassFactory, which like all ATL classes must derive from one of the CComObject classes. In this case its CComCachedObject because we want to cache the housing's class factory instances. The pointer to the CComClassFactory class is then stored in the pCF element of the object map entry for &CLSID_CMATH.

COM (via CoCreateInstance) or the client (CoGetClassObject/CreateInstance) uses CComClassFactory::CreateInstance to create component instances. This function actually calls m_pfnCreateInstance passing pUnkOuter as a parameter. If the pUnkOuter parameter is null, which indicates the client is not aggregating, the CComCreator<CComObject<CMath>>::CreateInstance method is used. If pUnkOuter is non-null, indicating creation as a aggregate, then the CComCreator<CComAggObject<CMath>>::CreateInstance is used instead.

Okay, now let's step through that in a bit more detail.

DECLARE_CLASSFACTORY

First, let's take a look at the DECLARE_CLASSFACTORY macro.

```
// From ATLCOM.H
...
#define DECLARE_CLASSFACTORY() DECLARE_CLASSFACTORY_EX(CComClassFactory)
#define DECLARE_CLASSFACTORY_EX(cf) \
    typedef CComCreator< CComObjectCached< cf > > _ClassFactoryCreatorClass;
```

As you can tell from the above definitions, the class factory macro declares a typedef for something called _ClassFactoryCreatorClass, but what is going on with those nested templates? Well, let's expand it out. Here's what it eventually looks like:

```
typedef CComCreator< CComObjectCached< CComClassFactory > >
_ClassFactoryCreatorClass
```

ATL uses something called a "creator" class that actually creates instances of our components when requested from an external client. ATL also uses the creator classes to create a component's class factory. The above typedef is used to specify the a creator class that will create instances of the CComObject type specified. The creator class will create instances of a class factory using the CComObjectCached implementation. Instances of CComObjectCached are cached and so a component's class factory is only created when a client asks for it. It then hangs around until the housing is destroyed. Here's what our CComCoClass looks like now:

```
class CComCoClass
{
public:
    //DECLARE_CLASSFACTORY()
    typedef CComCreator< CComObjectCached< CComClassFactory > >
            _ClassFactoryCreatorClass;

    DECLARE_AGGREGATABLE( CMath )
    typedef CMath _CoClass;
    static const CLSID& WINAPI GetObjectCLSID() {return &CLSID_Math;}
    static LPCTSTR WINAPI GetObjectDescription() {return NULL;}
    static HRESULT WINAPI Error(LPCOLESTR lpszDesc,
                        const IID& iid = GUID_NULL,
                        HRESULT hRes = 0)
    {
        return AtlReportError(GetObjectCLSID(), lpszDesc, iid, hRes);
    }
...
};
```

CComCreator

What does CComCreator look like? Good question.

```
// From ATLCOM.H
template <class T1>
class CComCreator
{
public:
```

```
static HRESULT WINAPI CreateInstance(void* pv, REFIID riid, LPVOID* ppv)
{
    _ASSERTE(*ppv == NULL);
    HRESULT hRes = E_OUTOFMEMORY;
    T1* p = NULL;
    p = new T1( pv )
    if (p != NULL)
    {
        p->SetVoid(pv);
        p->InternalFinalConstructAddRef();
        hRes = p->FinalConstruct();
        p->InternalFinalConstructRelease();
        if (hRes == S_OK)
            hRes = p->QueryInterface(riid, ppv);
        if (hRes != S_OK)
            delete p;
    }
    return hRes;
}
};
```

As you can see, the most important aspect of CComCreator is that it has a static method called CreateInstance that creates an instance of the class that is specified as the template parameter. It's here, in CComCreator, that the new operator is used on an ATL component. However, so far we've just provided a way for ATL to create an instance of our component's class factory. How is the component actually created? Before we get to that, let's look at the implementation of CComClassFactory.

CComClassFactory

Most components built using ATL will get their class factory through inclusion of the CComCoClass class. As we've seen above, the class factory is handled by the DECLARE_CLASSFACTORY macro. The macro provides a typedef that is used in the component's OBJECT_ENTRY macro entry. The typedef is used to specify the type of CComObject implementation that we want. Remember, our ATL implementation must ultimately derive from one of the CComObject classes.

As described above, we now have a CComCreator that "knows" how to create our class factory when necessary. In other words, when the housing is loaded, it doesn't have to instantiate class factories immediately for each component that it supports. The creation of a class factory object is deferred until a client explicitly asks for it via DllGetClassObject. This is another example of how ATL allows you to build efficient COM objects.

Here's a look at `CComClassFactory`. It provides the two standard class factory methods: `CreateInstance` and `LockServer`. What we're interested in is that strange `SetVoid` function and the `m_pfnCreateInstance` data member.

```
class CComClassFactory :
   public IClassFactory,
   public CComObjectRootEx<CComGlobalsThreadModel>
{
public:
   BEGIN_COM_MAP(CComClassFactory)
      COM_INTERFACE_ENTRY(IClassFactory)
   END_COM_MAP()

   // IClassFactory
   STDMETHOD(CreateInstance)(LPUNKNOWN pUnkOuter, REFIID riid, void** ppvObj);
   STDMETHOD(LockServer)(BOOL fLock);

   // helper
   void SetVoid(void* pv)
   {
      m_pfnCreateInstance = (_ATL_CREATORFUNC*)pv;
   }
   _ATL_CREATORFUNC* m_pfnCreateInstance;
};
```

As we'll see in a moment, the `m_pfnCreateInstance` member will hold a pointer to another creator class static method that provides the component creation mechanism for the class factory. If we look back at our class's implementation of `CComCoClass`, you'll see that we have one macro yet to expand. `DECLARE_AGGREGATABLE` will finally complete ATL's support for class factories—well, almost.

CComCreator2 and DECLARE_AGGREGATABLE

Again, here's a look at what we've got so far:

```
class CComCoClass
{
public:
   typedef CComCreator< CComObjectCached< CComClassFactory > >
         _ClassFactoryCreatorClass;

   DECLARE_AGGREGATABLE( CMath )
   typedef CMath _CoClass;
...
};
```

The default `CComCoClass` gives a component support for aggregation. To override this support, you can add one of several macros (for example, `DECLARE_NOT_AGGREGATABLE`) to your class. However, so as not to confuse the issue here, let's just plow ahead. The DECLARE_AGGREGATABLE macro looks like this:

```
#define DECLARE_AGGREGATABLE(x) public:\
    typedef CComCreator2< CComCreator< CComObject< x > >,\
            CComCreator< CComAggObject< x > > > _CreatorClass;
```

 I bet you thought MFC macros were hard to decipher!

N O T E

If we expand this template/macro in our class, we get this:

```
class CComCoClass
{
public:
    typedef CComCreator< CComObjectCached< CComClassFactory > >
            _ClassFactoryCreatorClass;

    typedef CComCreator2< CComCreator< CComObject< CMath > >,
            CComCreator< CComAggObject< CMath > > > _CreatorClass;

typedef CMath _CoClass;
...
};
```

Okay, we now have a typedef that describes a creator class (_CreatorClass) for our component class, which appears to provide two different creators. Here's the definition for CComCreator2.

```
template <class T1, class T2>
class CComCreator2
{
public:
    static HRESULT WINAPI CreateInstance(void* pv, REFIID riid, LPVOID* ppv)
    {
        _ASSERTE(*ppv == NULL);
        HRESULT hRes = E_OUTOFMEMORY;
        if (pv == NULL)
            hRes = T1::CreateInstance(NULL, riid, ppv);
        else
            hRes = T2::CreateInstance(pv, riid, ppv);
        return hRes;
    }
};
```

CComCreator2 is a template that takes two different creator classes as parameters. The CComCreator2 class provides two different ways to instantiate our CMath class. The first class (T1) uses ATL's standard, non-aggregatable CComObject implementation, and the second one (T2) uses CComAggObject, which supports aggregation. The first parameter provided to CreateInstance is the outer unknown, which indicates whether the client is attempting an aggregation.

The final detail is how the creators are accessed. We covered the OBJECT_ENTRY macros earlier in the chapter, but they should make a bit more sense now. Here's a look at them again:

```
#define BEGIN_OBJECT_MAP(x) static _ATL_OBJMAP_ENTRY x[] = {
#define OBJECT_ENTRY(clsid, class) {
          &clsid,
          &class::UpdateRegistry,
          &class::_ClassFactoryCreatorClass::CreateInstance,
          &class::_CreatorClass::CreateInstance,
          NULL, 0, &class::GetObjectDescription },
#define END_OBJECT_MAP()    {NULL, NULL, NULL, NULL}};
```

If we look back at our housing implementation, we'll notice this:

```
BEGIN_OBJECT_MAP(ObjectMap)
   OBJECT_ENTRY(CLSID_Math, CMath)
END_OBJECT_MAP()
...
BOOL WINAPI DllMain(HINSTANCE hInstance, DWORD dwReason, LPVOID /*lpReserved*/)
{
...
   _Module.Init(ObjectMap, hInstance);
...
}
```

The preceding code initializes our object map with the parameters provided via the macros. Ultimately, it looks something like this:

```
static _ATL_OBJECT_ENTRY ObjectMap[] =
{
   &CLSID_Math, &CMath::UpdateRegistry,
   &CMath::_ClassFactoryCreatorClass::CreateInstance,
   &CMath::_CreatorClass::CreateInstance,
...
}
```

Now we're getting somewhere. At least we recognize the second and third parameters as our creator class typedefs. Now, when COM asks for a specific component's class factory through DllGetClassObject, we can look up our class factory in the table.

```
STDAPI DllGetClassObject(REFCLSID rclsid, REFIID riid, LPVOID* ppv)
{
    // This eventually calls AtlModuleClassObject
    return _Module.GetClassObject(rclsid, riid, ppv);
}
```

Once the CLSID is found and the class factory instance is created via _ClassFactoryCreatorClass::CreateInstance, COM can then call through IClassFactory::CreateInstance to create an actual component instance. Here's a condensed implementation of CComClassFactory::CreateInstance, which is ultimately called.

```
// From ATLIMPL.CPP
STDMETHODIMP CComClassFactory::CreateInstance(
     LPUNKNOWN pUnkOuter,
     REFIID riid, void** ppvObj)
{
    HRESULT hRes;
    hRes = m_pfnCreateInstance(pUnkOuter, riid, ppvObj);
    return hRes;
}
```

The class factory creates an instance of our math component by calling its internal m_pfnCreateInstance function pointer. This data member is initialized via the SetVoid method, which is called when the class factory is initially created. Take a look at the highlighted lines in this code:

```
ATLAPI AtlModuleGetClassObject(_ATL_MODULE* pM,
                 REFCLSID rclsid,
                 REFIID riid, LPVOID* ppv)
{
    _ATL_OBJMAP_ENTRY* pEntry = pM->m_pObjMap;
    HRESULT hRes = S_OK;
    while (pEntry->pclsid != NULL)
    {
        if (InlineIsEqualGUID(rclsid, *pEntry->pclsid))
        {
            // We haven't created the class factory object yet, so do so
            if (pEntry->pCF == NULL)
            {
                // When we create the class object, pass in the address
                // of the ATL creator function for the actual component
                hRes = pEntry->pfnGetClassObject( pEntry->pfnCreateInstance,
                                                  IID_IUnknown,
                                                  (LPVOID*)&pEntry->pCF);
            }
        }
```

(code continued on next page)

```
      pEntry++;
   }
   return hRes;
}
```

The `m_pfnCreateInstance` member is set via the `pfnCreateInstance` member (`_CreatorClass::CreateInstance`) of the `ATL_OBJECT_MAP` structure. Later, when COM calls `IClassFactory::CreateInstance`, it will go directly into the `CreateInstance` implementation of `CComCreator2`.

 Here's one other detail concerning ATL's class factory support. If you look closely, you notice that the creator classes are never actually instantiated because the CreateInstance methods are static. Again, ATL is doing whatever it can to save space.

NOTE

Whew. I don't know whether you followed all that. If you didn't, you might try going through it again later. ATL is tough stuff and may not make sense on the first pass, but hang in there. One thing that will help is to run the example in debug mode and set break points in the following functions of the server.

- `DllGetClassObject`. Follow the code as it traverses the object map.
- `CComCreator::CreateInstance`. Watch as the `CComCreator2` address is passed via the `SetVoid` method
- `CComCreator2::CreateInstance`. Watch as an instance of the math component is created via `CComCreator::CreateInstance`.

SELF-REGISTRATION: THE REGISTRAR

All COM component housings should support *self-registration*, which is the ability of a housing to automatically add the COM registry entries for each of its housed components. In Chapter 2, we manually added these entries using a **.REG** file. In the real world, this isn't acceptable. Luckily, ATL makes support for self-registration easy to implement. When you create a basic ATL project with the wizards, the support is already provided.

DLL housings support self-registration by exporting two standard COM functions: `DllRegisterServer` and `DllUnregisterServer`. As their names imply, these functions cause the housing to either add or remove entries in the system registry.

If you've done any work with COM, OLE, or ActiveX, you have probably used the REGSVR32 utility. It takes a DLL as a parameter, as in this example:
`c:>REGSVR32 Chapter3_Server.dll`

The purpose of REGSVR32 is to register (or unregister via **/u**) components during installation on a local system. Following are the steps REGSVR32 follows to register the components in a specific housing.

1. Gets the name of the DLL from the command line and loads it using the Win32 API function `LoadLibrary`.
2. Gets the address of the `DllRegisterServer` function using the Win32 API function `GetProcAddress`.
3. Calls the entry point, which allows the DLL to add its entries to the registry.
4. Calls `FreeLibrary` to release the DLL.

In other words, you could write your own version of REGSVR32 with about 12 lines of code.

    We know how self-registration works with DLLs, but what about executables? The process differs slightly. Executables don't expose entry points, so the well-known entry point technique won't work. Instead, COM requires all executable housings to perform self-registration every time they execute. In that way, a user can self-register a component just by running the executable. Also, COM defines the **/RegServer** command-line option for those times when you want to register the components but don't want to leave the application running. The software installation process is a good example.

ATL's Registrar Component: `IRegistrar`

The Registrar is a simple, data-driven mechanism to update the registry with information about a housing's components. As you would probably guess, the Registrar is a COM object that implements the `IRegistrar` interface. Here's a look at `IRegistrar`.

```
interface IRegistrar : IUnknown
{
HRESULT AddReplacement(
    [in] LPCOLESTR key, [in] LPCOLESTR item);
HRESULT ClearReplacements();
HRESULT ResourceRegisterSz(
    [in] LPCOLESTR resFileName,
    [in] LPCOLESTR szID,
    [in] LPCOLESTR szType);
HRESULT ResourceUnregisterSz(
    [in] LPCOLESTR resFileName,
    [in] LPCOLESTR szID,
    [in] LPCOLESTR szType);
```

(code continued on next page)

```
HRESULT FileRegister([in] LPCOLESTR fileName);
HRESULT FileUnregister([in] LPCOLESTR fileName);
HRESULT StringRegister([in] LPCOLESTR data);
HRESULT StringUnregister([in] LPCOLESTR data);
HRESULT ResourceRegister(
    [in] LPCOLESTR resFileName,
    [in] UINT nID,
    [in] LPCOLESTR szType);
HRESULT ResourceUnregister(
    [in] LPCOLESTR resFileName,
    [in] UINT nID,
    [in] LPCOLESTR szType);
};
```

As you can see, `IRegistrar` provides methods to update the system registry with text files, resource files, and filenames. The implementation of the Registrar component is provided in **STATREG.H** and **STATREG.CPP** and can be delivered via **ATL.DLL** or as part of your executable. The `_ATL_STATIC_REGISTRY` preprocessor symbol controls this option, as we described earlier in the chapter.

ATL uses the Registrar throughout its implementation.

DECLARE_REGISTRY_RESOURCEID

If you look closely at the `Math` component's header file, you'll see a single line that handles self-registration for our component.

```
// Math.h : Declaration of the CMath

#include "resource.h"        // main symbols

////////////////////////
// CMath
////////////////////////
class ATL_NO_VTABLE CMath :
    public CComObjectRootEx<CComSingleThreadModel>,
    public CComCoClass<CMath, &CLSID_Math>,
    public IMath,
    public IAdvancedMath
{
...
DECLARE_REGISTRY_RESOURCEID(IDR_MATH)
...
};
```

The DECLARE_REGISTRY_RESOURCEID macro expands to a call to the Registrar. By default, the ATL Object wizard creates a ***ComponentName*.RGS** file (in our case, **MATH.RGS**) that contains a script for updating the registry. Here's what it looks like:

```
HKCR
{
  Chapter3.Math.1 = s 'Math Class'
  {
    CLSID = s '{8812699D-1CC8-11D1-883A-444553540000}'
  }
  Chapter3.Math = s 'Math Class'
  {
    CLSID = s '{8812699D-1CC8-11D1-883A-444553540000}'
    CurVer = s 'Chapter3.Math.1'
  }
  NoRemove CLSID
  {
    ForceRemove {8812699D-1CC8-11D1-883A-444553540000} = s 'Math Class'
    {
      ProgID = s 'Chapter3.Math.1'
      VersionIndependentProgID = s 'Chapter3.Math'
      InprocServer32 = s '%MODULE%'
      {
        val ThreadingModel = s 'Apartment'
      }
    }
  }
}
```

NOTE

Actually, it doesn't look exactly like the code shown. The line I've highlighted must be added manually for the version-independent ProgID to work. This is just a small bug in the Object wizard.

The script uses a special BNR (Backus-Nauer) syntax for describing each of the component's registry entries. The script is stored in the project's resource file (identified by IDR_MATH). The DECLARE_REGISTRY_RESOURCEID expands to this:

```
static HRESULT WINAPI UpdateRegistry(BOOL bRegister)
{
    return _Module.UpdateRegistryFromResource(IDR_MATH, bRegister);
}
```

This method is ultimately called by the `DllRegisterServer` and `DllUnregisterServer` functions in **CHAPTER3_SERVER.CPP**. A full discussion of the ATL registry component is beyond our scope (maybe we'll have more time in a later chapter). However, to modify your component's registry information, you need only edit the appropriate **.RGS** file and rebuild the project. It will be pulled in as a binary resource; when the component is registered, the information will be updated.

IMPLEMENTING OUR MATH COMPONENT USING ATL

What follows is a step-by-step process of creating the `Math` component using ATL's wizards. Most of the detail about the case is produced by the wizards was described in the preceding text. The following step-by-step approach should make it easier to create the example quickly. You can also download the code from WidgetWare.com.

Create the Visual C++ Project

Start Visual C++ and create a new project, selecting **ATL COM AppWizard**. Give it the name "**Chapter3_Server**". In Step 1 of 1, select **Dynamic Link Library** (see Figure 3.7). Select **Finish** and then **OK** to generate the project.

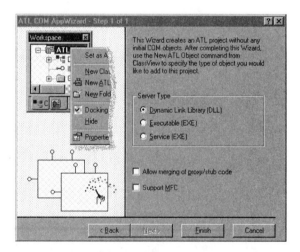

Figure 3.7 ATL COM AppWizard, Step 1 of 1.

The ATL COM AppWizard

The ATL COM AppWizard is a Visual C++ wizard that steps you through the initial creation of an ATL-based project. You will use AppWizard only once per project. After the project is created, you will use the ATL Object wizard to add components to your project.

The ATL Object Wizard

The initial project created using the ATL AppWizard provides only basic housing support for the Math component. We now need to create the component implementation files. To do that, we use the new ATL Object wizard. It is accessed through the Visual C++ **Insert/Add ATL Component** menu item.

The main Object wizard dialog box is shown in Figure 3.8. For our purposes we will add the Simple Object type from the ATL Objects section. After clicking the Next button, you should see a dialog box like that shown in Figure 3.9.

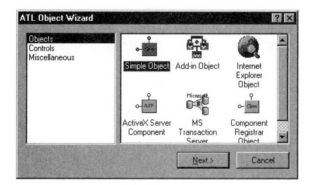

Figure 3.8 ATL Object wizard.

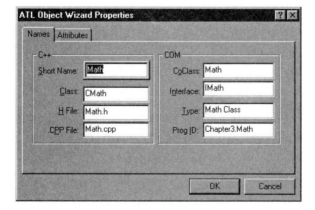

Figure 3.9 ATL Object Wizard Properties dialog box, **Names** tab.

Object Wizard Names

A series of dialog boxes is presented depending on the object type selected. For a simple COM object, information for two dialog boxes—Name and Attributes—must be populated. Figure 3.9 shows the Object wizard's Names dialog box with appropriate values for our project. We've set the **Short Name** to **Math** and changed the **Prog ID** to **Chapter3.Math**.

Object Wizard Attributes

The Attributes dialog box allows us to specify basic COM support options for our component. Figure 3.10 shows our selections. The only change from the defaults is that we're using a custom interface. After setting each option, click **OK** and the source files for our new object will be created.

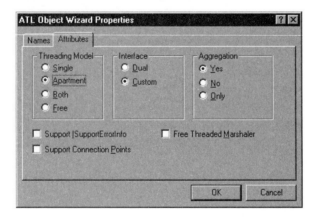

Figure 3.10 ATL Object Wizard Properties dialog box, **Attributes** tab.

The Object wizard adds the component implementation files to the project:

- **MATH.H.** CMath header file.
- **MATH.CPP.** CMath implementation file.
- **MATH.RGS.** Math component registrar script file.
- **CHAPTER3_SERVER.IDL.** The Object wizard also added entries to the server's IDL file.

Implementing the IMath Interface

To add interface methods to an ATL object, it's easiest to do it from Developer Studio's **ClassView** tab. In Class View, right click on the **IMath** interface and select **Add**

Method... This is shown in Figure 3.11 below. Complete the dialog entries for the **Add** method as shown in Figure 3.12, and then add the three other methods (Subtract, Multiply, and Divide) using the same technique.

Figure 3.11 Adding methods in the **ClassView** tab.

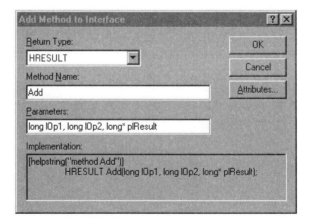

Figure 3.12 Add Method dialog box.

Now it's time to write some code. Load **MATH.CPP** and add the following highlighted code.

```
//
// Math.cpp : Implementation of CMath
//

#include "stdafx.h"
#include "Server.h"
#include "Math.h"

///////////////
// CMath
///////////////

// IMath interface
STDMETHODIMP CMath::Add( long lOp1, long lOp2, long* plResult )
{
   *plResult = lOp1 + lOp2;
   return S_OK;
}

STDMETHODIMP CMath::Subtract( long lOp1, long lOp2, long* plResult )
{
   *plResult = lOp1 - lOp2;
   return S_OK;
}

STDMETHODIMP CMath::Multiply( long lOp1, long lOp2, long* plResult )
{
   *plResult = lOp1 * lOp2;
   return S_OK;
}

STDMETHODIMP CMath::Divide( long lOp1, long lOp2, long* plResult )
{
   *plResult = lOp1 / lOp2;
   return S_OK;
}
```

That's all there is to adding our simple functionality. By using ATL's built-in COM function-ality, we've saved a lot of time.

Adding `IAdvancedMath` and Its Methods

When we used the Object wizard to add our math component, it allowed us to define only one interface (this is one of the deficiencies of the wizard). We must add the second inter-face by hand.

C++ interface declarations are built dynamically by compiling the project's IDL project with **MIDL.EXE**. In the earlier steps, the IDL entries for the `IMath` interface were added automatically. We'll have to do this manually for IAdvancedMath. Load **CHAPTER3_SERVER.IDL,** and add the following code. Before you do, though, you need to use the GUIDGEN utility to generate a GUID for IAdvancedMath.

```
//
// Chapter3_Server.idl : IDL source for Chapter3_Server.dll
//
...
import "oaidl.idl";
import "ocidl.idl";
   [
      object,
      uuid(8812699C-1CC8-11D1-883A-444553540000),
      helpstring("IMath Interface"),
      pointer_default(unique)
   ]
   interface IMath : IUnknown
   {
      // This was added automatically by the IDE
      HRESULT Add( [in] long, [in] long, [out, retval] long* plResult );
      HRESULT Subtract( [in] long, [in] long, [out, retval] long* plResult );
      HRESULT Multiply( [in] long, [in] long, [out, retval] long* plResult );
      HRESULT Divide( [in] long, [in] long, [out, retval] long* plResult );
   };

   [
     object,
     // We have to create this new GUID
     uuid(6AF3DF1E-C48F-11D0-A769-D477A4000000),
     helpstring("IAdvancedMath Interface"),
     pointer_default(unique)
   ]

   interface IAdvancedMath : IUnknown
   {
     HRESULT Factorial( [in] short sFact, [out, retval] long* pResult );
     HRESULT Fibonacci( [in] short sFib, [out, retval] long* pResult );
   };

[
   uuid(8812698E-1CC8-11D1-883A-444553540000),
   version(1.0),
   helpstring("Chapter3_Server 1.0 Type Library")
```

(code continued on next page)

```
]
library SERVERLib
{
    ...
    coclass Math
    {
        [default] interface IMath;
        // Add the interface to the component
        interface IAdvancedMath;
    };
};
```

Updating MATH.H

Once we've added the interface declaration to the IDL file, we declare and implement the interface in **MATH.H** and **MATH.CPP**. First, **MATH.H**:

```
// Math.h : Declaration of the CMath class

#ifndef __MATH_H_
#define __MATH_H_

#include "resource.h"       // main symbols

/////////////////////
// CMath
/////////////////////
class ATL_NO_VTABLE CMath :
   public CComObjectRootEx<CComSingleThreadModel>,
   public CComCoClass<CMath, &CLSID_Math>,
   public IMath,
   public IAdvancedMath
{
...

BEGIN_COM_MAP(CMath)
   COM_INTERFACE_ENTRY(IMath)
   COM_INTERFACE_ENTRY(IAdvancedMath)
END_COM_MAP()

// IMath
public:
   STDMETHOD(Divide)(long lOp1, long lOp2, long* plResult);
   STDMETHOD(Multiply)(long lOp1, long lOp2, long* plResult);
   STDMETHOD(Subtract)(long lOp1, long lOp2, long* plResult);
   STDMETHOD(Add)(long lOp1, long lOp2, long* plResult);
```

```
// IAdvancedMath
public:
   STDMETHOD(Factorial)( short, long* );
   STDMETHOD(Fibonacci)( short, long* );
};

#endif //__MATH_H_
```

Updating MATH.CPP

Next, we update **MATH.CPP**. This code is nearly identical to the code from the Chapter 2 example. It's the implementation of our component's interface.

```
//
// Math.cpp : Implementation of CMath
//

#include "stdafx.h"
#include "Server.h"
#include "Math.h"

////////////////
// CMath
////////////////

// IMath interface
STDMETHODIMP CMath::Add( long lOp1, long lOp2, long* plResult )
{
   *plResult = lOp1 + lOp2;
   return S_OK;
}
...

// IAdvancedMath interface
long calcFactorial( short n )
{
   if ( n > 1 )
      return n * calcFactorial( n - 1 );
   else
      return 1;
}

STDMETHODIMP CMath::Factorial( short sOp, long* pResult )
{
   *pResult = calcFactorial( sOp );
   return S_OK;
}
```

(code continued on next page)

```
long calcFibonacci( short n )
{
   if ( n <= 1 )
      return 1;

   return calcFibonacci( n - 1 ) + calcFibonacci( n - 2 );
}
STDMETHODIMP CMath::Fibonacci( short sOp, long* pResult )
{
   *pResult = calcFibonacci( sOp );
   return S_OK;
}
```

Build the Project

That's it—using ATL saved quite a bit of coding and we didn't have to worry about implementing the IUnknown methods or our component's class factory. ATL also provided self-registration code for the server. Now let's build the project. Before we move on to developing a client application, you should quickly test your new component using OLEVIEW. This is shown in Figure 3.13.

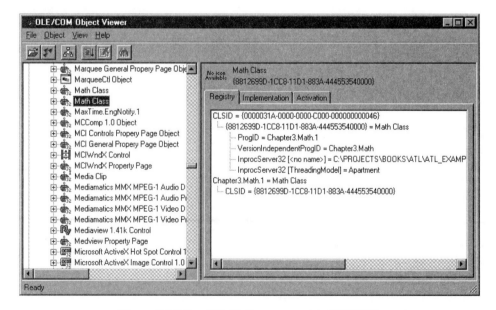

Figure 3.13 Our ATL Math component in OLEVIEW.

N O T E

Our component will show up under **All Objects** with the name `Math Class` instead of `Chapter3.Math`. This is because of the way the RGS file is created by the ATL Object wizard. Here's a look at the RGS file.

```
HKCR
{
  Chapter3.Math.1 = s 'Math Class'
  {
    CLSID = s '{8812699D-1CC8-11D1-883A-444553540000}'
  }
  Chapter3.Math = s 'Math Class'
  {
    CLSID = s '{8812699D-1CC8-11D1-883A-444553540000}'
    CurVer = s 'Chapter3.Math.1'
  }
  NoRemove CLSID
  {
    ForceRemove {8812699D-1CC8-11D1-883A-444553540000} = s 'Math
Class'
    {
      ProgID = s 'Chapter3.Math.1'
      VersionIndependentProgID = s 'Chapter3.Math'
      InprocServer32 = s '%MODULE%'
      {
        val ThreadingModel = s 'Apartment'
      }
    }
  }
}
```

Notice the `Chapter3.Math` entry. OLEVIEW uses the name of the ProgID entry if it is available. Of course, you can change this if you want to.

ANOTHER COM CLIENT

Our client application is similar to the one we developed in Chapter 2. The quickest way to build this project is to copy the project from your Chapter 2 directory and make the modifications highlighted next in **CLIENT.CPP**. Instead of using `CoGetClassObject`, we're now using `CoCreateInstance`, and that is the normal approach to instantiating

COM objects. Here's the complete code for Chapter3_Client. I've highlighted those lines that we need to discuss.

```cpp
//
// Chapter3_Client.cpp
//

#include <windows.h>
#include <tchar.h>
#include <iostream.h>

#include <initguid.h>
#include "..\Chapter3_Server\Chapter3_Server_i.c"
#include "..\Chapter3_Server\Chapter3_Server.h"
int main( int argc, char *argv[] )
{
   cout << "Initializing COM" << endl;

   if ( FAILED( CoInitialize( NULL )))
   {
      cout << "Unable to initialize COM" << endl;
      return -1;
   }

   // Use CoCreateInstance
   IMath* pMath;
   HRESULT hr = CoCreateInstance( CLSID_Math,
                                  NULL,
                                  CLSCTX_INPROC,
                                  IID_IMath,
                                  (void**) &pMath );
   if ( FAILED( hr ))
   {
      cout.setf( ios::hex, ios::basefield );
      cout << "Failed to create server instance. HR = " << hr << endl;
      return -1;
   }

   cout << "Instance created" << endl;

   long result;
   pMath->Multiply( 100, 8, &result );
   cout << "100 * 8 is " << result << endl;

   pMath->Subtract( 1000, 333, &result );
   cout << "1000 - 333 is " << result << endl;
```

```
   // Try IAdvancedMath, QI through IMath
   IAdvancedMath* pAdvMath = NULL;
   hr = pMath->QueryInterface( IID_IAdvancedMath, (LPVOID*)&pAdvMath );
   if ( FAILED( hr ))
   {
      cout << "QueryInterface() for IAdvancedMath failed" << endl;
      pMath->Release();
      CoUninitialize();
      return -1;
   }

   pAdvMath->Factorial( 10, &result );
   cout << "10! is " << result << endl;

   pAdvMath->Fibonacci( 10, &result );
   cout << "The Fibonacci of 10 is " << result << endl;

   cout << "Releasing IMath interface" << endl;
   pMath->Release();

   cout << "Releasing IAdvancedMath interface" << endl;
   pAdvMath->Release();

   cout << "Shuting down COM" << endl;
   CoUninitialize();

   return 0;
}
```

We have to make only a few adjustments to our client applications. First, we change how we reference the server's interface declarations. Because MIDL now generates them automatically from the IDL file, we include them instead. **CHAPTER3_SERVER.H** contains the IMath and IAdvancedMath interface declarations, and **CHAPTER3_SERVER_I.C** contains the definitions of the component's CLSIDs and IIDs.

The other difference is that we now use CoCreateInstance instead of CoGetClassObject. CoCreateInstance handles the details of getting the class factory and calling IClassFactory::CreateInstance. These details are always the same, so we let COM handle it.

Test the Server

After you make the preceding change, build the client project and run it in debug. It should behave just as it did in Chapter 2. The best way to learn COM and ATL is to step through this code in debug. When you get to an interface call, step into the call, and you'll begin debugging the server code.

On to IDL, Type Libraries, and Marshaling

That covers our introduction to ATL. We reimplemented our Math component using ATL, and I'm sure you can see that it's quite a bit easier that doing it with C++. In Chapter 4, we'll delve into what is required to house our components in executables instead of in DLLs. We'll take a look at *marshaling* as well as study the files produced by the MIDL compiler. Let's get started.

4

Interfaces, IDL, and Marshaling

At this point you should have an understanding of what COM is about and an idea of how ATL facilitates the creation of COM-based components. In this chapter we'll go a bit deeper into the various interface mechanisms provided by COM. In particular, we'll cover the Interface Definition Language (IDL) and marshaling. After that, we'll cover details such as COM error handling, COM memory management, and basic COM data types.

COM INTERFACE TYPES

In Chapter 2, we described COM interfaces by using the C++ Vtable structure as their implementation mechanism. Interfaces that use the Vtable structure exclusively are known as Vtable, or *custom*, interfaces. COM also supports two other interface: *dispinterfaces* (based on the standard IDispatch) and *dual* interfaces. In the next few sections we'll discuss each interface briefly.

Vtable Interfaces

You're familiar with the implementation of a Vtable interface. A COM component exposes its functionality through this Vtable interface. One of the drawbacks of a Vtable-style interface is that it requires some form of compile-time binding with the client (basically, the exact layout of the Vtable). In other words, the client must have compile-time knowledge of the interface methods and parameters. However, this static knowledge does not include the actual implementation of the methods in the component.

This is where COM's polymorphic behavior comes in. An interface's signature is defined at compile time, but the actual implementation of the interface methods is not. This allows you to "plug-in" component functionality at run time, as we've discussed.

IDispatch Interfaces: Dispinterfaces

What makes a dispinterface different from a Vtable interface is that its clients do not require any compile-time binding information (except to the IDispatch itself, which is well known). A client application can determine, at run-time, the method names and parameters. This arrangement removes any compile-time requirement on the client application. It sounds great, but the drawback is that dispinterfaces are much slower because they require an extra level of indirection in their implementation. We'll discuss this interface in detail in Chapter 6.

Dual Interfaces

Once you understand the concept of a Vtable and a dispinterface, a dual interface is easy. A dual interface is a combination of a regular COM Vtable interface and a dispinterface. This combination gives the client additional flexibility. A client of a component that supports a dual interface can choose the more efficient Vtable interface and bind to it at compile time, or it can choose to bind late (at run-time), which is less efficient but offers additional capabilities. We'll discuss implementing and accessing a dual interface in detail in Chapter 6.

DESCRIBING A COMPONENT AND ITS INTERFACES

Client applications that need to access a component's interface require a technique to obtain information about the interfaces. Interfaces must be described for several reasons. First, potential clients need to understand both the Vtable layout and the number and type of parameters in each method. Without this information, you would have to distribute language-dependent files (such as C++ header files) along with your component. Second, an interface description can be useful for generating language-specific bindings, something that is handy when you're developing components in particular language such as C++. Third, as we discussed in Chapter 2, COM-based components support the concept of location transparency. The client's ability to access a component's functionality across process and machine boundaries is important. However, to support this capability COM requires marshaling support for its interfaces. If you describe an interface in a canonical way, tools can automatically produce marshaling support code.

Type Information

Before a client application can access the services provided by a Vtable-based COM component, the client must know the structure of the component's interfaces. It must know information such as which interfaces are supported, which parameters each method takes, and so on. COM provides a way for components to describe their functionality through a binary, language-independent file called a type library.

As we discussed in Chapter 3, a component describes its interfaces with IDL. When you're using ATL, each component housing will have an associated IDL file that contains type information for components within the housing. This file is compiled into a type library using Microsoft's IDL compiler (**MIDL.EXE**). After compiling the type information, you distribute it along with the component either within the housing itself or as a separate **.TLB** file. The HKCR\TypeLib registry entry provides a way for client applications and object browsers to locate a component's type information. The type library provides all the needed information so that client applications can support compile-time type checking and early binding to a component's methods.

Language Bindings

IDL is also used to generate language-specific files for the described component. The MIDL compiler generates bindings (as **.H** and **.C** files) only for the C/C++ language. All other languages use the type library to generate compile-time bindings. Both Visual Basic and Visual J++ create wrapper classes for components by reading a component's type library and generating internal support code.

Proxy/Stub Generation

Another important aspect of IDL is its ability to produce proxy/stub DLLs for your component's interfaces. By describing your interfaces, methods, and parameters with IDL and compiling it with MIDL, you get code and a make file for a proxy/stub DLL. The proxy/stub DLL implements standard marshaling for each of your component interfaces.

MARSHALING

Marshaling is the process of transferring function arguments and return values across process and machine boundaries. Intrinsic types such as shorts and longs are easy to marshal, but most others, such as pointers to structures, are a bit more difficult. You can't just make a copy of a pointer because its value (an address) has no meaning in the context of another process, especially if that process is on another machine.

We've mentioned that COM objects are housed in either a Windows executable or a Windows DLL. When the component housing is a DLL it is called an in-process server to denote that the server component is executing within the context of the client's address space (executable). This method is the most efficient way to interact with a COM-based component, because marshaling usually is not necessary. However, as we'll see in a later chapter, COM uses marshaling to synchronize access to components in multithreaded applications. So in some cases you may need marshaling support even if your component supports only in-process execution.

COM's implementation of marshaling uses a *proxy* and a *stub*. When marshaling is required, COM creates a proxy object in the client's process space and a stub in the component's process space. The client application then interacts with the proxy just as if it had a direct connection to the component. The component also interacts with the stub just as if it were connected directly to the client. This important COM feature is what enables location transparency. The complexity of marshaling, which may require moving interface pointers from one machine to another, is hidden from the developer. Figure 4.1 shows the relationship of clients, proxies, servers, and stubs.

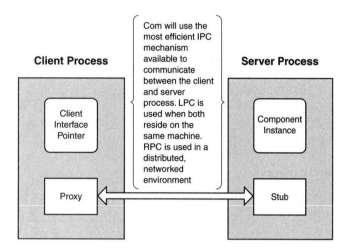

Figure 4.1 Proxies and stubs.

Marshaling is required in the following situations:

- When you're accessing a component in a different process on the same machine.
- When you're accessing a component on a different machine (DCOM).
- When you're passing interface pointers between single-threaded apartments in the same process.
- When you're passing interface pointers between multithreaded and single-threaded apartments in the same process.

COM handles the majority of these cases. By automatically managing the marshaling process between clients and components, COM makes module interoperability quite a bit easier.

Distributed COM

Distributed COM is COM's ability to distribute components and access them from different machines in a network. This means that we can deploy a COM-based component on a machine in New York and access its services on a client machine in Kansas City. The benefit is that the client software is oblivious to the location of the server component. It could reside locally on the client machine, on a different machine in Kansas City, or on a machine in New York.

The COM-client software doesn't care and doesn't need to know in what address space the server is executing. All this happens through the magic of marshaling. However, DCOM raises several additional issues—primarily security—that we will not discuss in this book. DCOM is mostly about getting the security right and managing component lifetimes in the more hostile, unstable network environment. See Dr. Richard Grimes's book, *Professional DCOM Programming* (Wrox Press, 1997) for much more detail.

Standard Marshaling

When you describe your component's interfaces via IDL, the MIDL compiler generates a series of files (shown in Table 4.1) that will produce a standard proxy/stub DLL. By building and registering the proxy/stub DLL, you provide standard marshaling for your components. For custom Vtable interfaces that you define, you must distribute and register the proxy/stub DLL with your components. Also, the proxy/stub must be registered on each client machine. Standard COM interfaces provided by Microsoft (such as `IClassFactory`) also have proxy/stub DLLs, but they are shipped as part of the operating system.

Table 4.1 MIDL-Generated Proxy/Stub Files

FILE	DESCRIPTION
ProjectNamePS.mak	The make file that will generate the proxy/stub DLL named *ProjectNamePS.DLL.*
ProjectName.h	A header file with the C and C++–compatible interface declarations.
ProjectName_p.c	The code that implements the proxy/stub.
ProjectName_i.c	A C file that contains the interface GUIDs.
DLLDATA.C	A C file that implements a DLL for the proxy/stub code.

Type Library (Universal) Marshaling

If you don't like the idea of shipping a proxy/stub DLL for each of your components, you have another option. *Type library marshaling* uses the standard automation marshaler that is part of the operating system. The one caveat with type library marshaling is that you can use only automation-compatible types in your interface methods, a topic we'll cover shortly.

To enable type library marshaling for your components, make sure that you use only automation types and add the `oleautomation` attribute to your interface declaration in your IDL file. Here's an example for our math component. The `IMath` interface uses automation-compatible types, so we can use type library marshaling.

```
[
    object,
    uuid(8C30BC10-B8F2-11D0-A756-B04A12000000),
    oleautomation,
    helpstring("IMath Interface"),
    pointer_default(unique)
]
interface IMath : IUnknown
{
    HRESULT Add( [in] long, [in] long, [out, retval] long* pResult );
    HRESULT Subtract( [in] long, [in] long, [out, retval] long* pResult );
    HRESULT Multiply( [in] long, [in] long, [out, retval] long* pResult );
    HRESULT Divide( [in] long, [in] long, [out, retval] long* pResult );
};
```

Another important step for type library marshaling is that you must register your component's type library via COM's RegisterTypeLibrary function. ATL automatically registers your type library as part of its normal registration process, so the changes to your interface declarations are all that is required when you're using ATL. Figure 4.2 shows the registry entries when you're using type library marshaling. Notice that the proxy/stub entry is **OLEAUT32.DLL,** which is the proxy/stub DLL provided by the OS.

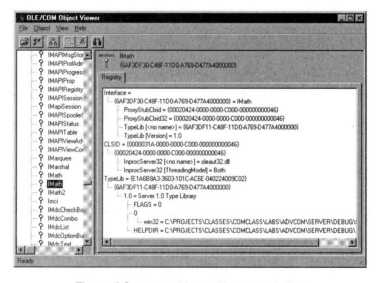

Figure 4.2 IMath with type library marshaling.

Custom Marshaling

If standard marshaling and type library marshaling do not meet your needs, you can always do your own custom marshaling. Custom marshaling requires that your component implement the IMarshal interface. When a component is created by a client, COM queries for the IMarshal interface. Standard and type library marshaling implement the IMarshal interface for the component, but with custom marshaling, the IMarshal interface returned is implemented directly within the component.

One of the benefits of custom marshaling is that you can use any mechanism for interprocess communication. For example, standard marshaling uses Microsoft's RPC implementation for cross-machine marshaling in a DCOM scenario. By implementing your own IMarshal interface, you can decide to use TCP/IP packets to marshal interface parameters from machine to machine.

A component developer will typically choose to implement custom marshaling either because COM does not support the desired behavior or because of the developer has intimate knowledge of the client/component interaction and wants to use this knowledge to increase performance.

Building the Proxy/Stub DLL

To build and register the proxy/stub DLL produced by the MIDL compiler you must work from the command line. First, locate the ***ProjectNamePS*.mk** make file and use **NMAKE** to create the DLL. It looks something like this:

```
c:\MyProject\NMAKE -f Chapter4_ServerPS.mk
```

Once the DLL is created, add it to the registry using **REGSVR32.**

```
C:\MyProject\REGSVR32 Chapter4_ServerPS.DLL
```

How COM Finds the Proxy/Stub DLL

COM locates the proxy/stub DLL for a component by looking it up in the registry. Whenever a client application queries for an interface (usually through CoCreateInstance or QueryInterface), COM will determine whether a proxy is required, and, if it is, will look up the location of the DLL via the registry. The HKCR\Interfaces key lists the proxy/stub DLLs for all interfaces on the system that support it. As an example, Figure 4.3 shows the entry for our math component.

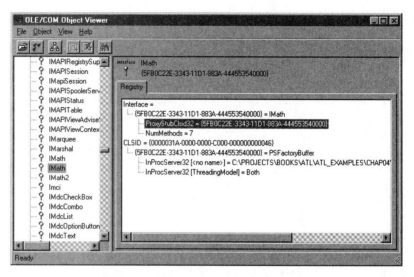

Figure 4.3 The proxy/stub registry entry.

When you're loading a component with the OLEVIEW utility, OLEVIEW determines which interfaces the component supports by calling `QueryInterface` with every potential interface under the `HKCR\Interfaces` Registry Key. (Yes, that's several hundred QIs, but remember that a component is defined by the interfaces it supports, and this is one way to check.) If your component does not show that it supports a certain implemented interface, add the IID under the `HKCR\Interfaces` key and it will show up.

THE INTERFACE DEFINITION LANGUAGE

We discussed IDL briefly in Chapter 3. In this chapter, we'll cover it in a bit more detail. In particular, we'll cover how IDL is used to produce type information, language bindings, and proxy/stub code for components.

Basic Syntax and Layout

The syntax of IDL is similar to standard C++ syntax. You can define structures, enums, and so on. One primary difference is that you declare interfaces instead of classes. In fact, there isn't any executable code within the IDL file. As its name implies, IDL describes an interface and its related details. The implementation of the resulting descriptions is done later using a specific language.

Keywords in IDL can be preceded by *attributes*, which are contained within a bracket pair and modify the keyword. For example, the `uuid`, `helpstring`, and `pointer_default` attributes modify the following interface.

```
[
   uuid(5FB0C22E-3343-11D1-883A-444553540000),
   helpstring("IMath Interface"),
   pointer_default(unique)
]
interface IMath : IUnknown
{
...
};
```

If the IDL file contains the `library` keyword, the MIDL compiler will generate a type library. As you can see in the following code, each IDL keyword is modified by its preceding attributes. The type library has a GUID, a version, and a help string.

```
[
   uuid(5FB0C221-3343-11D1-883A-444553540000),
   version(1.0),
   helpstring("Chapter4_Server 1.0 Type Library")
]
library CHAPTER4_SERVERLib
{
   importlib("stdole32.tlb");
   importlib("stdole2.tlb");

   [
      uuid(5FB0C22F-3343-11D1-883A-444553540000),
      helpstring("Math Class")
   ]
   coclass Math
   {
      [default] interface IMath;
      interface IMath2;
      interface IAdvancedMath;
      interface IComponentInfo;
   };
};
```

Items declared globally outside the library block generate C/C++ code when passed through the MIDL compiler.

Declaring Interfaces: Methods and Properties

Declaring interfaces in IDL follows the basic IDL syntax. You specify any special interface attributes prior to the `interface` keyword and then declare the methods that the interface supports. For example, here's the interface declaration for the `IMath` interface:

```
[
    object,
    uuid(5FB0C22E-3343-11D1-883A-444553540000),
    helpstring("IMath Interface"),
    pointer_default(unique)
]
interface IMath : IUnknown
{
    [helpstring("method Add")]
    HRESULT Add([in] long lOp1,[in] long lOp2, [out,retval] long* plResult);
    [helpstring("method Subtract")]
    HRESULT Subtract([in] long lOp1,[in] long lOp2, [out,retval] long*
plResult);
    ...
};
```

We described this interface in Chapter 3. COM also supports the concept of a *property:* a characteristic of the component that is usually handled internally by a data member. The data members of a class provide its *state,* and its methods operate on that state. COM components can expose their data members through standard accessor methods, but COM provides properties so that development tools can present them as explicit data members of the component. For example, if we add a `VersionNumber` property to our math component, we would describe it in IDL this way:

```
interface IMath2 : IUnknown
{
...
[propget, helpstring("property VersionNumber")]
    HRESULT VersionNumber([out, retval] long *pVal);
[propput, helpstring("property VersionNumber")]
    HRESULT VersionNumber([in] long newVal);
};
```

If we specify the `propget` and `propput` attributes for our accessor methods, client applications such as Visual Basic can provide a special syntax that allows the user to treat `VersionNumber` as a directly accessible data member of the component. The Visual Basic syntax looks like this:

```
Dim objMath as New Math
objMath.VersionNumber = 100
' or
txtVersion.Text = objMath.VersionNumber
```

The primary difference from a user's perspective is the use of the assignment operator instead of using method call syntax. Properties are used heavily in automation, which we'll discuss in Chapter 6.

 The native COM support in Visual C++ 5 also provides this syntax as part of its `#import` keyword implementation. See Appendix A for more details.

N O T E

IDL Data Types

IDL supports a number of built-in data types. The typical C++ data types are supported along with several others. Table 4.2 lists the base types support by IDL. When designing interfaces for your components, you should use these base types or structures based on these types. You can also use any of the automation-compatible types listed in Table 4.3. By limiting your interface parameters to automation types, you can use the built-in automation marshaler, as we described earlier.

Table 4.2 IDL Base Types

BASE TYPE	DESCRIPTION
boolean	8-bit data item
byte	8-bit data item
char	8-bit unsigned data item
double	64-bit floating-point number
float	32-bit floating-point number
handle_t	Primitive handle type
hypersigned	64-bit signed integer
int	32-bit signed integer
long	32-bit signed integer
short	16-bit signed integer
small	8-bit signed integer
void*	32-bit context handle pointer type
wchar_t	16-bit unsigned data item

Table 4.3 Automation types

Base Type	Description
boolean	Uses the VARIANT_BOOL type
unsigned char	8-bit unsigned data item
Double	64-bit IEEE floating-point number
Float	32-bit IEEE floating-point number
Int	Integer whose size is system-dependent
Long	32-bit signed integer
Short	16-bit signed integer
BSTR	Length-prefixed string
CY	8-byte fixed-point number
DATE	64-bit floating-point fractional number of days since December 30, 1899
SCODE	Built-in error type that corresponds to HRESULT
Enum	Signed integer, whose size is system-dependent
IDispatch *	Pointer to IDispatch interface (VT_DISPATCH)
IUnknown *	Pointer to an IUnknown interface

Arrays

Using IDL you can declare arrays of the basic types. It is easy to do because the declaration is similar to a declaration in C++. Here's an example of a method that takes an array of integers:

```
HRESULT Sum( [in] short sArray[5], [out, retval] long* plResult );
```

In this example, the component knows the size of the array in advance. More typically, it would be useful to sum a user-defined series of numbers. You can use the IDL size_is attribute to pass an arbitrary size to the server, something like this:

```
HRESULT Sum( [in] short sArraySize,
             [in, size_is( sArraySize )] short sArray[],
             [out, retval] long* plResult );
```

The server code is easy to implement:

```
STDMETHODIMP CMath::Sum( short sArraySize,
                         short sArray[],
                         long* plResult )
{
   *plResult = 0;
   while( sArraySize )
   {
      *plResult += sArray[—sArraySize];
   }

   return S_OK;
}
```

We use the method from the client just as easily.

```
short sArray[3] = { 3,4,5 };
long lResult = 0;
pMath2->Sum( 3, sArray, &lResult );
```

Strings

We use strings constantly when developing software. The IDL `string` attribute is a short-hand technique for describing a one-dimensional array. Following is a simple structure declaration that includes the `string` attribute:

```
typedef struct COMPONENT_INFO
{
    [string] char*    pstrAuthor;
    ...
} COMPONENT_INFO;
```

Structures

If COM interfaces allowed you to pass only native types back and forth, it would be difficult to build large, efficient components. Because IDL automatically generates proxy/stub code for our methods, we can build complex structures and the MIDL compiler will handle the details of marshaling the structures across processes and machines. For example, here's a simple structure that we'll use in our math component:

```
typedef struct COMPONENT_INFO
{
    [string] char*    pstrAuthor;
    short             sMajor;
    short             sMinor;
    BSTR              bstrName;
} COMPONENT_INFO;
```

We'll also add a new interface called `IComponentInfo` that returns details of a component to its user. Here's the declaration:

```
interface IComponentInfo : IUnknown
{
    [helpstring("method get_Info")]
        HRESULT get_Info( [out] COMPONENT_INFO** pInfo );
    [helpstring("method get_Name")]
        HRESULT get_Name( [out] BSTR* bstrName );
};
```

Wouldn't it be nice if every component implemented this interface? We would then have a standard way to query for version information directly from the component. The About box for each application would then be easy to write and could display information about each component within the application. This is a simple example of an interface that uses structures, but it also demonstrates the power of COM as a component architecture.

The get_Info method takes a COMPONENT_INFO** through which the component's information is returned. We've defined the get_Info method to take a pointer to a pointer because the component will allocate the structure and return it to the client. We'll discuss this process later when we describe how COM components manage memory.

Enums

IDL also supports enumerated types in a language-independent way. By describing your enumerated types in IDL, you can use them within your C++ projects as well as in Visual Basic, Java, and any language that can read a type library. Following is an example that we'll use in the Math component. We'll add a new method called Compute that takes as a parameter the type of computation to perform. The type is specified as one of the mathOPERATION constants.

```
typedef
[
    uuid(984D09A4-3379-11d1-883A-444553540000),
    helpstring("Math Operation Type"),
]
enum mathOPERATION
{
    [helpstring("Add")]        mathAdd      = 0x0001,
    [helpstring("Subtract")]   mathSubtract = 0x0002,
    [helpstring("Multiply")]   mathMultiply = 0x0003,
    [helpstring("Divide")]     mathDivide   = 0x0004
} mathOPERATION;
```

We can then use this new type in the declaration of the Compute method:

```
[helpstring("method Compute")]
HRESULT Compute( [in] mathOPERATION enumOp,
                 [in] long lOp1,
                 [in] long lOp2,
                 [out,retval] long* plResult );
```

After you run the preceding code through the MIDL compiler, it will produce a C construct as part of our **Chapter4_Server** header file.

```
// From Chapter4_Server.h
typedef /* [helpstring][uuid] */
enum mathOPERATION
    {       mathAdd      = 0x1,
      mathSubtract     = 0x2,
      mathMultiply     = 0x3,
      mathDivide       = 0x4
    }       mathOPERATION;
```

We can now use this type in the implementation of our component's method:

```
STDMETHODIMP CMath::Compute( mathOPERATION enumOp,
                             long lOp1,
                             long lOp2,
                             long * plResult)
{
   switch( enumOp )
   {
   case mathAdd:
      return Add( lOp1, lOp2, plResult );
   case mathSubtract:
      return Subtract( lOp1, lOp2, plResult );
   case mathMultiply:
      return Multiply( lOp1, lOp2, plResult );
   case mathDivide:
      return Divide( lOp1, lOp2, plResult );
   }
   return S_OK;
}
```

The type library that MIDL produces for our component also contains this definition, so non-C++ tools can also use the enumeration. Figure 4.4 shows the Object Browser in Visual Basic with our `mathOPERATION` type highlighted. The Visual Basic example at the end of the chapter will demonstrate the use of this type.

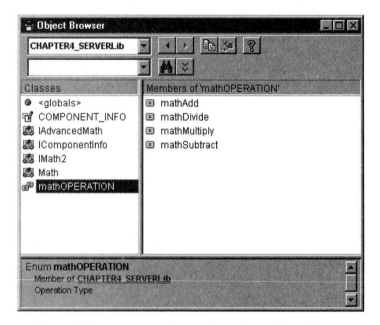

Figure 4.4 Our enumerated type in Visual Basic's Object Browser.

ATL AND COM DATA TYPES

When building COM components you will typically deal with several COM-based data types. In the next few sections we'll take a look at these basic data types and discuss how ATL provides wrapper classes for them. We'll begin with COM interface pointers and ATL's smart pointers and finish with the basic COM string type: the binary string, or BSTR.

Interface Pointers

The only way to access functionality in a COM component is through its interface. One of the most primitive types in COM is a `Vtable` interface. We've dealt with Vtables quite a bit, and we understand that interface pointers are really pointers to a C++ abstract class `Vtable`.

There are times when it is necessary to return interface pointers as part of your method or property implementations. The IDL syntax is straightforward. As an example, let's add a new property to the `IMath2` interface. The new `AdvancedMath` property returns a pointer to the `IAdvancedMath` interface within the `Math` component.

```
// IDL entry
[propget, helpstring("property AdvancedMath")]
    HRESULT AdvancedMath([out, retval] IAdvancedMath **ppVal);

// Implementation
STDMETHODIMP CMath::get_AdvancedMath(IAdvancedMath** ppVal)
{
    GetUnknown()->QueryInterface( IID_IAdvancedMath,
                                    (void**) ppVal);
    return S_OK;
}
```

The implementation uses ATL's GetUnknown function to get an IUnknown pointer through which we query for the IAdvancedMath interface. QueryInterface automatically increments the reference counter for the component, so we don't have to call IUnknown::AddRef explicitly. The client application is responsible for releasing the interface pointer.

C++ Smart Pointers

Smart pointers are C++ classes that hide many of the details of memory management when you're working with pointers. The smart pointer idiom can also be used with COM interface pointers. As we discussed in Chapter 2, interface pointers must be treated like a system resource. When the interface is retrieved, copied, or passed to another logical user, its reference count must be incremented. When we're finished using an interface pointer, we must release it. In this way, a component instance manages its own lifetime.

Smart pointers encapsulate the QueryInterface()/Release() and CoCreateInstance()/Release() pairs so that the user of the class doesn't have to worry about explicitly releasing COM pointers. Because the pointer operator is modified, access to the interface's methods proceeds as usual. ATL provides two smart pointer classes: CComPTR and CComQIPtr. Both classes are templatized to take an interface pointer type, and CComQIPtr also takes an IID to perform an implicit QueryInterface. We discuss these two classes in the next few sections.

 Visual C++ also provides a set of smart pointers for managing COM interfaces and in fact provides more functionality than that of ATL. However, the ATL classes were delivered before Visual C++ 5.0 and provide a compiler-independent smart pointer implementation.

N O T E

CComPtr

ATL's CComPtr template class provides basic smart pointer functionality. You can use the class as a COM interface pointer, with the added benefit that when it goes out of scope the class will call Release() automatically. Here's how you might use the CComPtr class:

```
CComPtr< IMath > ptrMath;
HRESULT hr;
// This time use CoCreateInstance
hr = CoCreateInstance( CLSID_Math,
                       NULL,
                       CLSCTX_LOCAL_SERVER,
                       IID_IMath,
                       (void**) &ptrMath );
...
// Access the IMath interface
long lResult;
ptrMath->Add( 134, 353, &lResult );
cout << "134 + 353 = " << lResult << endl;
...
}
```

In the example, we don't have to call `Release`. We could however, explicitly release by calling `CComPtr::Release` or by using the assignment operator:

```
ptrMath.Release();
// or
ptrMath = 0;
```

Smart pointers are useful, but they don't necessarily make it much easier to work with COM interfaces. Becaues `CComPtr` directly exposes a `Release` method, we might accidentally release an interface twice: explicitly (as we're used to) and again when the instance goes out of scope.

CComQIPtr

When you're working with COM (especially when you're a client), you often call `QueryInterface` on one interface pointer to get another one. We've done this in our client examples and will do it quite a bit more in our examples at the end of the chapter. ATL provides another smart pointer class that will perform a `QueryInterface` automatically when it's instantiated. `CComQIPtr` takes an additional parameter: the IID of the requested interface. Here's how you might use it.

```
// Access IAdvancedMath
CComQIPtr<IAdvancedMath,
         &IID_IAdvancedMath> ptrAdvancedMath( ptrMath );
if ( ptrAdvancedMath )
{
   ptrAdvancedMath->Factorial( 12, &lResult );
   cout << "12! = " << lResult << endl;
   ptrAdvancedMath->Fibonacci( 12, &lResult );
   cout << "The Fibonacci of 12 = " << lResult << endl;
}
```

BSTRs

COM uses a special string data type called a *binary* or *basic* string, or BSTR. A BSTR is declared as an OLECHAR*, which indicates that it's a Unicode string. However, COM provides a number of Win32 functions that act directly on the BSTR type. In other words, if you use these special APIs a standard Unicode or ANSI string can become a BSTR. The primary API, SysAllocString, creates and stores a DWORD value at the front of a Unicode string that describes its length. This is handy, because it allows the use of embedded nulls within the string. Also, by providing the string's length, you can perform marshaling more efficiently because there is no need to scan the string to determine its length.

BSTRs are Visual Basic strings and are described as automation-compatible types. Because the operating system provides APIs to manage them and because default marshaling code is also provided, the BSTR type is also the de facto COM string and is used extensively outside of its humble automation roots. Figure 4.5 depicts the structure of a BSTR.

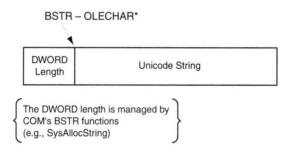

Figure 4.5 COM's binary string (BSTR).

Conversion of BSTRs into ANSI strings is easy because BSTRs are represented as OLECHAR pointers. To convert a BSTR to ANSI, you can use the standard Unicode-to-ANSI macros that we described in Chapter 2. Here's a quick excerpt from our chapter example.

```
BSTR bstrDescription = 0;
BSTR bstrSource = 0;

pEI->GetDescription( &bstrDescription );
pEI->GetSource( &bstrSource );
```

(code continued on next page)

```
USES_CONVERSION;
cout << OLE2T( bstrDescription ) << endl;
cout << OLE2T( bstrSource ) << endl;

::SysFreeString( bstrDescription );
::SysFreeString( bstrSource );
```

This example shows how we declare a BSTR and pass it to a COM method, which allocates and returns the BSTR. We then convert it to ANSI for display and deallocate the memory using the `SysFreeString` function. This is an example of COM's memory management rules that we'll discuss shortly.

CComBSTR

ATL's `CComBSTR` class acts as a wrapper around COM's BSTR data type. By using `CComBSTR` we can avoid looking up the BSTR APIs. However, `CComBSTR` is a thin wrapper around BSTR; many developers forgo it, instead using the BSTR type. We take the latter approach in this chapter, but we will use `CComBSTR` extensively in later chapters. Table 4.4 lists some of `CComBSTR`'s methods.

Table 4.4 CComBSTR methods

MEMBER	DESCRIPTION
CComBSTR(...)	The class has several constructors. There are constructors for each of the ANSI, Unicode, and BSTR string types.
Append	Appends an ANSI string to the BSTR.
AppendBSTR	Appends a BSTR.
Copy	Returns a copy of the BSTR.
Length	Returns the length of the string.

The `CComBSTR` class has a few useful operators. Two that are conspicuously missing, though, are the comparison and `char*` operators. If you want to compare two `CComBSTR` strings, you can use the following code or instead use the `CComVariant` class, which we'll describe in Chapter 6.

```
// BSTR comparison...
CComBSTR bstrA( "COM" );
CComBSTR bstrB( "COM" );
if ( ::SysStringByteLen( bstrA ) == ::SysStringByteLen( bstrB ) &&
     ::memcmp( bstrA, bstrB, ::SysStringByteLen( bstrA )) == 0 )
{
   cout << "bstrA == bstrB" << endl;
}
```

NOTE

Visual C++ also provides a native implementation of the BSTR type via the _bstr_t_ class. See Appendix A for more details.

COM MEMORY MANAGEMENT

In a distributed environment where clients and servers may be executing in different processes or on different machines, memory management is an important issue. In many cases, a component may have to allocate memory and return it to a client application, but the component does not know when the client is finished using the allocated memory. COM handles this situation by providing a few special APIs along with rules for how they should be used.

CoTaskMemAlloc and CoTaskMemFree

These two COM functions are helper functions for COM's IMalloc interface. IMalloc provides an abstraction of the familiar C run-time memory functions malloc and free. You won't typically use the interface directly, though, because CoTaskMemAlloc and CoTaskMemFree act as wrapper functions.

You use CoTaskMemAlloc and CoTaskMemFree just as you would the C run-time equivalents. Here's an example:

```
COMPONENT_INFO* pInfo = (COMPONENT_INFO *)
     CoTaskMemAlloc( sizeof( COMPONENT_INFO ));
ZeroMemory( pInfo, sizeof( COMPONENT_INFO ));
// Do something with the structure
...
// Now free it
CoTaskMemFree( pInfo );
```

The preceding example is easy to understand. Things get difficult, though, when we need to allocate and deallocate memory across processes, something that occurs all the time in COM. One other requirement is that the client and server applications be oblivious to each other's location. Again, because of COM's support for location transparency, the cooperating entities need hard and fast rules to follow. COM provides this through the IDL description of an interface's methods.

IDL and Memory Management

To determine who's responsible for allocating and deallocating memory, you must look at the declaration of the method in IDL. The entity responsible for allocating and freeing parameters of an interface method is specified via IDL's in and out parameter attributes. The following rules apply:

- For in-only parameters, the client (caller) is responsible for allocating and freeing the memory.

- For out-only parameters, the server (callee) is responsible for allocating the memory, and the client (caller) is responsible for freeing the memory.

- For in/out parameters, the client (caller) allocates the memory and is also responsible for freeing the memory. However, the component (callee) has the option of reallocating memory if it needs to.

You may also have to use COM's memory management functions when using certain COM APIs, particularly those functions that take a pointer to a pointer,such as COM's ProgIDFromCLSID function. Help for ProgIDFromCLSID indicates that the second parameter is an out parameter. Thus, we need to free the memory.

```
// Look up the ProgID
WCHAR* pProgID = 0;
ProgIDFromCLSID( guids[0], &pProgID );

// Add it to the listbox
USES_CONVERSION;
m_ControlList.AddString( W2A( pProgID ));

// Free the memory
CoTaskMemFree( pProgID );
```

COM ERROR HANDLING

All COM interface methods must return either void or an HRESULT, and void returns won't work until COM supports asynchronous calls in NT 5.0. For now, the primary mechanism of reporting errors from a component to its client is through the HRESULT return code. Recently, though, COM has added a rich error-handling model that allows a component to report detailed information. In this section we describe three new interfaces and three new API functions and discuss how clients and server applications use these facilities and how ATL makes error handling a bit easier to implement.

NOTE

Originally, the following interfaces and APIs were provided as part of automation's support for handling errors. However, error handling is now part of the whole of COM, so disregard any documentation that states otherwise.

ISupportErrorInfo

If a component wants to support COM error handling, its first step is to provide an implementation of the ISupportErrorInfo interface. ISupportErrorInfo has only one method, InterfaceSupportsErrorInfo. The component specifies, via its implementation of InterfaceSupportsErrorInfo, which of its interfaces can return rich error information. The method itself is easy to implement, especially when you're using ATL, as we'll see in a moment.

CreateErrorInfo and ICreateErrorInfo

Once a component indicates that it can return error information, it creates it by using the CreateErrorInfo function. The function returns an interface pointer to the created error object. Interaction with the error object proceeds through ICreateErrorInfo. ICreateErrorInfo contains a number of methods, all of which allow the setting of various attributes within the error object. Examples are, SetGUID, SetSource (which is the ProgID), SetDescription, and so on. The following example, which is adapted from ATL's implementation, demonstrates how to create and initialize an error object within a component.

```
ICreateErrorInfo* pICEI;
if ( SUCCEEDED( CreateErrorInfo( &pICEI )))
{
   // Set the GUID
   pICEI->SetGUID( iid );

   // Set the ProgID
   LPOLESTR lpsz;
   ProgIDFromCLSID( clsid, &lpsz );
   if (lpsz != NULL)
   {
      pICEI->SetSource( lpsz );
      CoTaskMemFree( lpsz );
   }

   // Set any help information
   if (dwHelpID != 0 && lpszHelpFile != NULL)
   {
      pICEI->SetHelpContext( dwHelpID );
      pICEI->SetHelpFile( const_cast<LPOLESTR>( lpszHelpFile ));
   }
```

(code continued on next page)

```
    // Set the actual description of the problem
    pICEI->SetDescription((LPOLESTR)lpszDesc);

    // Associate the error with the current execution context
    IErrorInfo* pErrorInfo;
    if ( SUCCEEDED(pICEI->QueryInterface( IID_IErrorInfo, (void**) &pErrorInfo
)))
        SetErrorInfo(0, pErrorInfo);

    // Release the interfaces
    pICIE->Release();
    pErrorInfo->Release();
}
```

SetErrorInfo and IErrorInfo

An error object is created using `CreateErrorInfo` and the `ICreateErrorInfo` interface. After everything is set up, the error object must be associated with the current thread of execution through the `IErrorInfo` interface and the `SetErrorInfo` function. This technique is demonstrated in the last few lines of the preceding code.

The `IErrorInfo` interface provides a corresponding `Get` method for each `Set` method in `ICreateErrorInfo`. In other words, `IErrorInfo` will ultimately be used by the client application to retrieve the error information.

Visual C++ 5.0 provides several native COM exception-handling classes. These classes encapsulate the details of working with the low-level details of COM error handling. See Appendix A for more details.

N O T E

Clients and GetErrorInfo

At this point we've examined how you implement error handling within the component itself. Next, we'll discuss how a client application retrieves the information. Initially, the client is notified that an error has occurred via an unsuccessful HRESULT return like this:

```
long lResult;
IMath* pMath;
...
if ( FAILED( pMath->Divide( 0, 0, &lResult ))
{
    HandleError( pMath, IID_IMath );
}
```

Once an error is indicated, as in preceding example, the client determines whether the component supports rich error information; the client queries for ISupportErrorInfo. If the QI succeeds, the client can continue retrieving the IErrorInfo interface. Following is the complete code for determining whether a component supports error info and, when it does, getting the COM error object and displaying the information.

```
void HandleError( IUnknown* pUnk, REFIID riid )
{
    HRESULT hr;

    // See if the object supports rich error info
    ISupportErrorInfo* pSEI = 0;
    hr = pUnk->QueryInterface( IID_ISupportErrorInfo, (void**) &pSEI );
    if (SUCCEEDED( hr ))
    {
        hr = pSEI->InterfaceSupportsErrorInfo( riid );
        if ( SUCCEEDED( hr ))
        {
            // Get the error info
            IErrorInfo* pEI;
            if ( SUCCEEDED( GetErrorInfo( 0, &pEI )))
            {
                USES_CONVERSION;

                BSTR bstrDescription = 0;
                BSTR bstrSource = 0;

                pEI->GetDescription( &bstrDescription );
                pEI->GetSource( &bstrSource );

                cout << OLE2T( bstrDescription ) << endl;
                cout << OLE2T( bstrSource ) << endl;

                ::SysFreeString( bstrDescription );
                ::SysFreeString( bstrSource );

                pEI->Release();
            }
        }
        pSEI->Release();
    }
}
```

Whew! That's a lot of work just to get the error information, but that's what we have to do. Once we determine that the component supports error information on the specified interface, we call the GetErrorInfo API, which returns the IErrorInfo interface. Through IErrorInfo we can retrieve and display the information passed by the server.

ATL's Support for Error Handling

When you initially create a component object using the ATL Object wizard, the first tabbed dialog gives you an option called: **Support ISupportErrorInfo**. By checking this option, you add an implementation of the ISupportErrorInfo interface to your component. The following code highlights the code added by the Object wizard.

```
// Math.h
...
class ATL_NO_VTABLE CMath :
    public CComObjectRootEx<CComSingleThreadModel>,
    public CComCoClass<CMath, &CLSID_Math>,
    public ISupportErrorInfo,
    public IMath
{
...
BEGIN_COM_MAP(CMath)
    COM_INTERFACE_ENTRY(IMath)
    COM_INTERFACE_ENTRY(ISupportErrorInfo)
END_COM_MAP()

// ISupportsErrorInfo
    STDMETHOD(InterfaceSupportsErrorInfo)(REFIID riid);
// IMath
public:
    // Added
    STDMETHOD(Add)( long, long, long* );
    ...
};

// Math.cpp
...
STDMETHODIMP CMath::InterfaceSupportsErrorInfo(REFIID riid)
{
    static const IID* arr[] =
    {
        &IID_IMath,
    };
    for (int i=0;i<sizeof(arr)/sizeof(arr[0]);i++)
    {
        if (InlineIsEqualGUID(*arr[i],riid))
            return S_OK;
    }
    return S_FALSE;
}
```

As you can see, it adds the new interface to our inheritance chain, adds our interface map, and then adds the declaration and definition for the InterfaceSupportsErrorInfo method. The method itself searches through a static table to determine whether the specified IID supports rich error handling. For our math component, we're adding error handling to the IMath interface. Specifically, we'll ensure that the client doesn't try to divide by zero.

CComCoClass::Error

Because ATL is mostly about creating components, it provides methods that encapsulate the creation of error information within components and doesn't do anything for the client side. The CComCoClass::Error method is overloaded to take every parameter that can be specified via ICreateErrorInfo. Here are a few of the overloaded Error methods:

```
static HRESULT WINAPI Error( LPCOLESTR lpszDesc,
   const IID& iid = GUID_NULL, HRESULT hRes = 0 )
{
   return AtlReportError( GetObjectCLSID(), lpszDesc, iid, hRes );
}
static HRESULT WINAPI Error( LPCOLESTR lpszDesc, DWORD dwHelpID,
   LPCOLESTR lpszHelpFile, const IID& iid = GUID_NULL, HRESULT hRes = 0)
{
   return AtlReportError( GetObjectCLSID(), lpszDesc, dwHelpID,
                      lpszHelpFile,iid, hRes );
}
static HRESULT WINAPI Error( UINT nID, const IID& iid = GUID_NULL,
   HRESULT hRes = 0, HINSTANCE hInst = _Module.GetResourceInstance())
{
   return AtlReportError(GetObjectCLSID(), nID, iid, hRes, hInst);
}
static HRESULT WINAPI Error( UINT nID, DWORD dwHelpID,
   LPCOLESTR lpszHelpFile, const IID& iid = GUID_NULL,
   HRESULT hRes = 0, HINSTANCE hInst = _Module.GetResourceInstance())
{
   return AtlReportError( GetObjectCLSID(), nID, dwHelpID,
                      lpszHelpFile, iid, hRes, hInst );
}
```

Each method ultimately calls an overloaded AtlReportError. If you look at **ATLIMPL.CPP** you will see that this method in turn calls AtlSetErrorInfo, which does basically what we did earlier in the server-side implementation. Following is an example of the use of CComCoClass::Error.

```
STDMETHODIMP CMath::Divide( long lOp1, long lOp2, long* pResult )
{
   // Handle divide-by-zero error
   if ( lOp2 == 0 )
   {
      return Error( "Divide by zero attempted." );
   }

   *pResult = lOp1 / lOp2;
   return S_OK;
}
```

ISupportErrorInfoImpl

ATL also provides an implementation class for adding ISupportErrorInfo functionality. However, it is limited in that it allows you to support error handling for only one interface. You specify the IID of the interface as a template parameter. Here's what it would look like in our math example:

```
// From MATH.H
...
class ATL_NO_VTABLE CMath :
   public CComObjectRootEx<CComSingleThreadModel>,
   public CComCoClass<CMath, &CLSID_Math>,
   public ISupportErrorInfo,
...
BEGIN_COM_MAP(CMath)
...
   COM_INTERFACE_ENTRY(ISupportErrorInfo)
END_COM_MAP()

// ISupportsErrorInfo
   STDMETHOD(InterfaceSupportsErrorInfo)(REFIID riid);
...

// From MATH.CPP
...
STDMETHODIMP CMath::InterfaceSupportsErrorInfo(REFIID riid)
{
   static const IID* arr[] =
   {
      &IID_IMath,
   };
   for (int i=0;i<sizeof(arr)/sizeof(arr[0]);i++)
   {
```

```
       if (InlineIsEqualGUID(*arr[i],riid))
          return S_OK;
   }
   return S_FALSE;
}
```

THE MATH COMPONENT IN AN EXE HOUSING

What follows is a step-by-step process of creating our Math component using ATL's wizards. The example that we develop is given the name **Chapter4_Server.** What follows, though, mostly describes how we modify our math component to reside within an executable housing instead of a DLL. We also add rich error handling and implement an IMath2 interface as well as a new IComponentInfo interface.

Create the Visual C++ Project

Start Visual C++ and create a new project, selecting ATL COM AppWizard. Give it the name **Chapter4_Server.** In Step 1 of 1, select **Executable (EXE).** Select **Finish** to generate the project.

The ATL Object Wizard

Next, using the ATL Object wizard, insert an object of type **Simple Object.** After clicking the **Next** button, populate the Names dialog box as follows:

- **Short Name:Math**. Take the defaults provided for Class, .H file, and .CPPfile.
- **CoClass:Math**.
- **Interface:**IMath.
- **Type:Math Class**.
- **ProgID:Chapter4.Math**.

Move to the Attributes dialog box and populate it with the following:

- **Threading Model:Apartment**.
- **Interface:Custom**.
- **Aggregation:Yes**.
- **Support** ISupportErrorInfo**:Yes**.
- **Support Connection Points:No**.
- **Free Threaded Marshaler:No**.

Adding the `IMath` and `IAdvancedMath`

At this point, you should follow the steps in Chapter 3 that describe how to implement the IMath and IAdvancedMath interfaces. We've already covered this process, so it doesn't need to be discussed here. Instead, we'll focus on adding support for rich error handling and implementing two additional interfaces in our math component.

Handling the Divide-By-Zero Problem

Because we checked the **Support ISupportErrorInfo** option when creating this project, ATL added the support for ISupportErrorInfo. To throw back an error in our Divide method, we need only use the CComCoClass::Error method. We described this in detail earlier.

```
STDMETHODIMP CMath::Divide( long lOp1, long lOp2, long* pResult )
{
    // Handle divide-by-zero error
    if ( lOp2 == 0 )
    {
        return Error( "Divide by zero attempted." );
    }

    *pResult = lOp1 / lOp2;
    return S_OK;
}
```

Adding the `IMath2` Interface

To demonstrate what is required to "version" an interface within a component, we'll add three new methods to the IMath interface. Remember, though, that COM interfaces should not change once they've been deployed. We follow this rule by adding a new interface, IMath2, to our component. Existing clients can continue to use IMath, but new clients can opt to use the feature-rich IMath2 interface instead. The following code updates the IDL, **MATH.H**, and **MATH.CPP** files.

```
// Chapter4_Server.idl
...
typedef
[
    uuid(984D09A4-3379-11d1-883A-444553540000),
    helpstring("Operation Type"),
]
enum mathOPERATION
{
    [helpstring("Add")]        mathAdd       = 0x0001,
```

```
        [helpstring("Subtract")]   mathSubtract = 0x0002,
        [helpstring("Multiply")]   mathMultiply = 0x0003,
        [helpstring("Divide")]     mathDivide   = 0x0004
} mathOPERATION;

[
    uuid(984D09A2-3379-11d1-883A-444553540000),
    helpstring("IMath2 Interface"),
    pointer_default(unique)
]
interface IMath2 : IUnknown
    {
        [helpstring("method Add")]
          HRESULT Add([in] long lOp1,[in] long lOp2,
                      [out,retval] long* plResult);
        [helpstring("method Subtract")]
          HRESULT Subtract([in] long lOp1,[in] long lOp2,
                           [out,retval] long* plResult);
        [helpstring("method Multiply")]
          HRESULT Multiply([in] long lOp1,[in] long lOp2,
                           [out,retval] long* plResult);
        [helpstring("method Divide")]
          HRESULT Divide([in] long lOp1,[in] long lOp2,
                         [out,retval] long* plResult);

        [helpstring("method Sum" )]
          HRESULT Sum( [in] short sArraySize,
                       [in, size_is( sArraySize )] short sArray[],
                       [out, retval] long* lResult );

        [helpstring("method Compute")]
         HRESULT Compute( [in] mathOPERATION enumOp,
                          [in] long lOp1,
                          [in] long lOp2,
                          [out,retval] long* plResult);

        [propget, helpstring("property AdvancedMath")]
          HRESULT AdvancedMath([out, retval] IAdvancedMath **ppVal);
    };

coclass Math
{
    [default] interface IMath;
    interface IAdvancedMath;
    interface IMath2;
};
```

(code continued on next page)

```
// Math.h
...
class ATL_NO_VTABLE CMath :
   ...
   public ISupportErrorInfo,
   public IMath,
   public IAdvancedMath,
   public IMath2
{
...
BEGIN_COM_MAP(CMath)
   COM_INTERFACE_ENTRY(IMath)
   COM_INTERFACE_ENTRY(IAdvancedMath)
   COM_INTERFACE_ENTRY(IMath2)
   COM_INTERFACE_ENTRY(ISupportErrorInfo)
END_COM_MAP()
...
// IMath2
public:
   STDMETHOD(Sum)( short sArraySize,
                   short sArray[],
                   long* plResult );
   STDMETHOD(Compute)( mathOPERATION enumOp,
                       long lOp1,
                       long lOp2,
                       long* plResult );
   STDMETHOD(get_AdvancedMath)(IAdvancedMath** ppVal);
...
};

// From Math.cpp
...
// New IMath2 methods
STDMETHODIMP CMath::Sum( short sArraySize,
                  short sArray[],
                  long* plResult )
{
   *plResult = 0;
   while( sArraySize )
   {
      *plResult += sArray[-sArraySize];
   }
   return S_OK;
}
```

```
STDMETHODIMP CMath::Compute( mathOPERATION enumOp,
                             long lOp1,
                             long lOp2,
                             long * plResult)
{
   switch( enumOp )
   {
   case mathAdd:
      return Add( lOp1, lOp2, plResult );
   case mathSubtract:
      return Subtract( lOp1, lOp2, plResult );
   case mathMultiply:
      return Multiply(  lOp1, lOp2, plResult );
   case mathDivide:
      return Divide( lOp1, lOp2, plResult );
   }
   return S_OK;
}

STDMETHODIMP CMath::get_AdvancedMath(IAdvancedMath** ppVal)
{
   GetUnknown()->QueryInterface( IID_IAdvancedMath, (void**) ppVal);
   return S_OK;
}
```

Adding the `IComponentInfo` Interface

To demonstrate marshaling structures from component to client, we'll add another interface to our example. `IComponentInfo` is implemented by the Math component so that it can pass back details concerning its author, name, and version number. Here are the major details from the IDL and CPP files. You can fill in the rest.

```
// From Chapter4_Server.idl
...
typedef struct COMPONENT_INFO
{
   [string] char*  pstrAuthor;
   short    sMajor;
   short    sMinor;
   BSTR     bstrName;
} COMPONENT_INFO;
```

(code continued on next page)

```
[
   uuid(1E405AA0-3396-11d1-883A-444553540000),
   helpstring("IComponentInfo Interface"),
   pointer_default(unique)
]
interface IComponentInfo : IUnknown
{
   [helpstring("method get_Info")]
       HRESULT get_Info( [out] COMPONENT_INFO** pInfo );
   [helpstring("method get_Name")]
       HRESULT get_Name( [out] BSTR* bstrName );
};

// From Math.cpp
STDMETHODIMP CMath::get_Info( COMPONENT_INFO** ppInfo )
{
   *ppInfo = (COMPONENT_INFO *)
             CoTaskMemAlloc( sizeof( COMPONENT_INFO ));
   ZeroMemory( *ppInfo, sizeof( COMPONENT_INFO ));

   // Make these globals or defines
   (*ppInfo)->sMajor = 1;
   (*ppInfo)->sMinor = 0;

   char szBuffer[128];
   if ( LoadString( _Module.GetResourceInstance(),
              IDS_AUTHOR,
              szBuffer,
              sizeof( szBuffer ) ))
   {
      (*ppInfo)->pstrAuthor = (unsigned char*)
               CoTaskMemAlloc( lstrlen( szBuffer ) + 1 );
      memcpy( (*ppInfo)->pstrAuthor,
              szBuffer,
              lstrlen( szBuffer ) + 1 );
   }

   if ( LoadString( _Module.GetResourceInstance(),
              IDS_NAME,
              szBuffer,
              sizeof( szBuffer ) ))
   {
      USES_CONVERSION;
      (*ppInfo)->bstrName = SysAllocString( A2W( szBuffer ));
   }
```

```
      return S_OK;
}

STDMETHODIMP CMath::get_Name( BSTR* pbstrName )
{
   char szBuffer[128];
   if ( LoadString( _Module.GetResourceInstance(),
                IDS_NAME,
                szBuffer,
                sizeof( szBuffer ) ))
   {
      USES_CONVERSION;
      *pbstrName = SysAllocString( A2W( szBuffer ));
   }

   return S_OK;
}
```

Build the Project

After adding the code described earlier (or downloading the example source from
WidgetWare.com), build the project. As part of the build process, a custom build step will
execute the server, which will add its entries to the registry.

Build and Register the Proxy/Stub DLL

When building an ATL project, the MIDL compiler produces a number of supporting files.
We're interested in those files that are used to build a proxy/stub DLL for our component.
Because our example in this chapter is implemented via an EXE housing, we must provide
a proxy/stub DLL for both client and component. The code is generated by MIDL; we
compile, link, and register it. Here's all it takes:

```
nmake -f serverps.mk
```

 To build the proxy/stub DLL on Windows 95, you must ensure that the VC++ binaries are in your path. The
best way is to expand the MS-DOS environment space using the **Properties** option; then execute the
VCVARS32.BAT file in the **\DevStudio\VC\BIN** directory.

NOTE

After the make finishes, register the DLL using **REGSVR32.EXE**.

```
REGSVR32 serverps.dll
```

This creates the necessary entries in the registry. Figure 4.6 shows the IMath interface and our new proxy/stub DLL. Look under the **Interfaces** section of OLEVIEW.

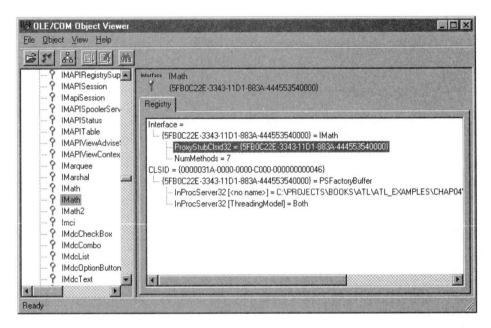

Figure 4.6 Proxy/stub DLL registered.

THE COM CLIENT

Our client application is similar to the one we developed in Chapter 3. The primary differences are that we now use CoCreateInstance instead of CoGetClassObject, implement error handling to catch the divide-by-zero error, and demonstrate the use of enumerators, properties, structures, and memory management. I've highlighted the new code and have commented it liberally.

```
//
// Chapter4_Client.cpp
//

#include <windows.h>
#include <tchar.h>
#include <iostream.h>
```

```cpp
// We include these for BSTR/ANSI conversions
#include <atlbase.h>
#include <atlimpl.cpp>

// GUIDs, enumerates types, interface declarations, etc.
// Remember, these files are generated by the MIDL compiler
#include "..\Chapter4_Server\Chapter4_Server_i.c"
#include "..\Chapter4_Server\Chapter4_Server.h"

void HandleError( IUnknown* pUnk, REFIID riid )
{
    HRESULT hr;

    // See if the object supports rich error info
    ISupportErrorInfo* pSEI = 0;
    hr = pUnk->QueryInterface( IID_ISupportErrorInfo, (void**) &pSEI );
    if (SUCCEEDED( hr ))
    {
        hr = pSEI->InterfaceSupportsErrorInfo( riid );
        if ( SUCCEEDED( hr ))
        {
            // Get the error info
            IErrorInfo* pEI;
            if ( SUCCEEDED( GetErrorInfo( 0, &pEI )))
            {
                USES_CONVERSION;

                BSTR bstrDescription = 0;
                BSTR bstrSource = 0;

                pEI->GetDescription( &bstrDescription );
                pEI->GetSource( &bstrSource );

                cout << OLE2T( bstrDescription ) << endl;
                cout << OLE2T( bstrSource ) << endl;

                ::SysFreeString( bstrDescription );
                ::SysFreeString( bstrSource );

                pEI->Release();
            }
        }
        pSEI->Release();
    }
}
```

(code continued on next page)

```
int main( int argc, char *argv[] )
{
   cout << "Initializing COM" << endl;

   if ( FAILED( CoInitialize( NULL )))
   {
      cout << "Unable to initialize COM" << endl;
      return -1;
   }

   IMath* pMath;
   HRESULT hr;
   // This time use CoCreateInstance
   hr = CoCreateInstance( CLSID_Math,
                          NULL,
                          CLSCTX_LOCAL_SERVER,
                          IID_IMath,
                          (void**) &pMath );

   if ( FAILED( hr ))
   {
      cout.setf( ios::hex, ios::basefield );
      cout << "Failed to create server instance. HR = " << hr << endl;
      CoUninitialize();
      return -1;
   }

   // Access the IMath interface
   long lResult;
   pMath->Add( 134, 353, &lResult );
   cout << "134 + 353 = " << lResult << endl;

   // Try to divide by zero
   hr = pMath->Divide( 0, 0, &lResult );
   if ( FAILED( hr ))
   {
      // Use our new HandleError function to
      // display any rich error information
      HandleError( pMath, IID_IMath );
   }

   // Access IMath2
   IMath2* pMath2;
   hr = pMath->QueryInterface( IID_IMath2,
                               (void**) &pMath2 );
   if ( SUCCEEDED( hr ))
```

```
{
    // Here's our new Compute method that
    // uses the mathOPERATOR enumerated type
    pMath2->Compute( mathAdd,
                     100,
                     200,
                     &lResult );
    cout << "100 + 200 = " << lResult << endl;

    // Our example of using arrays in an interface method
    short sArray[3] = { 3,4,5 };
    pMath2->Sum( 3,
                 sArray,
                 &lResult );
    cout << "3 + 4 + 5 = " << lResult << endl;
}
// Access IAdvancedMath
IAdvancedMath* pAdvancedMath = 0;
hr = pMath->QueryInterface( IID_IAdvancedMath,
                            (void**) &pAdvancedMath );
if ( SUCCEEDED( hr ))
{
    pAdvancedMath->Factorial( 12, &lResult );
    cout << "12! = " << lResult << endl;

    pAdvancedMath->Fibonacci( 12, &lResult );
    cout << "The Fibonacci of 12 = " << lResult << endl;
}

// Access IComponentInfo
IComponentInfo* pCompInfo;
hr = pMath->QueryInterface( IID_IComponentInfo,
                            (void**) &pCompInfo );
if ( SUCCEEDED( hr ))
{
    // Pass in a pointer. The component
    // will allocate and return the structure
    COMPONENT_INFO* pInfo = 0;
    pCompInfo->get_Info( &pInfo );
```

(code continued on next page)

```
      // Display the contents of the structure
      cout << "Component author is " << pInfo->pstrAuthor << endl;
      cout << "Component version is " << pInfo->sMajor << "." << pInfo-
>sMinor << endl;
      USES_CONVERSION;
      cout << "Component name is " << OLE2T( pInfo->bstrName ) << endl;

      // Free any memory allocated by the component
      if ( pInfo->pstrAuthor )
         CoTaskMemFree( pInfo->pstrAuthor );
      if ( pInfo->bstrName )
         SysFreeString( pInfo->bstrName );
      if ( pInfo )
         CoTaskMemFree( pInfo );
   }

   // Release all of our interfaces
   if ( pMath )
      pMath->Release();
   if ( pMath2 )
      pMath2->Release();
   if ( pAdvancedMath )
      pAdvancedMath->Release();
   if ( pCompInfo )
      pCompInfo->Release();

   CoUninitialize();

   return 0;
}
```

NOTE

The Chapter 4 examples include a project called **Chapter4_ATLClient** that implements the preceding code using ATL's `CComPtr` and `CComQIPtr` classes. The code in Appendix A also implements the preceding code, but it uses the Visual C++ native COM support. See **Chapter4_NativeClient** for details.

Test the Server

After typing in the preceding code (or downloading it), build the client project and run it in debug. It should behave just as it did in the Chapter 3 example. This time, however, the component resides in an executable and all the interface calls are being marshaled by the proxy/stub DLL that we developed.

A Visual Basic Client

To demonstrate COM's language independence, let's write a simple Visual Basic application that uses our Chapter 4 math component. Start Visual Basic, choose **Standard EXE**, and follow the steps listed next. (The project is also part of the example download. It's in the **Chapter4_VBClient** directory.)

Build the Form

Place three text boxes and eight command buttons on the form in an arrangement like that shown in Figure 4.7.

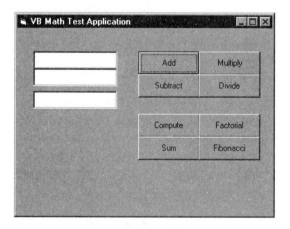

Figure 4.7 Our Visual Basic Form.

Be sure to use good Hungarian notation when naming the controls. Give the text boxes the names txtOp1, txtOp2, and txtResult. Name the command buttons in a similar fashion: cmdAdd, cmdSubtract, cmdMultiply, and cmdDivide, and so on.

Insert a Reference for the Math Component

From the **Project|References** menu, locate our math component's entry under **Server 1.0 Type Library**. Check the entry and add the reference to our Visual Basic project. This is shown in Figure 4.8.

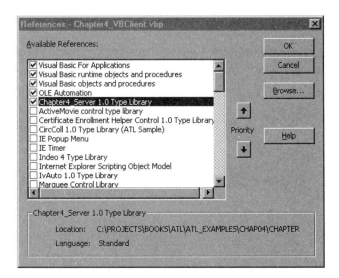

Figure 4.8 Adding the component reference.

Visual Basic will read the type library for the Math component and set up a new Visual Basic type that we can use. You can check this out using Visual Basic's Object Browser. Select **View|Object Browser** or press **F2**. Figure 4.9 shows our Math component in Object Browser.

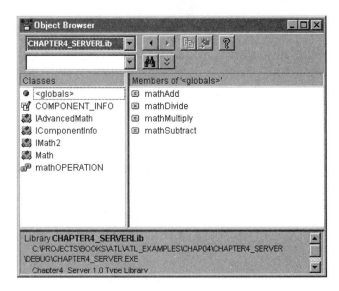

Figure 4.9 Visual Basic's Object Browser.

Adding the Code

We can now use the `Math` component and its `IMath`, `IMath2`, and `IAdvancedMath` interfaces from Visual Basic. Add the followingcode:

```
' this code goes in the "General" section
' We have to include the library name because
' "Math" is a reserved word in Visual Basic
Dim iMath As New CHAPTER4_SERVERLib.Math
Dim iAdvMath As CHAPTER4_SERVERLib.IAdvancedMath
Dim IMath2 As CHAPTER4_SERVERLib.IMath2

Private Sub cmdAdd_Click()
    txtResult = iMath.Add(txtOp1, txtOp2)
End Sub
Private Sub cmdDivide_Click()
    txtResult = iMath.Divide(txtOp1, txtOp2)
End Sub
Private Sub cmdMultiply_Click()
    txtResult = iMath.Multiply(txtOp1, txtOp2)
End Sub
Private Sub cmdSubtract_Click()
    txtResult = iMath.Subtract(txtOp1, txtOp2)
End Sub
```

Once you get the code working, add code for the `cmdFactorial` and `cmdFibonacci` buttons:

```
Private Sub cmdFactorial_Click()
    ' VB's Set command actually does a QueryInterface
    Set iAdvMath = iMath
    txtResult = iAdvMath.Factorial(txtOp1)
End Sub

Private Sub cmdFibonacci_Click()
    Set iAdvMath = iMath
    txtResult = iAdvMath.Fibonacci(txtOp1)
End Sub
```

Pretty cool. The Visual Basic Set keyword performs a `QueryInterface`. Let's use it again to access the `IMath2` interface:

```
Private Sub cmdCompute_Click()
    Set IMath2 = iMath
    ' Here's an example of using our enumerated type
    txtResult = IMath2.Compute(mathAdd, txtOp1, txtOp2)
End Sub
```

(code continued on next page)

```
Private Sub cmdSum_Click()
    Set IMath2 = iMath
    Dim sArray(3) As Integer
    sArray(1) = 3
    sArray(2) = 4
    sArray(3) = 5
    txtResult = IMath2.Sum(3, sArray(1))
End Sub
```

The application's behavior should be very similar to that of our C++ client example. When you attempt to divide by zero, the message will be passed to the Visual Basic run time and will be displayed as part of Visual Basic's exception mechanism. Figure 4.10 shows the error dialog box.

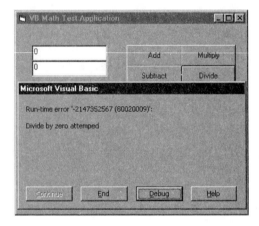

Figure 4.10 Divide by zero in Visual Basic.

COM's BINARY REUSE TECHNIQUES

Our purpose in this chapter was to understand how COM supports location transparency, which hides the details, from both the client and the server, of cross-process and cross-machine communication. COM does this by providing standard marshaling services. Marshaling takes care of the details of moving data from one process or machine to another.

We also discussed how COM manages memory and how to implement rich error handling in both a component and its clients. In Chapter 5 we'll describe COM's binary reuse mechanisms—containment and aggregation—in the context of ATL.

Containment and Aggregation

One important feature of COM is its support for software module reuse at a binary level. In this chapter we'll take a look at COM's binary reuse techniques: containment and aggregation. After a quick introduction to the two techniques, we'll examine how ATL provides support for developing components that support and use containment and aggregation.

BINARY REUSE

Binary reuse allows a developer to create a software component that can be used across languages, tools, and platforms by distributing only a binary component (such as a DLL). This approach is a boon for software developers, because they can choose the best language and tool to develop and deliver their components without worrying (as much) about which language or tool the user of the component might employ.

One aspect of binary reuse is that it gives COM language independence. We've already discussed this in detail. Another aspect of binary reuse is that developers can incorporate existing COM components directly within their own component implementations.

For example, say you're building a comprehensive text editor component that will provide spell checking and a thesaurus. You know that a full-featured spell checker component has been developed by a third party. You also know that the spell checking component exposes its functionality via a set of COM interfaces. By using either containment or aggregation, you can expose the spell checking component's interfaces directly from within your component as if your component implemented them directly. You must follow licensing requirements for the third-party component, but the potential is there.

Binary reuse isn't always as easy as it sounds. You must overcome several difficulties when implementing binary reuse. COM provides good support for it, but there are several limitations.

The first limitation is that you won't necessarily understand the implementation of the third-party component, and the public methods may have interdependencies that aren't documented (if you even have access to documentation). In other words, a method may change the internal state of a component, so we cannot directly replace the method. Also, if a component exposes a number of interfaces, you can't replace one interface with a new one because, again, the internal state of a component is not exposed.

Second, there is the issue of type information. Should a component that exposes another component's functionality describe this functionality as part of its description (i.e., in its own type library)? In most cases the answer is yes, but this adds complexity to the implementation.

COM CONTAINMENT

COM *containment* (also called *delegation*) is nearly identical to the C++ technique of class composition. You may not recognize the name for this C++ technique (it's also called *embedding*), but I'm sure you use it all the time when creating C++ classes. You typically use class composition when the relationship between a set of classes follows the "has a" relationship. For example, a car object "has an" engine. A C++ implementation would look something like this:

```
class Engine
{
public:
   void Start();
   void Stop();
};

class Car
{
public:
   // Use the embedded Engine implementation
   Go() { m_Engine.Start(); }

   // Expose Engine functionality directly
   Start() { m_Engine.Start(); }

private:
   Engine m_Engine;
};
```

The preceding example is rather abstract, but you get the idea. We contain an instance of the Engine class and use it internally as part of the Car implementation. The example also demonstrates what is required to expose some of the Engine class functionality directly through the Car class. To demonstrate real class composition, let's return to our simple math example.

```
class CSimpleMath
{
   long Add( long lOp1, long lOp2 )
```

```
           { return lOp1 + lOp2 };
    long Subtract( long lOp1, long lOp2 )
           { return lOp1 - lOp2 };
    long Multiply( long lOp1, long lOp2 )
           { return lOp1 * lOp2 };
    long Divide( long lOp1, long lOp2 )
           { return lOp1 / lOp2 };
};

class CMath
{
public:
    long Factorial( short sOp ) { ... };
    long Fibonacci( short sOp ) { ... };

private:
    CSimpleMath m_SimpleMath;
}
```

The CSimpleMath class contains the functionality of the earlier IMath interface. When implementing the CMath class, we want to use the functionality of CSimpleMath. To demonstrate containment, we embed an instance of CSimpleMath and re-expose its methods via CMath's public interface. We also use the instance as part of our Factorial and Fibonacci implementation. It looks something like this:

```
class CMath
{
public:
    long CalcFactorial( short n )
    {
        // Use our embedded class in our implementation
        if ( n > 1 )
            return m_SimpleMath.Multiply( n, calcFactorial( n - 1 ));
        else
            return 1;
    }
    long Factorial( short sOp )
    {
        CalcFactorial( sOp );
    };
    long Fibonacci( short sOp )
    {
        ...
    };
```

(code continued on next page)

```
// We explicitly expose the SimpleMath methods
long Add( long lOp1, long lOp2 )
   { return m_SimpleMath.Add( lOp1, lOp2 );
long Subtract( long lOp1, long lOp2 )
   { return m_SimpleMath.Subtract( lOp1, lOp2 );
long Multiply( long lOp1, long lOp2 )
   { return m_SimpleMath.Multiply( lOp1, lOp2 );
long Divide( long lOp1, long lOp2 )
   { return m_SimpleMath.Divide( lOp1, lOp2 );
private:
   CSimpleMath m_SimpleMath;
}
```

This example doesn't make much sense as a C++ implementation, but it describes COM containment accurately. Both composition and containment achieve reuse by using the services of a C++ class or COM component internally. The interface of the contained component is exposed only indirectly (if at all) via methods provided by the containing (or outer) component. The internal (or inner) COM component's interfaces are used by the "outer" COM object in the implementation of its interfaces. The outer component can, if it chooses, also expose the inner component's interfaces.

In COM containment, the lifetime of the inner object is controlled completely by the outer component, just as in C++ composition. An important aspect of containment is that a COM component supports being contained by default. It does not have to do anything to support being used as an inner or contained object.

When you're using containment with COM, the two (or more) components need not and typically don not follow the "has a" relationship. Instead, the important aspect is that you're gaining binary reuse of another component. Another way of looking at it is that the outer component is acting as a client of the inner component.

The component that you "contain" may have been developed by a third party. It doesn't matter who implemented the component or in what language the component was implemented because we're going to reuse it via COM's binary support for component interfaces and uniform instantiation. However, because we are reusing the component through its client interfaces, we do not have any special knowledge of its implementation, and this sometimes makes full reuse very difficult to achieve.

To demonstrate containment, our example at the end of the chapter again implements our Math component, this time it does so in a two-step process with two distinct components. To give you a preview of how containment is implemented, here's the most important step: the creation of the inner component and the implementation of the outer component's IMath interface.

```
// Instantiate the contained component
HRESULT FinalConstruct()
{
    HRESULT hr = CoCreateInstance( CLSID_SimpleMath,
                                   0,
                                   CLSCTX_INPROC_SERVER,
                                   IID_IMath,
                                     (void**) &m_pSimpleMath );
    return hr;
}

// Utilize the inner component's interface in our implementation
STDMETHODIMP CAdvancedMath::Add(long lOp1, long lOp2, long * plResult)
{
    return m_pSimpleMath->Add( lOp1, lOp2, plResult );
}
STDMETHODIMP CAdvancedMath::Subtract(long lOp1, long lOp2, long * plResult)
{
    return m_pSimpleMath->Subtract( lOp1, lOp2, plResult );
}

STDMETHODIMP CAdvancedMath::Multiply(long lOp1, long lOp2, long * plResult)
{
    return m_pSimpleMath->Multiply( lOp1, lOp2, plResult );
}

STDMETHODIMP CAdvancedMath::Divide(long lOp1, long lOp2, long * plResult)
{
    return m_pSimpleMath->Divide( lOp1, lOp2, plResult );
}
```

COM AGGREGATION

Aggregation is similar to component containment except that the inner component's interfaces are exposed directly. The aggregate object doesn't need or use the functionality of the contained object internally but instead exposes the inner object's interfaces directly as if they were its own.

The IUnknown interface of the outer object provides access to some or all the interfaces of the inner component. This little detail makes it complicated to implementing aggregation at times. The management of the lifetimes of the outer and inner objects must be coordinated through the outer component's IUnknown implementation. In other words, if a client calls AddRef through an interface on the inner component, it must increment the outer component's reference count. This is because the outer object manages the lifetime of the aggregate object, so clients of the aggregate never access the IUnknown of the inner component.

Successful lifetime management of the aggregate requires that the inner component provide support for a controlling unknown, the outer component in aggregation. When the inner component is created as part of an aggregate, it is passed a pointer to the outer object's IUnknown implementation. The inner component then delegates its IUnknown implementation to that of the outer component. This arrangement provides a consistent approach to the management of the aggregate object's lifetime.

Another requirement is that a QueryInterface on any interface of the aggregate must behave exactly the same way. Again, the inner component should delegate any QueryInterface calls to the outer component. The outer component can then determine whether the QI is for an interface it has implemented and if it is not, can pass the QI call back to the inner component.

COM components support being contained by default. They don't have to do anything special to handle being contained. However, with aggregation a component must explicitly provide support to act as an inner component in aggregation. To support being aggregated, a component must provide two different implementations of its IUnknown interface: one that behaves conventionally and one that delegates all IUnknown calls to an outer, aggregating component.

Supporting Aggregation

Developing a component that supports aggregation is easy when you're using a COM-capable framework such as MFC and ATL. In fact, with ATL, it's just a checkbox in the Object wizard dialog box, so we won't go to detail implementing an aggregatable object. It is instructional, though, to review the rules for developing a component that supports being aggregated.

- The component's implementation of the IUnknown interface methods must not delegate to the outer component's IUnknown implementation.

- QueryInterface, AddRef, and Release for all other interfaces must delegate their implementation to that of the outer object. This implementation uses the pUnkOuter parameter passed to the inner component during its creation via CoCreateInstance (and other) functions. The component should store this pointer and use it when delegating.

- The component must not call AddRef through the outer component's IUnknown pointer.

- When the component is initially created as an aggregate (indicated by the pUnkOuter parameter in IClassFactory::CreateInstance), it must fail if an interface other than IUnknown is requested.

ATL's aggregate implementation follows all of the preceding rules. As you will see, by adding a simple macro to your component's implementation you get support for aggregation.

Creating Aggregate Components

Most frameworks make it easy to develop aggregatable components. However, most of them lack support for creating aggregates. ATL, though, provides good support, and we'll cover it in a moment. Before we do, let's cover the rules for creating aggregate objects. The following rules are for those components that expose some of their functionality by aggregating another component.

- The inner component's lifetime is managed completely by the outer, aggregating component. When creating the inner component (usually via CoCreateInstance), we must explicitly ask for the inner's IUnknown. CoCreateInstance must return an IUnknown pointer.

- The outer component must protect its implementation of IUnknown::Release from reentrancy with an artificial reference count around its destruction code.

- The outer object must call its controlling IUnknown's Release if it queries for a pointer to any of the inner object's interfaces. To free this pointer, the outer object calls its controlling IUnknown's AddRef, followed by Release on the inner object's pointer.

- The outer component should not blindly delegate a QueryInterface to the inner component if it does not recognize the interface. The outer component can, however, do this if it is part of the design. This distinction is the difference between selective and blind aggregation.

SELECTIVE AGGREGATION

Microsoft recommends that you use selective aggregation when aggregating, and it is a good programming practice. With selective aggregation, you expose only those interfaces on the inner component that you want to. For example, here's how the outer component's QueryInterface is implemented for selective aggregation.

```
// Demonstrates selective aggregation
HRESULT COuterComponent::QueryInterface( REFIID riid, void** ppv )
{
   // Do we implement the interface?
   if ( IID_IAdvancedMath == riid || IID_IUnknown == riid )
   {
      *ppv = this;
```

(code continued on next page)

```
      ...
   }
   // Determine if it's one of the interfaces in our aggregate
   //
   else ( IID_IMath == riid )
   {
      // Get it from the inner component
      return pInnerUnk->QueryInterface( riid, ppv );
   }
   // The client asked for an interface we don't support
   return E_NOINTERFACE;
}
```

BLIND AGGREGATION

Blind aggregation is not recommended, but it is up to the implementer to decide whether to use it. Blind aggregation means that the outer component blindly passes all `QueryInterface` calls to the inner component if it does not recognize the requested interface. Here's an example of a blind aggregation `QueryInterface`.

```
// Demonstrates blind aggregation
HRESULT COuterComponent::QueryInterface( REFIID riid, void** ppv )
{
   // Do we implement the interface?
   if ( IID_IAdvancedMath == riid || IID_IUnknown == riid )
   {
      *ppv = this;
      ...
      return S_OK;
   }

   // Blindly ask the inner component if it
   // supports the requested interface
   return pInnerUnk->QueryInterface( riid, ppv );
}
```

That finishes our discussion of the basic concepts of containment and aggregation. In the next few sections we discuss containment and aggregation in the context of ATL. The code demonstrated is from our chapter examples. First, we develop a simple math component that implements only the IMath interface. Then, using this as our inner component we implement an AdvancedMath component using both containment and aggregation. The AdvancedMath component contains both IMath (from the inner component) and an IAdvancedMath interface (from the outer component).

ATL's Support for Containment

As we described earlier, a component doesn't have to do anything special to support being contained by another component. All of those components that you develop using ATL can be contained, and there isn't anything you can do to disable this support. ATL provides additional help when building a component that uses containment to expose the functionality of another component, and that's what we'll cover here.

The first step in containing another component is to create it. ATL provides two methods—FinalConstruct and FinalRelease—as part of the CComObjectRootEx class. Because the outer object's functionality depends on capabilities of the inner component, the inner component must be created as soon as possible. The outer component, however, can't necessarily do this creation in its constructor, because constructors don't have return values.

When a client attempts to instantiate a component (such as CoCreateInstance), an HRESULT is returned to indicate the success or failure of the creation. When a component implements containment, some mechanism must be provided so that this can be communicated back if a failure occurs when the inner component is created. ATL provides a *hook* in the creation process so that a component can indicate success or failure to the client.

FinalConstruct and FinalRelease

The creation of component in ATL proceeds via a two-step process. When a component is created via ATL's creator class static method, the class is instantiated. After instantiation and before returning to the client, ATL calls the component's FinalConstruct method, thereby giving the implementation a chance to perform any last-second initialization. Here's the code from CComCreator::CreateInstance that we studied in Chapter 3.

```
// From ATLCOM.H
template <class T1>
class CComCreator
{
public:
   static HRESULT WINAPI CreateInstance(void* pv, REFIID riid, LPVOID* ppv)
   {
      _ASSERTE(*ppv == NULL);
      HRESULT hRes = E_OUTOFMEMORY;
      T1* p = NULL;
      p = new T1( pv )
      if (p != NULL)
```

(code continued on next page)

```
      {
        ...
        hRes = p->FinalConstruct();
        ...
        if (hRes == S_OK)
            hRes = p->QueryInterface(riid, ppv);
        if (hRes != S_OK)
            delete p;
      }
      return hRes;
    }
};
```

The `FinalConstruct` method is the perfect place for us to create an inner component. The default implementation does nothing, so a simple override will work.

```
HRESULT FinalConstruct()
{
    HRESULT hr = CoCreateInstance( CLSID_SimpleMath,
                                   0,
                                   CLSCTX_INPROC_SERVER,
                                   IID_IMath,
                                   (void**) &m_pSimpleMath );
    return hr;
}
```

If creation of the inner component fails, we can return the error, which will also fail the creation of our outer component. The error propagates all the way back to the client application through its call to `IClassFactory::CreateInstance` (usually via `CoCreateInstance`).

ATL also provides a `FinalRelease` method whereby we can destroy the contained instance. This method needs only to be called if the creation succeeds. Here's a basic implementation of `FinalRelease`.

```
void FinalRelease()
{
    if ( m_pSimpleMath )
        m_pSimpleMath->Release();
}
```

We are managing the lifetime of our inner component by maintaining a pointer to its IMath interface. We also need this interface as part of our implementation, because containment requires that we re-implement each of the `IMath` methods by calling through the inner component's `IMath`. It looks something like this:

```
// Implementation needed with containment
// However, we just pass the call on to the contained component
STDMETHODIMP CAdvancedMath::Add(long lOp1, long lOp2, long * plResult)
{
   return m_pSimpleMath->Add( lOp1, lOp2, plResult );
}

STDMETHODIMP CAdvancedMath::Subtract(long lOp1, long lOp2, long * plResult)
{
   return m_pSimpleMath->Subtract( lOp1, lOp2, plResult );
}

STDMETHODIMP CAdvancedMath::Multiply(long lOp1, long lOp2, long * plResult)
{
   return m_pSimpleMath->Multiply( lOp1, lOp2, plResult );
}

STDMETHODIMP CAdvancedMath::Divide(long lOp1, long lOp2, long * plResult)
{
   return m_pSimpleMath->Divide( lOp1, lOp2, plResult );
}
```

As you can see, implementing containment using ATL is relatively straightforward. One of the tricks when modifying the IDL file is that you must use the correct interface ID for IMath. For containment to work, the IMath interface ID in the outer object must be the same as the one in the inner object. You must know the method signatures within the interface.

ATL's Support for Aggregation

ATL supports building a component that supports aggregation as well as building components that aggregate with other components. As we described in Chapter 3, a basic ATL component supports acting as an aggregate through the default implementation of CComCoClass. When you're using ATL, building a component that aggregates another one is similar to building our containment example. There are, however, a few additional details. We'll cover both aspects of aggregation in the next few sections.

Implementing Aggregatable Components

When initially creating a component using the ATL Object wizard, you are presented with three aggregation options in the **Attributes** dialog:

- **Yes—Support being aggregated**. The DECLARE_AGGREGATE macro is added by the wizard to the class declaration. This is the default provided by CComCoClass.

- **No—Disallow the component from being aggregated**. The DECLARE_NOT_AGGREGATABLE macro is added by the wizard to your class declaration.

- **Only—Allow the component's instantiation only as an aggregate**. The DECLARE_ONLY_AGGREGATABLE macro is added to your class declaration.

DECLARE_AGGREGATABLE

The DECLARE_AGGREGATABLE macro is added by default when you're creating an ATL component. CComCoClass adds the macro as part of its implementation:

```
#define DECLARE_AGGREGATABLE(x) public: \
    typedef CComCreator2< CComCreator< CComObject< x > >,
            CComCreator< CComAggObject< x > > > _CreatorClass;

template <class T, const CLSID* pclsid> class CComCoClass
{
public:
    DECLARE_AGGREGATABLE(T)
...
};
```

The creator class implementation provides a static CreateInstance method for both non-aggregate and aggregate creations. If the pUnkOuter parameter contains a value, the client is attempting aggregation. If it is NULL, normal, non-aggregate creation is occurring. The creator again handles this:

```
template <class T1, class T2>
class CComCreator2
{
public:
    static HRESULT WINAPI CreateInstance(void* pv, REFIID riid, LPVOID* ppv)
    {
        _ASSERTE(*ppv == NULL);
        HRESULT hRes = E_OUTOFMEMORY;
        if (pv == NULL)
            hRes = T1::CreateInstance(NULL, riid, ppv);
        else
            hRes = T2::CreateInstance(pv, riid, ppv);
        return hRes;
    }
};
```

DECLARE_NOT_AGGREGATABLE

By default, ATL's CComCoClass implementation provides support for aggregation. To disable aggregation in a basic ATL object, add the DECLARE_NOT_AGGREGATABLE macro to your implementation header file or select **No** in the **Aggregate** option of the **Attributes** tab when you're initially creating the component.

```
class ATL_NO_VTABLE CMath :
   public CComObjectRootEx<CComSingleThreadModel>,
   public CComCoClass<CSimpleMath, &CLSID_SimpleMath>,
   public IMath,
{
   DECLARE_NOT_AGGREGATABLE( CMath );
...
};
```

The macro works by using ATL's CComFailCreator class.

```
#define DECLARE_NOT_AGGREGATABLE(x) public:\
   typedef CComCreator2< CComCreator< CComObject< x > >,  \
   CComFailCreator<CLASS_E_NOAGGREGATION> > _CreatorClass;
```

If the client attempts to aggregate with the component by passing a valid pUnkOuter parameter to CoCreateInstance, ATL's implementation returns the CLASS_E_NOAGGREGATION error. It does so through its CComFailCreator implementation. Here it is:

```
template <HRESULT hr>
class CComFailCreator
{
public:
   static HRESULT WINAPI CreateInstance(void*, REFIID, LPVOID*)
   {
      return hr;
   }
};
```

There's nothing difficult here. The CComFailCreator::CreateInstance implementation just returns the HRESULT provided. No attempt is made to instantiate a component.

DECLARE_ONLY_AGGREGATABLE

The **Only** aggregation option implements your component so that it supports only being aggregated. Again, the CComFailCreator class is used, this time for the case when the client does not specify a value for the pUnkOuter parameter.

```
#define DECLARE_ONLY_AGGREGATABLE(x) public:\
   typedef CComCreator2< CComFailCreator<E_FAIL>,
   CComCreator< CComAggObject< x > > > _CreatorClass;
```

DECLARE_POLY_AGGREGATABLE

You can use the DECLARE_POLY_AGGREGATABLE macro for your component instead of the default DECLARE_AGGREGATABLE if you want to save space in your implementation. If you use the POLY macro, ATL will use CComPolyObject for your component's IUnknown implementation. The default implementation uses both a CComObject and a CComAggObject implementation to support the non-aggregating and aggregating cases. By using the POLY macro, you instead use CComPolyObject, which supports both cases in a single implementation. This approach may be beneficial if your component has several interfaces in its implementation.

```
#define DECLARE_POLY_AGGREGATABLE(x) public:\
        typedef CComCreator< CComPolyObject< x > > _CreatorClass;
```

Implementing Aggregation

The previous discussion focused on ATL's support for building components that support being aggregated. This section covers what is required to implement a component that aggregates another component. Aggregating another component is very similar to containment. We must first create the inner component in our FinalConstruct method. This time, however, we ask explicitly for the inner's IUnknown interface. This is a requirement for aggregation.

```
HRESULT FinalConstruct()
{
   HRESULT hr = CoCreateInstance( CLSID_SimpleMath,
                      GetControllingUnknown(),
                      CLSCTX_INPROC_SERVER,
                        IID_IUnknown,
                        (void**) &m_pSimpleUnknown );

return hr;
}
```

After we create the component and obtain its IUnknown implementation, we must decide which interfaces we want to expose directly. With aggregation, we don't have to re-implement any interface methods. Instead we expose them directly using a number of ATL macros. We must decide to either selectively or blindly expose the inner's interfaces.

Another requirement when you're aggregating a component is that the component must be in-process. Aggregation is currently not supported across process, so don't try it with local or remote servers.

COM_INTERFACE_ENTRY_AGGREGATE

For each interface in the aggregated object that you want to expose, you must add a COM_INTERFACE_ENTRY_AGGREGATE (or one of its counterparts) to your component's interface map. In our math example, we expose the IMath interface this way:

```
class ATL_NO_VTABLE CAdvancedMath :
    public CComObjectRootEx<CComSingleThreadModel>,
    public CComCoClass<CAdvancedMath, &CLSID_AdvancedMath>,
    public IAdvancedMath
{
...
BEGIN_COM_MAP(CAdvancedMath)
   COM_INTERFACE_ENTRY(IAdvancedMath)
   COM_INTERFACE_ENTRY_AGGREGATE( IID_IMath, m_pSimpleUnknown )
END_COM_MAP()
...
};
```

Here we are selectively exposing the IMath interface. The macro expands to this:

```
#define COM_INTERFACE_ENTRY_AGGREGATE(iid, punk)\
   {&iid,\
   (DWORD)offsetof(_ComMapClass, punk),\
   _Delegate},
```

COM_INTERFACE_ENTRY_AGGREGATE_BLIND

To blindly expose all interfaces of the aggregated component, you can use ATL's AGGRE-GATE_BLIND macro. The only parameter required is the IUnknown* pointer for the inner component. If an interface is not found in the outer component's map, the result of a QueryInterface on the inner's unknown is returned. Remember, though, that blind aggregation is not recommended unless you really understand the consequences. Here's how we would implement blind aggregation for the Math component example:

```
class ATL_NO_VTABLE CAdvancedMath :
    public CComObjectRootEx<CComSingleThreadModel>,
    public CComCoClass<CAdvancedMath, &CLSID_AdvancedMath>,
    public IAdvancedMath
{
...
BEGIN_COM_MAP(CAdvancedMath)
   COM_INTERFACE_ENTRY(IAdvancedMath)
   // Blindly expose all interfaces of the inner
   COM_INTERFACE_ENTRY_AGGREGATE_BLIND( m_pSimpleUnknown )
END_COM_MAP()
...
};
```

COM_INTERFACE_ENTRY_AUTOAGGREGATE and COM_INTERFACE_ENTRY_AUTOAGGREGATE_BLIND

The AUTOAGGREGATE macros are basically the same as the previous AGGREGATE macros except that the named component is instantiated automatically. By using the AUTOAGGREGATE macro, we skip the step of explicitly creating the component in the FinalConstruct method. Using AUTOAGGREGATE, our code would look like this:

```
class ATL_NO_VTABLE CAdvancedMath :
    public CComObjectRootEx<CComSingleThreadModel>,
    public CComCoClass<CAdvancedMath, &CLSID_AdvancedMath>,
    public IAdvancedMath
{
...
BEGIN_COM_MAP(CAdvancedMath)
   COM_INTERFACE_ENTRY(IAdvancedMath)
   COM_INTERFACE_ENTRY_AUTOAGGREGATE( IID_IMath,
                                      m_pSimpleUnknown,
                                      CLSID_SimpleMath )
END_COM_MAP()
...
};
```

DECLARE_GET_CONTROLLING_UNKNOWN

When you're creating the inner component of an aggregate, the outer component must pass its IUnknown implementation. ATL provides the DECLARE_GET_CONTROLLING_UNKNOWN macro for just this purpose.

```
#define DECLARE_GET_CONTROLLING_UNKNOWN() public:\
    virtual IUnknown* GetControllingUnknown() {return GetUnknown();}
```

You add the macro to your component's header file in order to use the GetControllingUnknown method when calling CoCreateInstance. It looks something like this:

```
DECLARE_GET_CONTROLLING_UNKNOWN()
HRESULT FinalConstruct()
{
   HRESULT hr = CoCreateInstance( CLSID_SimpleMath,
                       GetControllingUnknown(),
                       CLSCTX_INPROC_SERVER,
                       IID_IUnknown,
                       (void**) &m_pSimpleUnknown );

   return hr;
}
```

THE SIMPLE MATH COMPONENT

To demonstrate the two binary reuse mechanisms available in COM, we'll build our Math component using two COM components. First, we'll build a component that implements only the IMath interface. Then we'll build a component that implements IAdvancedMath and exposes IMath through aggregation. After that, we'll build the Math component using containment to expose the inner component's IMath interface.

Create the Simple Math Component That Implements IMath

Start Visual C++ and create a new project, selecting **ATL COM AppWizard**. Give it the name **Chapter5_Simple**. In Step 1 of 1, select a type of DLL. Select **Finish** to generate the project. Using **the** ATL Object wizard, insert a **Simple Component** with the following options.

- Use a Short Name of **SimpleMath**.
- Make sure the interface name is **IMath**.
- Change the **ProgID** to **Chapter5.SimpleMath**.
- On the **Attributes** tab, select a **Custom** interface. Take the defaults on the rest of the attributes.

Implement the `IMath` Interface

Using the **Add Method** option by right-clicking on the ClassView, add the methods from our previous `IMath` interface. Here is the implementation:

```
// SimpleMath.h : Declaration of the CMath

#ifndef __SIMPLEMATH_H_
#define __SIMPLEMATH_H_

#include "resource.h"        // main symbols

/////////////////////////////////////////////////////////////////////////////
// CSimpleMath
class ATL_NO_VTABLE CSimpleMath :
    public CComObjectRootEx<CComSingleThreadModel>,
    public CComCoClass<CSimpleMath, &CLSID_SimpleMath>,
    public IMath,
{
...

// IMath
public:
    STDMETHOD(Add)( long, long, long* );
    STDMETHOD(Subtract)( long, long, long* );
    STDMETHOD(Multiply)( long, long, long* );
    STDMETHOD(Divide)( long, long, long* );
};

//
// SimpleMath.cpp : Implementation of CSimpleMath
//
...
//////////////
// CSimpleMath
//////////////

// IMath interface
STDMETHODIMP CSimpleMath::Add( long lOp1, long lOp2, long* pResult )
{
    *pResult = lOp1 + lOp2;
    return S_OK;
}
```

```
STDMETHODIMP CSimpleMath::Subtract( long lOp1, long lOp2, long* pResult )
{
   *pResult = lOp1 - lOp2;
   return S_OK;
}

STDMETHODIMP CSimpleMath::Multiply( long lOp1, long lOp2, long* pResult )
{
   *pResult = lOp1 * lOp2;
   return S_OK;
}

STDMETHODIMP CSimpleMath::Divide( long lOp1, long lOp2, long* pResult )
{
   *pResult = lOp1 / lOp2;
   return S_OK;
}
```

Build the Project (Simple)

That's it. Now build the project. What we've done is to build a simple COM component that implements only our IMath interface. Next, we'll aggregate with this object to create a more advanced math component.

IMPLEMENTING THE MATH COMPONENT WITH AGGREGATION

Start Visual C++ and create a new project, selecting **ATL COM AppWizard**. Give it the name **Chapter5_Aggregate**. In Step 1 of 1, select a type of DLL. Select **Finish** to generate the project. Using the ATL Object wizard, insert a **Simple Component** with the following options.

- Use a **Short Name** of **AdvancedMath**.

- Make sure the interface name is **IAdvancedMath**.

- Change the **Prog ID** to **Chapter5.Aggregate**

- On the **Attributes** tab, make sure the interface type is **Custom.** You can take the defaults on the rest of the attributes.

- Add the **IAdvancedMath** declarations and definitions to the **AdvancedMath** component just as we did in the previous examples.

Implement the `IAdvancedMath` Interface

The implementation of the `IAdvancedMath` interface is the same as before. You can use your favorite technique to add the declarations to the **.IDL** and **.H** files. Here's the implementation:

```
// IAdvancedMath interface
long calcFactorial( short n )
{
   if ( n > 1 )
      return n * calcFactorial( n - 1 );
   else
      return 1;
}

STDMETHODIMP CAdvancedMath::Factorial( short sOp, long* plResult )
{
   *plResult = calcFactorial( sOp );
   return S_OK;
}

long calcFibonacci( short n )
{
   if ( n <= 1 )
      return 1;

   return calcFibonacci( n - 1 ) + calcFibonacci( n - 2 );
}

STDMETHODIMP CAdvancedMath::Fibonacci( short sOp, long* plResult )
{
   *plResult = calcFibonacci( sOp );
   return S_OK;
}
```

Aggregate with the Simple Math Component

All the prior work was familiar ground. Now we'll enhance the advanced math component to aggregate with the simple math component. This will allow `AdvancedMath` to directly expose the `IMath` interface along with its own `IAdvancedMath` interface. Follow these steps to implement the aggregation.

Include the Definitions for the Aggregate's CLSID and IID

To begin, we need the class ID and interface ID of the aggregate component.

```
//
// AdvancedMath.h : Declaration of the CAdvancedMath
//
...

// Include the CLSID and IID of the inner component
#include "..\Chapter5_Simple_i.c"

/////////////////////////////////////////////////////////////////////////////
// CAdvancedMath
class ATL_NO_VTABLE CAdvancedMath :
    public CComObjectRootEx<CComSingleThreadModel>,
...
```

Add an `IUnknown` Pointer to Your Class

One of the important steps in aggregation is to manage the lifetime of the aggregated (or inner) component. The best way is to maintain an interface pointer throughout the lifetime of the aggregating object, so we will add a member variable to hold the `IUnknown*` for the aggregate. We also need to maintain this `IUnknown` interface pointer so that we can delegate QueryInterface calls for the inner interfaces.

```
class ATL_NO_VTABLE CAdvancedMath :
    public CComObjectRootEx<CComSingleThreadModel>,
    public CComCoClass<CAdvancedMath, &CLSID_AdvancedMath>,
    public IAdvancedMath
{
{
public:
    CAdvancedMath() : m_pSimpleUnknown( 0 )
    {
    }

private:
    IUnknown* m_pSimpleUnknown;

};
```

Override `FinalConstruct`

Now that we have the `IUnknown` pointer, we need to create an instance of the simple component as soon as our advanced component is created. ATL provides an overridable member called `FinalConstruct` that provides the perfect place to create the instance. `FinalConstruct` is called right after `IClassFactory::CreateInstance` is called by a client, and it allows you to return an HRESULT to indicate any problems. Here's the code:

```
class ATL_NO_VTABLE CAdvancedMath :
    public CComObjectRootEx<CComSingleThreadModel>,
    public CComCoClass<CAdvancedMath, &CLSID_AdvancedMath>,
    public IAdvancedMath
{
public:
    CAdvancedMath() : m_pSimpleUnknown( 0 )
    {
    }

    DECLARE_GET_CONTROLLING_UNKNOWN()
    HRESULT FinalConstruct()
    {
        HRESULT hr = CoCreateInstance( CLSID_SimpleMath,
                            GetControllingUnknown(),
                            CLSCTX_INPROC_SERVER,
                            IID_IUnknown,
                            (void**) &m_pSimpleUnknown );

        return hr;
    }
```

Add the Aggregated Component's Interface to the Interface Map

When a client uses QueryInterface to query for either IMath or IAdvancedMath, it will occur through our advanced component's QI implementation. We need to add the aggregate's interface to ATL's interface map. ATL provides a special macro just for this purpose, COM_INTERFACE_ENTRY_AGGREGATE, which we described earlier. The macro takes two parameters.

```
class ATL_NO_VTABLE CAdvancedMath :
    public CComObjectRootEx<CComSingleThreadModel>,
    public CComCoClass<CAdvancedMath, &CLSID_AdvancedMath>,
    public IAdvancedMath
{
...
BEGIN_COM_MAP(CAdvancedMath)
    COM_INTERFACE_ENTRY(IAdvancedMath)
    COM_INTERFACE_ENTRY_AGGREGATE( IID_IMath, m_pSimpleUnknown )
END_COM_MAP()
```

Release the Aggregated Component

When our component is destroyed, we must also destroy the aggregated component. The best place to do this in ATL is in the `FinalRelease` call. When we release the inner component's `IUnknown`, its reference count will go to zero.

```
class ATL_NO_VTABLE CAdvancedMath :
    public CComObjectRootEx<CComSingleThreadModel>,
    public CComCoClass<CAdvancedMath, &CLSID_AdvancedMath>,
    public IAdvancedMath
{
...

   void FinalRelease()
   {
      if ( m_pSimpleUnknown )
         m_pSimpleUnknown->Release();
   }
...
}
```

Testing the Aggregation-Based Component

At this point you should be able to modify either the Chapter 3 or the Chapter 4 client to test the `AdvancedMath` component. If you need help, the downloadable examples contain a **Chapter5_Client** project that provides everything you need.

IMPLEMENTING THE ADVANCED MATH COMPONENT WITH CONTAINMENT

Once you've implemented aggregation, containment is a little easier. The following steps below modify our project to use containment instead of aggregation. The important point is that we still create the inner component when our advanced math component is created. However, we do not pass the `IUnknown*` to `CoCreateInstance`. Instead, we pass `null`, and ask for the `IMath` interface. We then maintain this pointer and use it to provide the `IMath` implementation.

Because the outer component exposes `IMath` directly, we must include the declaration for `IMath` and add `IMath` in our coclass entry to the IDL file. This example raises the issue of how to manage type information when using containment. We must again expose each parameter type and interface description for interfaces that we reuse from the contained component.

```
// Math.h : Declaration of the CAdvancedMath
#include "resource.h"        // main symbols

// This is needed for containment
// for the declaration of IMath
#include "..\Simple.h"

/////////////////////////////////////////////////////////////////////////
// CAdvancedMath
class ATL_NO_VTABLE CAdvancedMath :
    public CComObjectRootEx<CComSingleThreadModel>,
    public CComCoClass<CAdvancedMath, &CLSID_AdvancedMath>,
    public IAdvancedMath,
    // We have to include this for our implementation
    public IMath
{
public:
    CAdvancedMath() : m_pSimpleMath( 0 )
    {
    }

    // Don't need this anymore
    //DECLARE_GET_CONTROLLING_UNKNOWN()

HRESULT FinalConstruct()
    {
        HRESULT hr = CoCreateInstance( CLSID_SimpleMath,
                                // GetControllingUnknown(),
                                0,
                            CLSCTX_INPROC_SERVER,
                                IID_IMath,
                                //(void**) &m_pSimpleUnknown );
                                (void**) &m_pSimpleMath );

return hr;
    }
    void FinalRelease()
    {
        if ( m_pSimpleMath )
            m_pSimpleMath->Release();
    }
DECLARE_REGISTRY_RESOURCEID(IDR_ADVANCEDMATH)
BEGIN_COM_MAP(CAdvancedMath)
    COM_INTERFACE_ENTRY(IAdvancedMath)
    // COM_INTERFACE_ENTRY_AGGREGATE( IID_IMath, m_pSimpleUnknown )
    COM_INTERFACE_ENTRY(IMath)
END_COM_MAP()
```

```
private:
    //IUnknown* m_pSimpleUnknown;
    IMath* m_pSimpleMath;


// IMath - We now must explicitly implement these methods
// If you use ClassView/Add Method.. these will already be here
public:
    STDMETHOD(Divide)(long lOp1, long lOp2, long* plResult);
    STDMETHOD(Multiply)(long lOp1, long lOp2, long* plResult);
    STDMETHOD(Subtract)(long lOp1, long lOp2, long* plResult);
    STDMETHOD(Add)(long lOp1, long lOp2, long* plResult);

// IAdvancedMath
public:
    STDMETHOD(Fibonacci)(short sOp, long* plResult);
    STDMETHOD(Factorial)(short sOp, long* plResult);
};
```

Add the Implementation for `IMath`

Our `IMath` implementation is just a pass-through via the `m_pSimpleMath` interface
pointer. However, as described earlier, we need the declaration for `IMath` in our IDL file as
well as the header file of our implementation. It's easiest to add the methods using
ClassView/Add Method.

```
// Implementation needed with containment
// However, we just pass the call on to the contained component
STDMETHODIMP CAdvancedMath::Add(long lOp1, long lOp2, long * plResult)
{
    return m_pSimpleMath->Add( lOp1, lOp2, plResult );
}

STDMETHODIMP CAdvancedMath::Subtract(long lOp1, long lOp2, long *
plResult)
{
    return m_pSimpleMath->Subtract( lOp1, lOp2, plResult );
}

STDMETHODIMP CAdvancedMath::Multiply(long lOp1, long lOp2, long * plResult)
{
    return m_pSimpleMath->Multiply( lOp1, lOp2, plResult );
}

STDMETHODIMP CAdvancedMath::Divide(long lOp1, long lOp2, long * plResult)
{
    return m_pSimpleMath->Divide( lOp1, lOp2, plResult );
}
```

Testing the Containment-Based Component

The client application that you developed earlier to test the aggregation-based component should work just fine, even without a recompile, with your new containment-based AdvancedMath component. For a comparison of the two reuse techniques, the examples include two projects: **Chapter5_Aggregate** and **Chapter5_Contain**.

ATL AND AUTOMATION

That concludes our discussion of COM's binary reuse mechanisms. In Chapter 6 we cover an important aspect of COM: automation. Automation provides certain dynamic calling techniques that are not provided by Vtable interfaces. IDispatch, automation's primary interface, gives the implementer and user the ability to perform late binding of component functionality. Automation is also important because it is the only mechanism for exposing functionality in components that must work in Microsoft's scripting environments such as Internet Explorer.

Chapter 6

Automation

Automation is the COM-based technology that almost all Windows developers are familiar with, at least from a user's perspective. Visual Basic uses automation extensively, and ActiveX controls expose their functionality through automation. It's hard to be a Windows developer today without encountering these forms of automation.

Early in the history of COM and OLE, automation was the preferred technique for building components, primarily because it is supported well within MFC. Custom Vtable interfaces, which we've been exploring, aren't supported very well within MFC, especially via its wizards. As an example, MFC (version 4.21) still uses the older, automation-specific ODL technique of describing a component. You must use ATL to get built-in support for the more useful IDL.

Automation is still an important technology, but because of newer tools such as ATL, it isn't as important as it used to be. Many developers are using COM as an architecture with which to build their applications, and the most efficient and robust technique for this purpose is to use custom Vtable interfaces and IDL. However, automation is still required (and useful) in many cases (for example, ActiveX controls), so we'll cover it in this chapter. Also, when developing an ATL-based component, you can use either a custom or a dual interface, the latter of which depends heavily on automation.

Automation is supported by nearly every Windows development environment. Building a component that supports automation ensures that the component will work in every major development tool. For some developers this requirement is important, and for others it's not important at all. It all depends on your target market (in-house application architectures, shrink-wrap component market, and so on).

Another important aspect of automation is that it allows you to expose the functionality of a whole application. In other words, the application itself becomes a reusable component. If you need the services of a good word processor in your application, you can purchase a word processor that exposes its capabilities via automation and use it within your application. Microsoft Word, Microsoft Project, and Internet Explorer provide access to nearly all their capabilities through automation and can be used as components of other applications.

LATE BINDING

Late binding is what makes automation different from the other COM technologies that we've been discussing. Vtable interfaces require that the client bind to the Vtable structure at compile time; the client needs a header file or some other way of discovering how to build its call stack. Also, because COM interfaces are rigidly typed, parameter type checking is also performed at compile time. Certain types of dynamic behavior (such as dynamic instantiation of different implementations of an interface) are provided by Vtable interfaces, but they still require some compile-time knowledge.

Automation provides true late binding by adding a level of indirection to interface method invocations. The client still binds to a Vtable interface at compile time, but it binds to the standard IDispatch interface. The IDispatch implementation then provides run-time determination and invocation of a component's methods. Automation provides this late-binding mechanism not only within a single language but also across languages.

Late binding isn't typically the best technique when you're developing robust applications, because type checking isn't performed until runtime, and that makes effective testing difficult. However, certain Microsoft tools and technologies (such as Visual Basic for Applications and Internet Explorer's VBScript) require late-binding behavior because of their interpreted nature. In these cases, a component developer must expose functionality through automation so that the component can be used.

THE DISPINTERFACE

Automation is based on COM's IDispatch interface. IDispatch provides a series of methods that allow a client application to access functionality dynamically within an automation-based server. This dynamic invocation is different from the COM custom interface technique used in our custom interface–based math component. When using a custom interface, the client application requires some compile-time knowledge of the component's interface, either through a type library or by including the component's interface declaration at compile time (for example, **IMATH.H**). This approach implements *early binding* of the component's interface.

A component that implements its methods using IDispatch instead of a custom interface provides a number of additional capabilities. The interaction between the client and server applications must use late binding of the component's interface methods. This arrangement makes it easy for a server component to change its interface (even at run time!) without requiring client applications to be recompiled or relinked. If the interface methods are changed, it should be communicated to the client application so that it can take advantage of the new features.

Another significant feature you gain by using IDispatch is universal (or type library) marshaling. The default COM implementation provided by Windows contains a number of data types that can be used by components implementing the IDispatch interface. Intrinsic support for these data types makes it easy to build components that work across local and remote processes without the requirement of building and shipping a proxy/stub DLL.

Most COM interfaces are like our IMath example. They provide a structure that requires a rigid implementation of an abstract class. COM defines the abstract class (interface), but the application developer must provide a unique implementation of that abstract class. IDispatch is a little different, because it adds a level of indirection to the Vtable-style interfaces that we've studied so far. One term for this new interface type is *dispinterface*, for dispatch interface. That term succinctly describes how IDispatch differs from the standard Vtable implementation. The client does not access a component's functionality through the Vtable pointer as we did with IMath; instead, the client must first "look up" the function, provide an internal identifier for the desired function, and finally invoke or "dispatch" the function, as illustrated in Figure 6.1.

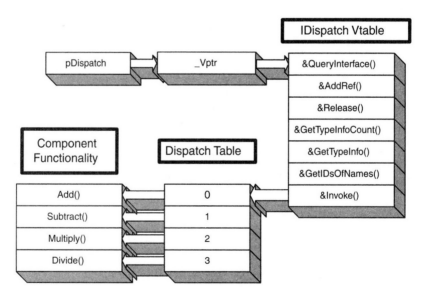

Figure 6.1 IDispatch Vtable and dispatch table.

The dispatch table in Figure 6.1 is an abstract construct. In code it's just a set of integers that uniquely identify each exposed method or property within a component.

NOTE

As you can see from the illustration, the IDispatch interface is more complicated than the usual Vtable interaction. The client still gets a Vtable pointer, but now the Vtable doesn't actually have direct access to the IMath methods. Instead, the call must first go through IDispatch::Invoke, which contains a parameter that maps the method call to a specific entry in the dispatch map. This additional level of indirection provides for late binding to a component's methods. Table 6.1 describes the four methods of the IDispatch interface.

Table 6.1 IDispatch Methods

METHOD	DESCRIPTION
Invoke	Invoke provides most of the functionality of the IDispatch interface. It takes eight parameters, the most important of which is the DISPID. The DISPID is mapped to a specific offset within the dispatch table and determines which component method is invoked.
GetIDsOfNames	GetIDsOfNames provides a facility for the client to map the textual automation server property or method name, such as "Add", to its numeric DISPID. The DISPID can then be used with the Invoke function to access the method in the component.
GetTypeInfo	A client that provides dynamic lookup and calling of automation methods typically does not have all the type information necessary to populate the Invoke DISPPARAMS structure. An automation client can call GetTypeInfoCount to determine whether the component can provide type information through this method.
GetTypeInfoCount	GetTypeInfoCount is used by the client to determine whether the component object implements the GetTypeInfo method. Setting the passed-in parameter to 1 indicates that type information is available; zero indicates that no type information is available.

To give you a brief example of how a dispinterface works, let's examine some common Visual Basic code that demonstrates late-binding functionality.

```
Dim objMath as Object
Dim nResult as Integer

Set objMath = CreateObject( "Chapter6.Math" )
nResult = objMath.Add( 100, 55 )
Set objMath = Nothing
```

The Object type in Visual Basic holds an IDispatch pointer, and the CreateObject procedure creates an instance of the component specified by the ProgID. Here are the steps in C++ code that Visual Basic goes through to perform the preceding function:

```
// Create an instance of the math component
// and QI for IDispatch
CLSIDFromProgID( "Chapter6.Math", &clsid );
IDispatch pDispatch = 0;
CoCreateInstance( clsid,
```

```
                ...
                IID_IDispatch,
                (void**) &pDispatch );
// Get the DISPID for Add
DISPID dispid;
pDispatch->GetIDsOfNames( "Add", &dispid );

// Build the parameters based on the context of the call
// and then invoke the method
pDispatch->Invoke( dispid, parameters, &result, ... );

// Release the pointer
pDispatch->Release();
```

The most important aspect of late binding is that the client gets the name of a method and the parameters that should be passed from the call itself. The preceding example does not use any compile-time bindings other than that for the standard IDispatch interface. Visual Basic gets the DISPID for the Add method at run time and determines which parameters to pass to the invoke method from the call itself. Suppose we had written it this way:

```
Dim objMath as Object
Dim nResult as Integer

Set objMath = CreateObject( "Chapter6.Math" )
nResult = objMath.Add( 100, 55, 77, 99 )
Set objMath = Nothing
```

In that case, we would get an "Invalid number of parameters" error *at run time* instead of at compile time, because the Add method does not accept four parameters. The important point is that this is true late binding of functionality, and it is what a dispinterface provides compared with a straight COM Vtable interface.

THE DUAL INTERFACE

We now have all the pieces we need to understand the concept of a *dual interface*. Dual interfaces are implemented by a server component and provide the client application two different ways to access its functionality. A dual interface combines a custom interface (such as IMath) with the standard IDispatch interface. This arrangement allows the client to choose the interface (and thus the binding technique) it wants to use.

Figure 6.2 depicts what our math component would look like with a dual interface. It is a combination of our custom interface (IMath) and the IDispatch that we'll implement using ATL. The math methods are exposed directly through our Vtable and indirectly through IDispatch.

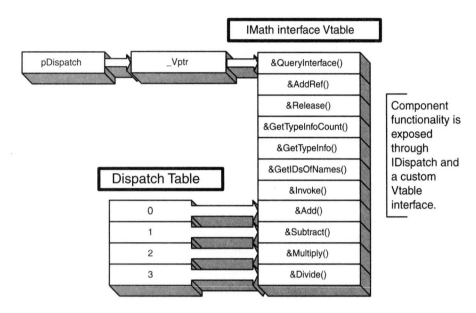

Figure 6.2 Math class with a dual interface.

Why should we expose two interfaces that provide basically the same functionality? The primary reason is performance. If the server has an in-process (DLL) implementation, no marshaling is required. The client can bind directly to the custom interface methods and make very efficient calls. The performance of this method is identical to that of direct C or C++ function bindings.

However, if the client requires late-binding functionality, it can use the IDispatch implementation. This technique is slower, because more of the work is done at run time instead of compile time, but in many instances late binding is necessary. We'll take another look at various client binding techniques later in this chapter.

AUTOMATION DATA TYPES

Automation provides standard marshaling of parameters and return values across process and apartment boundaries using the universal marshaler (**OLEAUT32.DLL**). This approach makes it a bit easier to implement your components within a local or remote server because you don't have to ship a proxy/stub DLL along with your component. To provide universal marshaling for automation, however, COM defines and limits the data types that can be used. We introduced these types in Chapter 4, and in this chapter we'll cover the major ones in more detail. To begin, Table 6.2 describes each of the automation data types.

Table 6.2 Automation Data Types.

TYPE	DESCRIPTION
BSTR	A binary string that stores the length of the string in the first four bytes of the structure and the actual string directly after. The string data is Unicode.
short, long, float, double	Intrinsic types.
Byte	An unsigned character.
BOOL	A Boolean value.
CURRENCY	A currency value stored in an eight-byte integer. Used for fixed-point representation of a number. The integer represents the value multiplied by 10,000.
DATE	A date stored in a double, where January 1, 1900, is 2.0, January 2 is 3.0, and so on. Functions are provided by COM to help in the manipulation of the date type.
IUnknown*	A pointer to an IUnknown interface.
IDispatch*	A pointer to an IDispatch interface.
SafeArray	An array of one of the preceding data types, including an array of Variants.
VARIANT	A structure containing any one of the preceding types, including a pointer to a safe array.

When designing a component that exposes its functionality through a dispinterface or dual interface, you can use only the data types described in Table 6.2. Many of the types are basic, and you probably use them all the time. The variant is special and is used frequently in automation so let's take a look at it.

The Variant Data Type

The VARIANT data type provides an effective mechanism to pass around arbitrary automation data, because the variant contains both the data type and its value. Also, because a variant can contain any of a number of different data types, it provides a rudimentary overloading mechanism, which we'll look at in a moment. In the following condensed version of the VARIANT structure, the comments indicate the symbol used for the VARTYPE value. A value of VT_EMPTY indicates that the variant does not contain a type or value.

```
struct tagVARIANT
{
   VARTYPE vt;
   union
   {
      LONG lVal;        // VT_I4
      SHORT iVal;       // VT_I2
      FLOAT fltVal;     // VT_R4
      DOUBLE dblVal;    // VT_R8
      VARIANT_BOOL boolVal;  // VT_BOOL
      SCODE scode;      // VT_ERROR
```

(code continued on next page)

```
      CY cyVal;          // VT_CY
      DATE date;         // VT_DATE
      BSTR bstrVal;      // VT_BSTR
      IUnknown *punkVal;      // VT_UNKNOWN
      IDispatch *pdispVal;    // VT_DISPATCH
      SAFEARRAY *parray;      // VT_ARRAY
      SHORT *piVal;      // VT_I2 | VT_BYREF
      LONG *plVal;       // VT_I4 | VT_BYREF
      FLOAT *pfltVal;    // VT_R4 | VT_BYREF
      DOUBLE *pdblVal;   // VT_R8 | VT_BYREF
      BSTR *pbstrVal;    // VT_BSTR | BT_BYREF
      SAFEARRAY **pparray; // VT_ARRAY | VT_BYREF
      VARIANT *pvarVal;     // VT_VARIANT | VT_BYREF
   }
};

typedef tagVARIANT VARIANT;
```

A VARIANT is just a big union of different types and an identifier indicating which type value is within the union. The vt member indicates the data type, and that allows the receiver to extract the data from the appropriate union element. Here's a simple example of initializing a variant to contain a long with a value of 1,045.

```
// Declare and initialize the variant
VARIANT varResult;
VariantInit( &varResult );

// Set the type to long (I4)
varResult.vt = VT_I4;

// Set its value to 1045
varResult.lVal = 1045;
```

We can now pass this variant through a COM interface method and the data will be marshaled automatically. There are several COM APIs and macros that make working with variants easier. Table 6.3 shows some of the common variant APIs.

Table 6.3 Variant-Based APIs

FUNCTION	PURPOSE
VariantInit	Initializes a variant to VT_EMPTY.
VariantClear	Initializes a variant by first freeing any memory used within the variant. This is useful for client-side applications when they need to clear a variant passed from a server.
VariantChangeType	Coerces a variant from one type to another. For example, this method will change a long (VT_I4) to a BOOL and even an IDispatch pointer to a BSTR.
VariantCopy	Makes a copy of a variant and frees any existing memory in the destination before making the copy.

I mentioned that variants can be used to overload automation methods. In the following example we'll rewrite our IMath methods to use variants, giving the client additional flexibility. For example, the client can now pass strings containing the numeric operands instead of pawwing only longs.

```
STDMETHODIMP CMath::Add(VARIANT varOp1, VARIANT varOp2, VARIANT *pvarResult)
{
    HRESULT hr;

    // Coerce the first variant into the desired type
    // In this case we would like a long
    hr = VariantChangeType( &varOp1,
                            &varOp1,
                            0,
                            VT_I4 );
    // If we can't get a long return invalid argument
    if ( FAILED( hr ))
        return( DISP_E_TYPEMISMATCH );

    // Coerce the second variant into the desired type
    // In this case we would like a long
    hr = VariantChangeType( &varOp2,
                            &varOp2,
                            0,
                            VT_I4 );

    // If we can't get a long return invalid argument
    if ( FAILED( hr ))
        return( DISP_E_TYPEMISMATCH );

    // Initialize the return value
    // If there isn't one, then just return
    if ( pvarResult )
    {
        VariantInit( pvarResult );
        pvarResult->vt = VT_I4;
        pvarResult->lVal = varOp1.lVal + varOp2.lVal;
    }

    return S_OK;
}
```

The Add method takes two variant parameters and returns a variant. By accepting a variant parameter, we allow a client to pass any automation type—for example, a BSTR instead of a long, or event a short or BOOL. We then use COM's variant coercion function, VariantChangeType, to ensure that we have a long before we do our calculations.

If the coercion fails, we return a type mismatch error. However, `VariantChangeType` can coerce almost anything. It will handle string-to-numeric, numeric-to-string, by-reference to value, value to by-reference, and a few other conversions automatically. In the preceding example, Visual Basic code such as this will actually work:

```
Dim result as Long
result = objMath.Add( "123", "345" )
```

This works because `VariantChangeType` can convert the BSTRs to `long`s. However, this behavior may not what we want. In other words, the component code can behave differently depending on the passed-in data types. If the client were to pass two strings, instead of coercing them to `long`s and performing addition we could create a new string by concatenating the string parameters. Here's an example:

```
// If we have two strings, append them
if ( varOp1.vt == VT_BSTR &&
     varOp2.vt == VT_BSTR )
{
   VariantInit( pvarResult );
   CComBSTR bstr( varOp1.bstrVal );
   bstr.AppendBSTR( varOp2.bstrVal );

   // Return the concatenated string
   pvarResult->vt = VT_BSTR;
   pvarResult->bstrVal = bstr.Copy();
   return S_OK;
}
```

The method provides different functionality based on the parameters, and because we also return our result via a variant, we can pass back either a `long` or a BSTR depending on our overloaded behavior.

The Safe Array

The *safe array* data type and its associated APIs provide a mechanism to move arrays of automation-compatible types between local and remote processes. The safe array began as a Visual Basic type but is now part of COM because it is an automation type. Here's a look:

```
typedef struct  tagSAFEARRAY
{
   USHORT cDims;
   USHORT fFeatures;
   ULONG cbElements;
   ULONG cLocks;
   PVOID pvData;
   SAFEARRAYBOUND rgsabound[ 1 ];
} SAFEARRAY;
```

```
typedef struct  tagSAFEARRAYBOUND
{
    ULONG cElements;
    LONG lLbound;
} SAFEARRAYBOUND;
```

A safe array can have multiple dimensions and also uses a reference counter to help with crossprocess memory management. When working with safe arrays, you shouldn't access the data members directly. Instead, you use a series of APIs provided by COM. Table 6.4 describes the basic safe array APIs.

Table 6.4 Safe Array APIs

FUNCTION	PURPOSE
SafeArrayCreate	Create a safe array.
SafeArrayDestroy	Destroy a safe array.
SafeArrayGetElement	Get a specified element from an array.
SafeArrayPutElement	Put an element into the array.
SafeArrayGetLBound	Get the lower bound.
SafeArrayGetUBound	Get the upper bound.

The lower and upper bound APIs are required because safe arrays do not necessarily begin at zero or 1. Instead, the bounds can be arbitrarily supplied by the developer. For example, a Visual Basic developer can create an array such as:

```
Private Sub cmdSum_Click()
    'Build a safe array of longs
    Dim longArray(-4 To 4) As Long
    For i = -4 To 4
        longArray(i) = i
    Next
    txtResult = objMath2.Sum(longArray)
End Sub
```

The corresponding component code looks like this:

```
STDMETHODIMP CMath::Sum(VARIANT varOp1, long * plResult)
{
    // Make sure we have an array of longs
    if (! (varOp1.vt & VT_I4 ))
        return DISP_E_TYPEMISMATCH;

    if (! (varOp1.vt & VT_ARRAY ))
        return DISP_E_TYPEMISMATCH;
```

(code continued on next page)

```
// The parameter may be a reference
SAFEARRAY* psa;
if ( varOp1.vt & VT_BYREF )
   psa = *(varOp1.pparray);
else
   psa = varOp1.parray;

// Get the lower and upper bounds
long lLBound, lUBound;
SafeArrayGetLBound( psa,
                    1, &lLBound );
SafeArrayGetUBound( psa,
                    1, &lUBound );

// Sum the elements of the array
long lSum = 0;
for( long i = lLBound; i <= lUBound; i++ )
{
   long lValue;
   SafeArrayGetElement( psa,
                        &i, &lValue );

   lSum += lValue;
}
*plResult = lSum;

return S_OK;
}
```

In our example we're accepting the safe array through a variant. Visual Basic likes to work with variants. Next, we check the variant type to make sure that it is an array of longs. We then check to see whether the safe array was passed by reference. If it is, we must extract the pointer from a different member of the union.

Another important point is that we don't access the safe array structure directly. Instead, we use the safe array API Functions to get the lower and upper bounds of the array and use these values to iterate over the elements and return the sum.

Passing a safe array in C++ is similar to what you do in Visual Basic, but you must use the APIs directly. Here's an example of passing a safe array to the Sum method.

```
// Try calling our Sum method
// We first have to build a safe array
// It's an array of 10 longs with
// the values 0,1,2,3,4...
SAFEARRAY       *psaArray = 0;
SAFEARRAYBOUND  rgsabound[1];
```

```
rgsabound[0].lLbound = 0;
rgsabound[0].cElements = 10;
psaArray = SafeArrayCreate( VT_I4,
                            1, rgsabound );

// Fill the array with values
for( int i = 0; i < 10; i++ )
{
    SafeArrayPutElement( psaArray,
                         (long *) &i, &i );
}
VARIANT varArray;
VariantInit( &varArray );
V_VT( &varArray ) = VT_ARRAY | VT_I4;
V_ARRAY( &varArray) = psaArray;

// Call the method
long lResult;
pMath2->Sum( varArray, &lResult );
```

We fill out the SAFEARRAY and SAFEARRAYBOUND structures and create the array by calling SafeArrayCreate. Next, we pack the array in a variant and pass it to the appropriate method. The V_VT and V_ARRAY macros are defined in **OLEAUTO.H** and provide a shorthand technique for setting the appropriate fields of the variant. Specifically, the two macros expand to this:

```
// V_VT( &varArray ) = VT_ARRAY | VT_I4;
(&varArray)->vt = VT_ARRAY | VT_I4;

// V_ARRAY( &varArray) = psaArray;
(&varArray)->pArray = psaArray;
```

IMPLEMENTING A DISPINTERFACE

Before we examine how ATL provides support for building automation components, let's look at how we would do it in C++. In this section we'll cover the server-side implementation of both a dispinterface and a dual interface, and then we'll examine how a client might access this functionality.

Implementing IDispatch

A component that exposes its functionality through IDispatch is considered an automation component. Microsoft recommends that components expose their functionality through a dual interface, which combines both the standard IDispatch and custom

Vtable interfaces into one Vtable. A component that implements only IDispatch is providing a dispinterface, and that's what we're going to describe here.

IDL provides a special interface type for IDispatch-based interfaces. The *dispinterface* keyword identifies an interface that implements only the four IDispatch methods. The description of a dispinterfaces is different from that of a straight Vtable interface, because a dispiniterface must provide the dispatch identifier (DISPID) for each method. As an example, here's how we might declare a dispinterface that implements our IMath functionality.

```
[
    uuid( B8721602-4A3D-11d1-883A-444553540000),
    helpstring("DMath dispinterface")
]
dispinterface DMath
{
    properties:
    methods:
        [id(1)] long Add( long lOp1, long lOp2 );
        [id(2)] long Subtract( long lOp1, long lOp2 );
        [id(3)] long Multiply( long lOp1, long lOp2 );
        [id(4)] long Divide( long lOp1, long lOp2 );
}
...
coclass Math
{
    [default] dispinterface DMath;
}
```

The convention is to prefix dispinterfaces with a D instead of an I. As you can see, the declaration is very similar to those of our earlier IMath interfaces. Notice, though, that dispinterface methods don't return HRESULTs as Vtable interfaces do. The dispinterface keyword comes from Microsoft's earlier Object Description Language (ODL) implementation, which did not have the retval attribute, so return values were handled this way. Alternatively, you can describe the same interface above using IDL:

```
[
    object,
    uuid(D6F16BC1-4B83-11d1-883A-444553540000),
    helpstring("IMath Dispinterface")
]
interface IMath : IDispatch
{
    [id(1)] HRESULT Add( [in] long lOp1,
                         [in] long lOp2,
```

```
                       [out,retval] long* plResult );
   [id(2)] HRESULT Subtract( [in] long lOp1,
                             [in] long lOp2,
                             [out,retval] long* plResult);
   [id(3)] HRESULT Multiply( [in] long lOp1,
                             [in] long lOp2,
                             [out,retval] long* plResult );
   [id(4)] HRESULT Divide( [in] long lOp1,
                           [in]long lOp2,
                           [out,retval] long* plResult );
}
...
coclass Math
{
   [default] interface IMath;
}
```

This technique is preferred because IDL syntax has replaced ODL, and, as we described in Chapter 4, IDL provides several additional capabilities. You implement the dispinterface (IDispatch) just as you would any COM Vtable interface. Here's an excerpt from **MATH.H** in the Chapter6_NativeServer example.

```
class CMath : public IDispatch
{
...
public:
   // IUnknown
   STDMETHOD(QueryInterface)( REFIID, void** );
   STDMETHOD_(ULONG, AddRef());
   STDMETHOD_(ULONG, Release());

   // IDispatch
   STDMETHOD(GetTypeInfoCount)( UINT* pctinfo );
   STDMETHOD(GetTypeInfo)( UINT itinfo,
                           LCID lcid,
                           ITypeInfo** pptinfo );
   STDMETHOD(GetIDsOfNames)( REFIID riid,
                             OLECHAR** rgszNames,
                             UINT cNames,
                             LCID lcid,
                             DISPID* rgdispid );
   STDMETHOD(Invoke)( DISPID dispid,
                      REFIID riid,
```

(code continued on next page)

```
                     LCID lcid,
                     WORD wFlags,
                     DISPPARAMS FAR* pDispParams,
                     VARIANT FAR* pvarResult,
                     EXCEPINFO FAR* pExcepInfo,
                     unsigned int FAR* puArgErr );
};
```

To implement a dispinterface, you typically need to implement only the GetIDsOfNames and Invoke methods. GetTypeInfoCount and GetTypeInfo allow a client to obtain type information. Most clients, though, get type information through a component's binary type library, so there isn't much need to implement these two methods. Getting a component's type information from its type library is more efficient anyway, because the client doesn't have to instantiate the component. So for our native automation implementation, we'll implement GetIDsOfNames and Invoke. Here's a look at GetIDsOfNames for the Math component.

```
// Method tokens (DISPIDs)
const DISPID_ADD = 1;
const DISPID_SUBTRACT = 2;
const DISPID_MULTIPLY = 3;
const DISPID_DIVIDE = 4;
...
STDMETHODIMP CMath::GetIDsOfNames( REFIID riid,
                       OLECHAR** rgszNames, UINT cNames,
                       LCID lcid, DISPID* rgdispid )
{
   // We only support one name at a time
   if ( cNames > 1 )
      return( E_INVALIDARG );

   // Convert the name to ANSI
   USES_CONVERSION;
   char* szAnsi = OLE2T( rgszNames[0] );

   if ( strncmp( "Add", szAnsi, 3 ) == 0 )
      rgdispid[0] = DISPID_ADD;
   else if ( strncmp( "Subtract", szAnsi, 8 ) == 0 )
      rgdispid[0] = DISPID_SUBTRACT;
   ...
   else
      return( DISPID_UNKNOWN );

   return S_OK;
}
```

With automation, the client application doesn't necessarily have any knowledge of a component's method signatures and DISPIDs at compile time. GetIDsOfNames provides the client with a way to specify a method name at run time and have the component pass back a token identifying the code associated with the method name.

The client calls this function to get the specific DISPID for a method within our math component. We map the member name to its DISPID. The rgszNames parameter is an array of member names provided by the client. The array consists of a method or property name in the first element, followed optionally by named parameter elements.

All COM method calls use native Unicode, so we convert the Unicode string to ANSI. Then we do a simple string compare, and if we get a match, we return the respective DISPID. If we don't get a match, we return the required DISPID_UNKNOWN error. After the client obtains a DISPID, it invokes the associated code by calling IDispatch::Invoke, passing the DISPID and any parameters needed for the method. Here's our implementation:

```
STDMETHODIMP Math::Invoke( DISPID dispid,
                           REFIID riid,
                           LCID lcid,
                           WORD wFlags,
                           DISPPARAMS FAR* pDispParams,
                           VARIANT FAR* pvarResult,
                           EXCEPINFO FAR* pExcepInfo,
                           unsigned int FAR* puArgErr )
{
   // All of our methods take two parameters
   if ( !pDispParams ||
        pDispParams->cArgs != 2 )
     return( DISP_E_BADPARAMCOUNT );

   // We don't support named arguments
   if ( pDispParams->cNamedArgs > 0 )
     return( DISP_E_NONAMEDARGS );

   // Break out the parameters and coerce them
   // to the proper type
   HRESULT hr;
   VARIANT varOp1;
   VARIANT varOp2;

   // Coerce the variant into the desired type
   // In this case we would like a long
   VariantInit( &varOp1 );
   hr = VariantChangeType(  &varOp1,
                      &(pDispParams->rgvarg[1]),
                      0,
                      VT_I4 );
   // If we can't get a long, return invalid argument
```

(code continued on next page)

```
    if ( FAILED( hr ))
       return( DISP_E_TYPEMISMATCH );

    // Coerce the variant into the desired type
    // In this case we would like a long
    VariantInit( &varOp2 );
    hr = VariantChangeType( &varOp2,
                            &(pDispParams->rgvarg[0]),
                            0,
                            VT_I4 );

    // If we can't get a long, return invalidate argument
    if ( FAILED( hr ))
       return( DISP_E_TYPEMISMATCH );
// Initialize the return value
    // If there isn't one, then just return
    if ( pvarResult )
    {
       VariantInit( pvarResult );
       pvarResult->vt = VT_I4;
    }
    else
       return S_OK;

    // Now, perform the appropriate calculation
    switch( dispid )
    {
       case DISPID_ADD:
          pvarResult->lVal = varOp1.lVal + varOp2.lVal;
          return S_OK;

       case DISPID_SUBTRACT:
          pvarResult->lVal = varOp1.lVal - varOp2.lVal;
          return S_OK;

       case DISPID_MULTIPLY:
          pvarResult->lVal = varOp1.lVal * varOp2.lVal;
          return S_OK;

       case DISPID_DIVIDE:
          pvarResult->lVal = varOp1.lVal / varOp2.lVal;
          return S_OK;

       default:
          return( DISP_E_MEMBERNOTFOUND );
    }
}
```

There's quite a bit going on here, but we discussed the use of Variants as parameters earlier, so that code should look familiar. The client must fill the DISPPARAMS structure with any method parameters (stored in variants) and will supply the pvarResult parameter if a return value is expected. We check these to ensure that they match our implementation, coerce the variants into longs, and finally perform the math computation. We then package the result in the provided variant and pass it back to the client.

As you can see, the server-side support code for automation is considerable. This is because we are handling things that would normally be managed by the compiler. The added complexity of breaking out a parameter structure is part of providing the flexibility of run-time binding.

The IDispatch API Functions

To make it easier to implement a dispinterface, Microsoft provides a set of APIs that handle some of the work. These APIs generate an IDispatch interface implementation automatically, based the component's type library. The type library contains nearly all the information needed to implement an IDispatch interface. It contains the type information for GetTypeInfoCount and GetTypeInfo, contains the DISPIDs for GetIDsFromNames, and knows the structure of the parameters for each method call. The primary API functions are shown in Table 6.5.

Table 6.5 Dispatch API Functions

FUNCTION	DESCRIPTION
CreateStdDispatch	Creates an IDispatch interface based on the provided type information.
CreateDispTypeInfo	Creates type information for use when implementing a simple IDispatch interface.
LoadTypeLib	Loads a type library and returns its description through an ITypeInfo interface.
DispGetIDsOfNames	Uses type information to convert a set of names into their respective DISPIDs.
DispInvoke	Automatically calls a method on an interface based on the type information for that interface.

IMPLEMENTING A DUAL INTERFACE

We covered how to implement Vtable interfaces in most of the chapters leading to this one, and from the preceding discussion, you now understand what is required to implement a dispinterface. Implementing a dual interface is a combination of both techniques. A dual interface implements the IDispatch methods as well as any methods provided by your component's custom interface. One key, is that the functionality exposed through both techniques must be the same. In other words, you don't want to expose methods through your Vtable that aren't available through your dispinterface. Here's how we describe the IMath interface as a dual interface:

```
[
    object,
    uuid(D6F16BC1-4B83-11d1-883A-444553540000),
    dual,
    helpstring("IMath Dual Interface")
]
interface IMath : IDispatch
{
    [id(1)] HRESULT Add( [in] long lOp1,
                         [in] long lOp2,
                         [out,retval] long* plResult );

    ...

    }
```

The only difference here is the addition of the dual keyword. The dual keyword requires the implementation of the described methods as part of the Vtable interface, and that is different from the dispinterface case. The preceding declaration requires us to implement both IDispatch and the IMath interface methods. Here's a look at the header file from our Chapter6_DualServer example.

```
class CMath : public IMath
{
public:
    // IUnknown
    STDMETHOD(QueryInterface)( REFIID, void** );
    STDMETHOD_(ULONG, AddRef());
    STDMETHOD_(ULONG, Release());

    // IDispatch
    STDMETHOD(GetTypeInfoCount)( UINT* pctinfo );
    STDMETHOD(GetTypeInfo)( UINT itinfo,
                            LCID lcid,
                            ITypeInfo** pptinfo );
    STDMETHOD(GetIDsOfNames)( REFIID riid,
                            OLECHAR** rgszNames,
                            UINT cNames,
                            LCID lcid,
                            DISPID* rgdispid );
    STDMETHOD(Invoke)( DISPID dispid,
                       REFIID riid,
                       LCID lcid,
                       WORD wFlags,
```

```
                    DISPPARAMS FAR* pDispParams,
                    VARIANT FAR* pvarResult,
                    EXCEPINFO FAR* pExcepInfo,
                    unsigned int FAR* puArgErr );

// IMath
STDMETHOD(Add)( long, long, long* );
STDMETHOD(Subtract)( long, long, long* );
STDMETHOD(Multiply)( long, long, long* );
STDMETHOD(Divide)( long, long, long* );

};
```

> **NOTE** This chapter uses code from three difference examples. Chapter6_NativeServer demonstrates implementing a dispinterface in straight C++, Chapter6_DualServer demonstrates implementing a dual interface in straight C++, and Chapter6_Server, which uses ATL, is shown at the end of the chapter. Only the Chapter6_Server example uses ATL. All of these examples are included in the downloadable package at www.widgetware.com.

The implementation of the preceding is the same as what we've already covered. However, the CMath class has only one Vtable with 11 functions. It's a dual interface with both IDispatch and IMath implementations in the same interface (IMath).

The client now has the flexibility of querying for the dispinterface (IDispatch) or the Vtable (IMath) interface to access our functionality. The implementation of QueryInterface is interesting:

```
STDMETHODIMP CMath::QueryInterface( REFIID riid, void** ppv )
{
    *ppv = NULL;

    if ( riid == IID_IUnknown  ||
         riid == IID_IDispatch ||
         riid == IID_IMath )
      *ppv = this;
    if ( *ppv )
    {
       ((IUnknown*)*ppv)->AddRef();
       return( S_OK );
    }
    return E_NOINTERFACE;
}
```

The one Vtable handles a request for any of our component's three implemented interfaces. This works because they are all lined up in the same Vtable. This will become clear when we cover the client side in the next section. The complete source for this example is provided in the Chapter6_DualServer project. It demonstrates implementing a dual interface using straight C++.

ACCESSING AN IDISPATCH-BASED INTERFACE

A client of either a dispinterface or a dual interface has several options on how it might bind to an automation component's functionality. If the component implements only a dispinterface and does not provide a type library, late binding is the only option. If the component implements a dispinterface and provides a type library, a component can choose late binding or something called ID binding. If the component implements a dual interface and provides a type library (which is basically a requirement with a dual), the client can choose between late binding, ID binding, and early binding. Each option has its strengths and weaknesses.

Late Binding (Dynamic Binding)

Late binding is one of the more powerful features of automation. It allows a client application to determine a component's functionality at run time. The method names and parameter types are not checked during the client development process. Instead, the functionality is queried for and called at run time. In other words, the client application will query for the DISPID of the method and will then populate the DISPPARAMS structure and call Invoke through the IDispatch interface. This is the most expensive technique and provides no compile-time type checking. All type checking is performed at run time by the server as the method is called. If an incorrect type is passed, a run-time error results.

Because of the run-time aspect of this technique, it is also the slowest technique. However, it is the most flexible. If the server interface changes, the client will not have to be recompiled to take advantage of these changes. The following code demonstrates the use of late binding in Visual Basic.

```
Dim objMath as Object
Dim nResult as Integer

Set objMath = CreateObject( "Chapter6.Math" )
nResult = objMath.Add( 100, 55 )
Set objMath = Nothing
```

We discussed this earlier in the chapter. Following is complete C++ that performs exactly as the preceding Visual Basic code.

```
IDispatch* pDispatch;
HRESULT hr = CoCreateInstance( CLSID_Math,
                    NULL,
                    CLSCTX_SERVER,
```

```
                              IID_IDispatch,
                              (void**) &pDispatch );
if ( FAILED( hr ))
{ ... }

// Get the DISPID
LPOLESTR lpOleStr = L"Add";
DISPID dispid;
hr = pDispatch->GetIDsOfNames( IID_NULL,
                      &lpOleStr,
                      1,
                      LOCALE_SYSTEM_DEFAULT,
                      &dispid );
if (FAILED( hr ))
{ ... }

// Call the Add method after setting up the parameters
DISPPARAMS dispparms;
memset( &dispparms, 0, sizeof( DISPPARAMS ));
dispparms.cArgs = 2;

// allocate memory for parameters
VARIANTARG* pArg = new VARIANTARG[dispparms.cArgs];
dispparms.rgvarg = pArg;
memset(pArg, 0, sizeof(VARIANT) * dispparms.cArgs);

// The parameters are entered right to left
dispparms.rgvarg[0].vt = VT_I4;
dispparms.rgvarg[0].lVal = 55;
dispparms.rgvarg[1].vt = VT_I4;
dispparms.rgvarg[1].lVal = 100;

// This method returns a value so we need a VARIANT to store it in
VARIANTARG vaResult;
VariantInit( &vaResult );

hr = pDispatch->Invoke( dispid,
                IID_NULL,
                LOCALE_SYSTEM_DEFAULT,
                DISPATCH_METHOD,
                &dispparms,
                &vaResult,
                0, NULL );

pDispatch->Release();
```

That's a lot of code to add two numbers, but there are no header files involved in the preceding implementation, except for those that are part of the development environment (such as **WINDOWS.H**).

To understand all of what's going on, we need to discuss the automation DISPPARAMS structure. DISPPARAMS is used to pass parameters to the method call. Here's its declaration:

```
typedef struct tagDISPPARAMS
{
    // An array of variants containing the arguments
    VARIANTARG *rgvarg;

    // An array of DISPIDs for named arguments
    DISPID  *rgdispidNamedArgs;

    // The number of arguments in the rgvarg array
    UINT cArgs;

    // The number of DISPIDs in the rgdispidNamedArgs array
    UINT cNamedArgs;
} DISPPARAMS;
```

In the preceding code, we first allocate space for two variants; we then set the cArgs count to 2 and fill the variant parameters. An important point is that the array holds the parameters in right to left order.

ID Binding (Early Binding)

In our example above, the client must call IDispatch::GetIDsOfNames before invoking our component's Add method. No type checking is performed, because the client has not used the component's type information. A second binding technique, called ID binding, provides increased performance and the benefit of compile-time type checking.

The Visual Basic **References** option will add a type library to your project. You can then treat the imported type as a native Visual Basic type. As your project is compiled, Visual Basic will check the syntax and parameter types against your component's type information. Also, Visual Basic will cache the DISPIDs for each method and property. This removes the run-time requirement to query for each member DISPID. One of the drawbacks of this approach is that a recompile is necessary if the interface to a component changes. Here's code that demonstrates ID binding.

```
Dim objMath as New Chapter6_Server.Math
Dim nResult as Integer
nResult = objMath.Add( 100, 55 )
```

In this case the component implements only a dispinterface. However, because it provides a type library, Visual Basic can load the DISPIDs and cache them as part of the build process. Visual Basic can also ensure that we are providing the correct number and types of parameters when calling the component's methods.

To demonstrate the C++ code that implements ID binding, we need to look at how MFC supports `IDispatch`. When you use ClassWizard's **Add Class.../From TypeLib** option, it produces a wrapper class for an automation component. This wrapper class provides ID binding, because it hard-codes the DISPID in the source. Compile-time type checking is supported, because the methods of the wrapper class mirror those described in the type library. Only the `Invoke` method is needed to access a component's functionality. Here's a peek at an MFC wrapper class method for the `Math` component:

```
//
// IMath wrapper class
//
class IOMath : public COleDispatchDriver
{
public:
    IOMath() {}
    IOMath( IDispatch* pDisp );

public:
    long Add( long lOp1, lOp2 );
    long Subtract( long lOp1, lOp2 );
    long Multiply( long lOp1, lOp2 );
    long Divide( long lOp1, lOp2 );
};
...
long IOMath::Add( long lOp1, lOp2 )
{
    static BYTE parms[] = VTS_I4 VTS_I4;
    long result;

    // The DISPID is hard-coded here in the Invoke method
    InvokeHelper( 0x1, DISPATCH_METHOD,
                  VT_I4, &result, parms,
                  lOp1, lOp2 );
    return result;
}
```

ATL also provides a wrapper generator called the ATL Proxy Generator. We'll cover it in Chapter 7.

N O T E

For more details on MFC's automation support, see my previous book: Designing and Using ActiveX Controls (M&T Books, 1997).

Early Binding Requirements

Early binding requires that a component provide type information and implement a dual interface. It is the most efficient binding technique and is also the least flexible. As always, there is a trade-off. Early binding provides type checking, because the client can use the type information to verify parameters and return types at compile time. The important thing, though, is that method binding works directly through the Vtable so there are no DISPIDs or calls to GetIDsOfNames or Invoke. The Visual Basic code for early binding is the same as for ID binding.

```
Dim objMath as New Chapter6_Server.Math
Dim nResult as Integer
nResult = objMath.Add( 100, 55 )
```

The difference is that the component supports a dual interface and so Visual Basic will Query for IID_IMath instead of IID_IDispatch and will use Vtable calls instead of IDispatch::Invoke. This is demonstrated in our C++ example:

```
// Create an instance of the math component
// and QI for IID_IMath
IMath* pMath;
HRESULT hr = CoCreateInstance( CLSID_ATLMath,
                    NULL,
                    CLSCTX_SERVER,
                    IID_IMath,
                    (void**) &pMath );

// Direct Vtable access to the method
long lResult;
pMath->Multiply( 9, 99, &lResult );
cout << "9 * 99 = " << lResult << endl;

pMath->Release();
```

This is the standard Vtable code that we've been using all along. The trick is that the client can choose whatever type of binding it requires.

ATL'S SUPPORT FOR AUTOMATION

ATL provides most if its automation support in terms of building components that implement an IDispatch. Built-in support for the client side in ATL is minimal. This follows from the design of ATL as a framework for building efficient components.

When building an ATL project, you have two options on the **Attributes** tab. You can choose to implement either a custom or a dual interface. As we've described, a dual interface adds IDispatch support to your Vtable implementation. Figure 6.3 shows the Object wizard's **Attributes** tab.

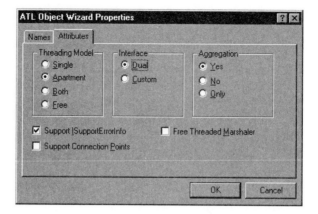

Figure 6.3 The **Attributes** tab.

IDispatchImpl

When you choose the default dual option, your component implementation includes the
IDispatchImpl class in its derivation hierarchy. The following code is from our chapter
example that implements the math component using ATL's dual interface support.

```
class ATL_NO_VTABLE CMath :
      public CComObjectRootEx<CComSingleThreadModel>,
      public CComCoClass<CMath, &CLSID_Math>,
      public IDispatchImpl<IMath, &IID_IMath, &LIBID_CHAPTER6_SERVERLib>
{
...
};
```

The IDispatchImpl template takes three parameters: the custom interface that describes
the Vtable interface of the dual, the interface IID of the custom interface, and the GUID of
the component's type library. When the template expands we get this:

```
class ATL_NO_VTABLE IDispatchImpl : public IMath
{
public:
   ...
   STDMETHOD(GetTypeInfoCount)(UINT* pctinfo)
   {
      *pctinfo = 1;
      return S_OK;
   }
```

(code continued on next page)

```
    STDMETHOD(GetTypeInfo)(UINT itinfo, LCID lcid, ITypeInfo** pptinfo)
    {
        return _tih.GetTypeInfo(itinfo, lcid, pptinfo);
    }

    STDMETHOD(GetIDsOfNames)(REFIID riid,
                LPOLESTR* rgszNames, UINT cNames,
                LCID lcid, DISPID* rgdispid)
    {
        return _tih.GetIDsOfNames(riid, rgszNames,
                                  cNames, lcid, rgdispid);
    }

    STDMETHOD(Invoke)(DISPID dispidMember, REFIID riid,
                      LCID lcid, WORD wFlags,
                      DISPPARAMS* pdispparams,
                      VARIANT* pvarResult,
                      EXCEPINFO* pexcepinfo,
                      UINT* puArgErr)
    {
        return _tih.Invoke((IDispatch*)this, dispidMember, riid, lcid,
                           wFlags, pdispparams,
                           pvarResult, pexcepinfo, puArgErr);
    }
protected:
    static CComTypeInfoHolder _tih;
    static HRESULT GetTI(LCID lcid, ITypeInfo** ppInfo)
    {
        return _tih.GetTI(lcid, ppInfo);
    }
};
```

ATL's IDispatchImpl implementation gets most of its functionality through the contained, static instance of CComTypeInfoHolder (_tih). The CComTypeInfoHolder instance wraps the component's type library via the ITypeInfo interface.

CComTypeInfoHolder

CComTypeInfoHolder is used by ATL to maintain an interface pointer to the type information for a component. As I mentioned earlier, COM provides APIs to make it easier to implement an IDispatch interface. These APIs, along with the ITypeInfo interface, enable a component to provide a default IDispatch implementation with only a little code. In other words, the component doesn't have to explicitly implement the standard IDispatch methods (such as Invoke).

The ITypeInfo interface provides a number of methods, many of which are used to extract information about an associated component interface. Through the various ITypeInfo methods, you can determine the following:

- The set of member functions (methods and properties) implemented by the described interface.

- Various data type descriptions, including enumerated types used in the interface's methods.

- The general attributes of the types described, including structures, interfaces, and enumerators.

There are two general uses of the ITypeInfo interface. Object browsers and development tools use the interface to obtain method and property names and method parameters in order to display them or use them as part of the compile process. Also, a component can use the ITypeInfo interface to provide an implementation of IDispatch, and this is precisely what ATL does.

The CComTypeInfoHolder maintains an ITypeInfo interface pointer and provides IDispatch support for any associated class. In our case, this is IDispatchImpl. IDispatchImpl delegates all the implementation details of IDispatch to that provided by the system through ITypeInfo. Table 6.6 describes some of the methods of ITypeInfo that CComTypeInfoHolder uses in its implementation.

Table 6.6 ITypeInfo Methods

FUNCTION	DESCRIPTION
GetIDsOfNames	Maps a member function to a specific DISPID. It's easy for ITypeInfo to implement this method, because it knows the DISPIDs of the interface.
Invoke	Invokes a method, or accesses a property of an object, that implements the interface described by the type description. This method has one more parameter than IDispatch::Invoke, which is the actual instance on which to invoke the method.

The implementation of CComTypeInfoHolder is provided primarily by the operating system through ITypeInfo. Initially, on first access, the GetTI method is used to load the type library of the component. Here's a condensed look at the CComTypeInfoHolder::GetTI method:

```
HRESULT CComTypeInfoHolder::GetTI(LCID lcid, ITypeInfo** ppInfo)
{
    *ppInfo = NULL;

    HRESULT hRes;
    if ( m_pInfo == NULL )
    {
        ITypeLib* pTypeLib;
        hRes = LoadRegTypeLib(*m_plibid, m_wMajor, m_wMinor, lcid, &pTypeLib);
        if (SUCCEEDED(hRes))
        {
            ITypeInfo* pTypeInfo;
            hRes = pTypeLib->GetTypeInfoOfGuid(*m_pguid, &pTypeInfo);
            if (SUCCEEDED(hRes))
                m_pInfo = pTypeInfo;
            pTypeLib->Release();
        }
    }
    *ppInfo = m_pInfo;
}
```

The `LoadRegTypeLib` function loads a component's type library based on the TypeLib registry entry. The library is located using the provided GUID. Once the library is loaded, ATL uses the `ITypeLib::GetTypeInfoOfGuid` method to retrieve the `ITypeInfo` interface for our dual interface (`IMath`) and then stores it in the `m_pInfo` member.

The actual implementation of the `IDispatch` methods is finally provided by COM through the `ITypeInfo` interface. Here's an example of the `GetIDsOfNames` method:

```
HRESULT CComTypeInfoHolder::GetIDsOfNames(REFIID riid,
                                          LPOLESTR* rgszNames,
                                          UINT cNames,
                                          LCID lcid,
                                          DISPID* rgdispid)
{
    ITypeInfo* pInfo;
    HRESULT hRes = GetTI(lcid, &pInfo);
    if (pInfo != NULL)
    {
        hRes = pInfo->GetIDsOfNames(rgszNames, cNames, rgdispid);
        pInfo->Release();
    }
    return hRes;
}
```

IDispatchImpl defers to CComTypeInfoHolder, and CComTypeInfoHolder defers to the system-provided ITypeInfo implementation. ITypeInfo builds the IDispatch implementation based on the information provided in the component's type library.

CComVariant

ATL provides a thin wrapper class for automation's VARIANT structure. CComVariant has just a handful of methods, most of which map directly to the underlying variant API calls. The Chapter6_Server example uses CComVariant. Here's an excerpt.

```
CComVariant varOne( varOp1 );

// Coerce the variant into the desired type
HRESULT hr = varOne.ChangeType( VT_I4 );
if ( FAILED( hr ))
    return( DISP_E_TYPEMISMATCH );
```

The CComVariant class members map closely to the variant APIs. The major members are described in Table 6.7.

Table 6.7 CComVariant Methods

METHOD/OPERATOR	DESCRIPTION
CComVariant(...)	Overloaded constructors are provided for most automation types.
ChangeType	Implements VariantChangeType.
Clear	Implements VariantClear.
Copy	Implements VariantCopy.
ReadFromStream, WriteToStream	Loads or saves a variant to a stream.
=	The equal operator is overloaded for most automation types.
==	Variant comparison.

The Visual C++ native COM support also provides the _variant_t type. See Appendix A for details.

N O T E

AUTOMATION AND INTERFACE VERSIONING

Automation is a useful COM technology and is used heavily in today's Windows development environments. However, straight dispinterfaces are slow because of the requirements of late binding. Dispinterfaces also require significantly more code within the client, again because of the requirements of late binding. Dual interfaces solve these problems by allowing a client to bind either early (to a Vtable) or late (via IDispatch), with the only drawback that the interface methods must use automation types.

Another drawback to automation is that it doesn't necessarily support COM's robust versioning. One of the most useful features of COM is the fact that you can easily add new functionality (for example, IMath2) to a component without breaking any existing clients. Robust versioning is handled through COM's support for multiple interfaces per component instance, and using IDispatch can sometimes make it more difficult to support multiple interfaces per component, at least when the various development tools (such as Visual C++, Visual Basic, and Visual J++) are factored in.

The next few sections describe versioning with dispinterfaces and dual interfaces and discuss it in the context of adding an IMath2 interface to our Math component. We did this in Chapter 4, but this time we'll discuss how dispinterfaces and duals affect the implementation.

Versioning IDispatch

If your component exposes only a dispinterface, then versioning is pretty easy to handle. When using a dispinterface, you can "upgrade" an interface by adding new members to the end of your dispatch map. Because each interface method is identified by a DISPID, you can add a new method by using a new DISPID. This technique of versioning does not break any existing client as long as you don't reorder the DISPIDs of the old methods. I've used this technique extensively when building automation servers with MFC.

The better technique for exposing a component's functionality is through a dual interface. By using duals we get both late and early binding flexibility, and, if the tool supports it, we can use the technique of multiple interfaces per component to handle versioning.

NOTE

As we described earlier, Visual Basic's CreateObject keyword creates an instance of a component and returns its IDispatch interface. However, a component can have only one default IDispatch, and this is the one Visual Basic uses. Visual Basic likes to view a component as having only one interface: its IDispatch identified by IID_IDispatch. Each dispinterface, though, has its own interface identifier (IID), so the QueryInterface implementation "decides" which dispinterface is the one that Visual Basic will use. So with automation components you must expose the majority of your component's functionality on one dispinterface, and that one of the most important COM design rules: Keep your interfaces discrete.

Versioning Duals

The addition of new DISPIDs works for a dispinterface, but when you introduce the concept of a dual, this technique no longer works. Dual interfaces expose both an IDispatch and a custom interface. By definition, custom interfaces are immutable, and in order to add members you must declare a new interface. So we can't just add a new DISPID to the IDispatch, because we can't do the same with its associated custom interface.

The solution to this problem is to implement multiple dual interfaces when you need to update an existing dual. For example, here's how we would use IDL to declare two dual interfaces in a component:

```
[
    object,
    uuid(DCA4F88E-4952-11D1-883A-444553540000),
    dual, helpstring("IMath Interface"),
    pointer_default(unique)
]
interface IMath : IDispatch
{
    [id(1), helpstring("method Add")]
            HRESULT Add([in] VARIANT varOp1,
                        [in] VARIANT varOp2,
                        [out,retval] VARIANT* pvarResult);
    // The rest of our IMath methods
    ...
};
[
    object,
    uuid(9F21BD41-4E25-11d1-883A-444553540000),
    dual, helpstring("IMath2 Interface"),
    pointer_default(unique)
]
interface IMath2 : IDispatch
{
    // Our IMath methods here
    ...
    // And our new method (Sum)
    [id(5), helpstring("method Sum")]
```

(code continued on next page)

```
        HRESULT Sum([in] VARIANT varOp1,
                    [out, retval] long* plResult);
};
...
library CHAPTER6_SERVERLib
{
    importlib("stdole32.tlb");
    importlib("stdole2.tlb");
    [
        uuid(DCA4F88F-4952-11D1-883A-444553540000),
        helpstring("Math Class")
    ]
        coclass Math
        {
                [default] interface IMath;
                interface IMath2;
        };
};
```

Visual Basic uses the coclass name to indicate the default interface within a component. You can add an underscore to your coclass name, and Visual Basic will show (in its Object Viewer) the default interface name instead, but this requires you to change all your ATL code that uses the coclass name when building symbols (for example, CLSID_Math). Still, this technique gives Visual Basic a cleaner view of your component's interfaces.

The MIDL compiler will generate two interface classes. To use them within an ATL implementation class, we use the IDispatchImpl class twice in our derivation:

```
class ATL_NO_VTABLE CMath :
    public CComObjectRootEx<CComSingleThreadModel>,
    public CComCoClass<CMath, &CLSID_Math>,
    public ISupportErrorInfo,
    public IDispatchImpl<IMath, &IID_IMath, &LIBID_CHAPTER6_SERVERLib>,
    public IDispatchImpl<IMath2, &IID_IMath2, &LIBID_CHAPTER6_SERVERLib>
{
...
};
```

We now have two interfaces that implement IDispatch, and we must decide which IDispatch should be exposed through QueryInterface. This is because many development tools query explicitly for IID_IDispatch instead of the IID of the dual.

When you're developing a component that has just one dual interface (such as IMath), its COM map looks like this:

```
BEGIN_COM_MAP(CMath)
    COM_INTERFACE_ENTRY(IMath)
    COM_INTERFACE_ENTRY(IDispatch)
    COM_INTERFACE_ENTRY(ISupportErrorInfo)
END_COM_MAP()
```

Even though our component has just one dual interface (IMath), we expose both IMath and IDispatch through ATL's QueryInterface implementation. Remember that our QueryInterface is special for a dual. It checks for both of the "interfaces" in the dual and returns either IDispatch or IMath through the same Vtalbe.

ATL uses the COM_MAP macros to specify which dual will provide the default interface for any queries for IID_IDispatch. The preceding macros work fine if there is only one dual in a component, but for multiple duals the implementer must decide which of many interfaces will provide the default IDispatch. ATL uses the COM_INTERFACE_ENTRY2 macro for this.

```
COM_INTERFACE_ENTRY2(IDispatch, IMath)
```

The COM_INTERFACE_ENTRY2 macro disambiguates multiple levels of inheritance. Instead of supplying only the interface that you want to expose, you must also supply the class through which to obtain the interface. For example, you can use the macro this way:

```
BEGIN_COM_MAP(CMath)
    COM_INTERFACE_ENTRY(IMath)
    COM_INTERFACE_ENTRY2(IDispatch, IMath)
    COM_INTERFACE_ENTRY(IAdvancedMath)
    COM_INTERFACE_ENTRY(ISupportErrorInfo)
END_COM_MAP()
```

We are specifying that ATL should return the IMath interface implementation when a client queries for IID_IDispatch. If instead we want to make the IAdvancedMath dual the default return from QI(IID_IDispatch) we would instead do this:

```
BEGIN_COM_MAP(CMath)
   COM_INTERFACE_ENTRY(IMath)
   COM_INTERFACE_ENTRY(IAdvancedMath)
   COM_INTERFACE_ENTRY2(IDispatch, IAdvancedMath)
   COM_INTERFACE_ENTRY(ISupportErrorInfo)
END_COM_MAP()
```

The ENTRY2 macro makes it easy to implement components that have multiple dual interfaces.

NOTE   Using multiple dual interfaces to solve the versioning problem works in nearly all cases. However, with Visual Basic (version 5.0), we still have one problem. Visual Basic doesn't support the concept of multiple dispinterfaces on one component, at least when using its late binding (for example, CreateObject) features. When using CreateObject, Visual Basic queries for IID_IDispatch, and there can only be only one default IDispatch interface on an object. You then must create an instance using its default interface and then use the SET keyword to query for the newer interface. Visual Basic works great if you bind early (to any of the component's multiple duals) using its type library.

THE MATH COMPONENT USING AUTOMATION

In this example we implement our math component using automation via a dual interface. We also demonstrate how to add an additional dual to support our IAdvancedMath functionality. The example, Chapter6_Server, contains three duals (IMath, IMath2, and IAdvancedMath), but we focus on the implementation of IMath and IAdvancedMath here. We've already discussed most of the implementation of IMath2; it demonstrates the use of a safe array.

Create the Math Component

Start Visual C++ and create a new project, selecting **ATL COM AppWizard.** Give it the name Chapter6_Server. In Step 1 of 1, select a type of DLL. Then select **Finish** and **OK** to generate the project. Using the ATL Object wizard, insert a **Simple Component** with the following options.

- Use a **Short Name** of **Math.**
- Make sure the interface name is **IMath.**
- Change the ProgID to **Chapter6.Math.**
- On the **Attributes** tab, enable the **Support ISupportErrorInfo** option and make sure that the **Dual** interface option is selected. This is shown in Figure 6.4.

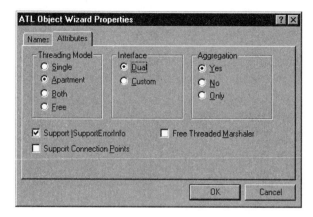

Figure 6.4 Math attributes

Implement the `IMath` Interface

Using the **Add Method** option by right-clicking on the ClassView, add the four methods from our previous `IMath` interface. This time, though, be sure to enter the parameter types as variants. We're using variants in this example to demonstrate how they are used. The implementation is shown as follows:

```
//
// Math.cpp : Implementation of CMath
//
#include "stdafx.h"
#include "Chapter6_Server.h"
#include "Math.h"

/////////////////
// CMath
/////////////////
...
STDMETHODIMP CMath::Add(VARIANT varOp1, VARIANT varOp2, VARIANT *pvarResult)
{
    // Coerce the variant into the desired type
    // In this case we would like a long
    HRESULT hr = VariantChangeType( &varOp1,
                     &varOp1,
                     0,
```

(code continued on next page)

```
                            VT_I4 );
   // If we can't get a long, return invalidate argument
   if ( FAILED( hr ))
      return( DISP_E_TYPEMISMATCH );

   // Coerce the variant into the desired type
   // In this case we would like a long
   hr = VariantChangeType( &varOp2,
                           &varOp2,
                           0,
                           VT_I4 );

   // If we can't get a long, return invalidate argument
   if ( FAILED( hr ))
      return( DISP_E_TYPEMISMATCH );

   // Initialize the return value
   // If there isn't one, then just return
   if ( pvarResult )
   {
      VariantInit( pvarResult );
      pvarResult->vt = VT_I4;
      pvarResult->lVal = varOp1.lVal + varOp2.lVal;
   }

      return S_OK;
}

STDMETHODIMP CMath::Subtract(VARIANT varOp1, VARIANT varOp2, VARIANT *
pvarResult)
{
   CComVariant varOne( varOp1 );
   CComVariant varTwo( varOp2 );

   // Coerce the variant into the desired type
   HRESULT hr = varOne.ChangeType( VT_I4 );
   if ( FAILED( hr ))
      return( DISP_E_TYPEMISMATCH );

   // Coerce the variant into the desired type
   // In this case we would like a long
   hr = varTwo.ChangeType( VT_I4 );
   if ( FAILED( hr ))
      return( DISP_E_TYPEMISMATCH );

   // Initialize the return value
   // If there isn't one, then just return
   if ( pvarResult )
```

```
    {
        VariantInit( pvarResult );
        pvarResult->vt = VT_I4;
        pvarResult->lVal = varOne.lVal - varTwo.lVal;
    }

    return S_OK;
}
```

The implementation is different from what we've done before, because we're using variant parameters. I've shown the implementations only for Add and Subtract. Add uses the variant APIs, and Subtract uses ATL's CComVariant class instead. The implementations of Multiply and Divide are similar.

Set the IDL Attributes

Unless you included the method attributes when adding your method parameters with ClassView, the default IDL attributes may not be correct for our component's methods. If necessary, modify the **Chapter6_Server.IDL** file to include the appropriate in/out/retval attributes.

```
//
// Chapter6_Server.idl : IDL source for Chapter6_Server.dll
//
...
[id(1), helpstring("method Add")] HRESULT
        Add( [in] VARIANT lOp1, [in] VARIANT lOp2,
             [out, retval] VARIANT* plResult);
[id(2), helpstring("method Subtract")] HRESULT
        Subtract( [in] VARIANT lOp1, [in] VARIANT lOp2,
                  [out, retval] VARIANT* plResult);
[id(3), helpstring("method Multiply")] HRESULT
        Multiply( [in] VARIANT lOp1, [in] VARIANT lOp2,
                  [out, retval] VARIANT* plResult);
[id(4), helpstring("method Divide")] HRESULT
        Divide([in] VARIANT lOp1, [in] VARIANT lOp2,
               [out, retval] VARIANT* plResult);
```

Build the Project

That's it. Now build the Chapter6_Server project. We've just finished building an ATL-based, automation-compatible version of the Math component. As you can see, there isn't any additional work when implementing a dual with ATL.

Adding a Second `IDispatch` Interface

But what about our `IAdvancedMath` interface? Components can expose more than one `IDispatch`-based interface, but some automation-capable tools (such as Visual Basic) cannot take advantage of this. To demonstrate a component that contains multiple `IDispatch`-based interfaces, let's add another one to our component. The Visual C++ IDE doesn't have a quick way of adding interfaces to components, so we'll have to do it ourselves. Here's the code for **CHAPTER6_SERVER.IDL**:

```
// Chapter6_Server.idl : IDL source for Chapter6_Server.dll
//

// This file will be processed by the MIDL tool to
// produce the type library (Chapter6_Server.tlb) and marshaling code.

import "oaidl.idl";
import "ocidl.idl";

...
[
    object,
    uuid(4B58EB8D-0B21-11D1-883A-444553540000),
    dual,
    helpstring("IAdvancedMath Interface"),
    pointer_default(unique)
]
interface IAdvancedMath : IDispatch
{
    [id(1), helpstring("method Factorial")] HRESULT
            Factorial( [in] short sOp, [out, retval] long* plResult);
    [id(2), helpstring("method Fibonacci")] HRESULT
          Fibonacci( [in] short sOp, [out, retval] long* plResult);
};

...
library CHAPTER6_SERVERLib
{
...
coclass Math
{
    [default] interface IMath;
    interface IAdvancedMath;
};
```

We also must add the declarations and definitions for our methods to **MATH.H** and **MATH.CPP**.

```
// Math.h : Declaration of the CMath

#ifndef __MATH_H_
#define __MATH_H_

#include "resource.h"        // main symbols
...

///////////////// -
// CMath
/////////////////
class ATL_NO_VTABLE CMath :
        public CComObjectRootEx<CComSingleThreadModel>,
        public CComCoClass<CMath, &CLSID_Math>,
        public ISupportErrorInfo,
        public IDispatchImpl<IMath, &IID_IMath, &LIBID_CHAPTER6_SERVERLib>,
        public IDispatchImpl<IAdvancedMath, &IID_IAdvancedMath,
                             &LIBID_CHAPTER6_SERVERLib>
{
...
BEGIN_COM_MAP(CMath)
   COM_INTERFACE_ENTRY(IMath)
   COM_INTERFACE_ENTRY2(IDispatch, IMath)
   COM_INTERFACE_ENTRY(IAdvancedMath)
   COM_INTERFACE_ENTRY(ISupportErrorInfo)
END_COM_MAP()

public:
   STDMETHOD(Factorial)( short sOp, long* plResult);
   STDMETHOD(Fibonacci)( short sOp, long* plResult);
};
```

As described earlier, because our class derives from two IDispatchImpl classes we must use the COM_INTERFACE_ENTRY2 macro. The interface specified in the second parameter becomes the interface returned when a client queries for IDispatch. Finally, here's the implementation of the methods. You've now seen this several times.

```
// IAdvancedMath interface
long calcFactorial( short n )
{
   if ( n > 1 )
      return n * calcFactorial( n - 1 );
   else
      return 1;
}
```

(code continued on next page)

```
STDMETHODIMP CMath::Factorial( short sOp, long* plResult )
{
   *plResult = calcFactorial( sOp );
   return S_OK;
}

long calcFibonacci( short n )
{
   if ( n <= 1 )
      return 1;

   return calcFibonacci( n - 1 ) + calcFibonacci( n - 2 );
}

STDMETHODIMP CMath::Fibonacci( short sOp, long* plResult )
{
   *plResult = calcFibonacci( sOp );
   return S_OK;
}
```

Build the Project

When you're finished, build the project. We now have a Math component that implements two dual interfaces.

A Third Dual Interface

The Chapter6_Server example actually implements three dual interfaces. The third is IMath2, which includes the Sum method to demonstrate how to work with safe arrays. By now, you should be able to add this new interface with the Sum method implementation. Here's a hint:

```
STDMETHODIMP CMath::Sum(VARIANT varOp1, long * plResult)
{
   if (! (varOp1.vt & VT_I4 ))
      return DISP_E_TYPEMISMATCH;

   if (! (varOp1.vt & VT_ARRAY ))
      return DISP_E_TYPEMISMATCH;

   SAFEARRAY* psa;
   if ( varOp1.vt & VT_BYREF )
      psa = *(varOp1.pparray);
   else
      psa = varOp1.parray;

   // Sum the elements of the array
   long lLBound, lUBound;
   SafeArrayGetLBound( psa,
```

```
                              1, &lLBound );
    SafeArrayGetUBound( psa,
                              1, &lUBound );

    long lSum = 0;
    for( long i = lLBound; i <= lUBound; i++ )
    {
        long lValue;
        SafeArrayGetElement( psa,
                              &i, &lValue );

        lSum += lValue;
    }

    *plResult = lSum;

    return S_OK;
}
```

Both of our dual clients will access this method to demonstrate client-side work with safe arrays.

A C++ Dual Interface Client

Our client application is again a simple Win32 console application. Using AppWizard, create a **Win32 Console Application** and name it **Chapter6_Client**. Next, create a file called **CHAPTER6_CLIENT.CPP** and add the following code.

```
//
// Chapter6_Client.cpp
//

#include <windows.h>
#include <tchar.h>
#include <iostream.h>

#include <initguid.h>
#include "..\Chapter6_Server\Chapter6_Server_i.c"
#include "..\Chapter6_Server\Chapter6_Server.h"

// For ATL's variant support
#include <atlbase.h>
#include <atlimpl.cpp>

int main( int argc, char *argv[] )
{
    cout << "Initializing COM" << endl;
```

(code continued on next page)

```
if ( FAILED( CoInitialize( NULL )))
{
   cout << "Unable to initialize COM" << endl;
   return -1;
}

// Create the math component and return IUnknown
IUnknown* pUnk;
HRESULT hr = CoCreateInstance( CLSID_Math,
                     NULL,
                     CLSCTX_SERVER,
                     IID_IUnknown,
                     (void**) &pUnk );
if ( FAILED( hr ))
{
   cout.setf( ios::hex, ios::basefield );
   cout << "Failed to create server instance. HR = " << hr << endl;
   CoUninitialize();
   return -1;
}

cout << "Instance created" << endl;

// Here we demonstrate accessing a
// dispinterface by first querying for
// IDispatch (which returns the default)
// and then using GetIDsOfNames and Invoke
// to actually call the Add method
IDispatch* pDispatch;
hr = pUnk->QueryInterface( IID_IDispatch,
                           (void**) &pDispatch );
pUnk->Release();
if ( FAILED( hr ))
{
   cout.setf( ios::hex, ios::basefield );
   cout << "Failed to create server instance. HR = " << hr << endl;
   CoUninitialize();
   return -1;
}
// Get the DISPID
LPOLESTR lpOleStr = L"Add";
DISPID dispid;
hr = pDispatch->GetIDsOfNames( IID_NULL,
                     &lpOleStr,
                     1,
                     LOCALE_SYSTEM_DEFAULT,
                     &dispid );
```

```cpp
if (FAILED( hr ))
{
   cout.setf( ios::hex, ios::basefield );
   cout << "GetIDsOfNames failed. HR = " << hr << endl;
   CoUninitialize();
   return -1;
}

// Set up the parameters
DISPPARAMS dispparms;
memset( &dispparms, 0, sizeof( DISPPARAMS ));
dispparms.cArgs = 2;

// allocate memory for parameters
VARIANTARG* pArg = new VARIANTARG[dispparms.cArgs];
dispparms.rgvarg = pArg;
memset(pArg, 0, sizeof(VARIANT) * dispparms.cArgs);

// The parameters are entered right to left
// We are adding 123 to 456
dispparms.rgvarg[0].vt = VT_I4;
dispparms.rgvarg[0].lVal = 123;
dispparms.rgvarg[1].vt = VT_I4;
dispparms.rgvarg[1].lVal = 456;

// This method returns a value so we need a VARIANT to store it in
VARIANTARG vaResult;
VariantInit( &vaResult );

// Invoke the method in the local server
hr = pDispatch->Invoke( dispid,
                  IID_NULL,
                  LOCALE_SYSTEM_DEFAULT,
                  DISPATCH_METHOD,
                  &dispparms,
                  &vaResult,
                  0,
                  NULL );

// Free up our our variantargs
delete [] pArg;

if ( FAILED( hr ))
{
   cout.setf( ios::hex, ios::basefield );
   cout << "Unable to Invoke SetExpression. HR = " << hr << endl;
   CoUninitialize();
```

(code continued on next page)

```
      return -1;
   }

   // Display the result
   cout << "123 + 456 = " << vaResult.lVal << endl;

   // Next, we demonstrate using the IMath
   // dual interface. First QI then access
   // the methods through the Vtable interface
   IMath* pMath = 0;
   pDispatch->QueryInterface( IID_IMath, (void**) &pMath );
   pDispatch->Release();

   // We're using variants in this chapter
   CComVariant varResult;
   CComVariant varOp1( 9 );
   CComVariant varOp2( 99 );
   pMath->Multiply( varOp1, varOp2, &varResult );
   cout << "9 * 99 = " << varResult.lVal << endl;

   // Because this is a dual interface we
   // can access the IDispatch methods
   // from IMath as well
   lpOleStr = L"Multiply";
   hr = pMath->GetIDsOfNames( IID_NULL,
                     &lpOleStr,
                     1,
                     LOCALE_SYSTEM_DEFAULT,
                     &dispid );

   if (FAILED( hr ))
   {
      cout.setf( ios::hex, ios::basefield );
      cout << "GetIDsOfNames (IMath) failed. HR = " << hr << endl;
      CoUninitialize();
      return -1;
   }
   cout << "The DISPID for Multiply is " << dispid << endl;

   // Get the IMath2 dual interface
   IMath2* pMath2;
   hr = pMath->QueryInterface( IID_IMath2,
                              (void**) &pMath2 );
   if ( FAILED( hr ))
   {
```

```
      cout.setf( ios::hex, ios::basefield );
      cout << "Unable to QI( IMath2 ). HR = " << hr << endl;
      CoUninitialize();
      return -1;
   }

   // Try calling our Sum method
   // We first have to build a safe array
   // It's an array of 10 longs with
   // the values 0,1,2,3,4...
   SAFEARRAY       *psaArray = 0;
   SAFEARRAYBOUND  rgsabound[1];
   rgsabound[0].1Lbound = 0;
   rgsabound[0].cElements = 10;
   psaArray = SafeArrayCreate( VT_I4,
                               1, rgsabound );

   for( int i = 0; i < 10; i++ )
   {
     SafeArrayPutElement( psaArray,
                          (long *) &i, &i );
   }
   VARIANT varArray;
   VariantInit( &varArray );
   V_VT( &varArray ) = VT_ARRAY | VT_I4;
   V_ARRAY( &varArray) = psaArray;

   // Finally
   long lResult;
   pMath2->Sum( varArray, &lResult );

   cout << "The sum of 0,1,2,3...9 is " << lResult << endl;

   // Release the interfaces
   pMath->Release();
   pMath2->Release();

   cout << "Shutting down COM" << endl;
   CoUninitialize();

   return 0;
}
```

The comments in the code explain what is going on, and we covered it earlier in the chapter. Basically, we now have more flexibility in accessing our component's functionality. We can choose its dispinterface or straight Vtable implementation.

A VISUAL BASIC CLIENT

We've demonstrated the steps required to build Visual Basic clients. What makes this example a bit different is that we now have two ways of accessing the Math component's functionality, just as we did earlier in the C++ client.

I won't go into the details of building the Visual Basic form, but Figure 6.5 shows what it looks like.

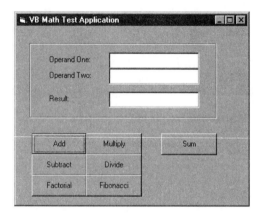

Figure 6.5 Our Visual Basic application.

Late Binding

To demonstrate late binding, use the following code:

```
Dim objMath as Object
Sub Form_Load ()
    ' Create the component via its ProgID
    Set objMath = CreateObject("Chapter6.Math.1")
End Sub
```

When we load the form, we create an instance of the math component. In this case, Visual Basic will query for IID_IDispatch. Then, when we call any of the four IMath methods, Visual Basic uses GetIDsOfNames and Invoke.

```
Private Sub cmdAdd_Click()
    txtResult = objMath.Add(txtOperand1, txtOperand2)
End Sub

Private Sub cmdDivide_Click()
    txtResult = objMath.Divide(txtOperand1, txtOperand2)
End Sub
```

```
Private Sub cmdMultiply_Click()
    txtResult = objMath.Multiply(txtOperand1, txtOperand2)
End Sub

Private Sub cmdSubtract_Click()
    txtResult = objMath.Subtract(txtOperand1, txtOperand2)
End Sub
```

How do we access `IAdvancedMath`? We can't, at least not through Visual Basic's late-binding support. Visual Basic's `Set` keyword does a `QueryInterface`, but to do so it must bind to the interface at compile time. So Visual Basic supports late binding only on the primary dispatch of a component. There are ways to get around this problem, but they involve additional work in the server.

Early Binding

Using late binding, which we demonstrated in Chapter 4, is easy. Early binding requires you to use the **Project/References** menu option to import the type library, but it gives you the ability to use any of the three interfaces within the math component.

```
Dim objMath As New CHAPTER6_SERVERLib.Math
' The IMath2 interface is implemented in the Chapter6_Server example
' and is needed for the Sum method below
Dim objMath2 As CHAPTER6_SERVERLib.IMath2
Dim objAdvancedMath As CHAPTER6_SERVERLib.IAdvancedMath

Private Sub cmdAdd_Click()
    txtResult = objMath.Add(txtOp1, txtOp2)
End Sub

Private Sub cmdDivide_Click()
    txtResult = objMath.Divide(txtOp1, txtOp2)
End Sub

Private Sub cmdFactorial_Click()
    Set objAdvancedMath = objMath
    txtResult = objAdvancedMath.Factorial(txtOp1)
End Sub

Private Sub cmdFibonacci_Click()
    Set objAdvancedMath = objMath
    txtResult = objAdvancedMath.Fibonacci(txtOp1)
End Sub

Private Sub cmdMultiply_Click()
    txtResult = objMath.Multiply(txtOp1, txtOp2)
End Sub
```

(code continued on next page)

```
Private Sub cmdSubtract_Click()
    txtResult = objMath.Subtract(txtOp1, txtOp2)
End Sub

Private Sub cmdSum_Click()
    Set objMath2 = objMath
    'Build a safe array of longs
    Dim longArray(-4 To 4) As Long
    For i = -4 To 4
        longArray(i) = i
    Next
    txtResult = objMath2.Sum(longArray)
End Sub
```

EVENTS AND CONNECTION POINTS

That covers automation in detail; we need it, because in Chapter 7 we'll cover COM's techniques for implementing callbacks within components. Callbacks (or events) provide a way for two components to signal each other asynchronously. Asynchronous behavior is central to development of efficient client/server applications, and, as you'll see, COM and ATL provide good support.

Chapter 7

Events and Connection Points

In the first six chapters we discussed various COM techniques for both implementing and using interfaces. In all these examples there was a clear delineation between the client (or consumer) and the server (producer) of an interface's implementation. Client applications query for a specific interface and then call through that interface to access functionality in the server (a component). An important point is that the interaction between client and server is synchronous. The client invokes a method and must wait until the call returns.

Today, this behavior is required because COM does not support explicit asynchronous method calls through its interfaces. However, COM provides pseudo asynchronous behavior through its support for interface callbacks and *connection points* , also called connectable objects. These techniques allow a client application to pass an interface to the server; the server can then call back into the client and notify it of various events. By using this technique, a client becomes a server and a server becomes a client. The entities maintain a peer-to-peer relationship as opposed to the master-slave relationship required by synchronous, one-way method calls. The trick is to pass an interface pointer from the client to the component, and that's what we'll cover in this chapter.

NOTE

When Windows NT version 5.0 is released, COM will have explicit support for asynchronous method calls. Until then, the techniques described here and in Chapter 10 should provide ample support for most applications.

INTERFACE CALLBACKS

In this first section we will discuss a standard way of implementing component-to-client communication. So far we have discussed only client-to-component communication through the interfaces implemented by the component. Now we want to open the communication channel and provide a richer environment. Follow these general steps to provide a component with callback (or notification) capabilities.

253

- The component describes several interfaces, some of which it implements (for example, IMath) and some of which a potential client might implement (for example, ICallback).
- The client implements one of the interfaces described by the component (for example, ICallback) using its favorite technique.
- The component provides a method (IMath::Advise) on one of its incoming interfaces through which the client can pass its implemented interface pointer (ICallback).
- The component then provides notifications to the client by calling methods through the interface implemented by the client.

Figure 7.1 illustrates this process.

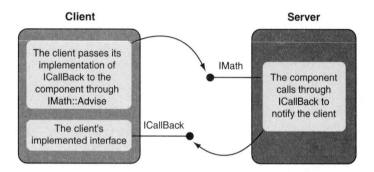

Figure 7.1 Out math component with a callback interface.

Incoming and Outgoing Interfaces

In the preceding scenario, the term *interface* isn't sufficient to describe what's going on. COM uses the terms *incoming interface* and *outgoing interface* to describe the two types of interfaces that a component can support. An incoming interface is an interface implemented by the component. The IMath interface that we're familiar with is an incoming interface, because it is implemented by our component. An outgoing interface is described in the component's type library but is actually implemented by a client of the Math component.

The client application must obtain a description of the component's outgoing interfaces and then implement them using whatever mechanism it chooses; for example, Visual Basic uses the implements keyword. After the interface is implemented, a pointer to it must somehow be communicated to the component. The standard technique is to have the component expose an `Advise` method on one of its main incoming interfaces, though which the client will pass its pointer.

The `Advise` Method

The `Advise` method is easy to implement. It takes just one parameter: an interface pointer for the outgoing interface. Internally, the component will store this pointer so that it can use it at any time to "call back" the client. Here's the IDL and implementation of a simple `Advise` method:

```
interface IMath : IUnknown
{
...
   [helpstring("method Advise")]
      HRESULT Advise([in] ICallBack* pCallBack);
...
};

STDMETHODIMP CMath::Advise(ICallBack * pCallBack)
{
   m_pCallBack = pCallBack;
   return S_OK;
}
```

`Advise` takes the client's interface point and stores it. Later, when we need to notify the client of an event within the component, we call through the stored pointer. It works something like this:

```
STDMETHODIMP CMath::Subtract(long lOp1, long lOp2)
{
   long lResult = lOp1 - lOp2;

   if ( m_pCallBack )
     m_pCallBack->ComputationComplete( lResult );

return S_OK;
}
```

There's only one problem with our implementation. How does the component determine when the callback pointer becomes invalid? In the simple case, the client and component can manage the callback pointer as part of their own lifetimes,so the callback pointer must remain valid until the component is destroyed. However, in more complex and useful cases, it is appropriate to have a standard way of disconnecting an outgoing interface.

The `Unadvise` method is the standard way of breaking an interface connection between cooperating entities. Here's a simple implementation of `Unadvise`:

```
interface IMath : IUnknown
{
...
   [helpstring("method Unadvise")] HRESULT Unadvise();
};

STD METHODIMP CMath::Unadvise()
{
   m_pCallBack = 0;
   return S_OK;
}
```

More-complex implementations (as we'll see in a moment) add a cookie to both the `Advise` and `Unadvise` methods so that multiple connections can be managed at the same time.

Visual Basic's `Implements` Keyword

Visual Basic (version 5) provides a new keyword that allows a client to implement COM interfaces described in a type library. First, you add the component's type library as a reference to the Visual Basic project. Next, you add a class module to the project and add the `implements` statement, specifying the interface that you will implement. You then implement each public member using Visual Basic code. Here's a simple example:

```
// From the CallBack.CLS module
Implements CHAPTER7_CALLBACKSERVERLib.ICallBack

Private Sub ICallBack_ComputationComplete(ByVal lResult As Long)
    frmMain.txtResult = lResult
End Sub
```

Once an interface is implemented in a class module, you create an instance of the class and pass it the component. It looks something like this:

```
Dim objCallBack As New CallBack

Private Sub Form_Load()
    objMath.Advise objCallBack
End Sub
```

Passing the `objCallBack` instance through the `Advise` method provides the component with a pointer to the `ICallBack` interface implemented in the Visual Basic class module.

Visual Basic is a worthy development tool for working with COM interfaces. We're focusing on ATL in this book, but in many cases Visual Basic applications are the target users of the components you build with ATL. The next section provides all the details of building an ATL/Visual Basic callback client and server.

THE CallBack EXAMPLE

To demonstrate the callback technique of providing notifications to a client, let's modify the Math component to describe a new interface through which it can notify a client when a computation is completed. This new interface, ICallback, is implemented by any client that wants to receive these notifications.

Create the Chapter7_Server Project and Math Component

Start Visual C++ and create a new project , selecting **ATL COM AppWizard**. Give it the name **Chapter7_CallbackServer**. In Step 1 of 1, select a type of DLL. Then select **Finish** to generate the project. Using the ATL Object wizard, insert a **Simple Component** with the following options:

- Use a Short Name of **Math**.
- Make sure the interface name is **IMath**.
- Change the ProgID to **Chapter7.CallbackMath**.
- On the **Attributes** tab, make sure the **Custom** interface option is selected.

Implement the IMath Interface

Using the **Add Method** option by right-clicking on the ClassView, add the typical four methods for the IMath interface. The IDL signatures for each method are shown next. Notice that this time we don't return the result of the computation via an out parameter. Instead, we will notify the client of the result through a callback method.

```
[helpstring("method Add")] HRESULT
    Add( [in] long lOp1, [in] long lOp2 );
[helpstring("method Subtract")] HRESULT
    Subtract( [in] long lOp1, [in] long lOp2 );
[helpstring("method Multiply")] HRESULT
    Multiply( [in] long lOp1, [in] long lOp2 );
[helpstring("method Divide")] HRESULT
    Divide([in] long lOp1, [in] long lOp2 );
```

Add the Advise Methods

For our callback example, we need to add two more methods to IMath interface: Advise and Unadvise. These two methods provide a way for the client to pass an interface pointer to the component. We then store this pointer as part of our implementation and will "fire" notifications to the client through it. The Unadvise method provides a way for the client to disconnect the notification interface. Following is the IDL and implementation.

```
// Chapter7_CallBackServer.IDL
interface IMath : IUnknown
{
...
    [helpstring("method Advise")]
      HRESULT Advise([in] ICallBack* pCallBack);
    [helpstring("method Unadvise")]
      HRESULT Unadvise();
};

// Math.H
...
class ATL_NO_VTABLE CMath :
    public CComObjectRootEx<CComSingleThreadModel>,
    public CComCoClass<CMath, &CLSID_Math>,
    public IMath
{
public:
    CMath()
    {
      m_pCallBack = 0;
    }
...
// IMath
public:
    STDMETHOD(Add)(long lOp1, long lOp2);
    STDMETHOD(Multiply)(long lOp1, long lOp2);
    STDMETHOD(Subtract)(long lOp1, long lOp2);
    STDMETHOD(Divide)(long lOp1, long lOp2);
    STDMETHOD(Advise)(ICallBack* pCallBack);
    STDMETHOD(Unadvise)();

private:
    ICallBack* m_pCallBack;
};

// Math.CPP
...
STDMETHODIMP CMath::Advise(ICallBack * pCallBack)
{
    m_pCallBack = pCallBack;
```

```
   return S_OK;
}

STDMETHODIMP CMath::Unadvise()
{
   m_pCallBack = 0;
   return S_OK;
}
```

Define the Outgoing Interface

Next, we declare the outgoing interface in our component's IDL file. We'll name the interface ICallBack and it has just one method: ComputationComplete. You'll need to use GUIDGEN to create a unique GUID for the interface; then add it to the coclass entry so that it will become part of the type library.

You should also mark the interface with the default and source attributes to signify that this is our component's default outgoing interface. However, to use it with Visual Basic's implements keyword, it cannot be marked as source, so it's commented out in the following code.

```
// Chapter7_CallBackServer.IDL
...
[
   object,
   uuid(48CD3740-50A3-11d1-B5EC-0004ACFF171C),
   helpstring("ICallBack Interface"),
]
interface ICallBack : IUnknown
{
   [helpstring("method ComputationComplete")]
      HRESULT ComputationComplete( long lResult );
};
...
library CHAPTER7_CALLBACKSERVERLib
{
...
   coclass Math
   {
      [default] interface IMath;
      /* [source, default] Visual Basic doesn't like these */
      interface ICallBack;
   };
};
```

Notify the Client

To receive the results of our math component's computations, clients must implement our outgoing `ICallBack` interface. To perform this notification, we need to add the callback code to each of the basic operation methods of `IMath`.

```
// IMath interface
STDMETHODIMP CMath::Add(long lOp1, long lOp2)
{
   long lResult = lOp1 + lOp2;
   if ( m_pCallBack )
     m_pCallBack->ComputationComplete( lResult );

    return S_OK;
}
STDMETHODIMP CMath::Subtract(long lOp1, long lOp2)
{
   long lResult = lOp1 - lOp2;
   if ( m_pCallBack )
     m_pCallBack->ComputationComplete( lResult );

return S_OK;
}
STDMETHODIMP CMath::Multiply(long lOp1, long lOp2)
{
   long lResult = lOp1 * lOp2;
   if ( m_pCallBack )
     m_pCallBack->ComputationComplete( lResult );

return S_OK;
}
STDMETHODIMP CMath::Divide(long lOp1, long lOp2)
{
   long lResult = lOp1 / lOp2;
   if ( m_pCallBack )
     m_pCallBack->ComputationComplete( lResult );

return S_OK;
}
```

This design probably isn't the most flexible, because it requires a client to provide a callback implementation if it wants to use our functionality. The better technique would be to pass back a return value as well as fire the notification with the result. We'll use this approach in the next example, which uses connection points, COM's general notification technique.

A Visual Basic Client

To test the `Math` component, let's write a Visual Basic application that supports result notifications. Again, the initial form is based on many of our previous Visual Basic examples. It is shown in Figure 7.2. The form uses the same control names that we've used previously. Also, be sure to give the form the name **frmMain.**

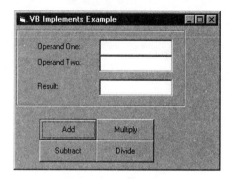

Figure 7.2 Our Visual Basic form.

Reference the Type Library for Chapter7_CallBackServer

Once you've built the form, add the type library of our math component using **Project|References** menu. The Math component and its interfaces is shown in Figure 7.3. Then, add the code below to the form:

```
Dim objMath As New CHAPTER7_CALLBACKSERVERLib.Math

Private Sub cmdAdd_Click()
    objMath.Add txtOp1, txtOp2
End Sub

Private Sub cmdDivide_Click()
    objMath.Divide txtOp1, txtOp2
End Sub

Private Sub cmdMultiply_Click()
    objMath.Multiply txtOp1, txtOp2
End Sub

Private Sub cmdSubtract_Click()
    objMath.Subtract txtOp1, txtOp2
End Sub
```

This code is slightly different from what we've done before, because the methods do not actually return the result of the computation. To get the results we must implement the ICallBack interface and pass the pointer to the component.

Figure 7.3 shows the Math component and its interfaces.

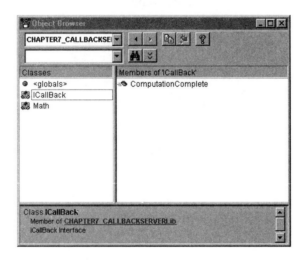

Figure 7.3 Math in Visual Basic's Object Browser.

Add the CallBack Class

Visual Basic supports the use of class modules, which behave just like the component classes that we've developed using ATL. A Visual Basic class module is implemented using either an IDispatch or an IUnknown-based interface. By using Visual Basic's implements keyword, we can provide an implementation for an interface described in a type library (as long as it derives from IUnknown or IDispatch).

When we referenced our Math component's type library, the definition for ICallBack was added to Visual Basic's known types. Using the **Project|Add Class Module**, add a new class module to your project and give it the name **CallBack**. This is shown in Figure 7.4.

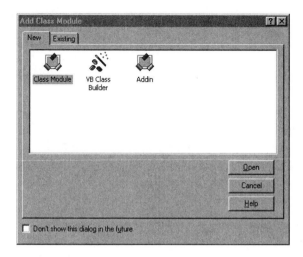

Figure 7.4 Visual Basic's Add Class dialog box.

Next, use the `implements` keyword to indicate that the class will implement the `Chapter7_CallBackServerLib.ICallBack` interface:

```
Implements CHAPTER7_CALLBACKSERVERLib.ICallBack
```

Figure 7.5 shows the interface.

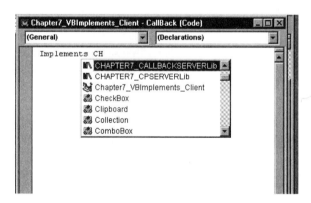

Figure 7.5 Using the implements keyword.

After you use the `implements` keyword, the module's left combo box will have **ICallBack** as an option. Choose **ICallBack**. This will add shell functions for each interface member. Add the following highlighted code:

```
Private Sub ICallBack_ComputationComplete(ByVal lResult As Long)
    frmMain.txtResult = lResult
End Sub
```

This code implements the `ComputationComplete` method of our `ICallBack` interface. After this interface is passed to the component, it will "call back," notifying the client of the result of any calculations. We then display the result in the result field on our form.

Advising the Component

All that's left is to create an instance of our class that implements `ICallBack` and pass it into the component via the `IMath::Advise` method. We create an instance of the `CallBack` class and pass it to the component when the application is started (the form is loaded). On shutdown, we call the `Unadvise` method.

```
Dim objCallBack As New CallBack

Private Sub Form_Load()
    objMath.Advise objCallBack
End Sub

Private Sub Form_Unload(Cancel As Integer)
    objMath.Unadvise
End Sub
```

That's all there is to it. We now have an application that implements bidirectional communication using COM interfaces. This technique is very useful in many development situations and is relatively easy to implement. However, both the client and the server need an understanding of the notification interface. COM also provides a more general technique for establishing outgoing interfaces in your components. This technique is more complex because of its generality but is used extensively by technologies such as ActiveX controls.

CONNECTABLE OBJECTS

Implementing and passing interface pointers through an interface method is a basic technique for handling notifications. COM also provides a general solution for the notification problem; it's called connection points, or connectable objects. In our callback example, both the client and the server required some specific knowledge of the call back interface. Using connectable objects, which is based on a number of standard COM interfaces (`IConnectionPoint`), a component can describe its outgoing interfaces in a general way and also provide a standard way for a client to implement and connect these interfaces to a component.

Connectable object technology supports the following set of features:

- Allows a component to define its outgoing interfaces.
- Provides the ability for a client to enumerate the outgoing interfaces supported by a component.
- Provides the ability to connect (Advise) and disconnect (Unadvise) outgoing interfaces to a component.
- Provides the ability for a client to enumerate the connected, outgoing interfaces on a particular component instance.

The general flow of connectable object negotiation proceeds as follows:

1. The client queries for IConnectionPointContainer through a well-known interface on the component. If this succeeds, the component supports connection points.

2. The client uses one of two techniques to retrieve an IConnectionPoint interface, through which it will set up the connection. The client can use the FindConnectionPoint method to locate a specific connection point by its interface identifier (IID). This is the technique used most frequently. The second IConnectionPointContainer method, EnumConnectionPoints, returns a COM enumerator with a list of all IConnectionPoint interfaces implemented within a component. The client can then iterate through this list to determine which connection point (if any) it would like to use.

3. If the client finds an acceptable outgoing interface, it must then implement it. Otherwise, the process ends. Implementing the outgoing interface is similar to what we did earlier with the Visual Basic implements keyword. However, because connection points are a more general technique, in many cases the outgoing interface will be derived from IDispatch.

4. Next, the client uses the IConnectionPoint::Advise method to pass an IUnknown pointer to its interface implementation. The interface implementation is also called a *sink*.

5. In the component's IConnectionPoint::Advise implementation, it will use QueryInterface to obtain the interface pointer to the client's implementation of the component's outgoing interface. Once this has been performed, the connection has been established. The component can now fire notifications by calling through this interface implemented within the client.

6. When the client no longer wants to be notified, it calls IConnectionPoint::Unadvise to shut down the connection.

IConnectionPointContainer

The `IConnectionPointContainer` interface is implemented by the component and is available from its main `QueryInterface` implementation. A client uses `IConnectionPointContainer` to determine whether a component supports connection points. If the `QueryInterface` succeeds, the client can then use `FindConnectionPoint` to return an `IConnectionPoint` interface for a specific outgoing interface. The signature of `FindConnectionPoint` is as follows:

```
HRESULT FindConnectionPoint( REFIID riid,
                             IConnectionPoint **ppCP );
```

The client calls `FindConnectionPoint`, passing the GUID of the component's outgoing interface. There are at least two ways the client can obtain this GUID. The first is to look through the component's type library for its outgoing interfaces. The second approach requires the component to implement the `IProvideClassInfo2` interface, which we'll discuss in a moment. The client can obtain the type information as well as the GUID of the component's default outgoing interface through the methods of `IProvideClassInfo2`.

The second method of `IConnectionPointContainer` returns a list of all the connection points within a component. The client can then decide which specific connection point it wants to use. Here's its signature:

```
HRESULT EnumConnectionPoints( IEnumConnectionPoints **ppEnum );
```

IConnectionPoint

An `IConnectionPoint` interface acts as a point of connection for each outgoing interface supported in a component. It is through this interface that a client connects its implementation of the component's outgoing interfaces. The `GetConnectionInterface` method passes back the interface identifier for the interface managed by this specific connection point, and the `GetConnectionPointContainer` method provides the component's `IConnectionPointContainer` interface implementation.

```
Interface IConnectionPoint : IUnknown
{
   HRESULT GetConnectionInterface( IID *pIID );
   HRESULT GetConnectionPointContainer( IConnectionPointContainer **ppCPC )
   HRESULT Advise( IUnknown *pUnk, DWORD *pdwCookie );
   HRESULT Unadvise( DWORD dwCookie );
   HRESULT EnumConnections( IEnumConnections **ppEnum );
};
```

The more interesting `IConnectionPoint` methods are `Advise`, `Unadvise`, and `EnumConnections`. Connectable object technology allows a component to maintain multiple connections to its outgoing interfaces. In other words, a component may have any number of clients connected to any one instance. To manage this, each connection must have a unique identifier called a *cookie*. A cookie is a 32-bit value that is unique in the context in which it is used. Cookies are used throughout the Win32 API.

The `Advise` method returns a cookie that uniquely identifies the client's connection. The cookie must then be passed back to the `Unadvise` method. The `EnumConnections` method returns a list of outstanding client connections on the specific connection point. In other words, it provides access to the `IUnknown` pointers provided by the clients for this connection point.

Connection Points, Automation, and `IProvideClassInfo2`

The connection point technique of implementing notifications was initially designed for and used in the development of ActiveX controls. As you'll see in Chapter 8, ActiveX controls expose their functionality through automation, usually with dual interfaces. Today, many development tools (such as Visual Basic) work only with components that describe their outgoing interfaces as dispinterfaces. This because dispinterfaces are easier to implement at run time.

As we described in the last chapter, `IDispatch`-based interfaces only have to implement `IDispatch::GetIDsOfNames` and `IDispatch::Invoke`. And in the case of connection points, where the component already knows the DISPIDs and the methods that it will call, there isn't really a need for the client to implement anything other than `IDispatch::Invoke`.

In these situations, in which a client will implement an outgoing interface at run time, it is important that there be an effective way for the client to identify a component's outgoing interfaces, methods, and parameters. An additional interface is specified by COM for just this purpose. The `IProvideClassInfo2` interface provides a simple mechanism whereby a client can obtain both the type information for a component and the interface identifier for its default, outgoing interface. We want this because we can then use `FindConnectionPoint` to get a connection point for this interface, and then call advise. Following is the definition of the `IProvideClassInfo2` interface as well as the `GUIDKIND` structure that is used to identify a default outgoing interface.

```
interface IProvideClassInfo2 : IUnknown
{
   HRESULT GetClassInfo( ITypeInfo** ppTI );
   HRESULT GetGUID( DWORD dwGuidKind, GUID* pGUID );
);
typedef enum tagGUIDKIND
{
   GUIDKIND_DEFAULT_SOURCE_DISP_IID = 1,
} GUIDKIND;
```

IProvideClassInfo2Impl

ATL provides a basic implementation of IProvideClassInfo2 via its
IProvideClassInfo2Impl class. The IProvideClassInfo2 interface should be pro-
vided by those components that implement outgoing interfaces through connection points.
Using ATL, implementing this interface takes just a few lines of code.

```
class ATL_NO_VTABLE CMath :
   ...
   public IProvideClassInfo2Impl<&CLSID_Math, &IID_IMathEvents,
                            &LIBID_CHAPTER7_CPSERVERLib>
{
...
BEGIN_COM_MAP(CMath)
   COM_INTERFACE_ENTRY(IProvideClassInfo2)
END_COM_MAP()
...
};
```

The first and third parameters provide information for ATL to load the type library, and the
second parameter signifies the component's default outgoing interface. The implementation of IProvideClassInfo2Impl is very similar to that of IDispatchImpl. It exposes
the type library using an instance of CComTypeInfoHolder.

ATL and Connection Points

When you're creating an ATL component using the Object wizard, one of the options is
Support Connection Points. The **Attributes** tab with this option is shown in Figure 7.6.
If you select **Support Connection Points**, the wizard adds several lines of code to your
component's header file, each one of which is highlighted next. These lines add basic support for outgoing interfaces in your component.

```
class ATL_NO_VTABLE CMath :
   public CComObjectRootEx<CComSingleThreadModel>,
   public CComCoClass<CMath, &CLSID_Math>,
   public IDispatchImpl<IMath, &IID_IMath, &LIBID_CHAPTER7_CPSERVERLib>,
   public IConnectionPointContainerImpl<CMath>
{
public:
...
BEGIN_COM_MAP(CMath)
   COM_INTERFACE_ENTRY(IMath)
   COM_INTERFACE_ENTRY(IDispatch)
```

```
    COM_INTERFACE_ENTRY_IMPL(IConnectionPointContainer)
END_COM_MAP()

BEGIN_CONNECTION_POINT_MAP(CMath)
END_CONNECTION_POINT_MAP()
```

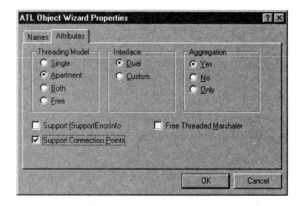

Figure 7.6 The Attributes tab.

First, our component gets an implementation of the IConnectionPointContainter interface. This interface is added to our interface map, and the wizard adds two macros that create a connection point map. This is just the start, because we still have to add code to support connection points within the component. Before we examine that, though, let's go over ATL's Proxy Generator and ATL's various connection point classes.

The ATL Proxy Generator

ATL provides a component, ATL Proxy Generator, that generates wrapper classes based on a component's type library. Proxy Generator can create either a smart pointer wrapper class or a wrapper class derived from IConnectionPointImpl, which we'll describe in a moment. The smart pointer functionality is simple. Proxy Generator reads the type library and produces a class derived from ATL's CComPtr class. In this chapter, we're interested in the Proxy Generator's ability to produce wrapper classes for a component's outgoing interfaces.

To run Proxy Generator, you first need a type library. With ATL projects, this means that you must add the interface declarations to your IDL file and build the project before you can use Proxy Generator. Once you've defined a component's outgoing interface, you run Proxy Generator to produce a class similar to this:

```
////////////////////////
// CProxyIMathEvents
////////////////////////
template <class T>
class CProxyIMathEvents :
    public IConnectionPointImpl<T, &IID_IMathEvents, CComDynamicUnkArray>
{
public:
    HRESULT Fire_ComputationComplete( long lResult)
    {
        T* pT = (T*)this;
        pT->Lock();
        HRESULT ret;
        IUnknown** pp = m_vec.begin();
        while (pp < m_vec.end())
        {
            if (*pp != NULL)
            {
                IMathEvents* pIMathEvents = reinterpret_cast<IMathEvents*>(*pp);
                ret = pIMathEvents->ComputationComplete(lResult);
            }
            pp++;
        }
        pT->Unlock();
        return ret;
    }
};
```

The purpose of this proxy class is to provide the component with a convenient way to call through an interface pointer provided by a client application. Connection point technology allows multiple outgoing (or sink) interfaces per component instance. ATL manages these connections in a simple vector of IUnknown pointers. The vector class is implemented in the CComDynamicUnkArray class and is part of ATL.

When developing a connection point–based component, you include the wrapper class in the implementation. It looks something like that shown below (the highlighted lines show the necessary changes).

```
// Our proxy class to fire events
#include "CPChapter7_CPServer.h"
...
class ATL_NO_VTABLE CMath :
    ...
    public CProxyIMathEvents<CMath>
{
```

```
...
BEGIN_CONNECTION_POINT_MAP(CMath)
   CONNECTION_POINT_ENTRY(IID_IMathEvents)
END_CONNECTION_POINT_MAP()
...
};
```

To fire an event (notify a client through its incoming interface), you use the methods provided by the proxy class.

```
STDMETHODIMP CMath::Add(long lOp1, long lOp2, long * plResult)
{
   *plResult = lOp1 + lOp2;
   Fire_ComputationComplete( *plResult );
   return S_OK;
}
```

A component can support any number of outgoing interfaces, and ATL provides a set of macros to help in this implementation. These macros create something called a *connection map.* Remember, each outgoing interface supported by a component must provide a connection point (an object that implements IConnectionPoint) through which a client can provide its implementation. The connection map lists each outgoing interface.

Connection Maps

If your ATL component supports connection points, it must have a connection map. The connection map manages a table of connection points, one for each outgoing interface that a component supports. A component exposes only IConnectionPointContainer interface from its QueryInterface implementation, and a client must obtain an outgoing interfaces' IConnectionPoint interface through IConnectionPointContainer.

   Here's a simple connection map declaration for a component that exposes one outgoing interface.

```
BEGIN_CONNECTION_POINT_MAP(CMath)
   CONNECTION_POINT_ENTRY(IID_IMathEvents)
END_CONNECTION_POINT_MAP()
```

IConnectionPointImpl

For each outgoing interface that your component supports, you need an implementation of the IConnectionPointImpl class. In most cases, you will use Proxy Generator to create a class derived from IConnectionPointImpl to include in your component's inheritance chain. In other cases, you can create a connection point using a standard COM interface such as IPropertyNotifySink. Here's an example of a component that supports two outgoing interfaces using both of these techniques.

```
// Math.h : Declaration of the CMath
...
// Our proxy class to fire events
#include "CPChapter7_CPServer.h"

class ATL_NO_VTABLE CMath :
    ...
    public IConnectionPointContainerImpl<CMath>,
    public CProxyIMathEvents<CMath>,
    public CConnectionPointImpl<CMath, &IID_IPropertyNotifySink>
{
public:
...
BEGIN_COM_MAP(CMath)
    COM_INTERFACE_ENTRY_IMPL(IConnectionPointContainer)
    ...
END_COM_MAP()

BEGIN_CONNECTION_POINT_MAP(CMath)
    CONNECTION_POINT_ENTRY(IID_IMathEvents)
    CONNECTION_POINT_ENTRY(IID_IPropertyNotifySink)
END_CONNECTION_POINT_MAP()
...
};
```

IConnectionPointContainerImpl

As you would expect, ATL's IConnectionPointContainerImpl class provides a default implementation of IConnectionPointContainer. To demonstrate how it works, we'll focus on the FindConnectionPoint method. The EnumConnectionPoint method uses similar techniques.

A client calls IConnectionPointContainer::FindConnectionPoint passing the IID of the outgoing interface that it is looking for. ATL's FindConnectionPoint implementation spins through the connection map looking for the associated IConnectionPoint implementation. Here's a concise version of the implementation.

```
template <class T>
class ATL_NO_VTABLE IConnectionPointContainerImpl
{
...
    STDMETHOD(FindConnectionPoint)(REFIID riid, IConnectionPoint** ppCP)
    {
        HRESULT hRes = CONNECT_E_NOCONNECTION;
```

```
          const _ATL_CONNMAP_ENTRY* pEntry = T::GetConnMap(NULL);
          IID iid;
          while (pEntry->dwOffset != (DWORD)-1)
          {
             IConnectionPoint* pCP =
                    (IConnectionPoint*)((int)this+pEntry->dwOffset);
             if (SUCCEEDED(pCP->GetConnectionInterface(&iid)) &&
                          InlineIsEqualGUID(riid, iid))
             {
                *ppCP = pCP;
                pCP->AddRef();
                hRes = S_OK;
                break;
             }
             pEntry++;
          }
       return hRes;
   }
};
```

Except for using some difficult offset calculations, the implementation corresponds to what we know about IConnectionPointContainer. ATL loops through the connection map until it finds a matching IID. If it finds a match, it returns the connection point implementation.

AtlAdvise

ATL provides the AtlAdvise method as a shortcut for clients that support connection points. AtlAdvise takes four parameters: the IUnknown* of the component, the IUnknown* of the client's outgoing interface implementation (for example, IMathEvents), the IID of the outgoing interface that it implements (IID_IMathEvents), and a variable to store the cookie returned by IConnectionPoint::Advise. Here's the implementation:

```
ATLAPI AtlAdvise(IUnknown* pUnkCP, IUnknown* pUnk,
                 const IID& iid, LPDWORD pdw)
{
   CComPtr<IConnectionPointContainer> pCPC;
   CComPtr<IConnectionPoint> pCP;
   HRESULT hRes = pUnkCP->QueryInterface(IID_IConnectionPointContainer,
                                         (void**)&pCPC);
   if (SUCCEEDED(hRes))
      hRes = pCPC->FindConnectionPoint(iid, &pCP);

if (SUCCEEDED(hRes))
      hRes = pCP->Advise(pUnk, pdw);

return hRes;
}
```

There's nothing difficult here. AtlAdvise performs the steps detailed earlier. It queries for the IConnectionPointContainer interface, calls FindConnectionPoint with the provided IID, and finally calls the Advise method with the IUnknown* of the client's implemented interface. Here's how a C++ client might use AtlAdvise:

```
CComPtr<IMath> ptrMath;
HRESULT hr;
hr = CoCreateInstance( CLSID_Math, NULL, CLSCTX_SERVER,
                       IID_IMath, (void**) &ptrMath );

CComObject<CMathEvents>* ptrMathEvents = new CComObject<CMathEvents>;
CComPtr<IUnknown> ptrEventsUnk = ptrMathEvents;

DWORD dwCookie;
hr = AtlAdvise( ptrMath,
                ptrEventsUnk,
                IID_IMathEvents,
                &dwCookie );
```

We'll see this again in our example later.

Visual Basic's WithEvents Keyword

Before release 5.0 of Visual Basic, only ActiveX controls enabled a Visual Basic developer to harness events through the connection point mechanism. With release 5.0, however, Visual Basic has a new keyword that enables it to handle events fired from arbitrary COM components. The WithEvents keyword provides functionality similar to that provided by the AtlAdvise method.

The WithEvents keyword requires early binding to components that support connection points, but this is hardly an issue. Hooking up events is now as easy as adding one keyword to an object's dimension statement. Here's an example:

```
Dim WithEvents objMath As CHAPTER7_CPSERVERLib.Math

Private Sub Form_Load()
    Set objMath = New CHAPTER7_CPSERVERLib.Math
End Sub

Private Sub objMath_ComputationComplete(ByVal lResult As Long)
    MsgBox "Computation result is " & lResult
End Sub
```

We'll use this technique later in our Visual Basic client example.

THE CONNECTION POINT EXAMPLE

In this example, we'll first implement our math component using a dual interface just as we did earlier in the chapter. This time, though, we'll use connection points to expose the outgoing notification interface. Once we implement the component, we'll then develop clients using both C++ and Visual Basic.

Create the Math Component

Start Visual C++ and create a new project, selecting **ATL COM AppWizard**. Give it the name **Chapter7_CPServer**. In Step 1 of 1, select a type of DLL. Then select **Finish** to generate the project. Using the ATL Object wizard, insert a **Simple Component** with the following options:

- Use a **Short Name** of **Math**.
- Make sure the interface name is **IMath**.
- Change the ProgID to **Chapter7.CPMath.**
- On the **Attributes** page, enable **Support Connection Points** option and make sure the **Dual** interface option is selected. This attributes tab is shown in Figure 7.6.

Implement the IMath Interface

Using the **Add Method** option by right-clicking on the ClassView, add the four methods for our IMath interface:

```
// IMath interface
STDMETHODIMP CMath::Add( long lOp1, long lOp2, long* plResult )
{
    *pResult = lOp1 + lOp2;
    return S_OK;
}
STDMETHODIMP CMath::Subtract( long lOp1, long lOp2, long* plResult )
{
    *pResult = lOp1 - lOp2;
    return S_OK;
}
```

(code continued on next page)

```
STDMETHODIMP CMath::Multiply( long lOp1, long lOp2, long* plResult )
{
    *pResult = lOp1 * lOp2;
    return S_OK;
}

STDMETHODIMP CMath::Divide( long lOp1, long lOp2, long* plResult )
{
    *pResult = lOp1 / lOp2;
    return S_OK;
}
```

You should also update the IDL file with the correct attributes for each method as follows:

```
[helpstring("method Add")] HRESULT
      Add( [in] long lOp1, [in] long lOp2,
         [out, retval] long* plResult);
[helpstring("method Subtract")] HRESULT
     Subtract( [in] long lOp1, [in] long lOp2,
              [out, retval] long* plResult);
[helpstring("method Multiply")] HRESULT
     Multiply( [in] long lOp1, [in] long lOp2,
              [out, retval] long* plResult);
[helpstring("method Divide")] HRESULT
     Divide([in] long lOp1, [in] long lOp2,
            [out, retval] long* plResult);
```

Define the Event Interface

We've seen all that before. Next, we need to declare our outgoing interface in our component's IDL file. We name the interface IMathEvents, and it has one method, ComputationComplete. Most tools require outgoing interfaces to be dispinterfaces, so that's what we use. We also must add the interface to our coclass description and mark with the default and source attributes to signify that this is our component's default outgoing interface.

```
// Chapter7_CPServer.IDL
...
[
   object,
   uuid(AEB18821-53A3-11d1-883A-444553540000),
   helpstring("IMathEvents Interface"),
   pointer_default(unique)
]
interface IMathEvents : IDispatch
```

```
{
   [id(1), helpstring("method ComputationComplete")]
         HRESULT ComputationComplete([in] long lResult);
};
...
library CHAPTER7_CPSERVERLib
{
...
coclass Math
{
   [default] interface IMath;
   [default, source] interface IMathEvents;
};
```

Before we run ATL Proxy Generator, we need to compile the IDL file to produce the type library, so build the project before continuing or right-click on the IDL File in the FileView and select **Compile...** from the pop-up menu.

Run the ATL Proxy Generator

As we described earlier, Proxy Generator produces a proxy or wrapper class that derives from ATL's `IConnectionPointImpl` class. Find Proxy Generator using **Project/Add To Project/Components and Controls**. Select **Developer Studio Components** and double-click on the **ATL Proxy Generator** component. This is shown in Figure 7.7.

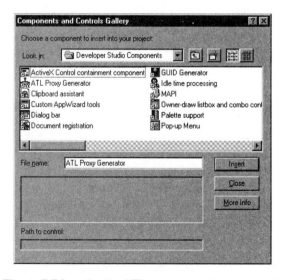

Figure 7.7 Inserting the ATL proxy generator component.

Next, we provide the path to our example's type library. Select the IMathEvents interface and click the **Insert** button. Accept the default filename of **CPCHAPTER7_CPSERVER**.H and save it. Figure 7.8 shows Proxy Generator dialog box.

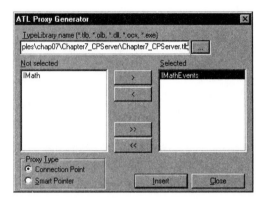

Figure 7.8 Building the IMathEvents proxy class.

We now need to include the proxy class in our component's implementation. The following code adds the implementation of our IConnectionPoint object as well as the IProvideClassInfo2 implementation.

```
// Math.h : Declaration of the CMath
...
// Our proxy class to fire events
#include "CPChapter7_CPServer.h"

class ATL_NO_VTABLE CMath :
    public CComObjectRootEx<CComSingleThreadModel>,
    public CComCoClass<CMath, &CLSID_Math>,
    public IDispatchImpl<IMath, &IID_IMath, &LIBID_CHAPTER7_CPSERVERLib>,
    public IConnectionPointContainerImpl<CMath>,
    public IProvideClassInfo2Impl<&CLSID_Math, &IID_IMathEvents,
                                  &LIBID_CHAPTER7_CPSERVERLib>,
    public CProxyIMathEvents<CMath>
{
public:
...
BEGIN_COM_MAP(CMath)
    COM_INTERFACE_ENTRY_IMPL(IConnectionPointContainer)
    COM_INTERFACE_ENTRY(IMath)
```

```
   COM_INTERFACE_ENTRY(IDispatch)
   COM_INTERFACE_ENTRY(IProvideClassInfo2)
END_COM_MAP()

BEGIN_CONNECTION_POINT_MAP(CMath)
   CONNECTION_POINT_ENTRY(IID_IMathEvents)
END_CONNECTION_POINT_MAP()
...
};
```

Update each method call to fire the ComputationComplete event. The proxy class provides the Fire_ComputationComplete method.

```
//
// Math.cpp : Implementation of CMath
//
...
STDMETHODIMP CMath::Add(long lOp1, long lOp2, long * plResult)
{
   *plResult = lOp1 + lOp2;
   Fire_ComputationComplete( *plResult );
   return S_OK;
}
STDMETHODIMP CMath::Subtract(long lOp1, long lOp2, long * plResult)
{
   *plResult = lOp1 - lOp2;
   Fire_ComputationComplete( *plResult );
   return S_OK;
}
STDMETHODIMP CMath::Multiply(long lOp1, long lOp2, long * plResult)
{
   *plResult = lOp1 * lOp2;
   Fire_ComputationComplete( *plResult );
   return S_OK;
}
STDMETHODIMP CMath::Divide(long lOp1, long lOp2, long * plResult)
{
   *plResult = lOp1 / lOp2;
   Fire_ComputationComplete( *plResult );
   return S_OK;
}
```

Now build the project, and we'll move on to accessing the connection point functionality with a couple of client examples.

A C++ Connection Point Client

Our C++ client application is a bit different from those that we've developed previously. This time we'll use ATL on the client side. To use ATL, we need to create a simple Win32 application instead of the typical Win32 console application that we've used in the past. The primary reason for this switch is that ATL requires an HINSTANCE, and the best way to get access to this is by implementing WinMain.

Using AppWizard, create a **Win32 Application** project and name it **Chapter7_Client**. Next, create a file called **Chapter7_Client.cpp** and add the following code.

```
//
// Chapter7_Client.cpp
//
#include <windows.h>
// Include ATL
#include <atlbase.h>
CComModule _Module;
#include <atlcom.h>
#include <atlimpl.cpp>

BEGIN_OBJECT_MAP(ObjectMap)
END_OBJECT_MAP()

#include "..\Chapter7_CPServer\Chapter7_CPServer.h"
#include "..\Chapter7_CPServer\Chapter7_CPServer_i.c"
...
```

Our client code now includes the ATL implementation files and declares a global CComModule instance. It also includes an empty ATL object map, which we will need to initialize CComModule. Next, we add two helper functions to display messages as our application runs. Here they are:

```
...
void DisplayMessage( char* szMsg )
{
   MessageBox( 0, szMsg, "Chapter7_Client", MB_OK );
}
void HandleError( char* szMsg, HRESULT hr )
{
   char szMessage[128];
   sprintf( szMessage, "%s. HR = %x", szMsg, hr );
   DisplayMessage( szMessage );
   CoUninitialize();
}
...
```

These functions are simple, but they support only ANSI builds. Next, we have an ATL class that will implement the client side, outgoing interface for our math component.

```
...
class CMathEvents :
   public IDispatchImpl<IMathEvents, &IID_IMathEvents,
                       &LIBID_CHAPTER7_CPSERVERLib>,
   public CComObjectRoot
{
public:
   CMathEvents() {}
BEGIN_COM_MAP(CMathEvents)
   COM_INTERFACE_ENTRY(IDispatch)
   COM_INTERFACE_ENTRY(IMathEvents)
END_COM_MAP()
// IMathEvents
public:
   STDMETHODIMP ComputationComplete(long lResult)
   {
      char szMsg[128];
      sprintf( szMsg, "The result is %d", lResult );
      DisplayMessage( szMsg );
      return S_OK;
   }
};
...
```

You've seen code similar to this before. We have an IDispatch-based component that implements the IMathEvents interface. We implement the only method in IMathEvents—ComputationComplete—a nd display a message box with the result of the computation.

Next, we have the implementation of WinMain and the CoInitialize call. Then we initialize ATL by calling the CComModule::Init method, passing in the HINSTANCE of our app and the object map.

```
...
int WINAPI WinMain(HINSTANCE hInst, HINSTANCE, LPSTR, int)
{
   if ( FAILED( CoInitialize( NULL )))
   {
      DisplayMessage( "Unable to initialize COM" );
      return -1;
   }
```

(code continued on next page)

```
// Initialize the ATL module
_Module.Init( ObjectMap, hInst );
CComPtr<IMath> ptrMath;
HRESULT hr;
hr = CoCreateInstance( CLSID_Math,
                       NULL,
                       CLSCTX_SERVER,
                       IID_IMath,
                       (void**) &ptrMath );
if ( FAILED( hr ))
{
   HandleError( "Failed to create server instance", hr );
   return -1;
}
...
```

After instantiating the math component, we next create an instance of the CMathEvents class, which will provide the IMathEvents implementation.

```
...
#ifdef NEED_FINAL_CONSTRUCT
   CComObject<CMathEvents>* ptrMathEvents;
   CComObject<CMathEvents>::CreateInstance( &ptrMathEvents );
#else
   CComObject<CMathEvents>* ptrMathEvents = new CComObject<CMathEvents>;
#endif
   CComPtr<IUnknown> ptrEventsUnk = ptrMathEvents;
...
```

I've provided two techniques for instantiating CMathEvents to demonstrate how they are different. By using the static CreateInstance method, we are assured that the component's FinalConstruct method will be executed. (We covered CreateInstance in Chapter 3 and FinalConstruct in Chapter 5.) ATL's default implementation of FinalConstruct does nothing, so the second technique will also work. The second technique is one that you would typically use in C++ development, but you should probably use the first technique when working with ATL.

Another important point is that in the preceding instantiation code, the instance's reference count is initially zero. After the instantiation, we use an ATL smart pointer to query for IUnknown, and that will bump the count to 1.

```
...
// Set up the connection
DWORD dwCookie;
hr = AtlAdvise( ptrMath,
                ptrEventsUnk,
                IID_IMathEvents,
                &dwCookie );
if (FAILED( hr ))
{
   ptrMath = 0;
   ptrEventsUnk = 0;
   HandleError( "Unable to setup the connection for IMathEvents", hr );
   return -1;
}
...
```

The preceding code uses the `AtlAdvise` method to set up the connection with the math component. We have to pass in several things: pointers to both interfaces, the IID of the outgoing interface, and the address of a DWORD to receive the returned cookie.

```
...
// Access the IMath interface
long lResult;
ptrMath->Add( 300, 10, &lResult );
ptrMath->Subtract( 300, 10, &lResult );
ptrMath->Multiply( 300, 10, &lResult );
ptrMath->Divide( 300, 10, &lResult );
...
```

Next, we call the methods in the math component. As they execute, the math component will notify the client of the result through the `IMathEvents::ComputationComplete` method. This will display a message box similar to Figure 7.9.

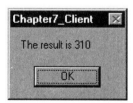

Figure 7.9 The result of a computation.

When we're finished, we shut down the connection, release our pointers, and uninitialize COM, just as we've done in the past.

```
...
// Shut down the event connection
AtlUnadvise( ptrMath,
             IID_IMathEvents,
             dwCookie );
// Release all of our interfaces
if ( ptrMath )
   ptrMath = 0;
if ( ptrEventsUnk )
   ptrEventsUnk = 0;
CoUninitialize();
return 0;
}
```

That concludes our C++ client example. Next, we'll do the same using Visual Basic.

A Visual Basic Connection Point Client

As we described earlier, Visual Basic provides native support for connection points via its WithEvents keyword. When you use this keyword, writing a client with Visual Basic is nearly identical to our previous example , which used Visual Basic's implements keyword.

To begin, start a Visual Basic executable project and build a form similar to our previous one in Figure 7.2. Next, using Visual Basic's **Project\References** dialog box add the type library for our Chapter7_CPServer server. All that's left is to add the following code:

```
Dim WithEvents objMath As CHAPTER7_CPSERVERLib.Math
Private Sub cmdAdd_Click()
    objMath.Add txtOp1, txtOp2
End Sub
Private Sub cmdDivide_Click()
    objMath.Divide txtOp1, txtOp2
End Sub
Private Sub cmdMultiply_Click()
    objMath.Multiply txtOp1, txtOp2
End Sub
Private Sub cmdSubtract_Click()
    objMath.Subtract txtOp1, txtOp2
End Sub
Private Sub Form_Load()
    Set objMath = New CHAPTER7_CPSERVERLib.Math
End Sub
Private Sub objMath_ComputationComplete(ByVal lResult As Long)
```

```
    txtResult = lResult
    MsgBox "Computation result is " & lResult
End Sub
```

Figure 7.10 shows the application in action.

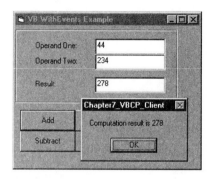

Figure 7.10 Our Visual Basic connection point client.

ACTIVEX CONTROLS

That concludes our coverage of COM events and connection points. In Chapter 8, we will cover another important COM technology: ActiveX controls. An ActiveX control will typically implement 20 or so COM interfaces. To this point, our components have implemented only a few interfaces, but as we continue to add functionality we must implement more and more interfaces. Frameworks such as ATL allow us to continue on this road of increased functionality by providing default implementations for the most important interfaces.

Oh, one other thing. You'll be happy to know that we're finally going to use a different example. I'm sure you're getting tired of our math component example, and the next few chapters will not use it. However, when we get to the threading chapter, we'll once more have a look at the math component.

Chapter 8

ActiveX Controls

ActiveX controls play a major role in Microsoft's component-based future. From a small start in 1993, ActiveX controls have grown into a tremendous demonstration of component-based software development. ActiveX controls are COM components that implement a number of standard interfaces. Some ActiveX controls implement only a handful of interfaces, whereas others implement more than 20.

It's hard to articulate what an ActiveX control is, primarily because the definition has changed frequently over the years. Today, ActiveX controls are used extensively in Microsoft's client-side (the Active Desktop) and server-side (for example, IIS) technologies. There are run-time and design-time controls as well as controls that work in Visual Basic and those that work only in Internet Explorer.

In this chapter we'll investigate what is required to implement a full ActiveX control that works in popular development environments such as Visual Basic. Books have been written on ActiveX controls, and in this chapter we'll only scratch the surface. My goal is to introduce you to as many ActiveX control interfaces as possible. That will make it easier to implement components based on their underlying functionality, which in COM is always based on your ability to implement (or understand how to use) a series of COM interfaces.

ACTIVEX CONTROLS AND CONTAINERS

ActiveX controls are discrete software elements similar to discrete hardware components. In most cases, a control must provide its functionality in conjunction with a cooperating software entity (called a container). Control containers (such as Visual Basic) make it easy to tie together various ActiveX controls into more complex and useful applications. One important feature of an ActiveX control container is the presence of a built-in language (such as VBScript) that can be used to provide programmatic interaction with the various controls within the container.

ActiveX control containers are similar to OLE document containers (such as Microsoft Word) in that they implement similar interfaces. Although OLE document containers and

ActiveX control containers share many internal characteristics, the ultimate goals of each type of container are different. OLE document containers focus on the assembly of documents for viewing and printing, typically they are typically complete applications. ActiveX control containers are used as *forms* that contain controls that are tied together with a scripting language to create an application. Figure 8.1 shows a Visual Basic form that contains a number of ActiveX controls.

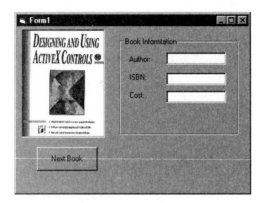

Figure 8.1 A Visual Basic form with some ActiveX controls.

Container Modalities

In typical visual development environments the container operates in various *modes*. When the developer is designing the application or Web page, the control behaves differently than it does when the application is executing. For example, when a Visual Basic developer needs a listbox control, he or she clicks the listbox icon on the tool palette, drags a representation of the listbox control, and drops it on a form. The listbox representation is merely a rectangle with a name in the upper-left corner. During design time, there is no need to create a window just to provide a representation of the control. When the Visual Basic form and its associated code are executed by a user of the application, the listbox control window is actually created and therefore must behave like a listbox and perform any special functions through its exposed properties, methods, and events. These two modes are described as *design-time* mode and *run-time* mode.

Control and Container Interfaces

An ActiveX control is an in-process server that supports a number of standard COM interfaces. An ActiveX control container is also a COM-based component that implements a set of standard COM interfaces. The trick is to hook up these interface implementations. In other words, when a control is embedded within a container, the container and control negotiate and exchange pointers to provide functionality.

A control container is really just a client of an ActiveX control, and at times a control is a client of the control container. As we described in Chapter 7, a control and container maintain a peer-to-peer relationship by exchanging interface pointers. Controls and containers support incoming and outgoing interfaces.

When you drag and drop a control on a Visual Basic form, the typical COM instantiation technique is used. The container calls CoCreateInstance with the CLSID of the control. After instantiation, the container calls QueryInterface for those interfaces that it expects the control to implement. Some of these control interfaces provide methods through which the container can pass interface pointers for those interfaces that *it* implements. In this way, the control and container interact, providing significant functionality for users. This process will become clearer as we work our way through the chapter. Figure 8.2 shows many of the interfaces that we'll discuss in this chapter.

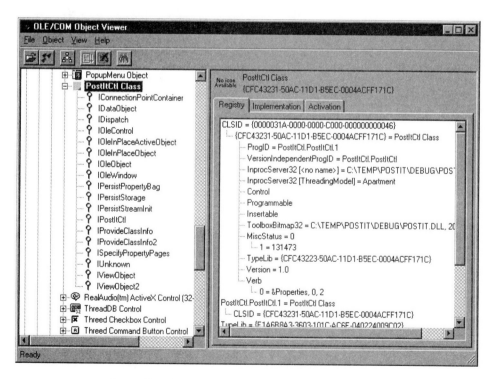

Figure 8.2 Control-implemented interfaces in OLEVIEW.

WHAT IS AN ACTIVEX CONTROL?

The definition of ActiveX has changed over the years. In late 1993, Microsoft introduced ActiveX controls (called *OLE controls* at the time) as a 32-bit replacement for the popular Visual Basic custom control (VBX) standard. The proprietary VBX specification was tied strongly to the 16-bit platform and was discarded for the new COM-based solution.

This initial version of the OLE control specification, now called the OLE Controls '94 specification, required that a control implement approximately 15 COM-based interfaces. Most of these interfaces were part of the OLE document specification; a control was just an in-process OLE document server with a couple of new, control-specific interfaces.

In early 1996, after more than two years' experience with implementing and using OLE controls, Microsoft modified the specification significantly and released the OLE Controls '96 specification. (Shortly after this document was released, Microsoft coined the term *ActiveX*.) The new specification addressed a number of performance issues inherent in the earlier '94 specification controls. It also added significant new features and capabilities for controls and containers.

Along with the OLE Control '96 specification, Microsoft released another document called *OLE Control and Container Guidelines 2.0*. This document changed significantly the definition of the term *ActiveX control*. The next few sections cover these changes in more detail.

From this point, I'll use the term ActiveX control except when referring to document titles. However, the term OLE control was used before April, 1996.

NOTE

The OLE Control '94 Specification

The original ActiveX control architecture was specified as an extension to the existing OLE document specification. An ActiveX control had to implement all the interfaces required by an embedded OLE document server with in-place activation capabilities. Additionally, ActiveX controls had to implement several new control-specific interfaces. In all, a control that meets the OLE Control '94 specification would implement more than 15 interfaces.

Implementing a component, such as an ActiveX control, that requires 15 interface implementations is a lot of work. Fortunately, MFC provided an implementation for the majority of these interfaces, so building ActiveX controls based on this early specification wasn't overwhelming as long as you used MFC.

One of the problems with the control specification was that it provided only guidelines as to how a control and container should implement their interfaces. Early on, there were several problems in getting controls to behave similarly in each of the available containers (most control developers would say that this situation still exists). To help with this situation, Microsoft released a document that described how a container and its controls should interact with one another.

Much of this coordination was already described via the OLE document specification, but there was still a need for a document that would help developers understand the complex relationship between a control and its container. The resulting document was titled *OLE Controls and Container Guidelines* Version 1.1 (circa late 1995). The guideline puts forth the minimum requirements that a control or control container must meet. It describes the interfaces that are mandatory and those that are optional.

OLE Controls '96 Specification

Although ActiveX controls provided a wonderful new technology that validated the concept of component-based development, they weren't perfect. The large number of interfaces and methods that a control had to implement, coupled with the requirement that most controls create a window when executing, made them somewhat "heavy."

Building an application with a large number of ActiveX controls could be problematic. There were also some functionality holes that needed to be filled. To address these issues, Microsoft released in early 1996 the OLE Controls '96 specification. The changes to the existing control specification are embodied mostly in a series of new interfaces.

Control and Container Guidelines

Along with the OLE Controls '96 specification, Microsoft released a new version of the control and containers guidelines document. By following the guidelines, developers can ensure that their controls and containers work reliably together. The ActiveX control is becoming ubiquitous within development tools and applications. The large number of controls and containers, with their specialized functionality, makes it imperative for certain guidelines to be followed. By following the guidelines, a developer makes the control or container useful within the largest number of development environments.

One of the major changes in the new guidelines document is a new definition of what an ActiveX control is. The document states that an ActiveX control is any specialized COM object that supports the IUnknown interface and self-registration. The trouble with this definition is that every COM object fits it. In other words, every component that we've developed in this book is technically an ActiveX control! The definition is so broad that it is useless. Most developers use the term *ActiveX control* to describe those controls that work in most commercial ActiveX control containers (Visual Basic, Visual C++, and so on), a definition that is quite different from the one in this document.

Listed next are the various control functional categories detailed in the guidelines document.

- **A COM object.** An ActiveX control is just a specialized COM object. The only true requirement for a control is that it support self-registration and the IUnknown interface. However, such a control could not provide much functionality. According to the guidelines, a control developer should add only those interfaces that the control needs, with the ultimate purpose being to make the control as lightweight as possible.

- **Self-registration.** A control must support self-registration by implementing the DllRegisterServer and DllUnregisterServer functions, and it must add the appropriate OLE document and automation server entries in the registry. A control must also use the component categories API to indicate which services are required to host the control.

- **Interface support.** If a control supports an interface, it must support it at a basic level. The document provides guidelines for each potential ActiveX control and container interface. It describes which methods must be implemented within each interface that is implemented.

- **Persistence support.** If a control needs to support persistence, it must implement at least one IPersist* interface and should support more than one if possible. This arrangement makes it easier for a container to host the control. Support for IPersistPropertyBag is highly recommended, because most of the major containers provide a **Save as text** capability.

- **Ambient properties.** If a control supports ambient properties, it must support a certain number of ambient properties exposed by the container. They are LocalID, UserMode, UIDead, ShowGrabHandles, ShowHatching, and DisplayAsDefault.

- **Dual interfaces.** ActiveX controls and containers are strongly encouraged to support dual interfaces. If you recall from Chapter 6, a component implements a dual interface by providing both an IDispatch interface and a custom interface for its methods and properties.

- **Miscellaneous.** ActiveX controls should not use the WS_GROUP or WS_TABSTOP window flags, because it may conflict with the container's use of these flags. A control should honor a container's call to IOleControl::FreezeEvents. When events are frozen, a container will discard event notifications from the control.

The control and containers guideline document made a significant change in what is required for a COM object to be an ActiveX control. The only requirement for an ActiveX control is that it support self-registration and IUnknown. That's it! This is quite a change from the earlier specification and guidelines, which required a control to implement at least 15 interfaces. What the document is saying is that any COM object that provides self-registration *is* an ActiveX control.

This means that a control now has tremendous flexibility in choosing which interfaces it should implement. If you want your component to function as an ActiveX control, you usually need to implement a number of interfaces. The new guidelines have basically put all the pressure on container developers. Because a control can pick and choose the interfaces it wants to implement, the container must be very careful about what it assumes a control can do.

This new definition has caused much consternation in the developer community, and as of this writing this issue hasn't been completely resolved. It's not all bad, because frameworks such as MFC and ATL make it easy to implement *full-function* controls, which implement the 20 or so interfaces that allow them to work in most containers. However, as described earlier, the guidelines document details what functionality a control might provide by describing those interfaces that actually provide the control's functionality. It's a good way to group the interfaces that a control should implement, and that is how we'll go through the next few sections.

ACTIVEX CONTROL FUNCTIONAL CATEGORIES

An ActiveX control is a COM object that supports those interfaces required to implement any desired functionality. In the next few sections we will cover each of these functional categories. At the end of this chapter we will implement a full-function ActiveX control; as we go through each functional category, code fragments from our control example will be presented.

BASIC COM SUPPORT

An ActiveX control is first and foremost a COM object and must provide the most basic COM service: an implementation of the IUnknown interface. To create an instance of a control, the control housing (a DLL in our case) must also expose a class factory. We've already discussed this process in detail.

Self-Registration

A control must also support self-registration. As we've discussed, ATL provides support for self-registration through its Registrar component. ATL provides a default **.RGS** file for a control that adds several new registry entries that controls will typically use. Following is the RGS file for our example control.

```
HKCR
{
    PostItCtl.PostItCtl.1 = s 'PostItCtl Class'
    {
        CLSID = s '{CFC43231-50AC-11D1-B5EC-0004ACFF171C}'
    }
    PostItCtl.PostItCtl = s 'PostItCtl Class'
    {
        CurVer = s 'PostItCtl.PostItCtl.1'
    }
    NoRemove CLSID
    {
        ForceRemove {CFC43231-50AC-11D1-B5EC-0004ACFF171C} = s 'PostItCtl Class'
        {
            ProgID = s 'PostItCtl.PostItCtl.1'
            VersionIndependentProgID = s 'PostItCtl.PostItCtl'
            ForceRemove 'Programmable'
            InprocServer32 = s '%MODULE%'
            {
                val ThreadingModel = s 'Apartment'
            }
            ForceRemove 'Control'
            ForceRemove 'Programmable'
            ForceRemove 'Insertable'
            ForceRemove 'ToolboxBitmap32' = s '%MODULE%, 202'
            'MiscStatus' = s '0'
            {
                '1' = s '131473'
            }
            'TypeLib' = s '{CFC43223-50AC-11D1-B5EC-0004ACFF171C}'
            'Version' = s '1.0'
            'Verb'
            {
                '0' = s '&Properties, 0, 2'
            }
        }
    }
}
```

Control Registry Entries

Self-registration is basically the act of adding a number of registry keys and values to the Windows registry. As you can tell by the RGS file, ActiveX controls have a number of special registry entries that we have not encountered before. Each of the following control entries is a subkey under \HKEY_CLASSES_ROOT\CLSID.

Control

The Control entry indicates that the component is an ActiveX control. This entry allows containers to easily identify the ActiveX controls available on the system by searching through the registry looking only for CLSIDs with a Control subkey. This mechanism for marking a control is now obsolete, and you should instead use a specific component category (we'll discuss these in a moment). However, for backward compatibility, the Control entry should still be added to the registry.

Programmable

The Programmable key specifies that the component supports automation. Most ActiveX controls support automation through an IDispatch or dual interface. This has also been replaced with a new component category.

Insertable

The Insertable entry indicates that the component can be embedded within an OLE document container. This is the entry used by OLE document containers such as Visio, Word, and Excel. OLE document containers populate the Insert Object dialog box by spinning through the registry looking for components marked with the Insertable key. Controls should add this subkey only if they can provide functionality when embedded within an OLE document container.

MiscStatus

The MiscStatus entry specifies options of interest to the control container. These values can be queried before the control is embedded. The value for this entry is an integer equivalent of a bit mask value composed of optional OLEMISC flags. The MiscStatus values are described in Table 8.1.

Table 8.1 Control OLEMISC Status Bits

NAME	PURPOSE
ACTIVATEWHENVISIBLE	Set to indicate that the control prefers to activate when visible. This option can be very expensive when there are a large number of controls. The new Controls '96 specification makes it possible for controls to perform most functions even when not active. This flag should be set so that the control will work in containers that do not support the new specification.
IGNOREACTIVATEWHENVISIBLE	Added by the Controls '96 specification. If a control supports the new optimized control behavior, it should set this flag to inform new containers that they can safely use the Controls '96 specification enhancements.
INVISIBLEATRUNTIME	Indicates that the control should be visible only during the design phase. When running, the control should not be visible. Any control that provides only nonvisual services will fit in this category.

(continted)

Table 8.1 *(continued)*

NAME	PURPOSE
ALWAYSRUN	The control should always be running. Controls such as those that are invisible at run time may need to set this bit to ensure that they are loaded and running at all times so that their events can be communicated to the container.
ACTSLIKEBUTTON	The control is a button and so should behave differently if the container indicates to the control that it should act as a default button.
ACTSLIKELABEL	The container should treat this control as a static label. For example, it should always set focus to the next control in the tab order.
NOUIACTIVE	Indicates that the control does not support UI activation. The control may still be in-place activated but does not have a UI-active state.
ALIGNABLE	Indicates that the control would like for the container to provide a way to align the control in various ways, usually along a side or at the top of the container.
IMEMODE	Indicates that the control understands the input method editor mode. This is used for localization and internationalization within controls.
SIMPLEFRAME	The control uses the ISimpleFrameSite interface (if supported by the container). ISimpleFrameSite allows a control to contain instances of other controls. This is similar to group box functionality.
SETCLIENTSITEFIRST	Controls set this bit to indicate to the container that they would like their site within the container to be set up before the control's construction. This enables the control to use information from the client site (particularly ambient properties) during loading.

Verb

A control should have the Verb key with a Properties entry. The Properties entry allows a container to display the control's property page.

ToolboxBitmap32

The ToolboxBitmap32 entry value specifies the filename and resource ID of the bitmap used for the toolbar of the container. ATL does not provide a default bitmap for its controls, but it is easy to add one yourself.

TypeLib

The TypeLib entry value specifies the GUID and actual location of the type library for the component. All components that have a type library should add this registry entry.

Component Categories

Early in the days of ActiveX controls, the preceding registry entries were all that were needed to specify the functionality of a control. The Control registry key indicated that a component was a control, and the `Insertable` key indicated whether the control could function as a simple OLE document server. Today, however, the functional capabilities of all COM-based components (especially controls) continues to expand rapidly. A more efficient and descriptive mechanism for categorizing the capabilities provided by these objects is needed. The control guidelines require that new controls support something called *component categories*. Component categories are used to describe two things within a component: first, those capabilities that a component implements (for example, that it's an ActiveX control), and second, categories that describe which facilities are required from its client to provide its functionality (for example, that the container must support a certain interface).

The CATID

Component categories are identified using a category ID (CATID). A CATID is just another name for a GUID. Along with the CATID there is a locale ID, which is specified by a string of hexadecimal digits and a human-readable string. The known CATIDs are stored in the registry under the `HKEY_CLASSES_ROOT\Component Categories` key. Figure 8.3 shows some of the registry entries under this key. The OLEVIEW utility can display components by their component categories.

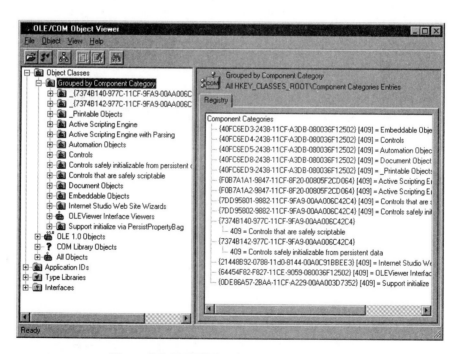

Figure 8.3 OLEVIEW and component categories.

For backward compatibility, older registry entries that were previously used to categorize components are supported. As you can see from Figure 8.3, some registry entries have an OldKey entry. This provides a way to map the older registry mechanism to component categories. Table 8.2 lists the CATIDs associated with the old registry entries.

Table 8.2 Category IDs for Old Registry Entries

OLD REGISTRY ENTRY	CATID SYMBOL FROM COMCAT.H	GUID
Control	CATID_Control	40FC6ED4-2438-11cf-A3DB-080036F12502
Insertable	CATID_Insertable	40FC6ED3-2438-11cf-A3DB-080036F12502
Programmable	CATID_Programmable	40FC6ED5-2438-11cf-A3DB-080036F12502
DocObject	CATID_DocObject	40FC6ED8-2438-11cf-A3DB-080036F12502
Printable	CATID_Printable	40FC6ED9-2438-11cf-A3DB-080036F12502

Categorizing Your Components

You categorize components in two different ways: by the component's capabilities and by the capabilities required by its potential client (its container). Two new registry entries are used to communicate this information. The Implemented Categories entry lists those category capabilities that your component provides, and the Required Categories entry lists those categories that your component requires from its client. These subkeys are added below the CLSID of a component. Figure 8.4 shows the categories for our example control.

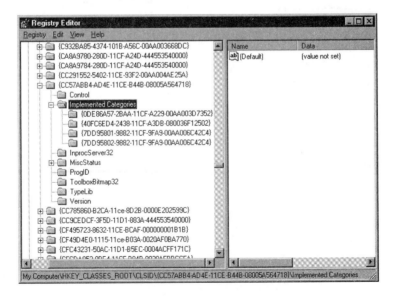

Figure 8.4 A component's categories in REGEDIT.

Currently, the Component Categories specification describes a few standard categories. Additional categories will be added as the technologies require them. For example, the ActiveX scripting model uses two component categories to indicate scripting support within controls. Table 8.3 shows some of the defined categories as of this writing.

NOTE Component categories do not have to be predefined by Microsoft. You are welcome to create your own categories for your own components. At DST Systems, where I work, we have defined several categories for the different types of components we develop.

Table 8.3 Component Categories

CATID SYMBOL FROM COMCAT.H	PURPOSE
CATID_PersistsToMoniker, CATID_PersistsToStreamInit, CATID_PersistsToStream, CATID_PersistsToStorage, CATID_PersistsToMemory, CATID_PersistsToFile, CATID_PersistsToPropertyBag	Used by Internet-aware controls to indicate which persistence methods they support. These categories can be used to indicate that an inter face is required if the control supports only one persistence method.
CATID_SimpleFrameControl	The control implements or requires the container to provide ISimpleFrameSite interface support.
CATID_PropertyNotifyControl	The control supports simple data binding.
CATID_WindowlessObject	The control implements the new windowless feature of the Controls '96 specification.
CATID_VBFormat, CATID_VBGetControl	The control uses one or both of these Visual Basic–specific interfaces.
CATID_VBDataBound	The control supports the advanced data binding interfaces.
CATID_RequiresDataPathHost	The control expects help from the container with its data path properties. The container must support IBindHost.
CATID_InternetAware	The control implements or requires some of the Internet-specific functionality, in particular the new persistence mechanisms for Web-based controls. The control also handles large property values with the new data path property type. This includes support for asynchronous downloads.
CATID_SafeForScripting	The control is safe for use within scripting environments.
CATID_SafeForInitializing	The control can safely be initialized.

To support component categories, Microsoft has defined two new COM interfaces—ICatRegister and ICatInformation—that make working with component categories easier, because there is no need to muck with the registry directly. Also, Microsoft has provided a system-level component that implements these interfaces; it's called Component Categories Manager.

Component Categories Manager

The Component Categories Manager (CCM) is a simple in-process server that implements the ICatRegister and ICatInformation interfaces. Component categories are defined registry entries, and CCM provides a simple way to maintain these entries within the registry. To create an instance of CCM, you use the COM CoCreateInstance function and pass the defined CCM CLSID: CLSID_StdComponentCategoriesMgr. You can request either of the two interfaces it implements.

ICatRegister

The ICatRegister interface provides methods for registering and unregistering categories at both the system and the component level. Here's its definition.

```
interface ICatRegister : IUnknown
{
    HRESULT RegisterCategories(
        ULONG cCategories,
        CATEGORYINFO rgCategoryInfo[]);

    HRESULT UnRegisterCategories(
        ULONG cCategories,
        CATID rgcatid[]);

    HRESULT RegisterClassImplCategories(
        REFCLSID rclsid,
        ULONG cCategories,
        CATID rgcatid[]);

    HRESULT UnRegisterClassImplCategories(
        REFCLSID rclsid,
        ULONG cCategories,
        CATID rgcatid[]);

    HRESULT RegisterClassReqCategories(
        REFCLSID rclsid,
        ULONG cCategories,
        CATID rgcatid[]);

    HRESULT UnRegisterClassReqCategories(
        REFCLSID rclsid,
        ULONG cCategories,
        CATID rgcatid[]);
};
```

There are six registration methods, but three are used to reverse the registration process. The RegisterCategory method takes the count and an array of CATEGORYINFO entries and ensures that they are registered on the system as valid component categories. This means placing them below the HKEY_CLASSES_ROOT\Component Categories key. In most cases, the category will already be in the registry, but it doesn't hurt to make sure. Here's the definition of the CATEGORYINFO structure and some simple code that shows how to use the RegisterCategory method.

```
typedef struct  tagCATEGORYINFO
{
   CATID catid;
   LCID lcid;
   OLECHAR szDescription[ 128 ];
} CATEGORYINFO;

// Include the component category interfaces and symbols
#include "comcat.h"
...
HRESULT CreateComponentCategory( CATID catid, WCHAR* catDescription )
{
   ICatRegister* pcr = NULL;
   HRESULT hr = S_OK;

   // Create an instance of the category manager.
   hr = CoCreateInstance( CLSID_StdComponentCategoriesMgr,
                     NULL,
                     CLSCTX_INPROC_SERVER,
                     IID_ICatRegister,
                     (void**) &pcr );
   if (FAILED(hr))
      return hr;

   CATEGORYINFO catinfo;
   catinfo.catid = catid;
   // English locale ID in hex
   catinfo.lcid = 0x0409;

   // Make sure the description isn't too big.
   int len = wcslen(catDescription);
   if (len>127)
      len = 127;
   wcsncpy( catinfo.szDescription, catDescription, len );
   catinfo.szDescription[len] = '\0';

   hr = pcr->RegisterCategories( 1, &catinfo );
   pcr->Release();

   return hr;
}
```

The preceding code creates an instance of the CCM and queries for ICatRegister. If everything works, a CATEGORYINFO structure is filled with the component information, and the RegisterCategory method is called.

To add \Implemented Categories registry entries for a specific component, you use the RegisterClassImplCategories method. The method takes three parameters: the CLSID of the component, a count of the number of CATIDs, and an array of CATIDs to place under the \Implemented Categories key. Here's some code to mark a control as implementing the Control category.

```
ICatRegister* pcr = NULL ;
HRESULT hr = S_OK ;

// Create an instance of the category manager.
hr = CoCreateInstance( CLSID_StdComponentCategoriesMgr,
                       NULL,
                       CLSCTX_INPROC_SERVER,
                       IID_ICatRegister,
                       (void**)&pcr );
if (SUCCEEDED(hr))
{
   // Register that we support the  "Control" category
   CATID rgcatid[1];
   rgcatid[0] = CATID_Control;
   hr = pcr->RegisterClassImplCategories(clsid, 1, rgcatid);
}

if (pcr != NULL)
   pcr->Release();
```

To add \Category Required entries for a component, you use the RegisterClassReqCategories method. The method takes the same parameters as RegisterClassImplCategrories, so the code is nearly identical to that just shown.

Component Categories and ATL

The ATL Registrar component allows us to add component categories for our controls without writing any (C++) code. To add an entry to the Implemented Categories or Category Required key to the registry for your control, add the key and value to your control's **.RGS** file under the CLSID section.

```
NoRemove CLSID
{
   ForceRemove {CFC43231-50AC-11D1-B5EC-0004ACFF171C} = s 'PostItCtl Class'
   {
      ...
      'Implemented Categories'
      {
        '{40FC6ED4-2438-11cf-A3DB-080036F12502}'
      }
      'Implemented Categories'
      {
        '{40FC6ED5-2438-11cf-A3DB-080036F12502}'
      }
      'Category Required'
      {
        '{40FC6ED7-2438-11cf-A3DB-080036F12502}'
      }
   }
}
```

OLE DOCUMENT INTERFACES

The technology that allows an ActiveX control to be embedded within a container has been around a long time. The OLE document standard (called Compound Documents at the time) was created in 1991 and was the major part of OLE. Actually, OLE at the time was an acronym for object linking and embedding. When ActiveX controls came along, the OLE document standard was enhanced to allow document servers to expose programmatic functionality.

Today, if your control needs to provide a visual representation and basic interaction with the user through mouse clicks and similar means, it must support the basic OLE document interfaces, including IOleObject, IOleInPlaceObject, IOleInPlaceActiveObject, IDataObject, and IViewObject2. Each of these interfaces is discussed briefly in Table 8.4. We'll see them again when we discuss ATL's control support classes.

Table 8.4 OLE Document Interfaces

INTERFACE	DESCRIPTION
IOleObject	IOleObject provides the essence of the OLE document architecture. Through this interface, the container and component communicate to negotiate the size of the embedded object (the control, in our case) as well as get the MiscStatus bits for the control.
IOleInPlaceObject	A control must implement IOleInPlaceObject to support the ability to be activated and deactivated in place within the container. The interface also provides a method to notify the control when its size changes or is moved within the container.
IOleInPlaceActiveObject	A control must implement IOleInPlaceActiveObject to provide support for the use and translation of accelerator keys within the control. Many of IOleInPlaceActiveObject's methods are not required for ActiveX controls.
IOleControl	IOleControl is a new interface added to support ActiveX controls. It provides methods to enhance the interaction with the control's container. IOleControl primarily adds functionality to let the control and container work together when handling keyboard input.
IDataObject	A control implements this interface to provide graphical renderings to the container. IDataObject is also used to provide a property set for its persistent properties.
IViewObject2	IViewObject2 is implemented by controls that provide a visual aspect. IViewObject2 provides the container with methods to ask the control to render itself within the container's client area.

AUTOMATION SUPPORT: `IDispatch`

We discussed automation and the IDispatch interface in detail back in Chapter 6. An ActiveX control is required to expose its functionality (methods and properties) through an IDispatch-based interface. The guidelines recommend that controls implement IDispatch using duals, because they provide the most efficient and flexible implementation.

Automation is used in other areas of ActiveX controls. An ActiveX control container exposes its ambient properties though a dispinterface. Also, control events are implemented with automation through COM's connectable object technology, which we covered in Chapter 7. We'll touch on this briefly in a moment.

Standard and Stock Properties

The ActiveX control specifications provide a set of standard properties that should be used when you're implementing a property that provides some common control functionality. This approach provides a uniform interface for the control user. Examples of such common properties include Font and BackColor. Table 8.5 lists the standard properties currently defined by the standard. You will also encounter the term *stock* property. Frameworks such as MFC and ATL provide default implementations of most standard properties. When they do, they are termed stock properties.

Table 8.5 Standard Control Properties

PROPERTY	DESCRIPTION
Appearance*	Appearance of the control (such as 3-D).
AutoSize*	If TRUE, the control should size to fit within its container.
BackColor*	The background color of the control.
BorderStyle*	The style of the control's border; a short that currently supports only two values. A 0 indicates no border, and 1 indicates a normal, single-line border around the control. More styles may be defined in the future.
BorderColor*	The color of the border around the control.
BorderWidth*	The width of the border around the control.
BorderVisible*	Show the border.
DrawMode*	The mode of drawing used by the control.
DrawStyle*	The style of drawing used by the control.
DrawWidth*	The width of the pen used for drawing.
FillColor*	The fill color.
FillStyle*	The style of the fill color.
Font*	The font used for any text in the control.
ForeColor*	The color of any text or graphics within the control.
Enabled*	TRUE indicates that the control can accept input.
HWnd*	The hWnd of the control's window.
ReadyState*	Indicates the readiness state of a control. Used with data bound or asynchronous properties. We'll cover this in Chapter 9.
TabStop	The control's participation in the tab stop scheme.
Text*, Caption*	A BSTR that indicates the caption or text of the control. Both properties are implemented with the same internal methods. Only one of the two may be used.

* INDICATES STOCK IMPLEMENTATION PROVIDED BY ATL

When implementing properties in your controls, you should use one of the standard property names whenever possible. If you need a property that indicates the background color of your control, use the BackColor standard property. This makes things easier on the control user who already understands the purpose of the BackColor property.

Ambient Properties

ActiveX controls usually exist within the context of a control container. The container provides the environment through which the control provides its functionality. A control, however, can learn a lot about this environment by communicating with the container. The control standard specifies that containers should expose a set of *ambient* properties, which allow the control to query for certain container characteristics. An example of an ambient property is UserMode. As we've discussed earlier, a container has two modes of operation: design-time mode and run-time mode. A control can determine the container's current mode by checking the UserMode ambient property.

Ambient properties are provided by the default IDispatch of the container. As a control is loaded into the container, the ambient dispatch is passed to the control through IOleObject::SetClientSite. The control saves this pointer, and, when it needs an ambient property value, it calls through the IDispatch pointer. Each of the ambient properties has a specified DISPID, so access to the property is easy. Table 8.6 lists the standard ambient properties. Note that containers do not have to expose all of these properties, although most of the good containers do.

Table 8.6 Ambient Properties

PROPERTY	DESCRIPTION
BackColor	Default background color for the control.
DisplayName	The name of the control as given by the container. This name should be used when the control needs to display information to the user.
Font	The default font for the control.
ForeColor	Foreground color for text.
LocaleID	The container's locale identifier.
MessageReflect	If this property is TRUE, the container supports reflecting messages back to the control.
ScaleUnits	A string name for the container's coordinate units (such as twips or cm).
TextAlign	Indicates how the control should justify any textual information.
	0: Numbers to the right, text to the left 1: Left justify 2: Center justify 3: Right justify 4: Fill justify
UserMode	Returns TRUE if the container is in run mode; otherwise, the container is in design mode.
UIDead	Indicates to the control that it should not accept or act on any user input directed to the control. Containers may use this property to indicate to the control that it is in design mode or that it is running but the developer has interrupted processing during debugging.
ShowGrabHandles	If TRUE, the control should show grab handles when UI active.
ShowHatching	If TRUE, the control should show diagonal hatch marks around itself when UI active.
DisplayAsDefault	The container sets this property to TRUE for a button style control when it becomes the default button within the container. This occurs when the user tabs to the specific control or when the control is the default button on the form and the focus is on a nonbutton control. The button should indicate that it is the default button by increasing the thickness of its border.
SupportsMnemonics	If TRUE, the container supports the use of mnemonics within controls.
AutoClip	If TRUE, the container automatically clips any portion of the control's rectangle that should not be displayed. If FALSE, the control should honor the clipping rectangle passed to it in the IOleInPlaceObject's SetObjectRects method.

ATL and Ambient Properties

The container's ambient properties can be accessed by an ATL-based control through the GetAmbient* methods provided by the CComControl class. Each method name begins with GetAmbient and is followed by the appropriate ambient name. For example, the following code uses several ambient properties when a control is drawing its representation.

```
BOOL bUserMode = FALSE;
GetAmbientUserMode( bUserMode );
if ( bUserMode == FALSE )
{
    HFONT hOldFont = 0;
    IFont* pFont = 0;
    if ( SUCCEEDED( GetAmbientFont( &pFont )) && pFont )
    {
        HFONT hFont;
        pFont->get_hFont( &hFont );
        hOldFont = (HFONT) SelectObject( hdc, hFont );

        pFont->Release();
    }

    BSTR bstr;
    if ( SUCCEEDED( GetAmbientDisplayName( bstr )))
    {
        DrawText( hdc,
                  OLE2A( bstr ),
                  -1,
                  &rc,
                  DT_TOP | DT_SINGLELINE );
    }

    if ( hOldFont )
        SelectObject( hdc, hOldFont );
}
```

The code first gets the ambient UserMode, which indicates whether the container is currently in the design phase or the run phase. When in design mode, most controls draw their ambient display name as part of the design-time representation. Next, we get the ambient font and ambient display name and render it using the DrawText Win32 API function.

Standard Control Methods

The ActiveX control specification recommends three standard control methods that controls should implement if they provide the specific behavior. Each method is shown in Table 8.7.

Table 8.7 Standard Control Methods

Method	Description
AboutBox	Show the About box for the control.
Refresh	Forces a redraw of the control's representation.
DoClick	Fires the standard Click event within the control.

Connectable Objects and Control Events

To support events, an ActiveX control uses the connectable objects technology that we described in Chapter 7. A control's events are specified through its outgoing IDispatch-based interface, just as we did with the Chapter 7 connection point example. Here's a look at our example control's event interface. Notice that it is marked with the source and default interface attributes.

```
[
    uuid(5010B641-6516-11d1-B5F7-0004ACFF171C),
    helpstring("_PostItEvents Interface"),
]
dispinterface _PostItEvents
{
    properties:
    methods:
        [id(DISPID_CLICK)] void Click();
};
[
    uuid(CFC43231-50AC-11D1-B5EC-0004ACFF171C),
    helpstring("PostItCtl Class")
]
coclass PostItCtl
{
    [default] interface IPostItCtl;
    [default, source] dispinterface _PostItEvents;
};
```

A control must also implement the IConnectionPointContainer interface on its main QueryInterface. It will also provide a connection point object that implements IConnectionPoint. This allows the container to pass its implementation of the control's outgoing dispinterface.

Standard Events

Just as it does with properties and methods, the ActiveX control standard describes a set of standard events that a control can implement. The events are primarily for graphical controls. Each of the standard events is listed in Table 8.8.

Table 8.8 Standard Events

EVENT	DESCRIPTION
Click	Fired by a BUTTONUP event for any mouse button.
DblClick	Fired by BUTTONDBLCLK message for any mouse button.
Error	Fired by the control when an error occurs.
KeyDown	Fired by the WM_SYSKEYDOWN or WM_KEYDOWN message.
KeyPress	Fired by the WM_CHAR message.
KeyUp	Fired by the WM_SYSKEYUP or WM_KEYUP message.
MouseDown	Fired by the BUTTONDOWN event for any mouse button.
MouseMove	Fired by the WM_MOUSEMOVE message.
MouseUp	Fired by the BUTTONUP event for any mouse button.

PROPERTY PAGES

One of the most important aspects of a control's functionality is its properties. ActiveX controls have the option of providing a series of control-specific property pages, which let you present control-specific information. The guidelines recommend that all controls that expose properties also implement property pages. Property pages are typically used during the design phase to provide a rich environment in which the control user manipulates the properties of the control. Figure 8.5 shows the property page for the control we will build at the end of the chapter.

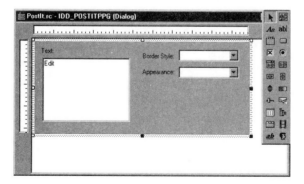

Figure 8.5 Our example control's property page.

Each property page is itself a COM component and is instantiated independently by the container application. Development frameworks may include certain standard property pages. For example, ATL provides an implementation of three common property pages: fonts, colors, and pictures. However, you will typically implement a custom property page for each of your controls for those properties that are not of the preceding types.

Most development tools (such as Visual Basic) provide a property window for showing and setting your control's properties, but this is not always the case. For this reason you should always provide a complete set of property pages for your control.

During the application design process, the control user can modify a control's properties. When the user selects to edit a control's properties, the container will ask the control for its list of property pages. The container then instantiates each property page component individually and merges them to form a property sheet. As property values are modified, the property page communicates directly with the control (through its IDispatch) to update any values. Figure 8.6 shows our complete control's property sheet, and Table 8.9 describes each property page interface.

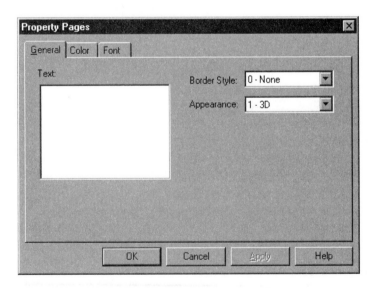

Figure 8.6 Our control's property sheet.

Table 8.9 Property Page Interfaces

INTERFACE	DESCRIPTION
ISpecifyPropertyPages	A control implements this interface to provide the container with a list of its associated property pages. The GetPages method returns an array of CLSIDs, one for each property page.
IPropertyPageSite	IPropertyPageSite facilitates communication between the property page component and the property sheet frame as implemented by the container. An IPropertyPageSite pointer is provided to each property page after it has been instantiated through IPropertyPage::SetPageSite. The OnStatusChange method is used by the property page to indicate to the frame that one or more properties have been modified.
IPropertyPage2	IPropertyPage2 is implemented by each property page component and provides the container with methods to get the size of, move, create, destroy, activate, and deactivate the component's property page window. The container creates a frame for each property page and uses these methods to manage the display of the property sheet. This allows the property sheet to appear and behave as if driven by one application; in fact, a property sheet comprises individual components housed within a frame window created by the container.

PROPERTY PERSISTENCE

One of the most important aspects of ActiveX controls is the ability of their state to persist. As part of the design process, control users will modify a control's state by manipulating its properties (through its property pages). A control embedded within a container is an instance of that control. Each control within the container has its own set of property values that makes the instance unique. For a control to maintain the state of its properties after the container shuts down, it must support a persistence mechanism.

Since its inception, the OLE document standard has provided support for component persistence. The container provides the environment whereby embedded servers (such as controls) can save and restore their internal states. Controls require assistance from the container because the container is in charge of the complete document or development environment. For example, when you're using a Visual Basic form, the form itself maintains the state of any embedded controls in the **.FRM** file. The embedded controls have very little knowledge of how the form saves their states.

All this is done through a series of COM interfaces. There are a number of such interfaces, because they have evolved over the years. For ActiveX controls, the three most important persistence interfaces are IPersistStream, IPersistStreamInit, and IPersistPropertyBag.

IPersistStream

IPersistStream is part of the OLE document specification and provides a simple mechanism for a component to maintain the persistence of state. A stream is a simple file structure, defined by OLE, that provides a stream-oriented structure to the component. The component (a control) implements the IPersistStream interface, which contains methods such as Load and Save. The client application (our container) determines whether the component supports persistence by querying for one of the IPersist* interfaces. In our example, the control would return a pointer to its implementation of IPersistStream. The container would then create and open a stream and pass it as a parameter to the IPersistStream::Load and IPersistStream::Save methods.

IPersistStreamInit

The IPersistStreamInit interface was added with the ActiveX control specification and provides a way for the control to initialize its state (i.e. set any default property values) before its properties are initialized by the container. A new method, InitNew, was added to support this capability. By implementing InitNew, a control can initialize its state (as a constructor does) before any persistent information is loaded.

IPersistPropertyBag

A new persistence interface, IPersistPropertyBag, was added as part of the Controls '96 specification, which now allows "textual" persistence. IPersistPropertyBag and the container-side interface, IPropertyBag, provide an efficient method of saving and loading text-based properties. The control implements IPersistPropertyBag, through which the container calls Load and Save. Instead of providing a stream for the control to write to, the container provides an implementation of the IPropertyBag interface. The control and retrieves saves its property values by calling IPropertyBag::Read and IPropertyBag::Write. The property bag persistence mechanism is very effective in a Web-based environment, where a control's property information must be stored within the HTML document.

When you're using a control in Web environments, support for IPersistPropertyBag allows the control to use the HTML PARAM element. If a control implements IPersistStreamInit instead, the persistence of its properties is implemented using the HTML DATA element. By default, ATL-generated controls get support for IPersistStreamInit. In Chapter 9 we'll add the implementation for IPersistPropertyBag so that our controls will work effectively in Web environments.

ATL's Support for ActiveX Controls

At this point, we understand a lot of what goes into developing an ActiveX control. A control is an in-process component that implements a series of Microsoft-defined interfaces, most of which we have described. ATL gives you significant support for developing controls, because it provides default implementations for the majority of those interfaces a component must implement to be classified as a control.

In the next series of sections, we will cover ATL's support for developing ActiveX controls. We'll begin with coverage of the ATL Object wizard. After that we'll work our way through ATL's support classes for controls. We'll look at each interface that a fully functional control must implement. After we've examined each of ATL's support classes, the final part of the chapter will walk you through the development of a complete ActiveX control.

ATL's ActiveX Control Support Files

The implementation of ATL's ActiveX control support is provided in the **ATLCTL.H** and **ATLCTL.CPP** files in the ATL\INCLUDE directory. Both files are included in **STDAFX.CPP**. ATL's control implementation also depends on ATL's window support classes. These classes are similar to MFC's CWnd class and provide basic windowing support with very little overhead. The implementation of these classes is in **ATLWIN.H** and **ATLWIN.CPP**.

ATL Object Wizard

We've covered and used the ATL Object wizard in most of the chapters leading to this one. However, we haven't covered the **Controls** category of the wizard. Figure 8.7 shows the wizard's **Controls** category.

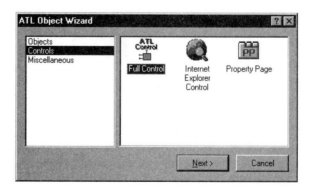

Figure 8.7 ATL Object wizard control types.

Three component types are provided here. A full ActiveX control provides default implementations of nearly all control-related interfaces. An Internet Explorer control implements those interfaces required to be embedded within Internet Explorer along with a property page component, which most controls should provide. We'll describe the implementation of a full control, because it demonstrates most of the interfaces implemented by a control.

The Names and Attributes Tabs

The Object wizard provides a series of four tabbed dialog boxes for setting the characteristics of an ActiveX control. We covered the options available on the first two tabs—**Names** and **Attributes**—in earlier chapters. When inserting a full control, you get two additional tabbed dialog boxes.

The Miscellaneous Tab

The **Miscellaneous** tab is used to provide ActiveX control–specific information to the Object wizard. The various options presented here are used only by ActiveX controls. The Miscellaneous dialog box is shown in Figure 8.8. The following section describes each of the options on the **Miscellaneous** tab.

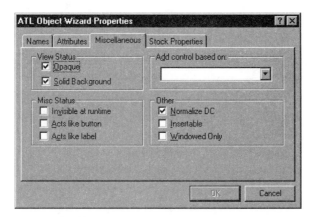

Figure 8.8 Object wizard's **Miscellaneous** tab.

VIEW STATUS AND TRANSPARENT CONTROLS

The **View Status** option indicates whether your control will act as an opaque control or as a transparent control. The OLE Control '96 specification added functionality that makes it easier to develop transparent controls, which can also be described as nonrectangular controls. The gist is that the background of the control can be transparent.

For example, Visual Basic has long had a *line* control whose purpose is to draw a simple line. Developing a control that mimics Visual Basic's line control was difficult using the earlier OLE Controls '94 specification. Graphical controls based on this specification used a window to render their graphical representation. Windows are rectangular creatures, and a difficulty arises when you're trying to draw items that do not completely "fill" a rectangle.

Controls based on the new specification typically do not require a window to do their work, so the creation of nonrectangular controls is much easier. If your control's representation can be drawn in a rectangular space, you should choose the **Opaque** option, which lets the container draw the background quickly. It makes a `FillRect` call with the background color. On the other hand, if you're developing a control that is transparent or nonrectangular, you should toggle off the **Opaque** option.

The **Solid Background** option is pertinent only when you choose the **Opaque** option. It indicates that your control has a solid background as opposed to a hatched pattern. It also allows the container to render your control more quickly.

Misc Status Bits

When a control is initially embedded within a container, negotiation occurs between the two entities. As the control and container negotiate, the control provides the container with a set of bits that describes certain characteristics of the control. There are a number of these MISC_STATUS bits, but only a few of them pertain directly to ActiveX controls and their containers. Earlier, Table 8.1 provided a list of those used by ActiveX controls.

The Object wizard's **Misc Status** frame allows you to specify three of these bits. **Invisible at runtime** indicates that your ActiveX control will be invisible during the runtime phase. An invisible control typically provides some nonvisual service. A good example is the timer control whose only purpose is to provide a series of events and no visual functionality. An invisible control, however, still provides some visual representation during the design phase.

The **Acts like button** and **Acts like label** bits are used by controls that provide functionality similar to that provided by buttons and labels. Because controls are small, independent components that have no knowledge of other controls in the container, they must rely on the container to provide container-wide information. For example, only the container knows whether a button is the current default button. Also, certain controls, such as labels, indicate to the container that they should be treated specially in the container's tabbing order. You will typically use these bits when implementing button-type and label-type controls.

ADD CONTROL BASED ON

The **Add control based on** option provides a skeletal project that superclasses an existing Windows control. You select the control to superclass from the drop-down list. You typically superclass a control because you need functionality that is similar to that provided by a standard Windows control—for example, an edit field that accepts only numbers, a Windows 95 tree view that allows multiple selections, a listbox that contains icons and text, and so on. By superclassing an existing control, you get some of the drawing code and control structures already implemented. Of course, if you owner-draw the control, you must do most of the drawing yourself.

NOTE

When developing ActiveX controls using MFC, you can instead subclass an existing Windows control. The techniques are very similar. Both subclassing and superclassing allow you to modify the behavior of an existing window class. Superclassing gives you a bit more control over the process, but it also requires more work to implement.

OTHER

The **Other** section allows you to customize certain aspects of your control. Each of the three options is described in Table 8.10.

Table 8.10 Other Options

OPTION	DESCRIPTION
Normalize DC	Checking this option will cause ATL to pass a normalized device context to your control. This option makes drawing easier but is less efficient.
Insertable	When you check this option, ATL will add the `Insertable` registry entry for your control. This indicates that the control can be embedded within standard OLE containers such as Microsoft Word.
Windowed Only	Controls created using the ATL will behave as windowless controls whenever possible. Windowless controls are more efficient than controls that create a window. However, older containers (such as Visual Basic 4.0) were created before the newer control specifications and do not support windowless controls. By default, ATL will create a window for controls when embedded in older containers and will not create a window when instantiated in containers that support windowless controls. By checking this option, you are specifying that your control always requires the existence of a window.

The Stock Properties Tab

When you're adding an ActiveX control component with the Object wizard, an additional tab is provided to set up the control's initial properties. Properties are characteristics of the control that map to an attribute or data member of the underlying component implementation. ATL provides stock implementations for several standard properties. The potential properties and their descriptions were shown in Table 8.5. Figure 8.9 shows the Stock Property dialog box.

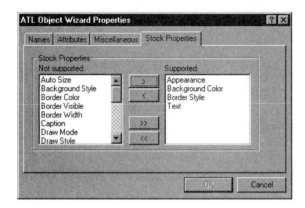

Figure 8.9 Adding stock properties.

For each property selected, the Object wizard adds property accessor methods to your control's IDL file and a data member of the appropriate type. The implementation of the property methods is provided by the CStockPropImpl class, which we'll discuss in a moment.

Files Created by the ATL Object Wizard

Just as in our previous examples, the Object wizard creates a number of files for our control's implementation. However, as you can see by the abbreviated listing that follows, the implementation classes now include a number of interfaces that we've not encountered before. These interfaces must be implemented by those controls that want to work in most commercial control containers (such as Visual Basic). We'll cover most of these classes in the next few sections.

```
class ATL_NO_VTABLE CPostItCtl :
    public CComObjectRootEx<CComSingleThreadModel>,
    public CComCoClass<CPostItCtl, &CLSID_PostItCtl>,
    public CComControl<CPostItCtl>,
    public CStockPropImpl<CPostItCtl, IPostItCtl, &IID_IPostItCtl,
    &LIBID_POSTITLib>,
    public IProvideClassInfo2Impl<&CLSID_PostItCtl,
                                  &DIID__PostItEvents, &LIBID_POSTITLib>,
    public IPersistStreamInitImpl<CPostItCtl>,
    public IPersistStorageImpl<CPostItCtl>,
```

(code continued on next page)

```
     public IQuickActivateImpl<CPostItCtl>,
     public IOleControlImpl<CPostItCtl>,
     public IOleObjectImpl<CPostItCtl>,
     public IOleInPlaceActiveObjectImpl<CPostItCtl>,
     public IViewObjectExImpl<CPostItCtl>,
     public IOleInPlaceObjectWindowlessImpl<CPostItCtl>,
     public IDataObjectImpl<CPostItCtl>,
     public IConnectionPointContainerImpl<CPostItCtl>,
     public IPropertyNotifySinkCP<CPostItCtl>,
     public ISpecifyPropertyPagesImpl<CPostItCtl>,
{
...
BEGIN_COM_MAP(CPostItCtl)
    COM_INTERFACE_ENTRY(IPostItCtl)
    COM_INTERFACE_ENTRY(IDispatch)
    COM_INTERFACE_ENTRY_IMPL(IViewObjectEx)
    COM_INTERFACE_ENTRY_IMPL_IID(IID_IViewObject2, IViewObjectEx)
    COM_INTERFACE_ENTRY_IMPL_IID(IID_IViewObject, IViewObjectEx)
    COM_INTERFACE_ENTRY_IMPL(IOleInPlaceObjectWindowless)
    COM_INTERFACE_ENTRY_IMPL_IID(IID_IOleInPlaceObject,
    IOleInPlaceObjectWindowless)
    COM_INTERFACE_ENTRY_IMPL_IID(IID_IOleWindow, IOleInPlaceObjectWindowless)
    COM_INTERFACE_ENTRY_IMPL(IOleInPlaceActiveObject)
    COM_INTERFACE_ENTRY_IMPL(IOleControl)
    COM_INTERFACE_ENTRY_IMPL(IOleObject)
    COM_INTERFACE_ENTRY_IMPL(IQuickActivate)
    COM_INTERFACE_ENTRY_IMPL(IPersistStorage)
    COM_INTERFACE_ENTRY_IMPL(IPersistStreamInit)
    COM_INTERFACE_ENTRY_IMPL(ISpecifyPropertyPages)
    COM_INTERFACE_ENTRY_IMPL(IDataObject)
    COM_INTERFACE_ENTRY(IProvideClassInfo)
    COM_INTERFACE_ENTRY(IProvideClassInfo2)
    COM_INTERFACE_ENTRY_IMPL(IConnectionPointContainer)
END_COM_MAP()
...
};
```

Some of the interfaces, such as IConnectionPointContainer and IProvideClassInfo2, should be familiar, but others may not be. The important point is that it requires quite a bit of work to implement an ActiveX control if you're not using a framework such as MFC or ATL. By examining the preceding code, you should now see why.

CComControl

ATL provides a lot of its ActiveX control functionality via the CComControl class. This class is similar to MFC's COleControl implementation. By deriving our implementation class from CComControl we get support for a number of COM interfaces, stock properties, property persistence, and basic windowing functionality. As you can see from the following code, though, the majority of CComControl's behavior comes from CComControlBase and CWndowImpl.

```
template <class T>
class ATL_NO_VTABLE CComControl :
     public CComControlBase, public CWindowImpl<T>
{
...
};
```

CComControlBase

The CComControlBase class provides most of the functionality of CComControl. A control implements several COM interfaces, and many of these interfaces have subtle dependencies on one another. The CComControlBase class centralizes data members and functionality that is shared by several interface implementations, such as IOleObject, IDataObject, IViewObjectEx, and IOleInPlaceObject.

CWindowImpl

The CWindowImpl class derives from CWindow, which provides a thin wrapper around the Win32 windowing functions, and from CMessageMap, which allows CWindowImpl to implement message mapping and chaining. CWindoSwImpl gives a control the ability to use a window in its implementation, although the control does not have to use this functionality. If it does, though, it will have a basic windowing class through which window messages can be mapped to member functions. This is similar to the functionality provided by MFC message maps.

For example, a control can trap window messages and act on them. Here's the message map from our example control:

```
BEGIN_MSG_MAP(CPostItCtl)
   MESSAGE_HANDLER(WM_PAINT, OnPaint)
   MESSAGE_HANDLER(WM_SETFOCUS, OnSetFocus)
   MESSAGE_HANDLER(WM_KILLFOCUS, OnKillFocus)
   MESSAGE_HANDLER(WM_LBUTTONDOWN, OnLButtonDown)
END_MSG_MAP()
```

The MESSAGE_HANDLER macros map window messages to member functions. ATL message maps, like MFC, allow an object to route or chain messages to other objects. This is useful if your controls comprise multiple windows.

CStockPropImpl

The CStockPropImpl class provides ATL's stock property implementation. This class is similar to the IDispatchImpl class that we discussed in Chapter 6. In fact, if your control does not implement any stock properties, your implementation class will derive from IDispatchImpl instead of CStockPropImpl.

Our example control uses several stock properties. When they were added using the Object wizard's stock property dialog box, it added accessor methods to the IDL file and data members to our implementation class. Here's a look at the BackColor property.

```
// PostIt.IDL
...
interface IPostItCtl : IDispatch
{
    [propput, id(DISPID_BACKCOLOR)]
        HRESULT BackColor([in]OLE_COLOR clr);
    [propget, id(DISPID_BACKCOLOR)]
        HRESULT BackColor([out,retval]OLE_COLOR* pclr);
...
};

// PostItCtl.h
...
public:
    OLE_COLOR m_clrBackColor;
```

When the BackColor property declaration is passed through the MIDL compiler, it outputs accessor methods of the form: get_*PropertyName* and put_*PropertyName*. Here's a look at the resulting header file.

```
// PostIt.h
...
IPostItCtl : public IDispatch
{
public:
    virtual HRESULT put_BackColor( OLE_COLOR clr) = 0;
    virtual HRESULT get_BackColor( OLE_COLOR *pclr) = 0;
...
};
```

The CStockPropImpl class uses a series of macros to produce the implementation of the preceding methods. The IMPLEMENT_STOCKPROP macro for BackColor expands to this:

```
//IMPLEMENT_STOCKPROP(OLE_COLOR, BackColor, clrBackColor, DISPID_BACKCOLOR)
// expands to this:

HRESULT STDMETHODCALLTYPE put_BackColor(OLE_COLOR clrBackColor)
{
   CPostItCtl* pT = (CPostItCtl*) this;
   if (pT->FireOnRequestEdit(DISPID_BACKCOLOR) == S_FALSE)
      return S_FALSE;
   pT->m_clrBackColor = clrBackColor;
   pT->m_bRequiresSave = TRUE;
   pT->FireOnChanged(DISPID_BACKCOLOR);
   pT->FireViewChange();
   return S_OK;
}

HRESULT STDMETHODCALLTYPE get_BackColor(type* pclrBackColor)
{
   CPostItCtl* pT = (CPostItCtl*) this;
   *pclrBackColor = pT->m_clrBackColor;
   return S_OK;
}
```

As you can see, the name of the stock property member variable is important, because it is hard-coded into the implementation. Another important aspect of ATL's implementation of stock properties is that the ATL team used a strange technique to save space. The macros in CStockPropImpl are there all the time, but our controls don't always implement them. Why, then, doesn't the compiler complain that the stock property data members (such as m_clrBackColor) are not defined?

Thanks to a technique of using a blind union to ensure that the symbols for all the stock properties are predefined, everything works—but it's confusing the first time you run into it. The following union is declared in the CComControlBase class, and the comments give us a hint as to what's really going on.

```
union
{
   // m_nFreezeEvents is the only one actually used
   int m_nFreezeEvents; // count of freezes versus thaws

   // These are here to make stock properties work
   IPictureDisp* m_pMouseIcon;
   IPictureDisp* m_pPicture;
   IFontDisp* m_pFont;
   OLE_COLOR m_clrBackColor;
   OLE_COLOR m_clrForeColor;
...
```

(code continued on next page)

```
    BSTR m_bstrText;
    BSTR m_bstrCaption;
    long m_nBackStyle;
    long m_nBorderStyle;
    long m_nReadyState;
};
```

By placing in the union the names of each stock property member, the compiler is tricked into thinking that storage is allocated. However, only `m_nFreezeEvents` is actually used. Whenever the control developer implements a stock property such as `BackColor`, the *real* `m_clrBackColor` variable is declared within the implementation. Yes, this approach saves space, but it causes lots of gray hairs for those of us trying to figure this stuff out.

Initializing Stock Properties

When adding stock properties, the Object wizard provides only a default implementation of the `get` and `put` methods. You must initialize your properties to a default value. A good place to do this is in the control's constructors. It looks something like this:

```
CPostItCtl()
{
    m_nAppearance = 1;
    m_nBorderStyle = 0;

    // Backcolor is blue
    m_clrBackColor = RGB( 0, 255, 255 );

    // Foreground color is black
    m_clrForeColor = RGB( 0, 0, 0 );
}
```

Font Properties

Initialization of the stock font property requires a bit more work. When you're working in COM environments, fonts are handled a bit differently than when you're working with Win32 API calls. COM provides several APIs and interfaces to make a Windows font object serializable. The interfaces also allow a font to be marshaled across processes and machines.

```
static FONTDESC _fontDesc =
        { sizeof(FONTDESC), OLESTR("MS Sans Serif"), FONTSIZE( 12 ), FW_BOLD,
          ANSI_CHARSET, FALSE, FALSE, FALSE };
OleCreateFontIndirect( &_fontDesc,
                       IID_IFontDisp,
                       (void **)&m_pFont);
```

We initialize our stock font property to MS Sans Serif by creating a FONTDESC structure and passing it to the OleCreateFontIndirect API. COM implements a special font object that provides a mechanism to persist and marshal fonts. ActiveX controls use these fonts through the IFontDisp interface. Our control maintains an IFontDisp pointer to the current stock font object.

IOleObjectImpl

The IOleObject interface provides basic embedded object support so that the component can communicate with the container. IOleObject contains 21 methods: most of them are easy to implement, and only a few are of interest to an ActiveX control implementer. The SetExtent and GetExtent methods are used to negotiate a control's extent or size, and the GetMiscStatus method returns the OLEMISC status bits that we covered earlier.

ATL provides a functional implementation of IOleObject through its IOleObjectImpl class. The class provides the basic functionality that most controls need. Although the interface has 21 methods, only a few are actually needed by a control, so ATL implements only that subset.

Restricting the Size of a Control

As an example of how you might modify a control's behavior, let's demonstrate how to override one of IOleObject's methods. Certain controls may need to restrict their size or shape. When a control user changes the extents of a control, the container notifies the control of the new size through the IOleObject::SetExtent method. The SetExtent method takes as a parameter a SIZEL structure containing the new extents for the control. To restrict the size of the control, we override the default SetExtent method, check the new extents, and modify them if we need to. Here's how to do it for our example control.

```
// PostItCtl.h
...
class ATL_NO_VTABLE CPPostItCtl :
...
   STDMETHOD(SetExtent)(DWORD dwDrawAspect, SIZEL *psizel)
   {
      ATLTRACE(_T("SetExtent sizing control to 1000x1000\n"));
      psizel->cx = psizel->cy = 1000;
      return IOleObjectImpl<CPostItCtl>::SetExtent(dwDrawAspect, psizel);
   }
...
};
```

The SIZEL structure provides the extents in OLE's favorite unit: HIMETRIC. In our example, we force the control size to always be a square of 1,000 HIMETRIC units.

IViewObjectImpl

If a control expects to provide a visual representation, it should implement the IViewObjectEx interface. The IViewObject, IViewObject2, and IViewObjectEx interfaces are all related. Each interface is an extension of the others. The IViewObject interfaces provide a way for the container to ask a control to render itself. A control implements this interface and draws its representation onto a device context provided by the container. The initial version of this interface, IViewObject, was part of the original OLE document specification. The OLE Controls '94 specification added GetExtent, which allowed the container to get a control's extents through this interface instead of IOleObject. Finally, as part of the OLE Controls '96 specification, IViewObject2 was enhanced to create IViewObjectEx. The new interface includes five new methods that facilitate flicker-free drawing, nonrectangular objects, hit testing, and additional control sizing options.

ATL provides an implementation and support for all three of these view interfaces through its IViewObjectImpl class. The most important method of IViewObjectEx is the Draw method. Control containers call this method whenever they need the control to render itself. A number of parameters are passed, most of which deal with how and where to render the control's representation. ATL provides a simplification of the drawing process and ultimately calls the CComControl::OnDraw method.

CComControl::OnDraw

At both design time and run time, the container will ask a control to draw its representation through this method. The Object wizard provides a simple implementation of this method that draws the text "ATL 2.0."

```
HRESULT CNoteCtl::OnDraw(ATL_DRAWINFO& di)
{
    RECT& rc = *(RECT*)di.prcBounds;
    Rectangle(di.hdcDraw, rc.left, rc.top, rc.right, rc.bottom);
    DrawText( di.hdcDraw,
              _T("ATL 2.0"),
              -1,
              &rc,
              DT_CENTER | DT_VCENTER | DT_SINGLELINE );

    return S_OK;
}
```

The container passes a device context as well as the bounding rectangle in which the control should draw its representation.

IDataObjectImpl

The IDataObject interface is used by embedded servers to provide the container with a method of rendering data to a device other than a device context. ActiveX controls typically use the IViewObject* interfaces instead of IDataObject, but it can be implemented if needed.

ATL provides a basic implementation of IDataObject in its IDataObjectImpl class. IDataObjectImpl implements the GetData method, which returns a metafile representation of the control, which is used for printing a view of the document. It also implements the DAdvise and DUnadvise methods. These methods set up a notification interface through which the control can notify the container if its representation needs to be updated.

IOleInPlaceObjectImpl

A control must implement the OLE document IOleInPlaceObject interface to support the ability to be activated and deactivated in place within the container. The interface also provides a method to notify the control when its size changes or is moved within the container.

IOleInPlaceActiveObjectImpl

A control must implement IOleInPlaceActiveObject to provide support for the use and translation of accelerator keys within the control. Many of IOleInPlaceActiveObject's methods are not needed for ActiveX controls.

IOleControlImpl

The IOleControl interface provides four methods, through which the container gets information about a control's support for mnemonics (GetControlInfo, OnMnemonic), informs the control about any changes to the container's ambient properties (OnAmbientPropertyChange), and informs the control when it should and should not fire events (FreezeEvents).

ATL's implementation (IOleControlImpl) does nothing for the first three methods, and the implementation of FreezeEvents is pretty basic. FreezeEvents maintains a member variable, m_nFreezeEvents, that contains the current freeze count. A control should not fire events if this count is greater than zero. However, there is no support in ATL for enforcing this rule; you must do it yourself.

If your control needs to be notified of any change in an ambient property, override `OnAmbientPropertyChange`:

```
// Demonstrate overriding OnAmbientPropertyChange
STDMETHOD(OnAmbientPropertyChange)(DISPID dispid)
{
    ATLTRACE(_T("An ambient property changed\n"));
    return S_OK;
}
```

`IPersistStreamInitImpl` and `IPersistStorageImpl`

If a control has property values that need to persist between instantiations, it must support one or more of COM's persistence interfaces. The control and container work together to store a control's property values in a file (such as **FORM.FRM** and **PAGE.HTM**) managed by the container. ATL provides default implementations for the `IPersistStreamInit`, `IPersistStorage`, and `IPersistPropertyPage` interfaces in their corresponding `Impl` classes.

The implementation of these classes is fairly straightforward. However, ATL uses a series of macros that the control developer must use to indicate which properties in a control should persist. Four macros are used: `BEGIN_PROPERTY_MAP`, `PROP_ENTRY`, `PROP_PAGE`, and `END_PROPERTY_MAP`. These macros combine to produce a *property map*.

Property Maps

The Object wizard adds a simple property map to your control's header file. The map is used for several things. It provides a list of properties that should persist, associates each property with its respective property page (if any), and also builds an array of CLSIDs for the `ISpecifyPropertyPage::GetPages` method described earlier. Here's an example of a property map.

```
BEGIN_PROPERTY_MAP(CPostItCtl)
    PROP_ENTRY( "Text", DISPID_TEXT, CLSID_PostItPpg )
    PROP_ENTRY( "Appearance", DISPID_APPEARANCE, CLSID_PostItPpg )
    PROP_ENTRY( "BorderStyle", DISPID_BORDERSTYLE, CLSID_PostItPpg )
    PROP_ENTRY( "BackColor", DISPID_BACKCOLOR, CLSID_StockColorPage)
    PROP_ENTRY( "ForeColor", DISPID_FORECOLOR, CLSID_StockColorPage )
    PROP_ENTRY( "Font", DISPID_FONT, CLSID_StockFontPage)
    PROP_PAGE(CLSID_StockFontPage)
    PROP_PAGE(CLSID_StockColorPage)
END_PROPERTY_MAP()
```

The `PROP_ENTRY` macro has three parameters: a description of the property, its DISPID, and the property page on which it resides. If there isn't an associated property page, the value `CLSID_NULL` is used. The `PROP_PAGE` macro specifies an ATL stock property page that should be included when the container constructs the control's property sheet.

ATL's Support for Property Pages

A control's property pages are independent COM objects. ATL provides three stock property pages: one each for fonts, colors, and pictures. If your control has properties of these types, you can easily include them by adding them to your control's property map as described earlier.

Controls should also implement a custom property page for those properties that are not one of the three stock property page types. ATL provides an Object wizard for adding custom property pages. It's included in the **Controls** tab. To add a custom property page in your control, insert this component into your control project.

A property page is simply a Windows dialog box that supports one COM interface, IPropertyPage. The Object wizard creates a component that derives from both CDialogImpl and IPropertyPageImpl. Here's the initial header file:

```
// PostItPpg.h : Declaration of the CPostItPpg
...
class ATL_NO_VTABLE CPostItPpg :
   public CComObjectRootEx<CComSingleThreadModel>,
   public CComCoClass<CPostItPpg, &CLSID_PostItPpg>,
   public IPropertyPageImpl<CPostItPpg>,
   public CDialogImpl<CPostItPpg>
{
public:
   CPostItPpg()
   {
      m_dwTitleID = IDS_TITLEPostItPpg;
      m_dwHelpFileID = IDS_HELPFILEPostItPpg;
      m_dwDocStringID = IDS_DOCSTRINGPostItPpg;
   }
   enum {IDD = IDD_POSTITPPG};

DECLARE_REGISTRY_RESOURCEID(IDR_POSTITPPG)

BEGIN_COM_MAP(CPostItPpg)
    COM_INTERFACE_ENTRY_IMPL(IPropertyPage)
END_COM_MAP()

BEGIN_MSG_MAP(CPostItPpg)
   CHAIN_MSG_MAP(IPropertyPageImpl<CPostItPpg>)
END_MSG_MAP()
};
```

Most of the preceding code should be familiar. The new classes are CDialogImpl and IPropertyPageImpl.

CDialogImpl

ATL's CDialogImpl class provides a basic implementation of a Windows dialog box. The dialog box can be modeless or modal, and it uses an associated dialog box resource. CDialogImpl derives from both CWindow and CMessageMap and so has all the methods provided by these classes. Most important is the ability to route Windows messages via ATL's message map mechanism. We discussed this earlier.

When inserting the property page component, the Object wizard also adds a dialog box resource to your project's **.RC** file. The next step is to add controls to the dialog box. You must also add a significant amount of code to manage moving property values to and from the dialog box controls.

When the property page is initially loaded, the control's property values must be retrieved and set in the dialog box. If any properties have enumerated types, you must also handle this. The best place to do all this is in the WM_INITDIALOG message. Here's some code from our example.

```
LRESULT CPostItPpg::OnInitDialog( UINT, WPARAM wParam, LPARAM lParam, BOOL& )
{
    USES_CONVERSION;

    if ( m_nObjects > 0 )
    {
        CComQIPtr<IPostItCtl, &IID_IPostItCtl> pPostItCtl( m_ppUnk[0] );
        BSTR bstrText;
        if SUCCEEDED( pPostItCtl->get_Text( &bstrText ))
            SetDlgItemText( IDC_TEXT, W2A( bstrText ));

        // Initialize the Appearance combo box
        SendDlgItemMessage( IDC_APPEARANCE,
                            CB_ADDSTRING,
                            0,
                            (long) "0 - Flat" );
        SendDlgItemMessage( IDC_APPEARANCE,
                            CB_ADDSTRING,
                            0,
                            (long) "1 - 3D" );

        // Get the current value of the Appearance property
        long lAppearance;
        if SUCCEEDED( pPostItCtl->get_Appearance( &lAppearance ))
            ::SendMessage( GetDlgItem( IDC_APPEARANCE ),
                        CB_SETCURSEL,
                        lAppearance,
                        0 );
        ...
    }
    return 1;
}
```

IPropertyPageImpl

As expected, the `IPropertyPageImpl` class implements the `IPropertyPage` interface. ATL also provides the `IPropertyPage2Impl` class, but it does not implement the extra method (`EditProperty`) added via `IPropertyPage2`, so it isn't used. The `IPropertyPage` interface has 11 methods. The most important methods are `SetObjects`, which passes an array of `IDispatch` interfaces for the associated controls; `Show`, which forces the page to display; and `Apply`, which is called when the user moves to another page or clicks the **Apply** button.

ATL doesn't provide a nice data exchange facility like MFC's DDX (dialog data exchange), so you must write a lot of Win32 code when developing property pages for your ATL controls. As an example, here is the code needed to update one property in a control when the user presses the **Apply** button on the page:

```
STDMETHODIMP CPostItPpg::Apply(void)
{
    USES_CONVERSION;
    for (UINT i = 0; i < m_nObjects; i++)
    {
        CComQIPtr<IPostItCtl, &IID_IPostItCtl> pPostItCtl( m_ppUnk[i] );
        BSTR bstrText;
        if ( GetDlgItemText( IDC_TEXT, bstrText ) )
        {
            if FAILED( pPostItCtl->put_Text( bstrText ))
            {
                HandleError();
                return E_FAIL;
            }
        }
    }

    m_bDirty = FALSE;
    return S_OK;
}
```

The code obtains an interface pointer to the control's custom interface (remember, it implements a dual interface), extracts the property value from the dialog box's control, and calls the appropriate `put` method to update the control's property. These steps must be performed for each property on the property page.

BUILDING AN EXAMPLE CONTROL

That finishes our whirlwind coverage of the ActiveX control specifications and ATL's support for building controls. Now we'll demonstrate what is required to develop an ActiveX control with ATL. We'll build a basic control that uses most of the control functionality provided by

ATL. It's hard to cover everything you can do with ATL and ActiveX controls in one chapter, but we'll try. By learning the basics of how controls work and how ATL implements the various control interfaces, you should have a solid foundation on which to develop your own controls. Also, you should visit www.WidgetWare.com and check out the ActiveX control FAQ area when you encounter problems developing your own controls. There, you'll find answers to more than 100 questions on COM, OLE, and ActiveX development.

Create the Control's Housing

Start Visual C++ and create a new project, selecting **ATL COM AppWizard**. Give it the name **PostIt**. In Step 1 of 1, select a type of DLL. Then select **Finish** and **OK** to generate the project.

ATL Object Wizard

Using the ATL Object wizard, insert a **Full Control** component into your server's housing. Then fill out the four tabbed dialog boxes with the information provided next.

THE NAMES AND ATTRIBUTES TABS

Take the default settings after giving the control a name of **PostItCtl.** Figure 8.10 shows the finished **Names** tab. On the **Attributes** tab, be sure to enable the **Support Connection Points** option, because we will be adding an event to our control.

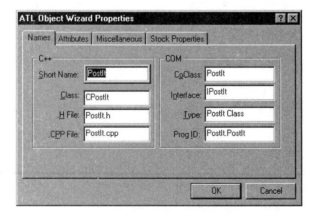

Figure 8.10 The Names dialog box.

THE MISCELLANEOUS TAB

The **Miscellaneous** tab is used to provide ActiveX control–specific information to the Object wizard. Take the defaults for each of the options. The **Miscellaneous** tab was shown earlier in Figure 8.8.

THE STOCK PROPERTIES TAB

When you're adding an ActiveX control component with the Object wizard, an additional tab is provided to set up the control's initial stock properties. The potential properties and their descriptions were shown in Table 8.5 earlier in the chapter.

For our example control, add the following properties on the **Stock Properties** tab. The resulting dialog box is shown in Figure 8.11.

- Appearance
- Background Color
- Border Style
- Font
- Foreground Color
- Text

After filling out the four tabbed dialogs, click **OK.**

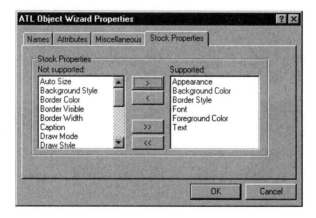

Figure 8.11 Adding stock properties.

A Basic Control

Our control isn't very functional right out of the box, but that gives us an opportunity to learn as we add functionality. The ATL Object wizard created a control that implements 17 interfaces. As we've described, a control that implements the majority of these control interfaces should work in almost any container that supports ActiveX controls. However, a control developer doesn't have to implement all these interfaces. The new control standards stipulate that a control need implement only those interfaces that it needs to supply its functionality. This is just fine, but most of today's containers expect a number of them to be there, and that's why we've chosen to implement a control that implements them all.

Initializing Our Stock Properties

When we added our control's stock properties through the ATL Object wizard, it basically did one thing: It created data members within our class to hold the values of our properties. Here's a look at the code:

```
// PostItCtl.H
...
class ATL_NO_VTABLE CPostItCtl :
   public CComObjectRootEx<CComSingleThreadModel>,
{
...
// IPostItCtl
public:
   HRESULT OnDraw(ATL_DRAWINFO& di);

   CComPtr<IFontDisp> m_pFont;
   OLE_COLOR m_clrBackColor;
   OLE_COLOR m_clrForeColor;
   CComBSTR m_bstrText;
   long m_nBorderStyle;
   long m_nAppearance;
};
```

However, that's all it did. We still need to set the initial values for the properties, because the default ATL implementation doesn't do that for us. A good place to do this is in the control's constructor.

```
CPostItCtl()
{
    m_nAppearance = 1;
    m_nBorderStyle = 0;
    m_clrBackColor = RGB( 0, 255, 255 );
    m_clrForeColor = RGB( 0, 0, 0 );

    static FONTDESC _fontDesc =
        { sizeof(FONTDESC), OLESTR("MS Sans Serif"), FONTSIZE( 12 ),
        FW_BOLD,
          ANSI_CHARSET, FALSE, FALSE, FALSE };
    OleCreateFontIndirect( &_fontDesc,
                           IID_IFontDisp,
                           (void **)&m_pFont);
}
```

We discussed initialization of properties earlier. In the preceding code we set the background color to blue, the foreground color to black, and the font to MS Sans Serif. Table 8.11 details the meaning of our integer properties.

Table 8.11 Property Values

PROPERTY	VALUES
Appearance	0: Flat 1: 3D
BorderStyle	0: None 1: Single Line

CComControl::OnDraw

Most ActiveX controls provide some sort of visual representation. Our PostIt control is basically an expensive Windows label control. Drawing text on the screen provides the majority of its functionality, but it demonstrates much of what you might do within an ActiveX control.

When our control is embedded, the container instantiates the control instance, loads any property values, and tells the control to render itself again. Whenever the control's region needs to be redrawn, the container again tells the control to render itself. The nice thing about all this is that the control is always notified through the OnDraw method. However, the default code provided by the Object wizard doesn't do much.

So the first thing we need to do is to add some drawing code. When the container asks the control to render itself, the container provides a device context on which to render. In most cases, the container will provide a DC that is part of its own window. With older tools, such as MFC, a control would get its own window. Today, though, that isn't always the case. It's not a big deal anyway; all we need is a device context to draw on. Replace the Wizard-provided code with this:

```
HRESULT CPostItCtl::OnDraw(ATL_DRAWINFO& di)
{
    USES_CONVERSION;
    COLORREF   colBack, colFore;
    HBRUSH     hOldBrush = 0;
    HBRUSH     hBackBrush = 0;
    HDC        hdc = di.hdcDraw;
    RECT&      rc = *(RECT*)di.prcBounds;

    // Convert the OLE_COLOR types into COLORREFs
    OleTranslateColor( m_clrBackColor, NULL, &colBack );
    OleTranslateColor( m_clrForeColor, NULL, &colFore );

    // Create a brush using the background color
    // and select it into the DC
    hBackBrush = (HBRUSH) CreateSolidBrush( colBack );
    hOldBrush = (HBRUSH) SelectObject( hdc, hBackBrush );

    // Fill the background with our new brush
    FillRect( hdc, &rc, hBackBrush );

    // If the BorderStyle is 1, draw
    // a border around the control
    if ( m_nBorderStyle )
    {
        HPEN hPen = (HPEN) CreatePen( PS_SOLID, 1, RGB( 0, 0, 0 ));
        HPEN hOldPen = (HPEN) SelectObject( hdc, hPen );
        Rectangle( hdc, rc.left, rc.top, rc.right, rc.bottom );

        if ( hOldPen )
            SelectObject( hdc, hOldPen );

        DeleteObject( hPen );
    }

    // If the appearance is 3-D draw an edge
    if ( m_nAppearance )
    {
        DrawEdge( hdc, &rc, EDGE_SUNKEN, BF_RECT );
```

```
      // Adjust our rectangle
      rc.left += 2;
      rc.top += 2;
      rc.bottom -= 2;
      rc.right -= 2;
   }

   // Get the user-selected font and select
   // it into our device context.
   CComQIPtr<IFont, &IID_IFont> pFont( m_pFont );
   HFONT hOldFont = 0;
   HFONT hFont = 0;
   if ( pFont )
   {
      pFont->get_hFont( &hFont );
      pFont->AddRefHfont( hFont );
      hOldFont = (HFONT) SelectObject( hdc, hFont );
   }

   // Check to see if we're in design mode or
   // run-time mode. If in design mode, get the
   // ambient display name and draw it within
   // the control.
   BOOL bUserMode = FALSE;
   GetAmbientUserMode( bUserMode );
   if ( bUserMode == FALSE )
   {
      BSTR bstr;
      if ( SUCCEEDED( GetAmbientDisplayName( bstr )))
      {
         SetBkMode( hdc, TRANSPARENT );
         SetTextColor( hdc, colFore );
         DrawText( hdc,
                   W2A( bstr ),
                   -1,
                   &rc,
                   DT_TOP | DT_SINGLELINE );
      }
   }

   // Draw the user-specified text
   if ( m_bstrText.Length() )
   {
      SetBkMode( hdc, TRANSPARENT );
```

(code continued on next page)

```
        SetTextColor( hdc, colFore );
        DrawText( hdc,
                  W2A( m_bstrText ),
                  -1,
                  &rc,
                  DT_CENTER | DT_VCENTER | DT_WORDBREAK );
    }

    // Release the IFont object. We don't
    // delete the font because the OLE font
    // object manages this
    if ( pFont )
       pFont->ReleaseHfont( hFont );

    // Restore the old font
    if ( hOldFont )
       SelectObject( hdc, hOldFont );

    // Restore the old brush and delete
    // the one we created earlier
    if ( hOldBrush )
    {
       SelectObject( hdc, hOldBrush );
       DeleteObject( hBackBrush );
    }

    return S_OK;
}
```

That's a lot of code, but I've commented it liberally so that we don't have to go over every line. Basically, we're using the stock properties that we set up to render the control. After adding the preceding code, rebuild the project, insert the control in Visual Basic, and you'll have a functional control.

After experimenting with the control, you should notice that if you set up a property value in design mode and then run the application, the properties don't persist. In other words, if you set the background color to red and press **F5** (run) in Visual Basic, the control's background isn't red. Why? Because we haven't caused the property values to persist. Whenever the control is destroyed and re-instantiated, it uses the defaults that we set in the constructor. To maintain state between design-time mode and run-time mode, we must implement property persistence.

Implementing Persistence of Your Control's Properties: Property Maps

For your control's properties to persist, they must be added to ATL's property map. The ATL Object wizard doesn't do this automatically, so you must do it yourself. For each property that you want to make persistent, add a PROP_ENTRY macro with a textual description of the property, the property's DISPID, and any associated property page. Our control doesn't yet have any property pages, so we use CLSID_NULL instead.

```
//
// PostItCtl.h : Declaration of the CPostItCtl
//
...
class ATL_NO_VTABLE CPostItCtl :
    public CComObjectRootEx<CComSingleThreadModel>,
...
BEGIN_PROPERTY_MAP(CPostItCtl)
    PROP_ENTRY( "Text", DISPID_TEXT, CLSID_NULL )
    PROP_ENTRY( "Appearance", DISPID_APPEARANCE, CLSID_NULL )
    PROP_ENTRY( "Border Style", DISPID_BORDERSTYLE, CLSID_NULL )
    PROP_ENTRY( "Background Color", DISPID_BACKCOLOR, CLSID_NULL)
    PROP_ENTRY( "Foreground or Text Color", DISPID_FORECOLOR, CLSID_NULL )
    PROP_ENTRY( "Font", DISPID_FONT, CLSID_NULL)
END_PROPERTY_MAP()
```

After entering this code, rebuild the control and build a simple Visual Basic application that uses it. You should notice that the property values persist as you toggle between design mode and run-time mode. But wait—we can make it even better.

Adding Stock Property Pages

As we described earlier, ATL provides three stock property pages for standard, often-used property types such as font, color, and picture. The stock property pages have standard CLSIDs, and we can use them directly within our control. Change the control's property map to this:

```
BEGIN_PROPERTY_MAP(CPostItCtl)
    PROP_ENTRY( "Text", DISPID_TEXT, CLSID_NULL )
    PROP_ENTRY( "Appearance", DISPID_APPEARANCE, CLSID_NULL )
    PROP_ENTRY( "BorderStyle", DISPID_BORDERSTYLE, CLSID_NULL )
    PROP_ENTRY( "BackColor", DISPID_BACKCOLOR, CLSID_StockColorPage)
    PROP_ENTRY( "ForeColor", DISPID_FORECOLOR, CLSID_StockColorPage )
    PROP_ENTRY( "Font", DISPID_FONT, CLSID_StockFontPage)
    PROP_PAGE(CLSID_StockFontPage)
    PROP_PAGE(CLSID_StockColorPage)
END_PROPERTY_MAP()
```

Now rebuild the control, insert it into a container, and finally launch the control's custom property sheet. You should see something like Figure 8.12.

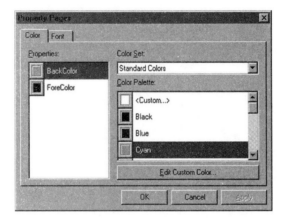

Figure 8.12 Stock property pages.

As we discussed earlier, a control should implement a custom property page for its properties. We have default property pages for three of our six properties, and we'll need a custom page for the remaining three.

Adding a Custom Property Page

Early in this example when we added the PostIt control to our project using the ATL Object wizard, only the control component was added. As you now understand, a property page is an independent COM object used by the container to interact with a control. To add a custom property page to the control, we'll use the Object wizard again. Fire it up using the **Insert/New ATL Object** menu item. Select **Controls** and **Property Page** and click **Next**. You'll see something like Figure 8.13.

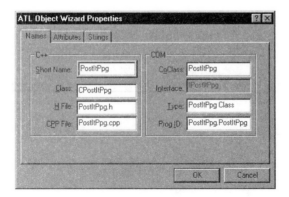

Figure 8.13 Property page properties.

Enter a short name of **PostItPpg** and take the defaults for the rest of the **Names** tab. Also take the defaults for the **Attributes** tab, and enter whatever you feel is appropriate in the **Strings** tab. When you're finished, click **OK**. The ATL Object wizard will create the files listed in Table 8.12.

Table 8.12 Property Page Files

FILE	DESCRIPTION
PostItPpg.h	The header file for our new property page class: CPostItPpg.
PostItPpg.cpp	The CPostItPpg class implementation.
PostItPpg.rgs	The registry script for our property page object.
PostIt.rc	A resource was added for the property page dialog box.

The ATL Object wizard added several new files to support the custom property page for our control. The first thing to do is to edit the dialog box resource and add controls for each of our three properties. Table 8.13 details the control type and identifier. Figure 8.14 shows how to build the dialog box with the Visual C++ resource editor.

Table 8.13 Property Page Controls and IDs

CONTROL TYPE	IDENTIFIER
Multi-line entry field	IDC_TEXT
Drop-list combo box	IDC_APPEARANCE
Drop- list combo box	IDC_BORDERSTYLE

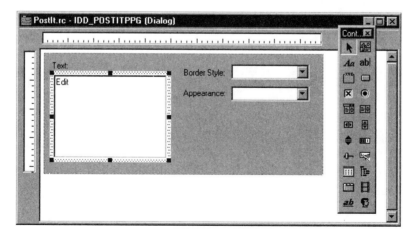

Figure 8.14 Building the property page.

After the dialog box is built, we need to populate the controls with valid property values. As the property page is loading, we must retrieve the current property values from the associated control instance. The best time to do this is when the dialog box is being created. Override WM_INITDIALOG by adding the following **PostItPpg.H** and **PostItPpg.CPP**.

```
// PostItPpg.h : Declaration of the CPostItPpg

#include "resource.h"

#include "PostIt.h"

class ATL_NO_VTABLE CPostItPpg :
     public CComObjectRootEx<CComSingleThreadModel>,
     public CComCoClass<CPostItPpg, &CLSID_PostItPpg>,
...

BEGIN_MSG_MAP(CPostItPpg)
   MESSAGE_HANDLER( WM_INITDIALOG, OnInitDialog )
   CHAIN_MSG_MAP(IPropertyPageImpl<CPostItPpg>)
END_MSG_MAP()

LRESULT OnInitDialog( UINT, WPARAM wParam, LPARAM lParam, BOOL& );
...
};

// PostItPpg.CPP
...
LRESULT CPostItPpg::OnInitDialog( UINT, WPARAM wParam, LPARAM lParam,
BOOL& )
{
   USES_CONVERSION;

   if ( m_nObjects > 0 )
     {
     CComQIPtr<IPostItCtl, &IID_IPostItCtl> pPostItCtl( m_ppUnk[0] );
     BSTR bstrText;
     if SUCCEEDED( pPostItCtl->get_Text( &bstrText ))
        SetDlgItemText( IDC_TEXT, W2A( bstrText ));

     // Initialize the Appearance combo box
     SendDlgItemMessage( IDC_APPEARANCE,
                         CB_ADDSTRING,
                         0,
                         (long) "0 - Flat" );
     SendDlgItemMessage( IDC_APPEARANCE,
                         CB_ADDSTRING,
                         0,
                         (long) "1 - 3D" );
```

```
      // Get the current value of the Appearance property
      long lAppearance;
      if SUCCEEDED( pPostItCtl->get_Appearance( &lAppearance ))
         ::SendMessage( GetDlgItem( IDC_APPEARANCE ),
                     CB_SETCURSEL,
                     lAppearance,
                     0 );

      // Initialize the BorderStyle combo box
      SendDlgItemMessage( IDC_BORDERSTYLE,
                     CB_ADDSTRING,
                     0,
                     (long) "0 - None" );
      SendDlgItemMessage( IDC_BORDERSTYLE,
                     CB_ADDSTRING,
                     0,
                     (long) "1 - Single Line" );

      // Get the current value of the BorderStyle property
      long lBorderStyle;
      if SUCCEEDED( pPostItCtl->get_BorderStyle( &lBorderStyle ))
         ::SendMessage( GetDlgItem( IDC_BORDERSTYLE ),
                     CB_SETCURSEL,
                     lBorderStyle,
                     0 );
   }
   return 1;
}
```

When the dialog box (property page) is initially created, we are doing two basic things. First, we query for the control's dual interface, IPostItCtl. Once we have a pointer to this interface, we can pull property values from the control. Also, we're populating our drop-list combo boxes with valid property values. Once they're populated we retrieve the value from the control and set the current selection.

The preceding code initially sets up the property page. However, if a user changes a value on the property page, we must pass the new value to the associated control. We must also enable the **Apply** button on the property sheet whenever a value has been changed. First, we must trap the CBN_CHANGE event so that we're notified every time one of the combo boxes is modified.

```
// PostItPpg.h
...
BEGIN_MSG_MAP(CPostItPpg)
   COMMAND_HANDLER( IDC_TEXT, EN_CHANGE, OnPropertyChange )
```

(code continued on next page)

```
   COMMAND_HANDLER( IDC_APPEARANCE, CBN_SELCHANGE, OnPropertyChange )
   COMMAND_HANDLER( IDC_BORDERSTYLE, CBN_SELCHANGE, OnPropertyChange )
   COMMAND_HANDLER( IDC_BACKSTYLE, CBN_SELCHANGE, OnPropertyChange )
   MESSAGE_HANDLER( WM_INITDIALOG, OnInitDialog )
   CHAIN_MSG_MAP(IPropertyPageImpl<CPostItPpg>)
END_MSG_MAP()

LRESULT OnPropertyChange( WORD wNotify, WORD wID, HWND hWnd,
                          BOOL& bHandled );
```

The following snippet of code sets the dirty flag for the page (thus enabling the **Apply** button) and notifies any attached property browsers (such as Visual Basic) that the property value has changed.

```
// PostItPpg.Cpp
...
LRESULT CPostItPpg::OnPropertyChange( WORD wNotify, WORD wID, HWND hWnd,
                                      BOOL& bHandled )
{
   SetDirty( TRUE );
   m_pPageSite->OnStatusChange( PROPPAGESTATUS_DIRTY |
PROPPAGESTATUS_VALIDATE );
   return 0;
}
```

All that is left is to implement the functionality of the **Apply** button. Here's what we need to add.

```
// PostItPpg.h
...
class ATL_NO_VTABLE CPostItPpg :
   public CComObjectRootEx<CComSingleThreadModel>,
{
...
STDMETHOD(Apply)(void);

private:
   void HandleError();
};

// PostItPpg.cpp
...
void CPostItPpg::HandleError()
{
   USES_CONVERSION;

   CComPtr<IErrorInfo> pError;
   CComBSTR strError;
   GetErrorInfo( 0, &pError );
```

```
        pError->GetDescription( &strError );
        MessageBox( OLE2T(strError),
                    _T("Error"),
                    MB_ICONEXCLAMATION );
}

STDMETHODIMP CPostItPpg::Apply(void)
{
    USES_CONVERSION;
    for (UINT i = 0; i < m_nObjects; i++)
    {
        CComQIPtr<IPostItCtl, &IID_IPostItCtl> pPostItCtl( m_ppUnk[i] );
        BSTR bstrText;
        if ( GetDlgItemText( IDC_TEXT, bstrText ) )
        {
            if FAILED( pPostItCtl->put_Text( bstrText ))
            {
                HandleError();
                return E_FAIL;
            }
        }

        enum enumAppearance eAppearance;
        eAppearance = (enum enumAppearance)
                                        SendDlgItemMessage( IDC_APPEARANCE,
                                        CB_GETCURSEL,
                                        0, 0 );
        if FAILED( pPostItCtl->put_Appearance( eAppearance ))
        {
            HandleError();
            return E_FAIL;
        }

        long lBorderStyle;
        lBorderStyle = SendDlgItemMessage( IDC_BORDERSTYLE,
                                        CB_GETCURSEL,
                                        0, 0 );
        if FAILED( pPostItCtl->put_BorderStyle( lBorderStyle ))
        {
            HandleError();
            return E_FAIL;
        }
    }
    m_bDirty = FALSE;
    return S_OK;
}
```

Now we must go back to the code for our control and update it with our new property page. We modify our property map to include the CLSID of our custom property page.

```
BEGIN_PROPERTY_MAP(CPostItCtl)
   PROP_ENTRY( "Text", DISPID_TEXT, CLSID_PostItPpg )
   PROP_ENTRY( "Appearance", DISPID_APPEARANCE, CLSID_PostItPpg )
   PROP_ENTRY( "BorderStyle", DISPID_BORDERSTYLE, CLSID_PostItPpg )
   PROP_ENTRY( "BackColor", DISPID_BACKCOLOR, CLSID_StockColorPage)
   PROP_ENTRY( "ForeColor", DISPID_FORECOLOR, CLSID_StockColorPage )
   PROP_ENTRY( "Font", DISPID_FONT, CLSID_StockFontPage)
   PROP_PAGE(CLSID_StockFontPage)
   PROP_PAGE(CLSID_StockColorPage)
END_PROPERTY_MAP()
```

We've made a lot of changes. Go ahead and rebuild the project. Fire up Visual Basic and check out the new functionality. The custom property page will allow you to change any of the control's properties. As soon as you press the **Apply** button, the control will redraw.

Adding Events to a Control

Controls implement events using COM's connectable object technology. We covered connection points and events in detail in Chapter 7. The following steps demonstrate what is required to add an outgoing interface to an ActiveX control. Our example control already had the default implementation of `IConnectionPointContainer` and `IProvideClassInfo2` provided by the Object wizard. We need to define our interface, use the proxy generator to create a wrapper class, and then fire the event through the client's interface implementation.

Define the Outgoing Interface

A control's outgoing event interface must be a dispinterface for most containers, and it must also be declared within the `library` section of your control's IDL file. Our example control will implement the stock `Click` event. First, we define it.

```
// PostIt.IDL
...
library POSTITLib
{
   importlib("stdole32.tlb");
   importlib("stdole2.tlb");
```

```
    [
        uuid(5010B641-6516-11d1-B5F7-0004ACFF171C),
        helpstring("_PostItEvents Interface"),
    ]
    dispinterface _PostItEvents
    {
        properties:
        methods:
        [id(DISPID_CLICK)] void Click();
    };

    [
        uuid(CFC43231-50AC-11D1-B5EC-0004ACFF171C),
        helpstring("PostItCtl Class")
    ]
    coclass PostItCtl
    {
        [default] interface IPostItCtl;
        [default, source] dispinterface _PostItEvents;
    };
...
};
```

We declare a dispinterface that has one method, Click. You will need to generate the preceding GUID manually using the GUIDGEN utility.

Use the Proxy Generator

Build the project to update the type library and then use the ATL Proxy Generator to generate a proxy for the outgoing interface. The steps to do this are outlined in Chapter 7. Accept the default name of **CPPostIt.CPP**. Next, include the file in your control's header file, update the IProvideClassInfo2Impl declaration, and add the class to the connection map. These steps are highlighted in this code:

```
//
// PostItCtl.h : Declaration of the CPostItCtl
//
...
#include "CPPostit.h"
```

(code continued on next page)

```
class ATL_NO_VTABLE CPostItCtl :
   public CComObjectRootEx<CComSingleThreadModel>,
   public CComCoClass<CPostItCtl, &CLSID_PostItCtl>,
   public CComControl<CPostItCtl>,
   public CStockPropImpl<CPostItCtl, IPostItCtl,
                       &IID_IPostItCtl, &LIBID_POSTITLib>,
   public IProvideClassInfo2Impl<&CLSID_PostItCtl, &DIID__PostItEvents,
                               &LIBID_POSTITLib>,
   ...
   public CProxyIPostItEvents<CPostItCtl>
{
...
BEGIN_CONNECTION_POINT_MAP(CPostItCtl)
   CONNECTION_POINT_ENTRY(IID_IPropertyNotifySink)
   CONNECTION_POINT_ENTRY(DIID__PostItEvents)
END_CONNECTION_POINT_MAP()
```

Fire the Event

All that's left is to trap the WM_LBUTTONDOWN message and fire the event through the outgoing interface. We add a message map entry and implement the method:

```
// PostItCtl.H
...
class ATL_NO_VTABLE CPostItCtl :
   public CComObjectRootEx<CComSingleThreadModel>,
{
...
BEGIN_MSG_MAP(CPostItCtl)
   ...
   MESSAGE_HANDLER(WM_LBUTTONDOWN, OnLButtonDown)
END_MSG_MAP()
...
private:
   LRESULT OnLButtonDown(UINT uMsg, WPARAM wParam,
                         LPARAM lParam, BOOL& bHandled);
...
};

// PostItCtl.CPP
...
LRESULT CPostItCtl::OnLButtonDown(UINT uMsg, WPARAM wParam,
                                 LPARAM lParam, BOOL& bHandled)
{
   Fire_Click();
   return 0;
}
```

Our control now supports the `Click` event. Build the project, and you will have a control that implements nearly every aspect of ATL's control support. Much of what's left, will be covered in Chapter 9.

The Visual Basic project included with the downloadable examples demonstrates the use of the example control. You can also use it in Visual C++ applications, Internet Explorer, and most other ActiveX control containers.

MORE ACTIVEX CONTROLS

That concludes our basic coverage of ActiveX controls. In Chapter 9, we'll cover two additional aspects of control development: transparent drawing and asynchronous property download. We'll also cover some of the requirements for implementing controls that work in the commercial Internet and corporate intranet environments.

Transparent Controls and Asynchronous Download

Microsoft's ActiveX strategy includes the use of ActiveX controls within the Web environment, both within a browser and on the server side as part of Internet Information Server (IIS) and the Active Server Page (ASP) technology. But ActiveX controls have not achieved widespread use in the commercial Internet environment because of security concerns. In the larger intranet environment, though, the use of ActiveX controls within browser-based applications is growing. This chapter describes how to build ActiveX controls that support transparency and asynchronous download, both of which are important in Web-based environments.

Transparency is the ability of a control to represent nonrectangular regions and to allow the background of its container to show through the representation. Asynchronous download refers to the ability of a component to store large property values (such as GIF images) separately from its normal persistence storage area. In the Web environment, this means storage on the Web sever instead of embedded in an HTML document.

The example in this chapter demonstrates the steps necessary to download and display a bitmap with a single transparent color. The control can be used with current versions of Internet Explorer, Netscape Navigator (if you use the ScriptActive plug-in), Visual Basic, and most other ActiveX control containers.

NOTE   This chapter is based on an article that I co-authored with Mark Nelson of Addisoft Consulting (www.addisoft.com). The article appeared in the March 1998 issue of Dr. Dobbs Journal. Mark is the author of several good books, including The Data Compression Book (M&T Books, 1995), The C++ Programmer's Guide to the Standard Template Library (IDG Books, 1995), and Serial Communications: A C++ Developer's Guide (M&T Books, 1998). I'd like to thank Mark for allowing me to use our article as the basis for this chapter.

TRANSPARENCY UNDER WINDOWS

When you're referring to bitmapped images, the term *transparency* has a straightforward meaning. A given image has an arbitrary number of transparent areas. When the image is drawn, the transparent areas don't obscure the area behind the image in the Z-order. In the simplest case, we've all seen transparency used to good effect on the Web, producing images of complex objects that appear to be floating on top of a background. Figure 9.1 shows a pair of transparent GIF files that float above a background on a typical Web page.

Figure 9.1 Transparent GIFs on the Web.

Sites such as Mr. Showbiz typically have a standard background pattern that shows up on many or all of their pages. In Figure 9.1, the GIF on the left side has navigation bars that are used in an image map. A GIF file with the site logo is shown on the right. Both images feature transparent areas that let them blend with the background of the page.

Windows Regions

After seeing this esthetically pleasing effect on the Web, we set ourselves the task of duplicating it in an ActiveX control. Investigation of the problem yielded two alternative solutions for obtaining control transparency. The most straightforward of these methods requires the developer to set up a Windows HRGN object to define a nonrectangular drawing area. Figure 9.2 shows a simple example of a drawing region. As long as you can define your region as a path created by connecting a series of points (or elliptical regions), you can create a drawing region that Windows understands.

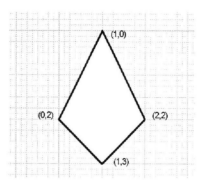

Figure 9.2 A Windows drawing region.

Once you have a drawing region defined, inmplementing transparency is easy. In the simplest case, you can take advantage of an existing Win32 capability by defining a nonrectangular window. Once that's done, you simply draw the window as you normally would. The areas outside the region will be drawn by whatever resides behind the window (the container's client area).

Defining a drawing region works well with containers that implement the OLE Control '96 specification (this is part of the Internet Client SDK). In the best case, you can implement two-pass drawing, which lets you draw the foreground part of your control first, and then lets the container draw the background. This provides fast and flicker-free drawing of controls.

The Gery Algorithm

Defining drawing regions is great for some applications, but it might not be the best general-purpose technique. We wanted to be able to draw any type of image with randomly configured transparent areas. This means having transparency controlled on a pixel-by-pixel basis. Attempting to define a region for any arbitrary bitmap is difficult.

For our control, we instead used a masking technique that is described by Ron Gery in a Microsoft Developer Network (MSDN) article. This approach uses a simple masking technique that makes it easy to use arbitrarily complex transparent regions. The Gery algorithm assumes that you have a bitmap with a single color that defines the transparent area. Given that, the drawing portion of your code must execute the following steps:

1. Create a monochrome bitmap the same size as the bitmap you are going to draw.
2. Set all the transparent pixels in the monochrome bitmap to 1, and set all the opaque pixels to 0.

3. XOR the screen region with the bits in your image.

4. AND the screen with your monochrome bitmap. This has the effect of leaving all the transparent areas unchanged and setting the opaque areas to black.

5. XOR the screen region with the image bits again. This sets all the transparent areas back to their original color, because the two XOR operations cancel each other. The opaque areas now contain the desired image bits, since and XORing with solid black is the same as simply setting the bits.

This drawing algorithm is simple to implement using standard Windows raster operations. If you step through the code in the example control and watch the effects when using the debugger, it will start to make sense after a few passes.

Internet Explorer and Windowless Controls

This drawing scheme works well with containers that adhere to the OLE Control '96 recommmendations, but it makes one important assumption: The XOR/mask sequence preserves the background behind transparent areas, but only if the background has already been drawn.

In those control containers that don't support windowless controls (such as Internet Explorer 3.0), an ActiveX control is simply a child window that is responsible for drawing its entire rectangular area. So when Internet Explorer is drawing the background for a Web page, it excludes the areas occupied by child windows, allowing them to draw their own background. If you've set up a pleasing background GIF, IE3 won't bother to draw it in any areas covered by an ActiveX control, thereby dooming any attempt at transparent drawing.

Microsoft has documented a way around this problem in Knowledge Base article Q165073. This article gives a code snippet that you can drop into a control's WM_ERASE-BKGND handler. The article includes MFC code for fixing the drawing problem.

```
BOOL CTransCtrl::OnEraseBkgnd(CDC* pDC)
{
  CWnd* pWndParent = GetParent();
  POINT pt;
  pt.x = pt.y = 0;
  MapWindowPoints(pWndParent, &pt, 1);
  OffsetWindowOrgEx(pDC->m_hDC, pt.x, pt.y, &pt);
  ::SendMessage( pWndParent->m_hWnd,
        WM_ERASEBKGND,
        (WPARAM)pDC->m_hDC,
        0 );
  SetWindowOrgEx( pDC->m_hDC, pt.x, pt.y, NULL );
  return 1;
}
```

In a nutshell, this code sends a WM_ERASEBKGND message to Internet Explorer along with the device context for the ActiveX control. This convinces Internet Explorer to draw the background behind the control as if it didn't belong to a child window. This code doesn't cause any trouble for more-sophisticated containers, such as Internet Explorer 4, because the WM_ERASE-BKGND never gets sent to the control. Newer containers that implement the OLE Control '96 specification support windowless controls and so don't create child windows for each embedded control. Instead, each control renders itself directly on the container's device context.

The Example Control

Our example control displays an eight-bit bitmap file and treats all solid white areas (RGB(255,255,255)) as transparent. To keep things simple, the control doesn't do any palette management, so if you are using it on 256-color displays you need to stick to the 20 system colors. (The system colors are usually present regardless of the remaining 236 colors in the palette.)

In this chapter we're not going to build the control step-by-step, because we covered that in Chapter 8. Instead, the following sections describe the implementation of transparent drawing and asynchronous downloading of a bitmap specified via a URL property.

The Image file

One of the goals of our control is to display an image. We need a property that gives us the file name of the image. We've chosen a property type of BSTR and a property name of ImageFile. Here's a glimpse at the implementation:

```
//
// TransCtl.h : Declaration of the CTransCtl
//
...
class ATL_NO_VTABLE CTransCtl :
...
{
public:
   CTransCtl()
   {
      m_bstrImageFile = "";
   }
...
BEGIN_PROPERTY_MAP(CTransCtl)
   PROP_ENTRY( "ImageFile", 1, CLSID_NULL )
END_PROPERTY_MAP()
```

(code continued on next page)

```
// ITransCtl
public:
    STDMETHOD(get_ImageFile)(/*[out, retval]*/ BSTR *pVal);
    STDMETHOD(put_ImageFile)(/*[in]*/ BSTR newVal);

private:
    CComBSTR m_bstrImageFile;
};

//
// TransCtl.cpp : Implementation of CTransCtl
//
...
STDMETHODIMP CTransCtl::get_ImageFile(BSTR * pVal)
{
    // We have an out parameter so we allocate the
    // storage and return the string
    *pVal = m_bstrImageFile.Copy();
     return S_OK;
}

STDMETHODIMP CTransCtl::put_ImageFile(BSTR newVal)
{
    m_bstrImageFile = newVal;

    // Only perform the download at runtime
    BOOL bUserMode;
    GetAmbientUserMode( bUserMode );
    if ( bUserMode )
    {
        // Inform the control that it can no longer
        // draw the old image
        put_ReadyState( READYSTATE_LOADED );

        // Reinitialize the DIB
        m_dib.Reset();

        // Start the asynchronous download
        COurBindStatusCallback<CTransCtl>::Download( this,
                                                     OnData,
                                                     m_bstrImageFile,
                                                     m_spClientSite,
                                                     FALSE );
    }
    return S_OK;
}
```

The put_ImageFile method must do more than just copy a string into our member variable. It clears the internal bitmap that holds the image, starts the download process, and informs the user that the control is in an incomplete state. We'll cover the details of this process in the next few sections.

Asynchronous Properties

Until recently, a control's property values, such as the bits of an image, had to be stored directly within a file managed by its container. As the control is instantiated within the container, its property values are passed to it by the container via the IPersist* interfaces. This process of *binding* a control's property values is a synchronous operation. The container opens its storage file, locates the control's persistent data, queries for the control's persistence interface (usually IPersistStreamInit or IPersistPropertyBag), and then calls IPersist*::Load, whereby the control sets its property values.

This technique works fine for most control properties such as background color, font, and so on, because the data is small. However, large property values such as the bits of an image can be quite large. In today's low-bandwidth environments, where 28.8 modems are considered fast, synchronously binding a control's properties isn't tolerated. For example, if a Web page contained four ActiveX controls, each of which displayed a 100K image, it would take several minutes before any aspect of the page would display. This is because a control's normal persistent data is stored in the HTML document.

In early 1996, when Microsoft finally realized that the Web was much more than a passing fad, it developed a COM-based technology to solve the synchronous binding problem. This new specification provided a way for controls and containers to bind their properties through an *asynchronous moniker*. Microsoft also provides an implementation of the specification, called a *URL moniker*.

Monikers are used to name specific instances of COM classes or storages. A moniker is itself a COM object that implements the IMoniker interface and whose purpose is to encapsulate the details of instantiating a particular object. The moniker hides (from the client) the process of locating, instantiating, and initializing a specific COM instance. In other words, clients work through the standard IMoniker interface or the MkParseDisplayNameEx API function and can ignore class-specific details.

Typically, monikers are used to bind to a specific instance of a COM object, but they can also be used to bind to a remote storage or stream. Microsoft's URL moniker implementation allows a client application to asynchronously bind to a Web resource specified by a URL. The client application, by implementing the IBindStatusCallback interface, can treat the resource as a stream of bytes (via an IStream pointer). In other words, a client can download a remote file in an asynchronous manner by specifying only its URL, and that is exactly what we need for our ImageFile property implementation.

The `ImageFile` property, then, becomes a string that holds only the URL for our bitmap file. The persistent data for our `ImageFile` property is no longer the bits of the image itself but rather is an embedded reference to them. To gain an idea of how this works in a Web page, examine the ImageFile property:

```
<HTML>
<HEAD>
<TITLE>Test page for TransCtl</TITLE>
</HEAD>
<BODY BACKGROUND="background.gif">
<OBJECT ID="TransCtl" WIDTH=128 HEIGHT=128
    CLASSID="CLSID:B25D9AF5-E760-11D0-A052-00A0247B7657"
    CODEBASE="TransparentControl.dll">
    <PARAM NAME="ImageFile" VALUE="http://www.widgetware.com/image01.bmp">
</OBJECT>
```

Loading the image proceeds as follows. As the control is instantiated by the container, it passes the image's URL as part of the synchronous property binding process. Once we have the URL, we initiate the asynchronous download process. The download occurs in a background thread, and when it is complete we render the transparent control using our image data.

CBindStatusCallback

As developers, we typically don't want to mess with all this detail, because the implementation is basically the same for any URL that we might access. That is why frameworks such as ATL are popular. ATL provides the `CBindStatusCallback` class for handling asynchronous downloads, and that's what we'll use to download our image data. The `CBindStatusCallback` class implements the `IBindStatusCallback` interface.

IBindStatusCallback

Clients that request an asynchronous download must provide a notification object that exposes the `IBindStatusCallback` interface. As the download proceeds, the asynchronous moniker passes data to the client through this callback interface. Table 9.1 shows the methods of `IBindStatusCallback`.

Table 9.1 IBindStatusCallback methods

METHOD	DESCRIPTION
GetBindInfo	Called by the asynchronous moniker to retrieve bind info from the client. This provides various download options (e.g., URL encoding technique).
OnStartBinding	Tells the client which callback methods it is registered for receiving.
GetPriority	Returns the priority during asynchronous bind operations.
OnProgress	Indicates the current progress of this bind operation.
OnDataAvailable	Receives the data as the download progresses.
OnObjectAvailable	This method is called by the moniker to pass an interface pointer to a potential client.
OnLowResource	An asynchronous moniker calls this method when it detects low resources.
OnStopBinding	An asynchronous moniker calls this method to indicate the end of the bind operation.

ATL's implementation of IBindStatusCallback provides default implementations of each of the methods in Table 9.1. The implementation of OnDataAvailable, however, requires that you implement a callback method in your component to receive the data as it downloads. As data is provided to the OnDataAvailable, the first parameter provides the status of the download via the BSCF enumerated type.

```
typedef enum tagBSCF {
    BSCF_FIRSTDATANOTIFICATION,
    BSCF_LASTDATANOTIFICATION,
    BSCF_INTERMEDIATEDATANOTIFICATION
} BSCF;
```

If you look closely at the implementation of get_Image, you'll notice that instead of using ATL's CBindStatusCallback class, we use a class named COurBindStatusCallback. The CBindStatusCallback implementation provided with version 2.1 of ATL isn't quite ready for prime time. We had to tweak a few of its methods to get everything to work properly. In particular, the implementation of IBindStatusCallback::OnDataAvailable does not provide a way to determine when a download has completed. The following highlighted code demonstrates the changes we made to CBindStatusCallback.

```
//
// BindStatusCallback.h
//
template <class T>
class ATL_NO_VTABLE COurBindStatusCallback :
    public CComObjectRootEx<T::_ThreadModel::ThreadModelNoCS>,
    public IBindStatusCallbackImpl<T>
{
    // -twa- Add the BSCF enum to the prototype
    typedef void (T::*ATL_PDATAAVAILABLE)(COurBindStatusCallback<T>* pbsc,
                            DWORD grfBSCF, BYTE* pBytes, DWORD dwSize);
...
STDMETHOD(OnDataAvailable)(DWORD grfBSCF, DWORD dwSize,
                        FORMATETC *pformatetc, STGMEDIUM *pstgmed)
{
    ...
    if (SUCCEEDED(hr))
    {
        pBytes[dwActuallyRead] = 0;
        if (dwActuallyRead>0)
        {
            // -twa- Pass the BSCF enum to the control
            (m_pT->*m_pFunc)(this, grfBSCF, pBytes, dwActuallyRead);
            m_dwTotalRead += dwActuallyRead;
        }
    }
...
    if (BSCF_LASTDATANOTIFICATION & grfBSCF)
    {
        // -twa- Make sure the control is notified
        if ( dwActuallyRead == 0 ) // -twa-
            (m_pT->*m_pFunc)(this, grfBSCF, 0, 0); // -twa-
        m_spStream.Release();
...
ATL_PDATAAVAILABLE m_pFunc;
...
}
```

The primary purpose of the changes was to pass the BSCF enumeration value to the implementation of the control's OnData method. The control can then determine when the download starts and when it completes.

The download begins with a call to COurBindStatusCallback::Download. The Download() method is shown next. The implementation is a little hard to understand at first, as is nearly every aspect of ATL, but with a look through ATL's source we can figure it out.

```
static HRESULT Download( T* pT, ATL_PDATAAVAILABLE pFunc,
            BSTR bstrURL,
            IUnknown* pUnkContainer = NULL,
            BOOL bRelative = FALSE)
{
   CComObject<COurBindStatusCallback<T> > *pbsc;
   HRESULT hRes =
   CComObject<COurBindStatusCallback<T> >::CreateInstance(&pbsc);
  if (FAILED(hRes))
    return hRes;

    return pbsc->StartAsyncDownload( pT, pFunc, bstrURL,
               pUnkContainer, bRelative);
}
```

COurBindStatusCallback is itself a COM object. Whenever we need to download a URL-based file, we call the static Download method. The Download method creates an instance of the callback class and then starts the download. The key point is that we pass our control's this pointer and the address of our callback method. As the download proceeds, we will be notified through our implementation of OnData.

```
void CTransCtl::OnData(COurBindStatusCallback<CTransCtl>* pbsc,
                      DWORD grfBSCF, BYTE* pBytes, DWORD dwSize)
{
   // If this is the first piece of data
   // make sure the buffer is empty
   if ( BSCF_FIRSTDATANOTIFICATION & grfBSCF )
   {
      if ( m_pbBuffer )
      {
         delete m_pbBuffer;
         m_pbBuffer = 0;
      }
   }

   // If we actually received some data
   // append it to our buffer
   if ( dwSize )
   {
      // If dwTotalRead is valued, it indicates
      // that this is not the first chunk, so we
      // append it
      if ( pbsc->m_dwTotalRead )
      {
```

(code continued on next page)

```
         BYTE* pbTemp = m_pbBuffer;
         m_pbBuffer = new BYTE[pbsc->m_dwTotalRead + dwSize]
         memcpy( m_pbBuffer,
                 pbTemp,
                 pbsc->m_dwTotalRead );
         memcpy( m_pbBuffer + pbsc->m_dwTotalRead,
                 pBytes,
                 dwSize );

         delete [] pbTemp;
      }
      else
      {
         // the first chunk of data
         m_pbBuffer = new BYTE[dwSize]
         memcpy( m_pbBuffer,
                 pBytes,
                 dwSize );
      }
   }

   // We have received all of the bitmap data
   // Inform the control (and user) that it
   // can now draw safely
   if ( BSCF_LASTDATANOTIFICATION & grfBSCF )
   {
      put_ReadyState( READYSTATE_COMPLETE );
   }
}
```

As data arrives, the OnData method is called with a buffer containing the remote data and a flag indicating whether this is the first, intermediate, or last data packet. We use the flag value to manage our download buffer. When the download is finished, we set the control's ReadyState property to complete. The rest of the code is general buffer management.

The ReadyState Property

Before the addition of asynchronous properties, a control was ready for use as soon as it was instantiated and initialized by its container. Now, for those controls with asynchronous properties, their internal state may not allow immediate use after initial loading. Controls that have asynchronous properties should implement the new standard control property *ReadyState*. A control uses this property to communicate its readiness to its users.

```
enum tagREADYSTATE
{
  READYSTATE_UNINITIALIZED = 0,
  READYSTATE_LOADING      = 1,
  READYSTATE_LOADED       = 2,
  READYSTATE_INTERACTIVE  = 3,
  READYSTATE_COMPLETE     = 4
} READYSTATE;
```

Most of the states are self-explanatory. The difference between the INTERACTIVE and COMPLETE states is up to the control implementer. Those controls that provide interaction with the user (such as mouse clicks) should move to the interactive state as soon as possible even if asynchronous downloading is still in progress.

For example, we might develop a button control that displays a bitmap. The control should move to the interactive state and allow its click event to fire even as the bitmap is downloading. Once the download is finished and the bitmap is rendered, the control moves into the complete state. A control developer should provide the user with interactive functionality as soon as possible.

For our transparent control, we don't really provide any interactive behavior, and so we stay in the loaded state until our bitmap has finished downloading. By examining the following OnDraw code, you can see that we defer rendering of the control until the bitmap download has completed.

```
HRESULT CTransCtl::OnDraw(ATL_DRAWINFO& di)
{
    USES_CONVERSION;
    ...
    // If we're drawing in design mode, just
    // fill the rectangle with a white background and add the control's name
    BOOL bUserMode;
    GetAmbientUserMode( bUserMode );
    if (! bUserMode )
    {
        USES_CONVERSION;
        HDC      hdc = di.hdcDraw;
        RECT& rc = *(RECT*)di.prcBounds;

        FillRect( hdc,
                  &rc,
                  (HBRUSH) GetStockObject( WHITE_BRUSH ));
```

(code continued on next page)

```
    // Now draw the ambient display name
    BSTR bstr;
    if ( SUCCEEDED( GetAmbientDisplayName( bstr )))
    {
        USES_CONVERSION;
        DrawText( hdc,
                  OLE2A( bstr ),
                  -1,
                  &rc,
                  DT_TOP | DT_SINGLELINE );
    }

    // At design time, we don't try to download
    // a remote image as it will not work in
    // most containers.
    return S_OK;
}

// If we're still downloading the image,
// draw some text and return
if ( m_nReadyState != READYSTATE_COMPLETE )
{
    DrawString( di.hdcDraw,
                "Downloading bitmap...",
                &rc );
    return S_OK;
}

...
    return S_OK;
}
```

A control implementer can use a new standard control event called ReadyStateChange to directly notify any users that the ReadyState property has change. Adding support for the ReadyState property to a control is easy. Just add a data member of type long with the name of m_nReadyState, and update the control's IDL file with the get and put methods.

```
interface ITransCtl : IDispatch
{
    [propget, id(DISPID_READYSTATE), helpstring("property ReadyState")]
        HRESULT ReadyState([out, retval] long *pVal);
    [propput, id(DISPID_READYSTATE), helpstring("property ReadyState")]
        HRESULT ReadyState([in] long newVal);
};
```

Constructing the Bitmap

URL monikers treat a URL resource as a stream of bytes. It is up to the client application to add meaning to the returned stream. In our example, the stream contains a Windows DIB, or bitmap. A DIB object is different from a **.GIF** file in that a DIB doesn't support progressive rendering, so our implementation requires the complete bitmap before we can draw the transparent image.

In most cases, working with DIBs involves reading the bitmap structure from a local file and working with a handle to the DIB. There's even an API function (LoadImage) that makes this process easy. However, in our case, we must manage a DIB structure in memory that is assembled asynchronously. Once the structure contains all of the necessary information, we need to realize the DIB within a Windows device context. To encapsulate this behavior we developed a DIB management class called CDib, which is based loosely on the WebImage example in the Win32 SDK. Here's the header file:

```
//
// Dib.h
//
class CDib
{
public:
    CDib();
    ~CDib();

void    Reset();
    BOOL    SetBitmapInfoHeader( BYTE* );
    DWORD   GetImageSize();
    DWORD   Create( HDC hdc );
    void    SetBits( BYTE* buffer );
    DWORD   DrawTo( HDC hdc );

operator HDC()
    {
        return m_memDC;
    }

DWORD GetHeaderSize()
    {
        return( m_dwHeaderSize );
    }
    long GetWidth()
```

(code continued on next page)

```
    {
        return m_lWidth;
    }
    long GetHeight()
    {
        return m_lHeight;
    }
    BOOL IsInitialized()
    {
        return m_bInitialized;
    }
private:
    union
    {
        BITMAPINFO*      p;
        BYTE*            pBytes;
    } m_uBMI;

BOOL        m_bInitialized;
    DWORD       m_dwHeaderSize;
    DWORD       m_dwImageSize;
    BYTE*       m_pbBits;
    HDC         m_memDC;
    HBITMAP     m_hSection;
    HBITMAP     m_hOldBitmap;
    LONG        m_lHeight;
    LONG        m_lWidth;
};
```

As data is downloaded it is stored in a buffer contained in our control's implementation class. Once the bitmap data is completely downloaded, the control's ReadyState transitions to complete, allowing the code from OnDraw to execute. The buffer information is passed to the DIB class, a device context is created based on the DC provided by the container, a DIB section is created, and the actual bits of the image are passed to the DIB section.

```
HRESULT CTransCtl::OnDraw(ATL_DRAWINFO& di)
{
...
    // If this is the first time through OnDraw,
    // we need to set up the DIB
    if (! m_dib.IsInitialized() )
    {
        m_dib.SetBitmapInfoHeader( m_pbBuffer );
        m_dib.Create( di.hdcDraw );
        m_dib.SetBits( m_pbBuffer );
    }
```

```
    int rows = m_dib.GetHeight();
    int columns = m_dib.GetWidth();

// Finally, draw the image
    ...
}
```

We are now ready to render our transparent image.

Drawing the Image

Once the image has been loaded into memory, all we have to worry about is displaying it. As we discussed earlier, for compatibility with IE 3.0 and other older containers we need a handler for WM_ERASEBKGND, and we use it to spoof the container into drawing the background for our control. Here's the code in our class that handles the WM_ERASEBKGND message:

```
BEGIN_MSG_MAP(CTransCtl)
    MESSAGE_HANDLER(WM_ERASEBKGND, OnEraseBackground)
END_MSG_MAP()

LRESULT OnEraseBackground( UINT,
                           WPARAM wParam,
                           LPARAM lParam,
                           BOOL& bHandled )
{
    //
    // Using the trick documented in KB article Q165073 to get the
    // parent window to erase using my device context
    //
    HDC dc = (HDC) wParam;
    HWND hParent = GetParent();
    int color_bits = ::GetDeviceCaps( dc, BITSPIXEL );
    HPALETTE hOldPalette = 0;
    if ( color_bits == 8 )
    {
        HPALETTE hpal;
        if ( GetAmbientPalette( hpal ) == S_OK )
        {
            hOldPalette = ::SelectPalette( dc, hpal, TRUE );
            ::RealizePalette( dc );
        }
        else
        {
            hOldpalette = 0;
```

(code continued on next page)

```
      }
   }
   POINT pt;
   pt.x = pt.y = 0;
   MapWindowPoints( hParent, &pt, 1 );
   OffsetWindowOrgEx( dc, pt.x, pt.y, &pt );
   ::SendMessage( hParent, WM_ERASEBKGND, (WPARAM) dc, 0 );
   SetWindowOrgEx( dc, pt.x, pt.y, NULL );

   if ( hOldPalette )
      ::SelectPalette( dc, hOldPalette, TRUE );
   return 0;
}
```

First, we add an entry to the message map for the control, and then we add the message handler itself. Essentially, all this handler does is to pass the WM_ERASEBKGND message to the parent window along with a copy of the control's device context.

The image is drawn in our OnDraw method. If you've slogged through this chapter wondering when we were going to show how to do transparent drawing, you have finally made it!

As we described in Chapter 8, the OnDraw method is called by the container, which passes a device context for the control to render its representation. Our implementation isn't much more complicated than it would be if we were simply displaying the BMP file. We simply add the code to create the monochrome bit mask, and then perform the XOR/AND/XOR drawing method discussed earlier.

The following code shown creates a monochrome bit mask in a compatible DC, relying on a Windows-specific characteristic of monochrome bitmaps. When you're copying from a color bitmap to a monochrome bitmap, any color pixel that is identical to the color bitmap's background color will get set to 1 in the monochrome bitmap. All other bits will get set to 0. With this knowledge in hand, you can see how the code will create the bitmap needed by the masking algorithm.

```
HDC hdcMask = ::CreateCompatibleDC( di.hdcDraw );
HBITMAP bmMask = ::CreateBitmap( columns, rows, 1, 1, NULL );
HBITMAP hOldMaskBitmap = (HBITMAP) SelectObject( hdcMask, bmMask );
SetBkColor( HDC( m_dib ), RGB( 255, 255, 255 ) );
SetTextColor( HDC( m_dib ), RGB( 0, 0, 0 ) );
BitBlt( hdcMask,
    0, 0,
    columns, rows,
    HDC( m_dib ),
    0,
    0,
    SRCCOPY );
```

Once the mask has been created, we can draw the image using three device contexts. di.hdcDraw contains the container's device context, HDC(m_dib) is the device context containing the color bitmap for the image file, and hdcMask is the device context containing the monochrome bitmap. Three consecutive BitBlt() function calls perform the transparent draw.

```
BitBlt( di.hdcDraw,
    rc.left, rc.top,
    columns, rows,
    HDC( m_dib ),
    0, 0,
    SRCINVERT );
BitBlt( di.hdcDraw,
    rc.left, rc.top,
    columns, rows,
    hdcMask,
    0, 0,
    SRCAND );
BitBlt( di.hdcDraw,
    rc.left, rc.top,
    columns, rows,
    HDC( m_dib ),
    0, 0,
    SRCINVERT );
```

Thanks to this special drawing code, each white pixel in a bitmap displays as if it were transparent. Figure 9.3 shows the control displaying a bitmap in Internet Explorer.

Figure 9.3 Our transparent control

INTERNET-AWARE CONTROLS

Controls that will work in Web-based environments must content with several other issues. Their persistent data should work well with HTML-based documents, they should ensure that a malicious user of the control will not harm a local system, and they must also be digitally signed to indicate that they come from a trusted source.

IPersistPropertyBagImpl

The `IPersistPropertyBag` interface allows a control and its container to work together to provide textual persistence. The older control persistence mechanism uses `IPersistStreamInit`, through which the container treats a controls property values as a stream of bytes. With `IPersistPropertyBag`, a control's properties can be saved in an HTML-friendly format. Implementing IPersistPropertyBag is easy with ATL; you simply include `IPersistPropertyBagImpl` in your derivation.

```
class ATL_NO_VTABLE CTransCtl :
...
    public IPersistPropertyBagImpl<CTransCtl>
{
...
BEGIN_COM_MAP(CNoteCtl)
...
    COM_INTERFACE_ENTRY_IMPL(IPersistPropertyBag)
END_COM_MAP()

};
```

These two lines of code give our control property bag support. Now when we load ActiveX Control Pad and add our control to an HTML page, the properties are saved this way:

```
<OBJECT ID="TransCtl" WIDTH=128 HEIGHT=128
    CLASSID="CLSID:B25D9AF5-E760-11D0-A052-00A0247B7657"
    CODEBASE="http://www.widgetware.com/TransparentControl.dll">
     <PARAM NAME="ImageFile"
VALUE="http://www.widgetware.com/image02.bmp">
</OBJECT>
```

Instead of this way:

```
<OBJECT ID="TransCtl" WIDTH=128 HEIGHT=128
    CLASSID="CLSID:B25D9AF5-E760-11D0-A052-00A0247B7657"
    CODEBASE="http://www.widgetware.com/TransparentControl.dll"

DATA="DATA:application/xoleobject;BASE64,L3R2EZC6nWlb+0AAAAu4UQEATZXJpZg==
">
</OBJECT>
```

IObjectSafety

A Web-enabled control implements IObjectSafety to inform its container that potential users cannot use it for malicious behavior. In other words, the control does not expose any functionality through which a user could harm the local system. Implementing IObjectSafety is only slightly more difficult, because ATL's version (2.1)of IObjectSafetyImpl doesn't work correctly. Instead of deriving directly from IObjectSafetyImpl, you can derive from IObjectSafety and provide implementations for its two methods: GetInterfaceSafetyOptions and SetInterfaceSafetyOptions.

```
class ATL_NO_VTABLE CTransCtl :
...
   public IObjectSafety,
{
...
BEGIN_COM_MAP(CNoteCtl)
...
   COM_INTERFACE_ENTRY(IObjectSafety)
END_COM_MAP()
...
// IObjectSafety
STDMETHODIMP GetInterfaceSafetyOptions( REFIID riid,
                                        DWORD *pdwSupportedOptions,
                                        DWORD *pdwEnabledOptions )
{
   *pdwSupportedOptions =  INTERFACESAFE_FOR_UNTRUSTED_CALLER |
                           INTERFACESAFE_FOR_UNTRUSTED_DATA;
   *pdwEnabledOptions = *pdwSupportedOptions;
   return S_OK;
}

STDMETHODIMP SetInterfaceSafetyOptions( REFIID riid,
                                        DWORD dwOptionSetMask,
                                        DWORD dwEnabledOptions )
{
   return S_OK;
}
```

The GetInterfaceSafetyOptions method sets the supported options parameter to include INTERFACESAFE_FOR_UNTRUSTED_CALLER, which indicates that the control does not expose any functionality that might allow a user to harm the local system.

For example, if you develop a control that exposes a CreateObject function that allows a script writer to create instances of automation objects within VBScript, the control is not safe. It would be easy for someone to use CreateObject to instantiate an external application (such as Microsoft Word) and use it to delete local files, install a virus, and so on.

In a browser environment, a control can also damage a local system if the data it downloads is from a malicious or untrusted source. When the control is instantiated on the local machine, the container provide an IPersist* interface to initialize any persistent data. Because the location of the data is provided by the control user, the data is also a potential security problem. The INTERFACESAFE_FOR_UNTRUSTED_DATA flag indicates that a control cannot harm the local system even when initialized with untrusted data.

Controls can also indicate that they are safe for scripting and safe for initializing by registering that they implement the corresponding component categories, CATID_SafeForScripting and CATID_SafeForInitializing.

Component Download

Browser's that support the embedding of ActiveX controls must also support a new Microsoft technology called component download. Component download is based on COM and provides automatic download, verification, and registration of ActiveX components. In other words, the component's object code is copied from a Web server to the local machine. Support for component download is provided via the new CoGetClassObjectFromURL API function, which uses URL monikers to perform the download.

After the component (typically an OCX or DLL file) is copied locally, the component download service ensures the validity of the component and, depending on the security level of the browser, registers it on the local machine. Once the component is registered, its functionality can be used within the browser. It's not always as simple as described here, because most controls require other files to execute, and this requires specific packaging of the component and these files.

Controls and Security

In an environment where executables are downloaded to a client machine, security is of major concern. An ActiveX control has full access to the Win32 API. This arrangement provides the highest degree of functionality for control writers, but it also creates a potential security problem. Java takes the sandbox approach of not allowing direct access to the local hardware. This approach helps with security, but it reduces functionality significantly. To maintain a high level of functionality, Microsoft uses the new WinVerifyTrust service to protect local machines from malicious components.

Microsoft approaches security in the Web environment in the same way it approaches that used in software retail channels. There is no guarantee that the software you buy from a local retailer is benign. There is no guarantee, but there is significant *trust*. When you purchase a software package from a vendor, such as Microsoft, you know where the software came from, and you're confident that it will not harm your machine.

Microsoft has taken the steps to set up such an environment of trust on the Web by providing technologies that ensure the authenticity and integrity of a component. A component is marked with a digital signature based on Microsoft's Authenticode technology. The component's signature is then maintained and verified by a trusted authority.

Digital Signatures

To ensure authenticity and integrity, each component is marked using a public-private key mechanism. This digital signature, which you can view as a complex checksum, is attached to a component. If the component is compromised in any way, the digital signature will become invalid. The signature also contains information about the individual or company that actually signed the component.

Code Signing

To sign your components using Authenticode so that they can be trusted in the Internet environment, you must register and obtain a certificate from one of the certification authorities such as VeriSign or GTE. After receiving your certificate, you can use the MAKECERT, SIGN-CODE, and CHKTRUST utilities provided with the Internet Client SDK to sign your controls.

Individual software developers can obtain certificates for $20 per year through VeriSign. The charge for software development companies is $400 per year for a companywide license. VeriSign can be reached at www.verisign.com.

NOTE

Internet Explorer Security Levels

Internet Explorer will not download and register components that have not been properly signed (unless you turn off security). Internet Explorer allows the user to specify the security level (see Figure 9.4). If the security level is set too high, your controls must be signed (if they are not already on the local machine) and they must be safe for scripting and safe for initializing. Your control specifies these characteristics through the component categories or by implementing the IObjectSafety interface that we discussed earlier.

Figure 9.4 Internet Explorer security levels.

ON TO COM THREADING

ActiveX controls provide a well-supported and effective technique for delivering software functionality in traditional Windows applications and in the new Web-based application environments. We took at look at the basics of ActiveX controls in Chapter 8, and in this chapter we examined techniques for developing controls for use in Web-based environments. In Chapter 10 we'll take a look at one of the more complicated areas of COM-based development: threading.

COM Threading

When I teach my five-day COM course, the students anxiously await the COM threading module. It seems that COM threading is one of the most misunderstood (and feared) COM topics. There's no doubt that multithreading is a difficult topic in itself, and introducing COM into the equation makes it even more difficult. There are those who will tell you that COM threading is easy, but that's because they've been working with COM a long time.

This chapter first covers the basics of COM threading and then moves into a discussion of ATL's support for the various COM threading models. The chapter ends with an example of a multithreaded math component. We haven't used the math component example since Chapter 7, and I'm sure you missed it. This chapter is, however, the last time you'll see it.

A Quick Summary of COM Threading

Let's begin with a summary of COM threading to introduce you to many of the terms and lay the groundwork for the coming sections. Before the release of Windows NT 3.51, COM did not support the concept of multiple threads accessing a COM object. When creating components, developers did not have to worry about concurrency issues. In other words, the components did not require thread safety. All component access occurred on the process's main (or primary) thread, so concurrency support was not required. Many components exist that are not thread-safe, and the need to support this legacy code contributes to the complexity of the various threading models.

NOTE

I'm using the term COM object to indicate an instance of a COM component somewhere in a process.

The Single-Threaded Apartment

Windows NT 3.51 (and Windows 95) introduced the *single-threaded apartment*, or STA, which allows COM objects to exist in different threads in the same process. The primary reason for introducing this new model was to improve the performance of applications that use several COM objects.

Before the release of the STA model, all component access proceeded through the main thread of an application, typically through the process's message pump. Consider an out-of-process server managing 100 clients via 100 instances of a component. Client access to an instance is serialized (through the message pump) because it must occur on the main thread. This arrangement is useful for component developers because they need not trouble themselves with concurrency issues, but in large client/server applications, this performance hit (forcing all client requests through a single queue) is not acceptable.

STA allows a client to create any number of threads to house COM objects. It also allows the development of components that use multiple threads in their implementation. Each thread that uses COM in any way becomes its own STA. An STA is an abstract entity that makes it easier to discuss relationships between clients and component instances. It also allows us to put forth rules that must be followed when working in COM multi-threaded environments.

In our example of 100 clients, our out-of-process server can now create an STA for each COM object. This means the creation of 100 threads, but it gives each client the appearance of multiple, simultaneous access to its component instance. In other words, we've enabled the development of higher-performance components.

One of the benefits of the STA model is that COM handles most of the details, and building a component that supports running in an STA is relatively painless. You still do not have to worry about concurrency when implementing your components.

The Multithreaded Apartment

The STA model provided good performance improvements, but there was room for more. With the release of Windows NT 4.0 (and the Windows 95 DCOM upgrade) a new threading model was introduced: the *multithreaded apartment*, or MTA. The MTA model allows COM objects in different threads to access one another directly.

In the STA model, cross-thread calls must be marshaled, and this is expensive. COM uses marshaling to synchronize access to those components that don't support concurrency. A COM object that resides in an STA must marshal its interface pointers when passed to another apartment (an STA or MTA).

This means that there are two COM threading models today: the STA model and the MTA model. The purpose of these models is to give component developers freedom in the way they develop components. If they want their components to be very efficient, they must ensure concurrency support and can code to the MTA model. If they are more concerned with functionality and less about concurrency, they can code to the STA model. Above all, though, the purpose of the two models is to allow both component types to work together regardless of the model chosen by a client application.

The Apartment

The COM apartment is a conceptual entity that allows us to think about components and their clients in a logical way. The term *apartment* indicates that some sort of separation (or wall) exists between the software entities within an apartment. An apartment is not a thread, but a thread belongs to only one apartment. An apartment is not an instance of a COM object, but each COM instance belongs to only one apartment. The wall that exists between apartments is the set of rules that COM clients and components must abide by. If either one breaks the rules, your application pays, usually by faulting.

A process can have one or more apartments, depending on its implementation. Apartments are created or entered by calling the `CoInitialize` or `CoInitializeEx` function. Each thread that calls `CoInitialize(0)` or `CoInitializeEx( 0, COINIT_APARTMENTTHREADED )` creates a new STA. Each thread that calls `CoInitializeEx( 0, COINIT_MULTITHREADED )` either creates or enters the MTA. A process can have only one MTA, and each MTA thread enters this apartment. Figure 10.1 shows a process with four threads and three apartments. COM's threading rules must be followed when you're crossing apartments, as indicated by the lines in the figure.

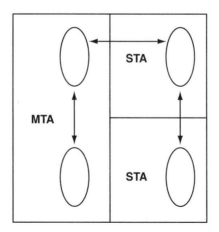

Figure 10.1 A process with three apartments.

Threading rule: You must call `CoInitialize` or `CoInitializeEx` for each thread (including your main thread) that will use COM. This call informs COM of your intentions and places your thread in a new STA, or you create or enter the MTA. Subsequently, when you create an instance of a component, COM will compare your threading model with that of the component and will place it in the appropriate apartment— hopefully, your own apartments, although that does not always happen.

In-Process Components

In-process components are loaded into an existing apartment when a client calls `CoCreateInstance`. The in-process component does not have an opportunity to call `CoInitializeEx` to instruct COM which apartment model it supports. Instead, in-process components indicate their threading model support through a new registry entry. The `ThreadingModel` entry is a named value stored under the component's `\HKCR\CLSID\InProcServer32` key. It can have one of the following four values:

- None. The absence of the value indicates that the component does not support any of the threading models and so must be created and accessed only on the client's primary thread (the first STA).

- `Apartment`. The component can execute in any STA in the client process and not just the primary STA. By marking your component as supporting the `Apartment` threading model you indicate that its class factory is thread-safe and that you protect any global data. This approach allows the client to load the component into any STA. It provides the client direct access to your component's interfaces as long as it accesses them from within the same STA in which it was created.

- `Free`. The component must reside in the MTA. Your component is thread-safe in every way and direct, simultaneous access by multiple threads is not a problem. The component can pass interface pointers directly to other threads, including STA threads. COM, however, will ensure marshaling of interface pointers when moving from the MTA to the STA.

- `Both`. The component is thread-safe in every way and can reside in either an STA or the MTA. The component understands that it may run in an STA and so marshals interface pointers to other apartments when necessary. However, at run time it won't know whether it's in an MTA or STA, so it should aggregate with the free-threaded marshaler, manually marshal its pointers, and let COM make the decision.

Threading rule: You must inform COM of your in-process component's threading model by adding a `ThreadingModel` value to the `HKCR\CLSID\InProcServer32` registry key.

SINGLE-THREADED APARTMENTS

An STA contains one thread on which all its components will be created. The component instances that reside within the STA may not be thread-safe and so COM must synchronize access to each of them within the STA. COM does this by creating a hidden window for every STA within a process. If the client and component instance reside within the same thread, everything is fine because the thread itself ensures synchronization. However, if an interface pointer is passed to another thread, be it an STA or MTA, someone must ensure synchronized access to the instances within the STA. COM handles this task in nearly all cases.

Through its marshaling process, COM ensures serialized access to components that don't support concurrency. COM's marshaling process uses the message pump of an STA to ensure serialized access. Every external call into an instance within an STA goes through the message pump. Just as window messages are serialized via a message pump, so is access to STA components. The only requirement for a component to be used within an STA is that it be reentrant. In other words, all global variable access must be protected using a critical section, semaphore, and so on, and local variables must be allocated on the stack.

NOTE

Threading rule: The reason COM needs to know your threading model so that it can ensure synchronized access to those components that do not support concurrency. COM ensures thread-safe access through marshaling. If your component does not support concurrency but protects its global data, it should use the STA model.

The Primary STA

The very first STA created in a process is special. Older components that have no knowledge of threading models must be created and accessed only on the primary STA. COM must assume that the components do not support concurrent access. In other words, all interaction with these components must occur on the primary STA even when accessing the component's class factory (for example, `DllGetClassObject`).

STA Component Requirements (Summary)

The component requirements for supporting execution in any STA are outlined in the following list. These requirements are mostly for in-process components except where noted. Out-of-process components are always accessed through COM's marshaling code and are much easier to implement. For this reason, this chapter concerns itself primarily with working with in-process components.

1. Because a component's class factory can be accessed simultaneously by multiple STAs, its exposed entry points (such as DllGetClassObject) must be thread-safe. In most cases, a component housing creates a unique class factory instance for each client request, thereby making the entry point safe. If only one instance of the factory supports all creation requests, however, it must be made thread-safe.

2. The component must protect access to any global data.

3. The internals of the component need not be thread-safe, because COM ensures serialized access to each component instance while in the STA.

4. If the component implements custom interfaces, it should provide a proxy/stub DLL (through either standard or universal marshaling) so that cross-apartment calls can be marshaled.

5. In-process components should mark themselves as supporting the any-STA model by setting the ThreadingModel value to "Apartment."

NOTE Threading rule: In-process components need a proxy/stub DLL for their custom interfaces if they expect to be used in multithreaded environments. Moving an interface pointer from one apartment to another requires marshaling.

MULTITHREADED APARTMENTS

Windows NT 4.0 introduced the multithreaded apartment model. The primary reason was to give component developers better performance and flexibility in their implementations. A process can have only one MTA, but this apartment can have any number of threads each with a number of component instances. The STA model requires that interface pointers be marshaled between apartment threads, something that reduces performance considerably. MTA allows each thread direct access to component instances in other MTA threads. Direct pointer access is much faster than marshaling.

However, this freedom comes at a price. For a component to operate in the MTA it must be thread-safe in every way. In the MTA, a COM object can be accessed simultaneously by multiple clients. These clients may or may not be in the same thread in which the component was created.

MTA Component Requirements (Summary)

The component requirements for supporting execution in the MTA of a process are outlined next. These requirements are for in-process components.

1. COM does not synchronize calls to a component, so the component must support simultaneous access by multiple clients. In other words, the component must be thread-safe.

2. The component can pass direct pointers to other threads in the MTA. This would typically be done when a component creates MTA-based worker threads. The component should use COM's marshaling APIs and let COM decide whether the pointers can be passed directly.

3. The component's class factory must be thread-safe, and global data must be protected, just as in the STA case.

4. The components should mark themselves as supporting the free-threading model by setting the `ThreadingModel` value to `Free`.

Mixed-Model Component Requirements

A component can choose to support both the STA and MTA models. This gives COM flexibility when deciding in which apartment a component instance should be created. An out-of-process component explicitly indicates its threading model to COM via the `CoInitializeEx` call, so only in-process components need deal with supporting both models.

NOTE

Threading rule: To use the CoInitializeEx function, you must be running NT 4.0 or higher, Windows 98, or Windows 95 with the DCOM upgrade. To use the new MTA functions (e.g., CoInitializeEx) in your code, you must define the _WIN32_DCOM preprocessor symbol.

The Free-Threaded Marshaler

The free-threaded marshaler is a system component provided by COM to help those in-process components that support both threading models (via the `ThreadingModel=Both` registry entry). The free-threaded marshaler aggregates with any client accessing the component, and custom marshals direct pointers to all apartments within the process.

NOTE

Threading rule: If your in-process component supports both STA and MTA, it should aggregate with the free-threaded marshaler via the CoCreateFreeThreadedMarshaler API. Care must be taken, though, if your component maintains direct pointers to objects in other STAs. See KB article Q150777 for more details.

CoMarshalInterThreadInterfaceInStream

One of the primary rules that you must follow when working in multithreaded COM environments is that you must marshal interface pointers when passed to another apartment. Luckily, COM handles this marshaling in most cases, including `QueryInterface` and `CoCreateInstance` and when you're moving interface pointers through a COM method call. As a developer, though, you must sometimes *manually* marshal interface pointers between apartments, primarily when COM isn't involved in the cross-apartment call. In other words, you move the pointer across apartments yourself.

Manually marshaling an interface pointer is as easy as using two COM API calls. The first one, `CoMarshalInterThreadInterfaceInStream` takes an interface pointer, marshals it into a stream, and returns the `IStream` pointer. This pointer can then be moved directly across an apartment boundary. In the other apartment, the `CoGetInterfaceAndReleaseStream` function is used to extract the marshaled interface pointer from the stream. Through this process, COM ensures synchronization of calls on the associated object.

Later in this chapter we'll develop a math component that uses a thread to perform its calculations. Each time the client calls one of `IMath`'s methods (such as `Add` or `Multiply`), the component creates a secondary thread to do the calculation. One of the parameters to the thread is a callback (`ICallBack`) interface pointer through which the thread will notify the client when the calculation is complete. This example represents the case when you must manually marshal an interface pointer from one apartment to another.

The `Add` method is similar to what we've seen before. This time, though, it calls `SimulateLongComputation`, which starts a thread. Here's a bit of the code.

```
STDMETHODIMP CMath::Add(long lOp1, long lOp2)
{
    SimulateLongComputation( mathAdd, lOp1, lOp2 );
    return S_OK;
}
...
HRESULT CMath::SimulateLongComputation( mathOPERATOR op,
                                        long lOp1, long lOp2)
{
    // Marshal the ICallBack interface into a stream
    IStream* pStream = 0;
    HRESULT hr = CoMarshalInterThreadInterfaceInStream( IID_ICallBack,
                                                        m_pCallBack,
                                                        &pStream );

    if( SUCCEEDED( hr ))
```

```
{
    // Create the thread parameters object and
    // fill it out with our parameters
    ThreadParameters* pTP = new ThreadParameters;
    pTP->op = op;
    pTP->lOp1 = lOp1;
    pTP->lOp2 = lOp2;
    pTP->pStream = pStream;

    // Create the thread
    HANDLE  hThread;
    DWORD   dwThreadID;
    hThread = CreateThread( 0, 0,
                            PerformComputation,
                            pTP,
                            0,
                            &dwThreadID);

    ...
}
    ...
    return hr;
}
```

Just as in the Chapter 7 CallBack example, the client implements an ICallBack interface and passes it to the component via the IMath::Advise method. The component stores the interface in the m_pCallBack member. The preceding code first marshals the ICallBack pointer into a stream. Next, it populates a thread parameters structure with the operator, operands, and IStream pointer. This structure is passed to the thread via the CreateThread call.

The PerformComputation function provides the code for execution by the thread. The first thing we do is to call CoInitialize with a NULL parameter, which creates a new STA. Interface pointers must be marshaled between apartments. In this case, we're moving the ICallBack pointer from the initial client apartment to the STA created directly by our component.

```
DWORD WINAPI PerformComputation( void *p )
{
    CoInitialize( 0 );

    // Get the thread parameters
    ThreadParameters* pTP = (ThreadParameters*) p;
```

(code continued on next page)

```
// Unmarshal the ICallBack pointer
ICallBack* pCallBack = 0;
HRESULT hr = CoGetInterfaceAndReleaseStream( pTP->pStream,
                                             IID_ICallBack,
                                             (void**) &pCallBack );

// We successfully retrieved the ICallBack interface
if( SUCCEEDED( hr ))
{
   // Perform the calculation and delay
   // to simulate doing some real work
   long lResult;
   switch( pTP->op )
   {
      case mathAdd:
         lResult = pTP->lOp1 + pTP->lOp2;
         break;

      ...
   }

   // Delay, but not too long
   Sleep( min( lResult, 5000 ));

   // Notify the client with the result of the computation
   pCallBack->ComputationComplete( lResult );
}

// Delete our thread parameters structure
delete pTP;

CoUninitialize();
return hr;
}
```

We extract the calculation parameters and stream from the thread structure and then use the CoGetInterfaceAndReleaseStream API to unmarshal the ICallBack interface pointer from the stream. After performing the calculation and delaying a bit for effect, we notify the client with the result through ICallBack. Finally, we shut down COM before the thread exits.

NOTE

Threading rule: You must marshal interface pointers between apartments. The easiest way is to use the marshaling APIs `CoMarshalInterThreadInterfaceInStream` and `CoGetInterfaceAndReleaseStream`. In a few cases you can get around this rule, but it's best to manually marshal every time and use the free-threaded marshaler in your components (marked as "`Both`") to ensure best performance.

Code-Based Examples

So far, in all our examples the client applications have created STAs by using the `CoInitialize` API with a `NULL` parameter. After initializing COM, we then called `CoCreateInstance` to create an instance of our component. It looked something like this:

```
int WINAPI WinMain(HINSTANCE hInst, HINSTANCE, LPSTR, int)
{
   // This creates the main STA
   CoInitialize( NULL );

   CComPtr<IMath> ptrMath;
   // By default ATL components are marked as Apartment if in-process
   HRESULT hr = CoCreateInstance( CLSID_Math,
                        NULL,
                        CLSCTX_SERVER,
                        IID_IMath,
                        (void**) &ptrMath );
...
}
```

Our process has only one thread, but we still must initialize COM to use its services. This creates a process with a single, primary STA. When we call `CoCreateInstance`, COM compares our threading model (STA) with that of the component. If the component is out-of-process, it can be viewed as another STA because COM marshals the calls in every case anyway. If the component is in-process, COM looks in the registry to determine which threading model the component supports. In our case, the math component supports the STA model, so COM creates the instance directly within our apartment. Access to the component (through its interfaces) is direct. There is no need for marshaling, because we have only one thread and threads are self-synchronizing.

The following code again demonstrates an application that initially creates an STA. This time, however, the math component can run only in the MTA. In other words, the registry is marked with ThreadingModel=Free.

```
int main( int argc, char *argv[] )
{
   // Create an STA
   CoInitializeEx( 0, COINIT_APARTMENTTHREADED );

   CComPtr<IMath> ptrMath;
   // The component is in-process and marked as "Free"
   // COM will create an MTA for the component
   HRESULT hr = CoCreateInstance( CLSID_Math,
                       NULL,
                       CLSCTX_SERVER,
                       IID_IMath,
                       (void**) &ptrMath );
...
}
```

COM recognizes that the component can reside only in an MTA, so it creates an MTA explicitly for the component. In this case, the math component requires a proxy/stub DLL for the IMath interface, because the interface pointer must be marshaled from the MTA to the STA. The STA thread will get a pointer to an interface proxy through the CoCreateInstance call.

Here's another example of the client creating an STA. This time, though, the math component can run in any STA or the MTA, because it has marked the registry with ThreadingModel=Both.

```
int main( int argc, char *argv[] )
{
   // Create an STA
   CoInitializeEx( 0, COINIT_APARTMENTTHREADED );

   CComPtr<IMath> ptrMath;
   // The component is in-process and marked as "Both"
   // COM will create the component in our STA,
   // so no marshaling is necessary
   HRESULT hr = CoCreateInstance( CLSID_Math,
                       NULL,
                       CLSCTX_SERVER,
                       IID_IMath,
                       (void**) &ptrMath );
...
}
```

As the comments indicate, because the component supports both threading models, COM creates the instance directly within the STA of the client. No proxy is needed for this example. Now let's look at some MTA examples. Our code examples will now demonstrate how the client creates an MTA with various math component configurations.

```
int main( int argc, char *argv[] )
{
   // Create an MTA
   CoInitializeEx( 0, COINIT_MULTITHREADED );

   CComPtr<IMath> ptrMath;
   // The math component is now marked as ThreadingModel=Apartment
   // COM must therefore create an STA for the component
   // The interface must be marshaled from the STA to the
   // MTA and so we need a proxy/stub DLL
   HRESULT hr = CoCreateInstance( CLSID_Math,
                      NULL,
                      CLSCTX_SERVER,
                      IID_IMath,
                      (void**) &ptrMath );
...
}
```

In the preceding CoCreateInstance call, COM will create an STA for the math component because it supports only the STA model. The component requires a proxy/stub DLL, because COM must marshal the pointer from the STA back to the client's MTA. Here's one more:

```
int main( int argc, char *argv[] )
{
   // Create an MTA
   CoInitializeEx( 0, COINIT_MULTITHREADED );

   CComPtr<IMath> ptrMath;
   // The math component is now marked as ThreadingModel=Free
   // COM creates the math component directly in the MTA
   // No marshaling support is required
   HRESULT hr = CoCreateInstance( CLSID_Math,
                      NULL,
                      CLSCTX_SERVER,
                      IID_IMath,
                      (void**) &ptrMath );
...
}
```

You should know by now what will happen. The client has created an MTA, and the component itself supports running in an MTA and so is created in the same thread as the client. No marshaling code is required.

We've gone over several examples of STA/MTA interaction, but there are several more. Table 10.1 outlines all the possible configurations. The important point is that COM manages these relationships. As developers, we just need to be aware of what's going on. If we follow the COM threading rules outlined in this chapter, our applications will behave appropriately.

Table 10.1 Component Access and Creation Based on Threading Model

CLIENT APARTMENT*	SERVER MARKED AS**	POINTER ACCESS/RESULT
Primary STA	Single	Direct access. Component is created in the primary STA
Nonprimary STA	Single	Proxy access. Component is created in the primary STA.
MTA	Single	Proxy access. Component is created in the primary STA. COM creates an STA if necessary.
Primary STA	Apartment	Direct access. Component is created in the primary STA.
Non-primary STA	Apartment	Direct access. Component is created in the client's STA.
MTA	Apartment	Proxy access. Component is created in an STA created by COM.
Primary STA	Free	Proxy access. Component is created in MTA, which may require creation by COM.
Nonprimary STA	Free	Proxy access. Component is created in MTA, which may require creation by COM.
MTA	Free	Direct access. Component is created in the MTA.
Primary STA	Both	Direct access. Component is created in the primary STA.
Non-primary STA	Both	Direct access. Component is created in client's STA.
MTA	Both	Direct access. Component is created in the MTA.

*PRIMARY STA INDICATES THE FIRST STA CREATED IN THE PROCESS

**SINGLE INDICATES THAT A SERVER SUPPORTS RUNNING ONLY IN THE PRIMARY STA. THIS IS INDICATED BY THE ABSENCE OF THE ThreadingModel REGISTRY VALUE.

The source for this table is Microsoft Knowledge Base article Q150177.

ATL AND COM THREADING

ATL currently supports all of COM's threading models and is the first framework to do so. MFC supports only the single-STA and multiple-STA models, because its classes are thread-safe only at the class level. When you initially create an ATL component using the ATL Object wizard, you are presented with several threading model options on the **Attributes** tab (see Figure 10.2).

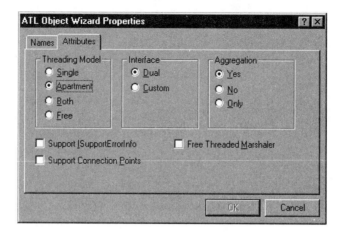

Figure 10.2 The **Attributes** tab.

Single and Apartment

Selecting either **Single** or **Apartment** instructs the Object Wizard to use the CComSingleThreadModel class as the template parameter for the CComObjectRootEx class. Both options use the same ATL implementation. A component that supports execution in the primary STA of a client is a subset of a component that supports any-STA execution.

```
class ATL_NO_VTABLE CMath :
    public CComObjectRootEx<CComSingleThreadModel>,
    public CComCoClass<CMath, &CLSID_Math>,
    public IMath
{
...
};
```

CComSingleThreadModel

Components that support the single or multiple-STA model do not have to be thread-safe, and ATL uses this fact to make these components more efficient. In Chapter 3 we discussed how CComObjectRootEx takes a template parameter that indicates what level of threading support is required by a component. Here's a concise look at its implementation:

```
template <class ThreadModel>
class CComObjectRootEx : public CComObjectRootBase
{
public:
   typedef ThreadModel _ThreadModel;
   typedef _ThreadModel::AutoCriticalSection _CritSec;

   ULONG InternalAddRef()
   {
      return _ThreadModel::Increment(&m_dwRef);
   }
   ULONG InternalRelease()
   {
      return _ThreadModel::Decrement(&m_dwRef);
   }
void Lock() {m_critsec.Lock();}
   void Unlock() {m_critsec.Unlock();}

private:
   _CritSec m_critsec;
};
```

The `ThreadModel` class provides the implementation of a component's `AddRef` and `Release` methods as well as `Lock` and `Unlock` methods, which manage the housing's global instance count. `CComSingleThreadModel` provides simple or no-op implementations of these methods, because the component developer is stating that multiple-threading support is not required. Here's a look at the `CComSingleThreadModel` class:

```
class CComSingleThreadModel
{
public:
   static ULONG WINAPI Increment(LPLONG p) {return ++(*p);}
   static ULONG WINAPI Decrement(LPLONG p) {return --(*p);}
   typedef CComFakeCriticalSection AutoCriticalSection;
   typedef CComFakeCriticalSection CriticalSection;
   typedef CComSingleThreadModel ThreadModelNoCS;
};
```

As you can see, the `Increment` and `Decrement` methods perform simple operations, and the critical section class is typedef'd to use ATL's `CComFakeCriticalSection` class. As you can guess, `CComFakeCriticalSection` does nothing. If you use the `CComSingleThreadModel` implementation, your component's code will be efficient but will not support the MTA model.

The only difference between selecting the **Single** or the **Apartment** option is that the Object wizard adds the `ThreadingModel=Apartment` string to the **Apartment** option component's RGS file.

Free and Both

If you chose the **Free** or **Both** option, the Object wizard will add the appropriate RGS entry for you and will also add the CComMultiThreadModel class to your component's CComObjectRootEx implementation.

```
class ATL_NO_VTABLE CMath :
    public CComObjectRootEx<CComMultiThreadModel>,
    public CComCoClass<CMath, &CLSID_Math>,
    public IMath
{
...
};
```

The CComMultiThreadModel class provides implementations of the reference counting methods that are thread-safe. Again, though, this provides thread safety only for the component's IUnknown and class factory implementations. The component developer must ensure the thread safety of the component's internal implementation.

```
class CComMultiThreadModel
{
public:
    static ULONG WINAPI Increment(LPLONG p) {return InterlockedIncrement(p);}
    static ULONG WINAPI Decrement(LPLONG p) {return InterlockedDecrement(p);}
    typedef CComAutoCriticalSection AutoCriticalSection;
    typedef CComCriticalSection CriticalSection;
    typedef CComMultiThreadModelNoCS ThreadModelNoCS;
};
```

Free-Threaded Marshaler

The free-threaded marshaler option automatically aggregates the free-threaded marshaler with your component. You should select this option only if you've marked your in-process component as supporting both the any-STA and MTA threading models (the **Both** option). The Object wizard adds the following highlighted code.

```
// Math.h
...
class ATL_NO_VTABLE CMath :
    public CComObjectRootEx<CComMultiThreadModel>,
    public CComCoClass<CMath, &CLSID_Math>,
    public IMath
{
```

(code continued on next page)

```
public:
    CMath()
    {
        m_pUnkMarshaler = NULL;
    }

BEGIN_COM_MAP(CMath)
    COM_INTERFACE_ENTRY(IMath)
    COM_INTERFACE_ENTRY_AGGREGATE(IID_IMarshal, m_pUnkMarshaler.p)
END_COM_MAP()

    DECLARE_GET_CONTROLLING_UNKNOWN()
    HRESULT FinalConstruct()
    {
        return CoCreateFreeThreadedMarshaler(
            GetControllingUnknown(), &m_pUnkMarshaler.p);
    }
    void FinalRelease()
    {
        m_pUnkMarshaler.Release();
    }
    CComPtr<IUnknown> m_pUnkMarshaler;
...
};
```

You've seen this code before. It is similar to our aggregation example from Chapter 5.

CComObjectRoot

ATL allows you to specify a global threading model for every component within a housing by defining one of three preprocessor symbols and by then deriving all your components from CComObjectRoot. CComObjectRoot is a simple typedef of CComObjectRootEx with a parameter of CComObjectThreadModel.

```
typedef CComObjectRootEx<CComObjectThreadModel> CComObjectRoot;
```

The CComObjectThreadModel parameter is defined via one of three preprocessor symbols.

```
// From ATLBASE.H
#if defined(_ATL_SINGLE_THREADED)
    typedef CComSingleThreadModel CComObjectThreadModel;
    typedef CComSingleThreadModel CComGlobalsThreadModel;
#elif defined(_ATL_APARTMENT_THREADED)
    typedef CComSingleThreadModel CComObjectThreadModel;
    typedef CComMultiThreadModel CComGlobalsThreadModel;
#else
```

```
        typedef CComMultiThreadModel CComObjectThreadModel;
        typedef CComMultiThreadModel CComGlobalsThreadModel;
#endif
```

By default, the ATL AppWizard defines _ATL_APARTMENT_THREADED in your project's **STDAFX.H** file. This has an effect only if you use CComObjectRoot instead of CComObjectRootEx when implementing your components.

The technique of defining the global preprocessor symbol was used in the initial versions of ATL. Today, however, you should define the threading model for your components at the component level using either the CComSingleThreadModel or CComMultiThreadModel parameter to CComObjectRootEx—unless, of course, you need the older technique.

NOTE The _ATL_ThreadingModel_ symbols also control certain global thread safety aspects of ATL's implementation. By defining the _ATL_APARTMENT_THREAD symbol, which ATL does by default, you will be fine. However, if you define the _ATL_SINGLE_THREAD symbol, none of your components get support for thread-safe class factories or module lock counts, so be careful.

THE THREADING EXAMPLE

We'll use our math component one more time. We discussed asynchronous behavior in Chapter 7, where we developed a math component example that used either a callback or a connection point interface to simulate asynchronous behavior through a COM interface. Our example in this chapter extends this notion by using a thread to perform the math calculations. This technique provides true asynchronous behavior, but we're doing most of the work. (When NT 5.0 is released, COM will do the work instead.) We'll first develop the component, and then we'll use the multithreaded component from a C++ client.

Create the Math Component

Start Visual C++ and create a new project selecting **ATL COM AppWizard**. Give it the name **Chapter10_Server**. In Step 1 of 1, select a type of DLL. Then select **Finish** and then **OK** to generate the project. Using the ATL Object wizard, insert a **Simple Component** with the following options.

- Use a **Short Name** of **Math**.
- Make sure the interface name is **IMath**.
- Change the ProgID to **Chapter10.Math**.
- On the **Attributes** page, make sure the **Custom** interface option is selected.

Implement the `IMath` Interface

Using the **Add Method** option, by right-clicking on the `IMath` interface in Dev Studio's ClassView, add the following six methods for the `IMath` interface. If you include the IDL attributes in the Add Method dialog box, Dev Studio will add them only to the IDL file. Figure 10.3 shows how to add the `Add` method.

```
STDMETHOD(Add)(/*[in]*/ long lOp1, /*[in]*/ long lOp2);
STDMETHOD(Subtract)(/*[in]*/ long lOp1, /*[in]*/ long lOp2);
STDMETHOD(Multiply)(/*[in]*/ long lOp1, /*[in]*/ long lOp2);
STDMETHOD(Divide)(/*[in]*/ long lOp1, /*[in]*/ long lOp2);
STDMETHOD(Advise)(/*[in]*/ ICallBack* pCallBack);
STDMETHOD(Unadvise)();
```

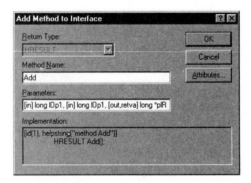

Figure 10.3 Adding methods with attributes.

Define the Event Interface

Just as in the Chapter 7 `CallBack` example, we'll define an outgoing interface for our math component. The client will implement the `ICallBack` interface and pass the pointer to the component through `IMath::Advise`. Our outgoing interface has two methods. `ComputationComplete` is called by the component when a client computation is finished. The `Error` method is called if an error occurs while the computation is being processed. In any event, the client is notified asynchronously of the result.

```
// Chapter10_Server.IDL
...
[
    object,
    uuid(9029D3B0-67FE-11d1-B5F9-0004ACFF171C),
    helpstring("ICallBack Interface"),
    pointer_default(unique)
]
interface ICallBack : IUnknown
{
    [helpstring("method ComputationComplete")]
        HRESULT ComputationComplete( [in] long lResult );
    [helpstring("method Error")]
        HRESULT Error( [in] BSTR bstrDescription );
};
...
library CHAPTER10_SERVERLib
{
    importlib("stdole32.tlb");
    importlib("stdole2.tlb");

[
        uuid(EBFEC173-67FA-11D1-B5F9-0004ACFF171C),
        helpstring("Math Class")
    ]
    coclass Math
    {
        [default] interface IMath;
        [default, source] interface ICallBack;
    };
};
```

Implement the Advise Methods

The Advise and Unadvise methods provide a way for the client to pass an interface pointer to the component. We then store this pointer as part of our implementation and fire notifications to the client through it. The Unadvise method allows a client to disconnect the notification interface. Following is the IDL and implementation.

```
// Math.H
...
class ATL_NO_VTABLE CMath :
    public CComObjectRootEx<CComSingleThreadModel>,
    public CComCoClass<CMath, &CLSID_Math>,
    public IMath
{
public:
    CMath()
    {
        m_pCallBack = 0;
    }
...
// IMath
public:
    STDMETHOD(Add)(/*[in]*/ long lOp1, /*[in]*/ long lOp2);
...

private:
    ICallBack* m_pCallBack;
};

// Math.CPP
...
STDMETHODIMP CMath::Advise(ICallBack * pCallBack)
{
    m_pCallBack = pCallBack;
    return S_OK;
}

STDMETHODIMP CMath::Unadvise()
{
    m_pCallBack = 0;
    return S_OK;
}
```

Perform the Computation in a Thread

To demonstrate how to build a multithreaded COM component, we'll start a thread for each computation that the math component will perform. For our simple computations this isn't necessary, but I'm sure you can imagine a method called Calculate_PI_To_x_Digits that might require a significant amount of time. What we're demonstrating here is that a COM method call can return immediately, and the actual work performed by the method can run in a background thread. When the work is done (the thread completes), the client is notified through its callback interface.

Performing the computation in a different thread adds complexity to our implementation, but not very much. We need a function that will execute as a thread, a thread parameter structure to pass thread-specific information, and a method to start the whole process. First, let's examine the header file.

```
//
// Math.h : Declaration of the CMath
//
...
typedef enum mathOPERATOR
{
    mathAdd,
    mathSubtract,
    mathMultiply,
    mathDivide
} mathOPERATOR;

struct ThreadParameters
{
    mathOPERATOR    op;
    long            lOp1;
    long            lOp2;
    IStream*        pStream;
};

class ATL_NO_VTABLE CMath :
    public CComObjectRootEx<CComSingleThreadModel>,
    public CComCoClass<CMath, &CLSID_Math>,
    public IMath
{
...
private:
    ICallBack* m_pCallBack;
    HRESULT SimulateLongComputation( mathOPERATOR op,
                                     long lOp1,
                                     long lOp2 );
};
```

We need an enumerated type to indicate the type of computation that the thread will perform, and the ThreadParameters structure contains everything the thread needs to carry out the computation. The IStream* parameter will contain our marshaled interface pointer through which the client will be notified. The SimulateLongComputation method will actually start the thread.

```
//
// Math.cpp : Implementation of CMath
//
...
STDMETHODIMP CMath::Add(long lOp1, long lOp2)
{
   SimulateLongComputation( mathAdd, lOp1, lOp2 );
   return S_OK;
}

STDMETHODIMP CMath::Subtract(long lOp1, long lOp2)
{
   SimulateLongComputation( mathSubtract, lOp1, lOp2 );
   return S_OK;
}
STDMETHODIMP CMath::Multiply(long lOp1, long lOp2)
{
   SimulateLongComputation( mathMultiply, lOp1, lOp2 );
   return S_OK;
}

STDMETHODIMP CMath::Divide(long lOp1, long lOp2)
{
   SimulateLongComputation( mathDivide, lOp1, lOp2 );
   return S_OK;
}
```

As you can see from the implementation, a thread is created each time the client calls one of our four computation methods. Here is the SimulateLongComputation method:

```
//
// Math.cpp : Implementation of CMath
//
...
HRESULT CMath::SimulateLongComputation(mathOPERATOR op,
                                       long lOp1, long lOp2)
{
   // Marshal the ICallBack interface into a stream
   IStream* pStream = 0;
   HRESULT hr = CoMarshalInterThreadInterfaceInStream( IID_ICallBack,
                                                       m_pCallBack,
                                                       &pStream );

   if( SUCCEEDED( hr ))
   {
```

```
    // Create the thread parameters object and
    // fill it with our parameters
    ThreadParameters* pTP = new ThreadParameters;
    pTP->op = op;
    pTP->lOp1 = lOp1;
    pTP->lOp2 = lOp2;
    pTP->pStream = pStream;

    // Create the thread
    HANDLE  hThread;
    DWORD   dwThreadID;
    hThread = CreateThread( 0, 0,
                            PerformComputation,
                            pTP,
                            0,
                            &dwThreadID);

    // If we have a hande, then everything
    // worked so close the handle
    if( hThread )
    {
        CloseHandle( hThread );
    }
    else
    {
        // Thread creation failed. Destroy
        // our parameters and release the stream
        delete pTP;
        pStream->Release();

        // Notify the client that an error occurred
        CComBSTR bstrMsg( "Unable to start computation thread" );
        m_pCallBack->Error( bstrMsg );
    }
}
else
{
    // If the marshaling fails, we probably don't have
    // the proxy/stub registered
    CComBSTR bstrMsg( "Unable to marshal the ICallBack interface. \
                      Make sure the proxy/stub is registered" );
    m_pCallBack->Error( bstrMsg );
}

return hr;
}
```

Because each thread will become a single-threaded apartment, we marshal the ICallBack interface pointer into a stream. If this succeeds, we create and initialize a ThreadParameters structure containing the operator, the operands, and the IStream pointer. Next, we create the thread, passing the address of our thread function and the ThreadParameters structure. If the thread creation fails, we clean up our structure, release the stream, and notify the client of the error through the ICallBack::Error method. If all goes well, the thread will execute the code specified in the PerformComputation function.

```cpp
//
// Math.cpp : Implementation of CMath
//
...
DWORD WINAPI PerformComputation( void *p )
{
   CoInitialize( 0 );

   // Get the thread parameters
   ThreadParameters* pTP = (ThreadParameters*) p;

   // Unmarshal the ICallBack pointer
   ICallBack* pCallBack = 0;
   HRESULT hr = CoGetInterfaceAndReleaseStream( pTP->pStream,
                              IID_ICallBack,
                              (void**) &pCallBack );

   // We successfully retrieved the ICallBack interface
   if( SUCCEEDED( hr ))
   {
      // Perform the calculation and delay
      // to simulate doing some real work
      long lResult;
      switch( pTP->op )
      {
         case mathAdd:
            lResult = pTP->lOp1 + pTP->lOp2;
            break;
         case mathSubtract:
            lResult = pTP->lOp1 - pTP->lOp2;
            break;
         case mathMultiply:
            lResult = pTP->lOp1 * pTP->lOp2;
            break;
         case mathDivide:
            lResult = pTP->lOp1 / pTP->lOp2;
            break;
      }
```

```
   // Delay, but not too long
      Sleep( min( lResult, 5000 ));

   // Notify the client with the result of the computation
      pCallBack->ComputationComplete( lResult );
   }

   // Delete our thread parameters structure
   delete pTP;

   CoUninitialize();
   return hr;
}
```

The preceding code implements the thread. We first initialize COM. As we discussed, the CoInitialize call creates a single-threaded apartment, and interface pointers must be marshaled between STAs, which we're demonstrating in this example. If an interface pointer crosses an STA through a COM API (such as CoCreateInstance) or interface method (such as QueryInterface), COM does the marshaling automatically. However, in our case, we're passing the pointer without COM's help, so we must manually marshal the pointer.

We get the thread parameters and unmarshal the ICallBack pointer. If this succeeds, we simulate a long computation and finally notify the client of the result through the ICallBack::ComputationComplete method.

Build the Project

That's all there is to building a multithreaded component. This example demonstrates what is required to build a component that moves an interface pointer between threads. In other words, the component itself contains multiple threads. In many cases, the clients will also be multithreaded, but this example demonstrates some of the useful techniques. Build the project, and next we'll develop a C++ client application.

A C++ CLIENT

In our C++ client example, we'll again use ATL on the client side as we did in Chapter 7. In fact, the client application is very similar to the Chapter 7 C++ connection point example. This time, instead of using connection points we're using a callback interface. In other words, we're implementing the Chapter 7 Visual Basic CallBack example in C++.

We use a Win32 application, because we need an HINSTANCE for initializing ATL. We also need a message loop in this example, because we must wait for the math component to complete its operations. A message loop is perfect for handling this asynchronous behavior. And as we have described, COM uses the message queue to implement much of its functionality anyway, so it's best to have one around.

Using AppWizard, create a **Win32 Application** project and name it **Chapter10_Client**. Next, create a file called **Chapter10_Client.cpp** and add the following code. We'll step through the code in sequential order.

```
//
// Chapter10_Client.cpp
//

#include <windows.h>

// Include ATL
#include <atlbase.h>
CComModule _Module;
#include <atlcom.h>
#include <atlimpl.cpp>

BEGIN_OBJECT_MAP(ObjectMap)
END_OBJECT_MAP()

#include "..\Chapter10_Server\Chapter10_Server.h"
#include "..\Chapter10_Server\Chapter10_Server_i.c"
...
```

Our client code includes the ATL implementation files and declares a global `CComModule` instance. It also includes an empty ATL object map, which we will need to initialize `CComModule`. Next, we have two helper functions to display messages as our application runs:

```
...
void DisplayMessage( char* szMsg )
{
    MessageBox( 0, szMsg, "Chapter10_Client", MB_OK | MB_TOPMOST );
}

void HandleError( char*szMsg, HRESULT hr )
{
    char szMessage[256];
    sprintf( szMessage, "%s. HR = %x", szMsg, hr );
    DisplayMessage( szMessage );
    CoUninitialize();
}
...
```

These functions are simple, but they support only ANSI builds. Next, we have an ATL class that will implement the client-side, outgoing interface for our math component.

```
...
class CCallBack :
   public CComObjectRoot,
   public ICallback
{

public:
   CCallBack() {}

BEGIN_COM_MAP(CCallBack)
   COM_INTERFACE_ENTRY(ICallBack)
END_COM_MAP()

// ICallBack
public:
   STDMETHODIMP ComputationComplete(long lResult)
   {
      char szMsg[128];
      sprintf( szMsg, "The result is %d", lResult );
      DisplayMessage( szMsg );

      // Terminate the application when we
      // get the result of the last computation
      if ( lResult == 3000 )
         PostQuitMessage( 0 );

      return S_OK;
   }

   STDMETHODIMP Error(BSTR bstrMessage)
   {
      USES_CONVERSION;
      DisplayMessage( W2A( bstrMessage ));
      return S_OK;
   }
};
...
```

You've seen similar code before. Our component, based on a custom interface, implements the ICallBack interface. We implement the two methods in ICallBack: ComputationComplete and Error. Both implementations display a message box.

Next, we implement WinMain, call CoInitialize, and initialize ATL by calling the CComModule::Init method, passing the HINSTANCE of our app and the object map.

```
...
int WINAPI WinMain(HINSTANCE hInst, HINSTANCE, LPSTR, int)
{
   CoInitialize(0);

   // Initialize the ATL module
   _Module.Init( ObjectMap, hInst );

   // Create an instance of our math component
   CComPtr<IMath> ptrMath;
   HRESULT hr;
   hr = CoCreateInstance( CLSID_Math,
                          NULL,
                          CLSCTX_SERVER,
                          IID_IMath,
                          (void**) &ptrMath );

   if ( FAILED( hr ))
   {
      HandleError( "Failed to create server instance", hr );
      return -1;
   }
...
```

After instantiating the math component, we next create an instance of the CCallBack component, which will provide the ICallBack implementation:

```
...
   // Create an instance of our CallBack component
   CComObject<CCallBack>* pCallBack;
   CComObject<CCallBack>::CreateInstance( &pCallBack );

   // QueryInterface for ICallBack and pass
   // it to the component
   CComPtr<ICallBack> ptrCallBack;
   pCallBack->GetUnknown()->QueryInterface( IID_ICallBack,
                                            (void**) &ptrCallBack );
   ptrMath->Advise( ptrCallBack );
...
```

After creating the instance, we query the interface for ICallBack, which bumps the reference count on the component to 1. Next, we pass the ICallBack interface implementation to the math component.

```
...
   // Access the IMath functionality
   // As the computations complete, the callback
```

```
// implementation will display a message box
ptrMath->Add( 300, 10 );
ptrMath->Subtract( 300, 10 );
ptrMath->Divide( 300, 10 );
ptrMath->Multiply( 300, 10 );
...
```

Finally, we call the methods in the math component. As they execute, the math component will create a thread to handle the computation. When the computation completes, the component notifies the client through ICallBack::ComputationComplete. Figure 10.4 shows the result of the four computations.

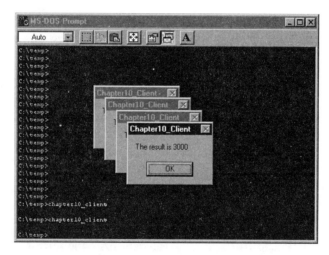

Figure 10.4 The result of several computations.

Because we've implemented asynchronous behavior, we need a message loop so that we can wait for the notifications to arrive. STAs are required to pump messages.

```
...
// Sit in a message loop until the
// last notification is fired
MSG    msg;
while (GetMessage( &msg, NULL, 0, 0 ))
{
    TranslateMessage( &msg );
    DispatchMessage( &msg );
}
...
```

When we're finished, we shut down the connection, release our pointers, and uninitialize COM, just as we've done in the past.

```
...
   // Shut down the connection
   ptrMath->Unadvise();

   // Release our interfaces
   if ( ptrMath )
      ptrMath = 0;
   if ( ptrCallBack )
      ptrCallBack = 0;

   CoUninitialize();

   return 0;
}
```

That completes our coverage of COM threading. I hope that you now have a better handle on the various threading models and what is required to build components that conform to them. As you can see, ATL does much of the hard work for you. The important point is to understand and obey the rules. Following are more resources for understanding COM threads.

- Microsoft Knowledge Base article Q150777, available at http://support.microsoft.com/support/kb/articles/Q150/7/77.asp.
- Microsoft's DCOM Architecture white paper.
- Don Box's COM/ActiveX Q&A articles in *Microsoft Systems Journal*.
- David Platt's threading articles in the February 1997 and August 1997 *MSJ*.
- Chapter 9 of Dale Rogerson's *Inside COM* (MS Press, 1996).

ATL AND MFC

When working on a large project, you typically use several different development tools. In Chapter 11, we'll cover some of the topics involved in working with ATL and MFC. Both MFC and ATL have their strengths and weaknesses, and you need to understand them in order to choose the correct framework for the job at hand. We'll also have a section on moving MFC-based controls to ATL.

Chapter

ATL and MFC

The primary focus of this book is ATL-based development. However, most Windows developers are already familiar with and probably use the Microsoft Foundation Class (MFC) libraries. MFC has been around for about five years and has become the most popular Windows development framework. In fact, working with MFC is probably many developers' first experience with COM, OLE, or ActiveX. In this chapter we discuss some of the pros and cons of developing your applications and components with ATL or MFC, cover how both frameworks can be used together, and discuss some of the issues encountered when converting MFC-based ActiveX controls to use ATL instead.

WHICH ONE SHOULD I USE?

In my five-day COM/ActiveX class, we cover both ATL- and MFC-based COM development. We go into great detail on how MFC and ATL implement their support for COM. As the week goes by, one of the most frequently asked questions is "Which one should I use? MFC or ATL?" My response is always a noncommittal "It depends."

As with most development projects, the tool to use to solve the problem at hand depends on what kind of developer you are, your level of experience, the long-term goals of the project, and so on. At the time of this writing there are some major differences between the two frameworks. What follows is a comparison of some of the differences between MFC and ATL. My hope is that it will help you make decisions about which tool to use for your projects.

 Of course, Visual Studio 98 will probably add significantly to both frameworks, and my opinion will probably change at that time. Check my Web site for updates.

NOTE

MFC versus ATL

Most Windows developers are already familiar with MFC, and many have even created some COM-based components (either ActiveX Controls or Automation servers) with MFC's

405

wizards. However, because MFC's wizards make it so easy to develop ActiveX controls and Automation servers, developers rarely understand what is actually going on underneath. They get something working and move on to the next project. This demonstrates how effective MFC is in hiding the complexity of COM's underlying implementation.

MFC provides a great environment for getting started in COM-based development. In particular, MFC is highly functional in the areas of ActiveX controls, OLE Document containers and servers, and OLE Drag-and-Drop. However, I do not recommend that you use it for anything other than basic development of these component types.

MFC's COM support was "tacked on" long after it was initially designed and developed, and this makes it difficult for MFC's developers to keep up with COM. ATL, though, as we discussed several times in this book, was developed solely for COM-based development. If you're serious about COM development, and you probably are if you purchased this book, ATL should be your framework of choice in the future.

With this said, MFC is not going away (at least for a few more releases), and it is still a great tool for application development, especially if the application has significant user-interface needs. Also, many of us have invested significant time in learning MFC's classes. Sure, they're just thin wrappers around Win32 API calls, but I sure don't miss writing reams of window procedure code. MFC will continue to be important for large Windows applications, and ATL will become more important as developer's realize that COM is not just a technology but a complete change in how applications should be designed and developed. Table 11.1 details some of the COM-related differences between ATL and MFC.

Table 11.1 ATL versus MFC (COM Functionality)

ATL	MFC
Supports dual interfaces directly, which are Microsoft's recommended method of exposing functionality from many components (e.g., ActiveX Controls).	Supports only dispinterfaces through its wizards. Moving to a dual interface requires lots of additional work to add dual interface support to a component. See MFC Technical Note 65 for details.
Supports all of COM's threading models	Does not support building MTA-based components because MFC classes are only thread safe at the class level.
Uses IDL to describe structures, interfaces, and components. The MIDL compiler then produces a C++ header file, a type library, and code for a proxy/stub DLL.	Uses the older ODL, which is Automation specific. The MkTypLib utility only produces a type library. Header files must be hand coded and ODL cannot produce a proxy/stub DLL for your interfaces.

General Recommendations

So, my general recommendations as to when to use ATL, MFC, or a mixture of both is as follows:

- MFC should be used to develop applications.

- ATL should be used to develop components, which are much smaller and in many cases will not provide any GUI aspect.

- If your applications have large GUI requirements, use MFC to build the GUI, but use ATL to implement as many internal components as possible. You can use these components within MFC-based applications through COM (CoCreateInstance) or C++ (new) bindings. The #import directive makes using COM bindings easy.

- If your application is mostly nonvisual and COM-based, then definitely use ATL as your primary framework. However, if you're comfortable with many of MFC's classes, go ahead and use them within your ATL implementation.

- If you find yourself using MFC's basic string (e.g., CString) and iterator classes (e.g., CObList), make an effort to move to the Standard Template Library (STL). The STL provides similar classes with more functionality, and it will eliminate your dependence on MFC40.DLL.

USING MFC WITH ATL PROJECTS

With the preceding as context, let's take a look at what is required to use MFC classes when developing ATL-based components. When creating a component housing with the ATL COM AppWizard (shown in Figure 11.1), you are presented with an option to **Support MFC** This option, as its name implies, allows the use of MFC classes within your ATL component implementations. The trick, though, is that this option is disabled, when you choose anything other than a **Dynamic Link Library (DLL)** project.

In other words, MFC can be used in DLL-based ATL projects but not in EXE projects. In the next two sections we'll take a look at each of these options, and you will see that in some cases you can use MFC classes in your ATL out-of-process servers.

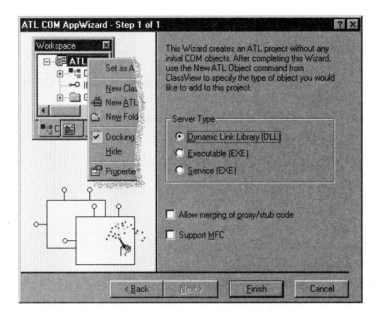

Figure 11.1 ATL COM AppWizard, step 1.

MFC with In-Process Servers

If you choose the **Support MFC** option when creating an ATL project, the wizard adds additional code to support the use of MFC's classes. In particular, MFC depends heavily on a global instance of its CWinApp class (Just as ATL depends on a global instance of CComModule). The wizard first adds the standard MFC includes to your component's **STDAFX.H** file.

```
// stdafx.h : include file for standard system include files,
...
#define STRICT

#include <afxwin.h>
#include <afxdisp.h>

#define _WIN32_WINNT 0x0400
#define _ATL_APARTMENT_THREADED

#include <atlbase.h>
extern CComModule _Module;
#include <atlcom.h>
#include <atlctl.h>
```

In the default housing code, the wizard adds the following highlighted code:

```
// Chapter11_Controls.cpp : Implementation of DLL Exports.
...
#include "stdafx.h"
...

CComModule _Module;

BEGIN_OBJECT_MAP(ObjectMap)
    OBJECT_ENTRY(CLSID_ListView, CListView)
END_OBJECT_MAP()

class CChapter11_ControlsApp : public CWinApp
{
public:
   virtual BOOL InitInstance();
   virtual int ExitInstance();
};

CChapter11_ControlsApp theApp;

BOOL CChapter11_ControlsApp::InitInstance()
{
   _Module.Init(ObjectMap, m_hInstance);
   return CWinApp::InitInstance();
}

int CChapter11_ControlsApp::ExitInstance()
{
   _Module.Term();
   return CWinApp::ExitInstance();
}

STDAPI DllCanUnloadNow(void)
{
   AFX_MANAGE_STATE(AfxGetStaticModuleState());
   return (AfxDllCanUnloadNow()==S_OK && _Module.GetLockCount()==0) ? S_OK :
S_FALSE;
}
...
```

The wizard first derived a project-specific instance of MFC's CWinApp class. It then over-rides and implements the InitInstance and ExitInstance methods. MFC applications are hidden from the standard DllMain entry point for a DLL. InitInstance and ExitInstance are called when MFC's DllMain entry is loaded. These methods corre-spond to a DllMain call with the DLL_PROCESS_ATTACH and DLL_PROCESS_DETACH flags.

In InitInstance we initialize both of our global objects We also call the appropriate application termination code in ExitInstance. Compare this to the code produced when *not* using MFC in an ATL DLL:

```
extern "C"
BOOL WINAPI DllMain(HINSTANCE hInstance, DWORD dwReason, LPVOID /*lpReserved*/)
{
   if (dwReason == DLL_PROCESS_ATTACH)
   {
      _Module.Init(ObjectMap, hInstance);
      DisableThreadLibraryCalls(hInstance);
   }
   else if (dwReason == DLL_PROCESS_DETACH)
      _Module.Term();
   return TRUE;    // ok
}
```

ATL does not have a wrapper around DllMain and the initialization and termination is handled there.

AFX_MANAGE_STATE

When using MFC with ATL, the ATL wizards add an AFX_MANAGE_STATE macro to the beginning of each COM method you implement. The preceding code also uses AFX_MAN-AGE_STATE in the DllCanUnloadNow entry point.

MFC maintains a small structure for each DLL within a process that is using MFC's runtime DLL. As the application's context switches between these DLLs, MFC must remember which module context it is running in. The AFX_MANAGE_STATE macro ensures that the module state is correct for the given DLL context. All entry points (e.g., DllGetClassObject), Window procedures, and COM method calls should use the AFX_MANAGE_STATE macro before any other code in the module. If you've done much MFC programming, I'm sure you've run into this before. For additional details, see MFC Technical Note 58.

Using MFC

With all of the above in place, using all of MFC's classes within a DLL-based server is easy. Just code along as if you're working with an MFC-based application, but don't expect ClassWizard to work correctly, at least not with release 5.0 of Developer Studio. You have to do most of your MFC work by hand, which isn't really a problem.

As an example of using MFC with ATL, one of the chapter examples is an ActiveX control that uses MFC within its implementation. The ActiveX control also demonstrates some features that we didn't have time for in other chapters. In particular, it superclasses the Windows 95 ListView control, demonstrates using a COM enumerator interface (IEnumCLSID), and shows how to use the ICatInformation interface.

CImageList

The control uses ATL's CContainedWindow class to support the ListView functionality. However, a list view can have an associated Image List control to support an array of images to display with each item in the list. So, we use MFC's CImageList class for this functionality. Its easier to work with, and if you already have experience with MFC, why not take advantage of it. Here's a part of the control's implementation.

```
// ListView.H
...
private:
   CImageList  m_ImageList;
...

// ListView.CPP
LRESULT CListView::OnCreate(UINT uMsg, WPARAM wParam, LPARAM lParam, BOOL&
bHandled)
{
   AFX_MANAGE_STATE(AfxGetStaticModuleState());

RECT rc;
   GetWindowRcc 2

m_ImageList.Create( IDB_STATE_BITMAP,
                    16, 2, RGB(255, 255, 25));

ListView_SetImageList( m_ctlSysListView32.m_hWnd,
                       m_ImageList.m_hImageList,
                       LVSIL_STATE );

...
   // Only list the components at runtime
   BOOL bUserMode = FALSE;
   GetAmbientUserMode( bUserMode );
   if ( bUserMode )
   {
      ListComponents( CATID_Control );
   }
return 0;
}
```

As you can see, we embed an instance of MFC's CImageList, create the image list, and associate it with the ATL ListView control. The example also uses MFC's CString class.

Using MFC with in-process servers is easy, but it's difficult to use with out-of-process servers.

MFC with Out-of-Process Servers

The ATL AppWizard does not allow you to include MFC support when building out-of-process servers. That isn't supported because only the nonvisual MFC classes work in executable-based ATL projects. Many times, all you really need is access to MFC's basic classes such as CString, CObList, CStringList, and so on. If you're interested only in using these classes, the following steps allow you to use MFC in an out-of-process ATL server.

1. Include **AFXWIN.H** and **AFXDISP.H** files in **STDAFX.H**. Be sure to include these files *before* the ATL include files. Also, you have to "un-define" the Windows includes so they won't be defined twice:

    ```
    #undef _WINDOWS
    #include <afxwin.h> // MFC core and standard components
    #include <afxext.h> // MFC extensions
    #include <afxdisp.h> // MFC Automation extensions
    #define _WINDOWS_
    ```

2. Change the project settings to use MFC in a shared DLL. From the Project Settings dialog, select the **General** tab, and change the setting in the Microsoft Foundation Classes drop-down box.

3. Add a CWinApp-derived class and provide overrides for InitInstance and ExitInstance. Also, provide a global instance of the new class. You'll need to do this in the housing implementation file.

    ```
    class CMyApp : public CWinApp
    {
    public:
       virtual BOOL InitInstance();
       virtual int ExitInstance();
    };

    CMyApp theApp;
    ```

4. Remove the AppWizard-generated _tWinMain function and replace it with the following InitInstance and ExitInstance code. This replaces ATL's WinMain with MFC's internal message pump:

    ```
    BOOL CMyApp::InitInstance()
    {
       // Initialize OLE libraries
       AfxOleInit();

    // Initialize the ATL Module
       _Module.Init(ObjectMap,m_hInstance);
    ```

```
        // This is important too. Without this line
        // the EXE won't terminate correctly. -twa-
        _Module.dwThreadID = GetCurrentThreadId();
#ifdef _AFXDLL
        Enable3dControls(); // Call this when using MFC in a shared DLL
#else
        Enable3dControlsStatic(); // Call this when linking
                                  // to MFC statically
#endif

        // Update the System Registry
        COleObjectFactory::UpdateRegistryAll(); // MFC Classes
        VERIFY(SUCCEEDED(_Module.RegisterServer(TRUE))); // ATL Classes

        // Register OLE Class Factories
        // MFC ones are for multiple as specified
        // by the IMPLEMENT_OLECREATE() macro
        COleObjectFactory::RegisterAll();

        // ATL ones specifically register with REGCLS_MULTIPLEUSE
        VERIFY(SUCCEEDED(_Module.RegisterClassObjects( CLSCTX_LOCAL_SERVER,
                                                       REGCLS_MULTIPLEUSE
                                                       )));

        // Parse the command line to see if launched as OLE server
        if (RunEmbedded() || RunAutomated())
        {
            // Application was run with /Embedding or /Automation.
            // Don't show the main window in this case.
            return TRUE;
        }
        // create dialog or other stuff here
        ...

        return FALSE; // Nothing to do, so exit.
        // return TRUE to execute CWinApp::Run()
    }

    int CMyApp::ExitInstance()
    {
        // MFC's class factory registration is
        // automatically revoked by MFC itself
        _Module.RevokeClassObjects(); // Revoke class factories for ATL
        _Module.Term(); // clanup ATL GLobal Module
        return CWinApp::ExitInstance();
    }
```

These steps will allow you to use MFC's nonvisual classes. Attempts at using other classes will most likely fail.

Using ATL with MFC Projects

You can also use ATL to create components that are part of an MFC project. This isn't as important as what we covered earlier (at least in my experience), but there may be cases in which you need to do it. MFC's support for COM-based components is quite different than that of ATL. As described earlier, MFC uses the older ODL to create type libraries for components. Also, MFC uses its CCmdTarget class to support IUnknown and COleObjectFactory to support class factory.

A sample application (MFCATL) is included with Visual C++ that demonstrates adding an ATL-based component to an MFC housing. The steps are similar to adding MFC support to an ATL housing that we described earlier. Basically, we have to include a global instance of ATL's module class and initialize it in the appropriate MFC CWinApp methods. The basic steps are as follows:

1. Include the basic ATL header files: **ATLBASE.H**, **ATLCOM.H**, and **ATLIMPL.CPP**.

2. Add a global class derived from CComModule and implement the Lock and Unlock methods. These methods defer to MFC's global module instance count implementation, as in the following:

```
class CAtlGlobalModule : public CComModule
{
public:
   LONG Lock()
   {
      if (GetLockCount()==0)
         AfxOleLockApp();
      return CComModule::Lock();
   }
   LONG Unlock()
   {
      LONG l = CComModule::Unlock();
      if (GetLockCount() == 0)
         AfxOleUnlockApp();
      return l;
   }
};
```

3. Add an ATL object map with the BEGIN_OBJECT_MAP and END_OBJECT_MAP macros.

4. Initialize and terminate the global ATL module in the corresponding MFC methods (InitInstance and ExitInstance). Also, add the self-registration and class factory reg-

istration code for the ATL components. This will differ based on the housing type. The code below demonstrates updating an executable housing. Changes for DLL housings would occur in `DllRegisterServer`. Also, DLL housings don't require explicit class factory registration.

```
BOOL CMFCApp::InitInstance()
{
    // Initialize OLE libraries
    if (!AfxOleInit())
    {
        AfxMessageBox(IDP_OLE_INIT_FAILED);
        return FALSE;
    }

    // Initialize the ATL Module
    _Module.Init( ObjectMap,m_hInstance );
    ...
    // Update the System Registry
    COleObjectFactory::UpdateRegistryAll();
    _Module.RegisterServer( TRUE );
    ...
    // Register MFC Class Factories
    COleObjectFactory::RegisterAll();
    // Register ATL Class Factories
    _Module.RegisterClassObjects(CLSCTX_LOCAL_SERVER,
                            REGCLS_MULTIPLEUSE)));
};

int CMfcAtlApp::ExitInstance()
{
    _Module.RevokeClassObjects(); // Revoke class factories for ATL
    _Module.Term();
    return CWinApp::ExitInstance();
}
```

5. At this point you can implement components using ATL's classes. However, you don't have wizard support, so you must do everything manually. This includes updating the projects ODL file, generating GUIDs when necessary, and adding `OBJECT_ENTRY` macros for each component class.

One particular reason you might want to use the preceding technique is to develop components that support dual interfaces. MFC has poor support for dual interfaces, and ATL's support is excellent. By using this technique you can add components to an existing MFC-based housing and slowly migrate to ATL.

CONVERTING MFC ACTIVEX CONTROLS TO ATL

The following sections will help you understand how the various functional elements in the MFC and ATL control implementations differ. It should help you convert existing controls from MFC to use ATL as well as help you decide which tool you might use when building your own ActiveX controls.

A General Comparison

In general, developing an ActiveX control is easier with MFC than with ATL. MFC provides better wizard support and has several classes that hide most of the complexity of developing a component that implements more than 20 interfaces. Also, today significantly more information is available about developing controls with MFC, and if you're developing a complex control with lots of functionality, this information can be a big help. ATL-based controls, on the other hand, are more efficient, don't require the MFC runtime, and support dual interfaces.

MFC versus ATL Housing Support

MFC and ATL controls both use the basic housing support provided by their frameworks. Both frameworks support all four COM entry points (`DllGetClassObject`, `DllCanUnloadNow`, `DllRegisterServer`, and `DllUnregisterServer`). However, because of ATL's registrar component and its use of RGS files, it provides better support for both registration and deregistration. The entries added by MFC's registration code are hard-coded and difficult to change. As an example, adding component categories to a control requires no coding with ATL, but it requires significant code with MFC.

Moving from ODL to IDL

MFC uses the older ODL, while ATL uses the newer IDL. When converting MFC controls to ATL, there are slight differences in how enumerated types are supported. The following example shows the correct syntax for IDL:

```
  [helpstring("Appearance")]
typedef enum Appearance
{
    [helpstring("Flat")] appearanceFlat = 0,
    [helpstring("3D")] appearance3D = 1
} Appearance;
```

Stock Property Support

MFC's support for stock properties is significantly better than ATL's. ATL provides only simple accessor methods for the properties. Initialization and implementation of any code based on the properties is left up to the developer. MFC, on the other hand, provides lots of implementation code. For example, when the BorderStyle property is changed, MFC actually draws or hides the border for you. In ATL you have to do the redraw. The Font, Appearance, Text, and ReadyState properties also have significant support code built-in by MFC.

Stock Method and Event Support

MFC provides default implementations of the Refresh and OnClick methods, whereas ATL does not. However, these methods are easy to implement. MFC also provides support for most of the standard ActiveX control events (e.g., Click, DblClick), while ATL does not. Again, those events can be implemented by hand.

Property Persistence

Adding persistence support for a property is similar in both frameworks. MFC uses the PX_*Type* functions and the DoPropExchange method where the developer provides the property name, member variable, and a default value:

```
void CClockCtrl::DoPropExchange(CPropExchange* pPX)
{
    ExchangeVersion(pPX, MAKELONG(_wVerMinor, _wVerMajor));
    COleControl::DoPropExchange(pPX);

    // TODO: Call PX_ functions for each persistent custom property.
    PX_Color( pPX, _T("TickColor"), m_clrTickColor, RGB( 0x00,0x00,0x00 ));
    PX_Color( pPX, _T("FaceColor"), m_clrFaceColor, RGB( 0xFF, 0xFF, 0xFF ));
    PX_Bool( pPX, _T("AllowResize"), m_bAllowResize, TRUE );
}
```

ATL uses a similar technique in its property map, but, you have to handle the stock properties explicitly, whereas MFC does it automatically.

Property Pages

MFC's property pages use the built-in Dialog Data Exchange (DDX) functionality. This makes development of custom property pages rather painless. MFC has significant wizard support for property page implementation, and in most cases you will not write any code at all. Here's all that is required to support three properties, all added by `ClassWizard`:

```
void CPostitPropPage::DoDataExchange(CDataExchange* pDX)
{
    //{{AFX_DATA_MAP(CPostitPropPage)
    DDP_Check(pDX, IDC_ENABLED, m_bEnabled, _T("Enabled") );
    DDX_Check(pDX, IDC_ENABLED, m_bEnabled);
    DDP_Text(pDX, IDC_TEXT, m_strText, _T("Text") );
    DDX_Text(pDX, IDC_TEXT, m_strText);
    DDP_Check(pDX, IDC_BORDER, m_bBorderStyle, _T("BorderStyle") );
    DDX_Check(pDX, IDC_BORDER, m_bBorderStyle);
    //}}AFX_DATA_MAP
    DDP_PostProcessing(pDX);
}
```

ATL requires the developer to write extensive code both to retrieve and set the properties values. If you are using ATL, be prepared to write lots of code for your property pages. We covered that back in Chapter 8.

Handling Control Events

MFC's support for control events is also wizard-driven. You simply pop up `ClassWizard`, go to the **Events** tab and add the event. Using ATL, though, you must manually edit the IDL file, build the type library, and then run the ATL proxy generator. All of this involves writing several lines of code.

Other Miscellaneous Differences

There are other, minor differences between an MFC and ATL-built control. Most do not affect general behavior but are little niceties provided by MFC. ATL was built to be mean and lean, and it leaves them out on purpose.

- An MFC control gets a default About Box implementation but an ATL control does not. If you want an About Box for your ATL control, you have to add the code manually. It isn't difficult, and the process is described in the ATL ActiveX Control FAQ at my site.

- An MFC control gets a default bitmap resource for the `ToolboxBitmap32` registry entry, and ATL controls do not. Again, this is easy to implement for your ATL-based controls. Just add a bitmap resource, size it to 16-by-15 (width by height) pixels, and draw a small representation of your control. Next, identifier the resource number of the bitmap and append this number to the ToolboxBitmap32 entry in the control's RGS file.

Appendix A

Visual C++ Native COM Support

Beginning with version 5.0 of Visual C++, the C++ compiler provides intrinsic support for COM-based development. This makes it easier for developers to use COM-based components in their applications. In many ways, native COM support is a preview of some of the capabilities that will be provided by COM+, a new version of COM that moves many of the details of COM development into the operating system. See Appendix B for more details.

Today, native COM support provides wrapper classes for the basic COM entities, such as interface pointers, BSTRs, and variants. The compiler provides this support with help from a number of header files—**COMUTIL.H**, **COMIP.H**, and **COMDEF.H**—and the new #import compiler directive.

SMART POINTERS: _com_ptr_t

We discussed smart pointers briefly in Chapter 4. Smart pointers act as wrappers to COM interface pointers and are an attempt to hide some of the tedium—such as having to explicitly release pointers—of working with straight COM interfaces. ATL provides a basic smart pointer class in CComPtr and CComQIPtr.

The Visual C++ smart pointer class _com_ptr_t implements additional smart pointer functionality. _com_ptr_t encapsulates CoCreateInstance functionality and uses C++ exceptions to indicate error conditions. The _COM_SMARTPTR_TYPEDEF macro is used to create a smart pointer for any COM interface.

```
_COM_SMARTPTR_TYPEDEF(IMyInterface, __uuidof(IMyInterface));
```

This macro produces a smart pointer class (using the _com_ptr_t template class) named IMyInterfacePtr. You then use an instance of the smart pointer class to instantiate a component that implements it, and from there you access the component's functionality just as you would through a COM interface pointer. The difference with smart pointers is that when they go out of scope, an implicit IUnknown::Release is called. Here's a simple example:

```
// From CHAPTER4_SERVER.TLI
...
//
// Smart pointer typedef declarations
//
_COM_SMARTPTR_TYPEDEF(IMath, __uuidof(IMath));
_COM_SMARTPTR_TYPEDEF(IMath2, __uuidof(IMath2));
_COM_SMARTPTR_TYPEDEF(IAdvancedMath, __uuidof(IAdvancedMath));
_COM_SMARTPTR_TYPEDEF(IComponentInfo, __uuidof(IComponentInfo));
...

IMathPtr ptrMath;

// Create an instance of the server
try
{
   HRESULT hr;
   hr = ptrMath.CreateInstance( CLSID_Math );
   if ( FAILED( hr ))
      _com_issue_error( hr );
}
catch( _com_error& e )
{
...
}

// Access the IMath interface
try
{
   long lResult;
   lResult = ptrMath->Add( 134, 353 );
   cout << "134 + 353 = " << lResult << endl;
}
catch( _com_error& e )
{
...
}
```

Notice that you use the dot (.) operator to access the smart pointer's functionality and the pointer operator (->) to access the underlying interface pointer methods. A smart pointer overloads the pointer operator to provide most of its functionality.

BSTRs (_bstr_t)

The _bstr_t type encapsulates COM's primary string type, the BSTR. As we described in Chapter 4, a BSTR is a length-prefixed Unicode string. The _bstr_t type provides constructors, methods, and operators that make it easier to work with BSTRs. Primarily, these constructs include ways of moving between ANSI strings, Unicode strings, and BSTRs.

```
_bstr_t name( pInfo->bstrName );
cout << "Component name is " << name << endl;
```

Variants (_variant_t)

The _variant_t class encapsulates COM's VARIANT data type. We discussed the variant type back in Chapter 6. _variant_t provides constructs, methods, and operators to make working with variants easier. To demonstrate the use of the _variant_t type, the downloadable examples include a simple client application (**Chapter6_NativeClient**) to access the Chapter6 math component. Here's a glimpse at some of the code.

```
_variant_t result;
_variant_t Op1( long( 100 ));
_variant_t Op2( long( 200 ));

result = ptrMath->Add( Op1, Op2 );
cout << "100 + 200 = " << long( result ) << endl;
```

We construct three variant_t objects to pass to our Add method. By casting the types, we initialize the variant to the correct type (for example, VT_I4). The default constructor creates an initialized, VT_EMPTY variant. The extraction operators work just like casting as the above example demonstrates.

Handling COM Errors (_com_error)

In most cases, the native COM wrapper classes handle COM errors through exceptions. When an error occurs (for example, an underlying CoCreateInstance fails), an exception of type _com_error is thrown. _com_error encapsulates an HRESULT and any associated IErrorInfo objects. The IErrorInfo methods are available only if the component supports rich error handling. The Error methods returns an HRESULT, Description returns the string message associated with an HRESULT (such as "Interface not registered" for

0x80040155), and the `ErrorInfo` method returns an `IErrorInfo` object if one exists. Here's an example of its use.

```
// Create an instance of the server
try
{
   HRESULT hr;
   hr = ptrMath.CreateInstance( CLSID_Math );
   if ( FAILED( hr ))
      _com_issue_error( hr );
}
catch( _com_error& e )
{
   cout << "Error creating instance" << endl;
   cout << "HRESULT message is " << e.ErrorMessage() << endl;

   // If rich error info is supported, display the description
   if ( e.ErrorInfo() )
      cout << e.Description() << endl;

   return -1;
}
```

Here we're using the smart pointer's ability to create an instance of a component. The `CreateInstance` method, however, does not throw an exception, so we check the HRE-SULT and use the `_com_issue_error` function to throw a `_com_error`. If any problems arise in the creation, we catch the error and display the message associated with the returned HRESULT. We determine next whether rich error information is supported, and, if it is, we display its description.

THE `#import` DIRECTIVE

The wrapper classes provide intrinsic compiler support for the basic COM types. The real power provided by Visual C++'s native support is through the use of the new `#import` directive. When the compiler encounters the `#import` directive, it produces wrapper classes for each interface described in the referenced component's type library. The type library can be read directly (for example, from a TLB file), or the compiler can locate it in an executable's (DLL, EXE) attached resources. The `#import` statement uses the `LoadTypeLib` API to load the type information for the module. Here's a brief example:

```
//
// Chapter4_NativeClient.cpp
//
#include <windows.h>
```

```
#import "Chapter4_Server.exe" no_namespace named_guids

int main( int argc, char *argv[] )
{
...
}
```

As just shown, `#import` has a number of optional attributes that affect its behavior. In our example, we've specified that the classes created by `#import` should not be defined within a namespace and that the GUIDs should be defined using the named format (for example, `CLSID_Math`) that we're familiar with.

THE TLI AND TLH FILES

The wrapper classes created by `#import` are placed in the output directory (such as **\DEBUG**) for the project. Two files are produced: a header file (**project.tlh**) and an implementation file (**projectname.tli**). Here's a glimpse of our header file for the math component:

```
// Chapter4_Server.TLH
// Created by Microsoft (R) C/C++ Compiler Version 11.00.0000 (eb20bb72).
//
// Debug/Chapter4_Server.tlh
//
// C++ source equivalent of Win32 type library Chapter4_Server.exe
// compiler-generated file created 11/25/97 at 06:47:31 - DO NOT EDIT!

#include <comdef.h>

...
//
// Smart pointer typedef declarations
//
_COM_SMARTPTR_TYPEDEF(IMath, __uuidof(IMath));
_COM_SMARTPTR_TYPEDEF(IAdvancedMath, __uuidof(IAdvancedMath));
...
struct __declspec(uuid("5fb0c22e-3343-11d1-883a-444553540000"))
IMath : IUnknown
{
    //
    // Wrapper methods for error-handling
    //
```

(code continued on next page)

```
    long Add ( long lOp1, long lOp2 );
    long Subtract ( long lOp1, long lOp2 );
    ...
    //
    // Raw methods provided by interface
    //
    virtual HRESULT __stdcall raw_Add (
        long lOp1,
        long lOp2,
        long * plResult ) = 0;
    virtual HRESULT __stdcall raw_Subtract (
        long lOp1,
        long lOp2,
        long * plResult ) = 0;
    ...
};
...
enum mathOPERATION
{
    mathAdd = 1,
    mathSubtract = 2,
    mathMultiply = 3,
    mathDivide = 4
};
...
//
// Named GUID constants initializations
//
extern "C" const GUID __declspec(selectany) CLSID_Math =
    {0x5fb0c22f,0x3343,0x11d1,{0x88,0x3a,0x44,0x45,0x53,0x54,0x00,0x00}};
extern "C" const GUID __declspec(selectany) IID_IMath =
    {0x5fb0c22e,0x3343,0x11d1,{0x88,0x3a,0x44,0x45,0x53,0x54,0x00,0x00}};
...
//
// Wrapper method implementations
//
#include "Debug/Chapter4_Server.tli"
```

Most of the preceding code should make sense. The compiler reads the type library and, using various macros and structures, it produces smart pointers for each of the interfaces, wrapper classes for both the "wrapped" and the "raw" interface methods, enumerated type declarations, and finally constants for the CLSID and IID GUIDs. The header file then includes the implementation file:

```
// Chapter4_Server.TLI
// Created by Microsoft (R) C/C++ Compiler Version 11.00.0000 (c4aee32c).
//
// Debug/Chapter4_Server.tli
//
// Wrapper implementations for Win32 type library Chapter4_Server.exe
// compiler-generated file created 11/25/97 at 05:43:34 - DO NOT EDIT!
//
// Interface IMath wrapper method implementations
//

inline long IMath::Add ( long lOp1, long lOp2 ) {
    long _result;
    HRESULT _hr = raw_Add(lOp1, lOp2, &_result);
    if (FAILED(_hr)) _com_issue_errorex(_hr, this, __uuidof(this));
    return _result;
}

inline long IMath::Subtract ( long lOp1, long lOp2 ) {
    long _result;
    HRESULT _hr = raw_Subtract(lOp1, lOp2, &_result);
    if (FAILED(_hr)) _com_issue_errorex(_hr, this, __uuidof(this));
    return _result;
}
...
//
// interface IAdvancedMath wrapper method implementations
//

inline long IAdvancedMath::Factorial ( short sFact ) {
    long _result;
    HRESULT _hr = raw_Factorial(sFact, &_result);
    if (FAILED(_hr)) _com_issue_errorex(_hr, this, __uuidof(this));
    return _result;
}
...
```

The implementation file creates a series of wrapper methods for each interface implemented by the component. The methods encapsulate some of the low-level behavior of the
interface. In particular, they provide a more friendly way of interacting with the interfaces.
In other words, the return value is not an HRESULT, but instead is the method parameter
marked as retval. This approach gives the C++ developer Visual Basic–like syntax. More
important, it allows us to develop using the C++ exception model. If an error occurs,
instead of checking the HRESULT we use try/catch blocks.

Which One Should I Use?

Good question. When developing components or client applications based on COM, you now have several choices. You can use interface pointers and native types (BSTR, VARI-ANT), or you can use ATL's wrapper classes (CComPtr, CComBSTR), and now you can use native Visual C++ support as well (_com_ptr_t, _bstr_t). It's nice to have so many choices, but which one should you use when developing your own applications?

The Visual C++ native COM types provide the most functionality. Its smart pointer classes and COM data type wrapper classes support exceptions and operations that are not part of the ATL implementation. So at first glance the native COM types are the ones to use. However, if you have any hope of ever moving your components or applications to non-Microsoft compilers and platforms, you probably should not use these classes. Classes such as _bstr_t and the #import directive are Microsoft-specific and will probably not be supported by other compilers (such as Borland). If this isn't an issue, using the native COM support classes is a preferred technique.

If you are worried about portability, I suggest that you use ATL's wrapper classes. In some situations, though, ATL's wrapper classes don't provide much functional improvement when compared with the straight types (for example, BSTR vs. CComBSTR). I expect, though, that ATL's implementations will become more functional in the future.

AN EXAMPLE CLIENT APPLICATION

Native COM supports both client-side and server-side development. However, in most cases, native support is most useful when you're *using* components, or acting as a client. For example, back in Chapter 4 we developed a math component that supported a number of interfaces. The #import directive makes it very easy to access the math component's functionality. The following example code shows how to access our Chapter 4 math component using Visual C++'s native COM support.

```
//
// Chapter4_NativeClient.cpp
//

#include <windows.h>
#include <tchar.h>
#include <iostream.h>

#import "..\Chapter4_Server\Debug\Chapter4_Server.exe" no_namespace named_guids

int main( int argc, char *argv[] )
{
    cout << "Initializing COM" << endl;
```

```
if ( FAILED( CoInitialize( NULL )))
{
   cout << "Unable to initialize COM" << endl;
   return -1;
}

IMathPtr ptrMath;

// Create an instance of the server
try
{
   HRESULT hr;
   hr = ptrMath.CreateInstance( CLSID_Math );
   if ( FAILED( hr ))
      _com_issue_error( hr );
}
catch( _com_error& e )
{
   cout << "Error creating instance" << endl;
   cout << "HRESULT message is " << e.ErrorMessage() << endl;
   // If rich error info is supported, display the description
   if ( e.ErrorInfo() )
      cout << e.Description() << endl;

   return -1;
}

// Access the IMath interface
try
{
   long lResult;
   lResult = ptrMath->Add( 134, 353 );
   cout << "134 + 353 = " << lResult << endl;

   // Try to divide by zero
   lResult = ptrMath->Divide( 0, 0 );
}
catch( _com_error& e )
{
   cout << "Error accessing IMath" << endl;
   cout << "HRESULT message is " << e.ErrorMessage() << endl;
   if ( e.ErrorInfo() )
      cout << e.Description() << endl;
   // Don't return, we forced the error with 0/0
}
```

(code continued on next page)

```cpp
// Access IMath2
try
{
   IMath2Ptr ptrMath2( ptrMath );

   long lResult;
   lResult = ptrMath2->Compute( mathAdd,
                                100,
                                200 );
   cout << "Compute( 100 + 200 ) = " << lResult << endl;

   // Sum an array
   short sArray[3] = { 3,4,5 };
   lResult = ptrMath2->Sum( 3, sArray );
   cout << "Sum( 3,4,5 ) = " << lResult << endl;
}
catch( _com_error& e )
{
   cout << "Error accessing IMath2" << endl;
   cout << "HRESULT message is " << e.ErrorMessage() << endl;
   return -1;
}

// Access IAdvancedMath
try
{
   IAdvancedMathPtr ptrAdvancedMath( ptrMath );
   if ( ptrAdvancedMath )
   {
     long lResult;

     lResult = ptrAdvancedMath->Factorial( 12 );
     cout << "12! = " << lResult << endl;

     lResult = ptrAdvancedMath->Fibonacci( 12 );
     cout << "The Fibonacci of 12 = " << lResult << endl;
   }
}
catch( _com_error& e )
{
   cout << "Error accessing IAdvancedMath" << endl;
   cout << "HRESULT message is " << e.ErrorMessage() << endl;
   return -1;
}
```

```
    // Access IComponentInfo
    try
    {
        IComponentInfoPtr ptrInfo( ptrMath );
        if ( ptrInfo )
        {
            COMPONENT_INFO* pInfo = 0;
            ptrInfo->get_Info( &pInfo );
            cout << "Component author is " << pInfo->pstrAuthor << endl;
            cout << "Component version is " << pInfo->sMajor <<
                                    "." << pInfo->sMinor << endl;
            _bstr_t name( pInfo->bstrName );
            cout << "Component name is " << name << endl;

            if ( pInfo->pstrAuthor )
                CoTaskMemFree( pInfo->pstrAuthor );
            if ( pInfo->bstrName )
                SysFreeString( pInfo->bstrName );

            if ( pInfo )
                CoTaskMemFree( pInfo );
        }
    }
    catch( _com_error& e )
    {
        cout << "Error accessing IComponentInfo" << endl;
        cout << "HRESULT message is " << e.ErrorMessage() << endl;
        return -1;
    }

    // We have to release the pointer here
    // because if we call CoUninitialize before
    // it goes out of scope, we'll get an exception
    ptrMath = 0;

    CoUninitialize();

    return 0;
}
```

CHAPTER6_NATIVECLIENT EXAMPLE

The downloadable examples also contain a client that demonstrates how to access the automation-based Chapter6 component. It demonstrates the use of the _variant_t class when you're working with variants.

An Introduction to COM+

At its September 1997 Professional Developer's Conference (PDC), Microsoft announced COM+, an evolutionary extension to the widely used Component Object Model (COM). COM+ builds on the success of COM, which boasts a current yearly market of around $410 million, with expectations of approximately $3 billion by the year 2001 (source: Giga Information Group). This appendix provides a high-level overview of this new technology and describes some of its important features. Currently, information about COM+ is scarce and vague, so we will avoid getting into the details (because they aren't available yet) and try to discuss it from a conceptual point of view.

NOTE This appendix was written with lots of help from Ron Patton (RonP@livewire-news.com) of Midwest Independent Consultant's Group. Thanks Ron. Also, this appendix is based on pre-alpha COM+ information. In other words, much of it may change in the final implementation.

WHAT IS COM+ AND WHY SHOULD I USE IT?

COM+ is a runtime set of services that makes it easier for developers to create and use COM components from any language or tool (at least it will if the tool developers agree to implement COM+ in their products). COM has long been considered difficult to learn, but its benefits (e.g., local transparency, binary compatibility, and language independence) make it worth the effort in most cases, especially if you are considering coding these features yourself. COM+ is a move away from having to understand much of what we've covered in the first few chapters of this book. Low-level COM concepts such as class factories, reference counting, and `QueryInterface` are part of the COM+ runtime. Developers will no longer have to wade through these details to implement and use COM-based components. Other features include:

- **COM+ is language neutral.** This makes it possible to develop COM components similar to the way you create objects in your native compiler language. The assumption here is that you already knows the native compiler language. Developing objects in COM+ should be very similar to developing objects in C++ if you are a C++ developer or Visual Basic if you are a Visual Basic developer. For example, in C++, rather than using `CoCreateInstance` to create an instance of a COM component we will use the new operator.

- **COM+ provides default behavior for otherwise repetitive tasks.** COM+ provides a default class factory, default class registration facilities, default object access and lifetime management, default `IDispatch` handler, and default Connection Point implementation. We say "default" because it is still possible to override this behavior. The point is that the default implementation works for most implementations, and it will give the developer more time to develop the business logic of the application.

- **COM+ has a variety of extensive services.** COM+ provides default extensible services including transactions, data binding, events, and load balancing.

- **COM+ will preserve existing COM components.** Today, there are a large number of COM-based components. It is very important that these legacy components continue to operate the same way they did before COM+. COM+ provides a runtime DLL that supports complete backward compatibility. Tools such as the Visual C++ compiler will target this DLL at development time and COM+ components will target it at runtime. The runtime will translate the language-specific code into normal COM SDK calls.

INTERCEPTION

COM+ implements extensible services such as transactions, security, load balancing, and memory management. Third-party developers can create new services or extend existing services through a concept known as interception.

Interception is a key concept of COM+. It provides the infrastructure necessary to extend the behavior of objects. Once you have registered an interceptor for an object, you are notified when the object is created and when methods within the object are called or returned. Obviously, that with this type of control, a developer can dynamically redefine a COM+ object.

This ability is absent from the current COM implementation. For example, it would be nice if a component could "monitor" all calls to a class factory on a specific system, maybe have some sort of object creation trace facility. Today, there is no mechanism, other than a series of hacks, to do this. COM+ provides such capabilities as part of its design.

DEVELOPING COM+ COMPONENTS

The development process begins by selecting a tool that supports COM+. This might be Visual C++, Visual J++, or Visual Basic. Next, you will type in the source code that defines your components and then run the compiler. So far it sounds very much like the usual process of developing any application. During the compilation/linkage stage COM+ steps in. The tool you are using will link to the COM+ runtime to build a metadata representation of the object, handle any system registration, and create the component's package (DLL or EXE).

Today, COM uses the IDL to describe components, interfaces, methods, and parameters. With COM+, the concept of an IDL file is gone. The native language will have special keywords that will produce underlying COM objects. For example, here's how our `Math` component might look in COM+ syntax:

```
cointerface IMath
{
   long Add( Add( long lOp1, long lOp2 );
   long Subtract( Add( long lOp1, long lOp2 );
   long Multiply( Add( long lOp1, long lOp2 );
   long Divide( Add( long lOp1, long lOp2 );
};

coclass CMath : implements IMath
{
   long Add( long lOp1, long lOp2  )
   {
      return lOp1 + lOp2;
   );
   long Subtract( long lOp1, long lOp2 )
   {
      return lOp1 - lOp2;
   );
   long Multiply( long lOp1, long lOp2 )
   {
      return lOp1 + lOp2;
   );
   long Divide( long lOp1, long lOp2 )
   {
      return lOp1 + lOp2;
   );
};
```

This is actually C++ syntax. In other words, existing C++ compilers will have to be extended to support COM+ (there are new keywords such as `coclass`). This will make your code very compiler-dependent, and that must be taken into account when deciding to whether to use a tool's built-in COM+ support. This issue as also discussed in Appendix A.

INHERITANCE

COM+ supports two types of inheritance, interface and implementation. Today, COM supports only interface inheritance at the binary level. COM+ will make COM fully object-oriented in the eyes of those who faulted COM's lack of support for implementation inheritance. Other features include:

- **Interface Inheritance.** In COM+, interfaces will be able to singly or multiply inherit from other interfaces. In C++, you would use the `implements` keyword to identify the interface your class will implement. It will be necessary to provide implementations for the methods defined in the interface as well as methods from any interfaces that are inherited.

- **Implementation Inheritance:** This type of inheritance has long been considered evil and error-prone by Microsoft. The idea of a fragile base class has been the source of many philosophical/religious debates in the COM newsgroups. All this has changed with COM+ because you can now singly inherit from within a process. This will allow the component developer to expose a component hierarchy within the component's package.

FIELDS AND PROPERTIES

COM+ objects can have fields and properties. Fields and properties usually represent the current state of an object. Internally, they are data members of the class., for which you can specify modifiers, attributes, and type. One major difference between fields and properties is that properties are implemented with accessor functions, so through interceptors you can tell when they are accessed or modified.

The modifiers can be broken down into two categories, access and storage modifiers. The access modifiers are similar to those in C++. Properties can have public, private, or protected access, but fields must always have private access. The storage modifiers are static and transient. The static storage modifier is similar to the C++ definition of a static modifier. If the variable is static, there is only one instance of it per class regardless of the number of instantiations. The transient storage modifier designates the variable as a transient variable, and as a result, it will not persist with the object. This is useful if you have a memory pointer in the object that could be different in another instance.

The attributes of a COM+ field or property can be very powerful. These attributes can provide the specified data to COM+ services during the runtime of the object. For example, an attribute is used by the COM+ data binding service to bind a property or field to a database column. Attributes can also be applied to the class. In COM+ you can also specify the threading model of an object through attributes.

The type can be any data type, but it is recommended that you stick to the COM+ standard data types to avoid marshalling conflicts and to provide the best support of potential tools (e.g., Visual Basic).

STANDARD DATA TYPES

COM+ has standardized a set of data types that will be used by the tools that support COM+. These standard data types will provide peace of mind when developing interfaces that will be used by other development tools. If you stick with these data types, other tools that support COM+ will always be able to understand them. In addition, you can define enumerations, structures, and classes based on these standard types. The COM+ data types are shown in Table B.1.

Table B.1 COM+ Data Types

TYPE	SIZE (BITS)
Boolean	8
BSTR	32
Byte	8
Char	16
ClassRef	32
COM interface pointer	32
Const (any native type)	
Currency	64
Date	64
Double	64
Float	32
HRESULT	32
Int	32
Java array	
Long	64
Pointer	32
Reference counted object reference	32
Safearray	
Short	16
Sized array	32
Unsigned char	8
Unsigned int	32
Unsigned long	64
Unsigned short	16
UUID	128
Variant	128
Void	0

METADATA

COM+ removes the requirement for using IDL. Because the tools will natively support COM+, component information previously placed in the IDL file will be garnered from the language in which it is developed. COM+ provides something called *metadata*, which has been described as a "type library on steroids." The metadata contains the basic IDL information we're familiar with, plus all of the new features of COM+:

- Class definitions including methods, arguments, fields and properties contained in the class.
- Interfaces implemented by the class.
- Events—both incoming and outgoing—and the event types.

Again, this metadata is generated and used by the COM+ tools. In other words, you get it for free when you compile your COM+ component, but it is an essential piece in the COM+ architecture. The COM+ runtime requires metadata for all COM+ objects. When you distribute your component package, this metadata is deployed with it.

INTERFACES

We've covered the concept of a COM interface in great detail in this book. As you know, the interface is the most important aspect of COM-based development. COM+ introduces two new interface features that should prove very useful:

- **Static data members**. COM+ allows interfaces to have static data members.
- **Multiple inheritance.** COM+ interfaces can now multiply inherit from other COM+ interfaces.

VERSIONING

COM+ provides the ability to version interfaces and classes. COM+ interface versioning builds on the current recommended methods of interface versioning. For example, let's say you have an interface called ICar and you want to add some new functionality to the interface. You would still call the new interface ICar2, or something other than Icar, but rather than refer to the interface as ICar2 , you could let the COM+ know that you want to refer to the new interface as ICar and the original ICar interface as something like ICarOld. That works because the interface identifiers (IIDs) that represent the two interfaces remain unique. Existing clients do not need to know that the human-readable name has changed because they have resolved to the IID, which remains the same, even though the name has changed.

Class versioning is more of an administrative issue. During the build process, a COM+ client stores the metadata information associated with all of the classes the client depends on. This will be used at runtime to identify, based on the CLSID, the appropriate class factory to load. The administrator will now be able to override this behavior.

EVENTS

COM+ supports three types of events. The first is basically the same as what we covered in Chapter 7, and the others are new features of COM+:

- **Interface-based events (tightly coupled).** These events mimic the connection point scenario used by many ActiveX controls. A major drawback to this type of event is that the sink object must implement every method of the connection point even if it isn't interested in all of the events. You end up with a lot of code that does nothing more than ignore the event altogether.

- **Method-based events (tightly coupled).** Method-based events fix drawbacks of interface-based events by requiring you to provide implementations for only the event methods you are interested in.

- **Persistent events.** These events are quite different from the tightly coupled interface-based and method-based events. Tightly coupled events know about the events that can occur from the source object. With persistent events, the source and the sink don't know very much about one another. The source object will publish all events the object is capable of firing, and sink objects will subscribe to these events, providing a dynamic way to receive events from an unknown object.

COMPONENT REGISTRATION AND DEPLOYMENT

COM+ will provide a registration database called the *class store* that will contain COM+ component registration information. For backward compatibility, the Windows registry can optionally be updated but eventually all COM components will be registered only in the COM+ registration database, which is distributed and will reside on a server.

Registration is automatic in COM+ thanks to the metadata, which describes the object. You do not have to write any code to perform object registration. During deployment to remote machines, the metadata is used to register the component. COM+ promises to drastically reduce the support issues associated with component registration.

Using COM+ Components from a C++ Client's Perspective

C++ developers should be able to use COM+ components in much the same way that we use type libraries in Visual C++ 5.0. You will simply import the type library (or metadata file) and use the classes as if you had included the header file that defined the class. From this point you can create a new instance by using the new operator. You can release the object by simply setting the object's pointer to NULL. You do not have to be concerned with class factories, reference counting, and so on.

As an example, here's a look at how we might access the Math component using COM+ support.

```
//
// AppendixB_Client.cpp
//

#include <windows.h>

#import "..\Math\math.dll"

int main(int argc, char* argv[])
{
    Math* pMath;
    pMath = new Math;

    long lResult;
    lResult = pMath->Add( 100, 200 );
    lResult = pMath->Subtract( 300, 200 );
    lResult = pMath->Multiply( 100, 200 );
    lResult = pMath->Divide( 100, 200 );

return 0;
}
```

This is similar to what we did back in Appendix A, but this time we don't have to use smart pointers, CreateInstance, and so on. COM support is built directly into the C++ language.

When/Where Can I get my Copy?

Microsoft is expected to ship COM+ in the fourth quarter of 1998. A preview version was distributed at the September PDC. A beta version is expected to be available in the first half of 1998. A good source of information about COM+ and COM development technology is http://www.microsoft.com/com.

Index

D

my2cents.idgbooks.com

Register This Book — And Win!

Visit **http://my2cents.idgbooks.com** to register this book and we'll automatically enter you in our monthly prize giveaway. It's also your opportunity to give us feedback: let us know what you thought of this book and how you would like to see other topics covered.

Discover IDG Books Online!

The IDG Books Online Web site is your online resource for tackling technology — at home and at the office.

Ten Productive and Career-Enhancing Things You Can Do at www.idgbooks.com

1. Nab source code for your own programming projects.

2. Download software.

3. Read Web exclusives: special articles and book excerpts by IDG Books Worldwide authors.

4. Take advantage of resources to help you advance your career as a Novell or Microsoft professional.

5. Buy IDG Books Worldwide titles or find a convenient bookstore that carries them.

6. Register your book and win a prize.

7. Chat live online with authors.

8. Sign up for regular e-mail updates about our latest books.

9. Suggest a book you'd like to read or write.

10. Give us your 2¢ about our books and about our Web site.

Not on the Web yet? It's easy to get started with *Discover the Internet,* at local retailers everywhere.